CHALLENGING THE
"APARTHEIDS" OF KNOWLEDGE
in Higher Education through **Social Innovation**

Joana Bezerra, Craig Paterson & Sharli Paphitis (Eds)

Challenging the 'Apartheids' of Knowledge in Higher Education through Social Innovation

Published by African Sun Media under the SUN PReSS imprint

First edition 2021

ISBN 978-1-991201-04-1
ISBN 978-1-991201-05-8 (e-book)
https://doi.org/10.52779/9781991201058

Set in Raleway Regular 10/15

Cover design, typesetting and production by African Sun Media

Cover photo: Tim Mossholder on Unsplash (https://unsplash.com/photos/zs-PAgqgenQ?utm_source=unsplash&utm_medium=referral&utm_content=creditShareLink)

SUN PReSS is an imprint of African Sun Media. Scholarly, professional and reference works are published under this imprint in print and electronic formats.

This publication can be ordered from:
orders@africansunmedia.co.za
Takealot: bit.ly/2monsfl
Google Books: bit.ly/2k1Uilm
africansunmedia.store.it.si *(e-books)*
Amazon Kindle: amzn.to/2ktL.pkL

Visit africansunmedia.co.za for more information.

Contents

Introduction

Sharli Paphitis, Joana Bezerra and Craig Paterson

RHODES UNIVERSITY
COMMUNITY ENGAGEMENT DIVISION

s.paphitis@ru.ac.za; j.bezerra@ru.ac.za;
craig.j.paterson@gmail.com

The apartheids of knowledge in *HE*

In their seminal paper 'An Apartheid of Knowledge in Academia: The Struggle Over the "Legitimate" knowledge of Faculty of Color' (2002), Bernal and Villalpando critically raise and discuss the issues of epistemic justice internal to academe, interrogating what they call the *'de facto'*-, gender- and, more importantly, race-based segregation of knowledges in academe.

Their paper was one of the first to highlight the statistics showing the slow speed of HE transformation in terms of racial demographics in academia, but more importantly showed distinct patterns of the segregation of knowledges across the academy along gender and race lines. Despite the grand assertions that HE is "objective, meritocratic, color-blind, race-neutral, and provides equal opportunities for all" (Bernal and Villalpando, 2002: 171), their study showed that these assertions serve to mask epistemic divisions, a literal apartheid of knowledge within the academy between those from dominant groups and those who have traditionally been marginalised within the knowledge economy. According to Bernal and Villalpando (2002:171), this is largely due to a global, and local, dominant European epistemological paradigm governing HE, which they claim leads to dominance of an epistemic perspective in HE that "can subtly – and not so subtly – ignore and discredit the ways of knowing and understanding the world that [black scholars and academics] often bring to academia."

Bernal and Villalpando set the scene and highlighted the problem in the global arena some 15 years ago, but little can be said to have changed in the modern academy, most notably perhaps in South Africa. Post-apartheid transformational work within institutions of HE has, until only recently, tended to focus on making universities more demographically inclusive and diverse, both in terms of students and staff (Soudien, 2010), and through the 'Africanisation' of university spaces (Metz, 2014).

At a national level, demographic transformation of the HE sector in terms of student enrolments in HE has shown the most progress: in 2013, 68% of honours student enrolments were black students, and in 2013, 52% of masters and doctoral student enrolments were black students. The enrolment of black students in HE overall increased from 64% to 70% between 2007 and 2013 (Council on Higher Education, 2013). Demographic transformation on the academic staff level, while slower, has also shown progress: in 2011 the ratio of white to black academics was almost 2:1 (9162:5077), and by 2013, the sector had 51% white academics (9205) and 34% black academics (5756), with similar increases in ratios of Indian and coloured academics (Council on Higher Education, 2013). These macro-level demographic transformations are largely, but not always, mirrored at the micro level of the individual disciplines themselves.

But overall, this transformation has been slow. Recent student-led activism – particularly in the form of the #FeesMustFall protests and the #RhodesMustFall movements – has demonstrated the growing discomfort with both the speed at which transformational efforts of these kinds occur and the lack of deeper transformation of epistemic norms governing academe.

In continuing to follow a Eurocentric, positivist paradigm, the South African HE sector has implicitly endorsed and perpetuated a number of important epistemic injustices beyond those discussed by Bernal and Villalpando. Epistemic injustices of this kind prevent the democratisation of the knowledge production process. They furthermore stunt the research potential of universities by delegitimising sources of knowledge deemed valid in mainstream research communities and limit access to HE in the face of already notorious economic barriers.

Continued positivist dominance in *HE*

The features of positivism dominating research and HE are views which held sway in the philosophy of science in the early twentieth century. In these views, the scientific enterprise was seen as predicated on the pursuit of value-free inquiries which transcended cultural and historical viewpoints, with the aim of producing objective, factual and dispassionate research (Fondacaro & Weinberg 2002; Karnilowicz *et al.*, 2014). The underlying assumption behind positivism is that objective methodology will give researchers access to the single, absolute 'truth' describing things as they 'really' are – thus, positivist research tends to emphasise generalisable outcomes while ignoring or marginalising the perceptions, lived experiences and realities and socio-cultural and political conditions experienced both subjectively and collectively by those being researched. Consequently, interactions between academics or researchers and subjects within this paradigm are typically impersonal (Potts & Brown, 2005; Karnilowicz *et al.*, 2014). Following this, in positivist research, academics or researchers are viewed as the credentialed, expert and only legitimate producers of knowledge, who are set in a hierarchical relationship of power and privilege above and detached from the objects of study or those being studied – who are seen merely as sources of data rather than bearers or creators of knowledge itself (Potts & Brown, 2005; Newman & Glass, 2015). Moreover, while academics and researchers are seen as primarily responsible for the outcomes of the knowledge production process, having the power and legitimacy to act on the knowledge produced, they are also seen as the primary beneficiaries of this process, lacking in epistemic agency and credibility from the perspective of academe (Potts & Brown, 2005).

The dominance of the positivist paradigm in research and within the HE sector is reflected in the governing norms and standards of the academy, which "privilege theoretical over practical knowledge" (Newman & Glass, 2015:226) – measuring impactful and meaningful research in peer-reviewed outputs, where editors, reviewers and audiences reinforce the paradigm with their overarching focus on objectivity and methodological validity, reliability, and, more recently, check-box exercises in ethical compliance still rooted in biomedical frameworks (Pizarro, 1998; Fine & Torre, 2008). Beyond the realm of research, positivism, as a dominant epistemic framework governing HE, is reflected in the norms and standards governing much of the teaching and learning at universities where students are predominantly invited to engage with the "official knowledge" (Brandt, 2004:95) constructed by academic and research experts. But the dominance of positivism has not only been in response to pressures internal to the academic community itself. It can also be seen as a response to pressures from research funders, programme evaluators and policy makers who tend to presume that academics have the necessary and sole expertise required for building and sustaining the knowledge economy (Karnilowicz *et al.*, 2014; Newman & Glass, 2015).

In the realm of policy making, the concept of 'epistemic communities' – first introduced by Peter Haas (1990; 1992) in the context of environmental policy debates, but now much more broadly used in reference to knowledge creation policy contexts – has taken prominence. Within this literature, and in practice, the original definition of an epistemic community, put forward by Haas as "a network of professionals with recognised expertise and competence in a particular domain and an authoritative claim to policy-relevant knowledge within that domain or issue area" (Haas, 1992:3) still primarily underpins debates in the field. The legitimacy and credibility of the advice and information aimed at influencing policy decisions provided by any epistemic community, within this framework, are derived primarily from the shared knowledge base within the community and the recognition of the expertise of the community of professionals (Sugden, 2006). While many groups of professionals (doctors, lawyers, accountants, etc.) can reasonably claim to constitute epistemic communities, researchers and academics comprise some of the most prominent epistemic communities which *in fact* impact on knowledge creation in policy contexts – providing reports, analysis, theories and frameworks from studies with scientific gravitas – where the expertise and power of credentialed researchers and academics play a large role in the politics of knowledge generation and knowledge application (Sohng, 1996; Sugden, 2006).

Predicated on an epistemologically positivist foundation, the concentration of 'knowledge' in epistemic communities comprising experts (predominantly communities of academic or scientific experts) resulted in a number of hierarchies dominating the modern knowledge economy, whereby: truth claims are generated through the discourses of credentialed academic experts rather than 'ordinary people'; individuals' understandings of their lived experiences are deferred to and become the province of expert academic analyses; academic experts colonise debates on development issues because technical, 'scientised' and jargon-laden discourses are either made inaccessible or assumed to be inaccessible to the broader public; and "practice principles and methods are developed by 'experts', often under controlled conditions, then imported into daily practice and tested against clients and the policy context" (Sohng, 1996: 82).

The developmental university

Debates on development are 'colonised' by 'experts' in the positivist paradigms and are thereby rendered inaccessible. This effectively prevents the 'knowledge' from having a significant impact on development at grassroots level and from being intelligible without the direct translation by members of the epistemic community that produced it. The academy as epistemic community is still expected to engage in these debates – assisting with knowledge production aimed towards so-called development is increasingly at the core of the 'post-apartheid' university. As the South African Department of Education White Paper 3 ("A Programme for Higher Education Transformation" (Department of Education, 1997)) directly states: university spaces are required to "promote and develop social responsibility and awareness amongst students of the role of higher education in social and economic development through community service programmes. (p. 14)" In other words, the universities, by policy, are not only required to engage with solving the social and economic development issues of the day, but also need to inculcate this approach into the teaching process. In theory – in theory! – this would mean a shift in the institutional culture of the university away from the positivist paradigm towards the paradigm of a socially valued 'developmental university.'

As noted above, this has failed to translate from theory into practice. And the important question to ask is: *why?* After all, the problem was diagnosed many years ago. Bernal and Villalpando wrote in 2002 and the White Paper 3 was published in 1997. And yet, rather than engaging in the two central roles of a university academic – teaching and research – to include these new 'developmental university' objectives, a 'third prong' emerged: community engagement (CE). While a number of ideas (and myriad acronyms) emerged within the teaching ('service learning') and research ('community-based research') spaces to accommodate these changes, their uptake has been slow. Rather, CE is regarded as a third, separate activity alongside the other two functions of the university. As Akpan, Minkley and Thakar pointed out in 2012, "while universities often present CE as a strategic and operational priority [including, for example, tying promotion to CE activities], in certain cases this recognition is more symbolism than reality." (Akpan *et al.*, 2012:2).

CE has been established "from above," as a "third branch" of the academic project, and has not become integrated into academic practice as was envisioned. While a handful of individual academics apply the methods and practices of CE in their work (through either research or teaching), it has not, as was mandated, changed the focus of academic practice to the creation of the 'developmental university'. Rather, each component of the academic project has formed into a niche body with CE divisions – deployed (sometimes reluctantly in order to secure promotion) as a component of the 'normal work' academics are required to do. Service-learning, for example, is seen as a CE component of teaching; community-based research methods are seen as a CE component of research;

and participatory methods are relegated to the margins. In other words, CE remains a third branch of the public university. Where it was envisioned that CE practices would become a central part of the academic project, these practices have remained separate from the core activities of teaching and research. At the present moment, academics who engage in CE-related activities are seen as doing just that. Community-based and service-learning work is seen as academics *coming to* CE, rather than CE practices entering the disciplines in which these academics work.

But why has this occurred? Or, put differently, why, when few would disagree that 'the university' should be conceived as a public good that contributes its expertise to the betterment of society as a whole, has the academic community been so reluctant to put CE-derived practices in a central position, and rather retained it as peripheral to standard academic practice? The reason for this failure is not simply hubris on the part of the positivist academic community, but also falls into the contemporary university structure. Envisioned as a community of practice, an epistemic community, safeguarded in its quasi-democratic autonomy by vague notions of 'academic freedom', the university-as-community carries out its task with a sometimes vicious collegiality. But the university is not only a community – it is also an institution that is increasingly managerial, bureaucratic and financially stretched. The public university is a state institution, following state directives; it is increasingly market-driven, a brand seeking endowments and capital while 'tightening the belt' to stay afloat during rough economic seas. In other words, two universities exist in one: the university is a community of scholars **and** the university is a legal person and a brand.

This gives rise to two competing logics of operation in universities. On one side you find a managerial, state-bureaucratic logic; on the other, a self-governing community of scholars striving for independent practice. These logics are mutually unintelligible and exist in constant tension with each other in the university. The objectives of the developmental university – specifically, the directives given to transform the public university into a developmental one – have on the one hand been established 'from above' through that managerial logic. When coming not 'from within' the academic community logics, it should be no surprise that increasingly strained, overworked, underpaid academics resist what is positioned as an addition and which seemingly falls outside of their already established mandates of teaching and research. On the other hand, much of the work to transform the university has been born from the work of individuals and collectives of academics who have embraced new ways of thinking about their own roles as researchers and teachers. While making strides in theorising CE or developing practice within their own discipline, they have seldom championed the institutionalisation of CE in an effort to radically transform HE establishments themselves. These academics have often been seen as the champions of CE in their disciplines or department, taking the role of CE on as others do with committee or administrative duties. Both of these developments, separately or together, have led to CE being forced into establishment as a 'third branch', rather than being embedded into teaching and research.

The mutual unintelligibility of the competing logics of universities may seem overstated, possibly exaggerated. Members of the academic community often feed from one space of predominating logic into another within the same institution through promotion from a teaching and research post into a managerial one: from Professor to Dean of Faculty, for example. Similarly, members of the academic community may effortlessly, and unconsciously, 'jump' between these logics, depending on the environment in the institution at a given time. Within an administrative committee meeting – perhaps as a representative on a university budget or infrastructure committee – the managerial logic is intelligible. To a university manager, a similar intelligibility of academic community logics may emerge in a curriculum discussion, for example. But a directive presented in a managerial or state-bureaucratic logic which impacts on the realm of teaching and research, governed by its competing logic, is unintelligible within that realm.

To understand just how unintelligible these competing logics might appear to each other, consider Felicity Wood's (2018) *Universities and the Occult Rituals of the Corporate World: Higher Education and Metaphorical Parallels with Myth and Magic* wherein she applies her experience as an anthropologist on myth and magic to the contemporary state of HE. In that work, Wood attempts an experiment in intelligibility through metaphor and analogy. Her approach is one that attempts to demystify the logics of HE's corporatisation through deliberately mystifying it; Wood takes the 'familiar' – day-to-day life inside a university – and makes it appear unfamiliar to the insider by way of metaphor. By 'defamiliarising', the problems and absurdities faced in that familiar thing (in this case, managerial and state-bureaucratic logics of universities) become more clear. In doing so, Wood, in a sense, 'translates' the managerial, state-bureaucratic logics for those operating in an academic logic, thereby clarifying it. That the analogy of myth, magic and the occult is so effective in this 'translation' indicates the degree to which mutual unintelligibility exists between the two logics of the university.

As individual teachers and researchers increasingly draw on CE-derived practices, however, a space is opening in which these practices can become embedded as envisioned. And an encouragement of this process – of kicking the leg out of CE as a separate activity of the academy – is what lies at the centre of this book. It is intended partly as an invitation to members of the academic community to embrace CE-derived practices in their daily business through the use of case studies that illustrate how some have done so. It is also partly an act of translation – from the managerial logics of the university-as-institution, to the logics of university-as-community – through which members of the academic community might draw CE-derived practices towards their core work instead of seeing CE practices as a separate branch of the academic project which draws the member away from their teaching and research practices.

In order to do so, a number of concepts require at least some elaboration. What is meant by, and what is the relevance of, 'social innovation'? What is 'epistemic injustice' and 'identity prejudice'? Why are these concepts important? How do they affect the 'knowledge' we, as members of the academic community, are expected (and determined) to produce? Below we will address these issues.

Undoing the logics of the apartheids of knowledge

The twenty-first century has seen a marked increase in diversity in the HE sector, both in terms of students and academic staff as well as disciplines and metho-dologies. This increased diversity has undoubtedly led to an increased awareness and appreciation of the complex interplay between the knowledges brought into the knowledge economy by those from different positionalities. But are all positions, and is all knowledge, equal when it comes down to it? Whose know-ledge counts? The disproportionate valuation of knowledge generated in the 'hard' sciences in contrast to the so-called 'soft' social sciences has long been a topic of debate. More recently, debates about the delegitimisation of contri-butions made by members of groups who are underrepresented in academe suggest that there is a segregation of knowledge (in terms of its value and legitimacy) such that it has been called an apartheid of knowledge.

As CE (encompassing volunteerism, service-learning and engaged research activities) has gained traction in the HE sector, two further apartheids of know-ledge have been highlighted. The first is between the knowledges internal to the academy and those beyond, while the second is between academic learning and the learning involved in developing so-called 'soft-skills', such as social awareness, critical citizenship, personal growth, etc. most commonly seen in engaged student learning. These apartheids of knowledge reveal a deep tension currently at the core of the HE sector, particularly in South Africa, between the commitment to preserving and furthering the traditional modes of knowledge generation and dissemination on the one hand, and the social and humanistic purposes of the academy (embodied in CE efforts) on the other.

The call for HE institutions to serve the public good – if seen as a call for these institutions to fulfil the political and moral imperative to actively contribute to social and epistemic justice and equality – can only be achieved if HE institutions themselves begin to shift from their traditional role as 'ivory tower' gatekeepers of knowledge to socially responsive and democratic institutions.

Given the post-apartheid calls for the transformation of the South African HE sector, it is surprising to find that higher education transformation "has not shown as much progress as might be expected" (Erasmus, 2014:105). While the call for HEIs to be more responsive to local communities and the challenges of local constituencies to serve the public good through CE has been widely accepted at policy levels throughout the higher education sector, community engagement has yet to become institutionalised in South Africa. The service-learning movement in particular has gained little traction since the release of the White Paper on Higher Education in 1997, and while 'graduate attributes' have been touted at institutions of higher learning as buzz words of the past two decades, academics struggle to integrate these learning outcomes into what they see as the 'core business' of their academic programmes. Most problematically, the question of the development of civically-minded graduates has been critically under-addressed in HE policy making at institutional, programmatic and curricular levels. As a result, the purposes of activities (such as CE) aimed at developing graduate attributes are often misunderstood, leading to "limited unequivocal support" (Erasmus, 2014:105) and remain relegated to the margins of academic activity. Similarly, engaged research, while gaining significant momentum in the sector (particularly in disciplines which already include extensive fieldwork components within their research methodologies and practice) is still subject to significant scepticism by those who continue to raise debates about "the specific forms of knowledge and understanding authorized by universities" (Glass & Newman, 2015:33).

CE activities (particularly in the form of service-learning and engaged research) have been purported as mechanisms of transforming the sector by breaking down the division between the academy and the communities in which they exist, as well as giving epistemic agency to both students and community partners in the knowledge production process. However, little research has been done on how effective such activities have been in promoting epistemic justice in both the academy and in broader society. There is also little evidence to suggest that these CE practices have been institutionalised in a manner which fundamentally alters institutional cultures in ways that would shift the governing epistemic paradigm of the sector more broadly.

CE activities have been purported to have transformative potential for students, staff and community partners who are involved in these activities. A vast body of literature on service-learning and (a smaller body of literature on) volunteerism suggests that students who are involved in these activities are epistemically transformed through having their beliefs, values, attitudes, and assumptions challenged, problematised and changed (where appropriate). In doing so, the epistemic transformation purportedly achieved through CE activities serves a moral and political transformation imperative in the struggle against race, gender and class oppression. Moreover, through involvement in CE activities, students are purported to become graduates who are more socially aware and who, on the basis of this awareness, become socially responsible, active citizens. Little research, however, shows how these transformations occur at an epistemic level, particularly in a South African context. Although it is also true that CE activities aim to achieve similar epistemic transformations in staff and community partners who are similarly involved, there is very little research that confirms that CE achieves the desired epistemic transformations in these target groups, particularly in a South African context.

The renewed calls for the transformation of the HE sector by student-led activism (in the form of the #RhodesMustFall and #FeesMustFall movements) provide a springboard for South African HE institutions to begin to engage more readily with the transformation project outlined in HE policy. Much of the scepticism about the transformative role of CE activities hinges on a reluctance to make appropriate shifts in the epistemic paradigm governing HE institutions. These epistemic shifts are both required and purported to be made possible through CE activities. Further debate and critical inquiry into these topics is important if the goals of epistemic justice are to be advanced. Central to this discussion is the willingness on the part of academics and researchers themselves to enter into a mode of critical reflexivity about the epistemic paradigms under which they operate, both explicitly and implicitly. Moreover, we suggest, this will require willingness on the part of academics and researchers to recognise their own biases and prejudices in the project of reimagining their own and other's roles in the knowledge production process – given that epistemic value is undoubtedly found not only within academic or dominant communities – and scholars have cautioned that within these debates "some local academics have come to the conclusion that what lies beyond the ivory tower is an … 'intellectual wasteland.'" (Erasmus, 2014:107)

Social innovation

The notion of 'social innovation' has become somewhat of a buzzword both within the academy and, more broadly, the society. Social innovation projects are transformative and have the ability to make profound and sustainable changes. Social innovation projects aim to meet social challenges and are for the benefit of all people. To this extent, many CE efforts undertaken in HE are social innovation projects, working to reorient the sector as a whole towards the public good. But to what extent can, and in what ways do, the engagement efforts – which bring together those within academe and those from broader society – introduce new ways of building and maintaining the knowledge economy, and thus serve to challenge the 'apartheids of knowledge' in HE?

In part, the answer to this can be found in recognising the often political, narrative, partnership-orientated and transdisciplinary nature of social innovation work. With social change and justice at the core of social innovation, new ways of knowledge production and dissemination are foregrounded in these projects. It is precisely the reimagining of the role players and rules of exchange in the knowledge economy inherent in social innovation which makes it instrumental in breaking down the apartheids of knowledge in HE. Social innovation is *social*, because it is often created by multiple forces and leads to systemic change (Moore *et al.*, 2012), change that enhances collective power resources (Pol & Ville, 2009). It is *innovation*, because it deliberately seeks new ideas and ways of thinking that may affect more than one social dimension (*Ibid.*), recognising an unmet need and finding new ways to address that need. Mulgan (2006:150) highlights an important point regarding social innovation: "Some of the most effective methods for cultivating social innovation start from the presumption that people are competent interpreters of their own lives and competent solvers of their own problems." Social innovation is thus underpinned by networks of community (Hazelkorn, 2009), and in order to be effective, there needs to be a recognition of the skills and capabilities of all concerned.

The practical – or grounded – nature of social innovation has two implications: (1) people from outside academia are necessarily part of knowledge creation; and (2) social and personal change to some degree will happen. Social innovation projects promote social inclusion and deep listening, stimulating and giving a space for knowledges from outside academia to flourish within the knowledge economy. CE as social innovation, as envisaged in this collection, thus continuously chips away at the apartheids of knowledge.

Epistemic justice and identity prejudice

Recently, epistemologists have paid some attention to the ethical implications of our epistemic practices. Most famously, philosopher Miranda Fricker (2007) has discussed issues of epistemic injustice in her work, which has received considerable attention since its publication in 2007. Much of the attention garnered by this work in relation to epistemic justice within the HE sector has focused on issues of inclusivity and exclusivity (particularly along race, class and gender lines) within the academy itself, but epistemic practices regarding research conducted with communities, and its ability to address the issue of epistemic justice in the knowledge production process, are not often discussed (Glass & Newman, 2015:25). Similarly, the relationship between the hegemony of Eurocentric positivism and epistemic injustice, perpetuated by researchers and academics while involved in the knowledge production process, remains largely underexplored in the social epistemology and HE literature. Recent discussions in the emerging discipline of the scholarship of engagement, by Glass and Newman (2015) and Leblanc and Kinsella (2016), have, to some extent, grappled with these issues. Glass and Newman, perhaps most strongly, suggest that HE institutions and academics are guilty of perpetuating both testimonial and hermeneutical injustices when they exclude from inclusion in the 'formal' knowledge production processes 'outside of the sphere of propositional knowledge' traditionally sanctioned by the academy. This is, at least in part, a by-product of operating under the dominant ideological paradigm of Eurocentric positivism as described above.

On Fricker's (2007) framework, an epistemic injustice is a kind of harm or injustice in which individuals or groups are wronged in their capacity as bearers of knowledge, or 'knowers'. Epistemic injustices are those which dehumanise both groups and individuals by delegitimising them as knowers – either in the eyes of society or the academy or in their own eyes. Our everyday epistemic practices, such as interpreting our social environment and experiences and reporting them to one another through knowledge claims, are compromised by the systematic prejudices and social inequalities which govern our societies (Fricker, 2007; Medina, 2012; Davies, 2016). Even as South African institutions and researchers become more inclusive of members of previously marginalised or structurally excluded groups in the academy, what Fricker calls persistent "identity prejudices" will remain in the institutions and those who work there through systems of social power in which epistemic trust are mirrored (Fricker 2007).

Negative identity prejudices undermine the credibility of testimonies given by members of marginalised or excluded groups by distorting the credibility judgements of hearers. In the wake of identity prejudice, knowledge claims, which should otherwise have been recognised by hearers, are lost (Leblanc & Kinsella, 2016). Epistemic encounters in which testimonial claims are devalued through identity prejudice serve to further oppress and marginalise members of groups who are already in epistemically less privileged positions, thereby excluding them from properly taking part in the knowledge economy (Leblanc & Kinsella, 2016). The systemic and structural testimonial injustice which arises from identity prejudice is, according to Fricker, a bias which operates at an individual level and is operational at a preconscious level in our everyday social interactions with one another, unless a conscious and deliberate disruption or intervention is made (Glass & Newman, 2015). While identity prejudices remain within the epistemic communities in HE itself – and important and significant work must still be done to disrupt the systemic and structural testimonial injustices which occur within academic institutions themselves – the epistemic relations between the epistemic communities within the academy and broader society are also significantly weakened not only by the social injustices pervasive in society, but by the overarching paradigm governing the HE sector. Here, too, important epistemic injustices occur.

Since academic and research epistemic communities enjoy privileged epistemic positions in society, they already and necessarily operate from a position of power and privilege when they engage with broader society, particularly in research settings, where, under the positivist framework, research participants are seen as lacking the epistemic credibility of their 'epistemically privileged counterparts' (Medina, 2012; Leblanc & Kinsella, 2016). Most problematically in the HE sector, such biases serve to further marginalise the voices and testimony of individuals and groups whose "knowledge claims enter the marketplace of ideas at a very substantial disadvantage" (Glass & Newman, 2015:27) when they are being received, evaluated and assessed by and assimilated into frameworks and paradigms determined by (for the most part) hearers from dominant groups. Testimonial injustices are committed when, because of identity prejudices stemming directly from the overarching positivist paradigm, "people's claims are dismissed as 'mere intuitions, vague feelings, or the like'" (Glass & Newman, 2015:29).

Similarly, both Fricker and Medina point to two further kinds of testimonial injustices – pre-emptive testimonial injustices and epistemic objectification – both of which seem to be perpetuated by the overarching paradigm. On the one hand, in cases of pre-emptive testimonial injustices, the opinions, views and knowledge claims of individuals and groups who are subjected to identity prejudice are not solicited because it is presumed that they will have little to contribute or that they do not possess the required knowledge, and consequently these individuals or groups are effectively silenced as their testimony is barred from consideration in formal knowledge production processes (Glass & Newman, 2015; Leblanc & Kinsella, 2016). When researchers and academics, often unwittingly, commit pre-emptive testimonial injustices, members of epistemically (and often not accidentally socio-economically) marginalised or oppressed groups have their research questions, interests and understandings systematically ignored and overlooked – which in turn has important ramifications for broader development and policy decisions (Glass & Newman, 2015). In cases of epistemic objectification, on the other hand, where the tenets of the positivist paradigm are perhaps most obviously operational, the epistemic harm committed does not accrue from being barred from having one's testimony enter the marketplace of ideas, but rather the harm that comes from relegating an "active epistemic agent (or subject) to that of passive object, to be studied, observed, and in many cases, exploited" (Leblanc & Kinsella, 2016:66).

Such exclusionary epistemic practices not only further the perception of the public that the academe is an elitist 'ivory tower', but serves to further separate the public from academics who are perceived to be detached 'experts'. A barrier is thus created between the public's access to knowledge in HE intuitions and, at the same time, a barrier is created between the academics who need to work with the public in non-exclusionary ways in order to further research and teaching goals.

Actors and actions challenging the apartheids of knowledge

In order to understand the relationship between social innovation and the reimagining of the knowledge economy necessary to reorientate HE most fully towards the public good, we must draw from the experiences of those working on the front lines of change. In May 2018, Rhodes University held their fourth annual Community Engaged Learning Symposium, with a specific focus on social innovation and bringing together academics, students and community partners from across South Africa to reflect critically and collectively on each other's work. This collection stems from the reflections in this setting. It does so as both a translation and illustration of translated practices; case studies through which examples of better – and broader – engagements may be made from within the academe by academics or from community partners with academe. This collection is aimed at the individual academic or practitioner and is intended to provide examples of how CE-derived practices might be incorporated into the core mandates of teaching and research. To this end, the chapters have been structured to guide the reader deeper into the realm of embedded CE-derived practices in that context.

An attempt has been made to draw together submissions which highlight, either tacitly or explicitly, ways to move beyond the issues of epistemic injustice, identity prejudice and positivist dominance in knowledge production. In selecting each submission, we deliberately sought to provide examples of the diversity of voices made available to us, and, as a collection of texts, provide examples of each of the themes and ideas discussed in this introduction. Our aim is to provide illustration of a collection which expands on the definition of 'expert', moving it away from the realm of (what Haas speaks of as) 'epistemic communities' and out of the positivist academic mode to include students', teachers', and community practitioners' voices alongside those of 'academics' and to include their voices *from that position*. In offering a diverse collection of knowledges perspectives in this way, the collection presents as kind of a hall of mirrors, showing the challenges and issues from a myriad angles and views, to raise important questions for the reader about where distortions or blind-spots in their own thinking may arise. As a result, the reader will find contained diversity, not just in the material or the position of the author, but also in the ways of writing and constructing writing which diverges from the formulaic model of academic publications. It includes work at proposal stage, reflections by those inside and outside the academy on their practices, explanations of research and research methods applied in an attempt to move the practices of disciplines. It brings questions, and intends to assist, not to necessarily provide answers, in encouraging readers to ask yet more questions and initiate discussions more widely in the academy, so that we might move to answer some questions collectively and, in doing so, transform HEIs into that envisioned in discussions on 'the developmental university'.

We have, in our selection, attempted to move beyond CE as a 'third branch' of the developmental university. In doing so, while we do take some of the work that has been done in CE into this collection, we deliberately selected work that does not. We also include submissions on work involving CE practitioners *outside* of CE, and practices that might not involve CE in higher education at all, but are programmes or reflections from which people in higher education might gain insight. In these instances, our goal is to ask how a developmental university might expand its practice beyond its epistemic community and engage with the community around it more broadly. Our goal is squarely to undo the logics of the apartheids of knowledge – it is also one reason for working with a broad understanding of social innovation: only by doing so can a multiplicity of voices be drawn into the project of expanding and diversifying the epistemic community of the academy. We focused on the principles outlined in this introduction – social inclusion, deep listening and creating spaces for knowledge outside of academia – in how we selected diverse voices, views, approaches and positions to highlight in this collection. Each chapter addresses these issues in its own way. Each chapter was selected because it was read as an invitation to find new ways of conducting teaching and research which breaks the epistemic mould of the academe, or, at the very least, adds another crack to, or chips away at, the manner that academics engage with the society in which they work.

In reading this collection, then, one should hold up a willingness to recognise the biases and prejudices of knowledge production processes in the academy; to give a generous reading to the myriad ways of knowing, writing and engaging with the world from inside the academy; and to avoid the common pitfall of evaluating and assessing according to frameworks and paradigms that are determined by the epistemic community of 'academic experts'. How to select and work with the texts that follow has been a challenge for the editors, and will necessarily be a challenge for the reader, but only through that challenge being accepted by the editors, and subsequently accepted by the reader, can we work towards challenging the apartheids of knowledge in higher education.

To facilitate this challenge, the collection is arranged into a number of parts. The first part comprises four chapters which illustrate the nexus of groups working in the Makhanda (formerly Grahamstown) education sector using CE-derived and social innovation orientated practices. We introduce six actors in these first four chapters. The first three are: Ashley Westaway, manager at GADRA Education, where educational programmes are conducted in the town; Nicola Hayes, former principal of Nombulelo High School, a Makhanda/Grahamstown public school; and, Benita Bobo, who runs the Engaged Citizen Programme for Rhodes University students through the university's CE Office. The position of each of these actors gives unique insights into the theoretical and practical problems and successes associated with education and volunteer programmes conducted by Rhodes University in the Makhanda/Grahamstown area.

Beginning with Bobo's discussion of the Engaged Citizen Programme (ECP) run by the Rhodes University Community Engagement Office, the chapter asks vital questions which highlight the importance, and justification, of CE and volunteerism by students in HE institutions. Bobo posits a number of pertinent questions which are vital for acquiring academic buy-in in social innovation projects: How do students at universities understand CE? What do students gain from such engagement? How do students change through CE activities? Bobo draws from the experience of working in ECP when asking these questions and illustrates how these questions have prompted the proposal for further research. This chapter highlights how we might take questions raised by our experiences of working in CE, identify what research needs to be done and produce a proposal from them.

How such 'engaged citizens' might collaborate through their organisations and institutions towards the formation of a 'coalition' aimed at positive change and social innovation is dealt with in Chapter 2. In this chapter, Westaway discusses some of the ways in which political power plays out in the public schooling sector of Makhanda/Grahamstown, and he reviews the efforts and effectiveness of varied collaborating actors to revitalise the sector. The chapter presents a robust theoretical scaffolding underlying the social innovation described, and highlights the wealth of expertise available beyond the ivory tower which can be harnessed for the knowledge generation project.

Chapter 3 is an autoethnographic reflection by Hayes, a school principal in Makhanda/Grahamstown's public schooling sector, and presents an important counter-narrative about power and the knowledge generation process to those seen in the pieces written from the perspective of academic practitioners. Hayes' reflections, covering the power dynamics of the school principals' position in relation to CE and volunteer programmes in the town, highlights the apartheid of knowledge through exploring "the reality of high power distance in the secondary education milieu and the perceived gap between those with 'valued knowledge' (in particular those within the academy) and those without." Hayes' chapter provides an important piece when read alongside Chapter 1, allowing the reader to think through the multiple layers of power and privilege which must be negotiated when facilitating spaces for co-development and co-reflection in community-based projects.

Three further actors in the town lead us deeper into the research arena in Makhanda/Grahamstown. Thandiswa Nqowana, a PhD candidate in the Rhodes University Pharmacy Department, along with Dr Roman Tandlich of that same department and Dr Sharli Paphitis of the Community Engagement Division, discuss their work in the field of public health and citizen science. Their case study of a community-based participatory research project at a Makhanda/Grahamstown public school emphasises the value of such interactions to researchers and community alike. They provide an outline of the community-based water quality monitoring programme in Makhanda/Grahamstown. Grade 9 learners from three high schools participated in this programme, which provided home testing kits to assess microbial counts in water, the results of which were used to pin-point water quality areas according the learners' water quality results. Here, research, education and citizen science converge in a public health programme in a town with notoriously poor water quality, introducing new technologies and ways of involving community members in the knowledge generation and dissemination process.

But these illustrations of some intersections and workings of CE and mutual benefits of participatory research are introductions, provocations and insinuations towards a different way in which HE can encounter the society it works within. Further exploration of certain aspects of these 'ways' are required. So we return to our point of departure and ask new questions in Part Two of the collection. From one high school programme to another, we turn to Diepsloot in Johannesburg where a participatory action research approach is used by Lourenço to find a way to empower learners through simultaneously focusing on English language – the medium of instruction in public schools – and mathematical proficiency in an online bilingual mathematics programme. Lourenço's chapter introduces Part Two, which focuses on education and the benefits which can come from service-learning and engaged research approaches in the education space. Continuing this line of thought, Bezerra and Paphitis, like Bobo in Chapter 1, provide an analysis of the effects of CE and volunteerism on university students. They argue that the discrepancies between reported personal growth and evidence of personal growth through engagements with the honours level service-learning programme hint towards a barrier to change in what is perceived as 'legitimate' or 'academic' knowledge. They then discuss some of the challenges posed to the widespread institutionalisation of service-learning programmes in HE.

Akhurst addresses another problem which emerges in the drive for new, more just, pedagogies and curricula in the course of changing the modes of knowledge production towards the public good. Akhurst effectively demonstrates how a service-learning component in community psychology training might also contribute towards new teaching methods and, importantly, curriculum transformation. In doing so, Akhurst addresses a key aspect of transformation in HE – how to move beyond the hard positivist paradigm in teaching and curricula and towards achieving the role envisioned of a developmental university, which trains students in addressing the needs of society – and provides concrete suggestions for how to do so through case study.

How, then, would one combine the *methodologies* of the academy towards social innovation? This question lies at the heart of Part Three, where authors suggest that effective social innovation must support local communities and contribute to capacity building of that community and its stakeholders. In Chapter 8 Ryan and Todd demonstrate such a process using the, now common, approach of systems theory in the opening chapter of Part Three of the collection. "What is clear," they say, "is that is there is a clear reliance on reliable information regarding the system itself. Access to such information is often difficult for South African researchers due to socio-political/cultural boundaries." Thus, they propose that the key to the effective application of systems theory is the development of trust through "stakeholder engaged research", using a case study of sports science research in a local soccer community to illustrate their point. This "stakeholder engaged research" acknowledges that trust comes through collaboration. Collaborative engagement, which was introduced by Bobo and Hayes in Part One, is expanded on in Chapter 9 by Haese *et al.*, who move away from a 'charity/deficit' approach to community engaged work through collaboration and developing along the grain of community members' strengths. They do so through a case study of visual literacy and a "wordless picturebook" project established in Mamelodi near Pretoria.

Such innovative 'new literacies' projects are becoming increasing popular in social innovation work and engaged research practices, as their use has shown itself to be effective in bringing out vital stories and connections through which participants can be empowered by personal reflection, as well as circumventing problems of low literacy levels (as understood by conventional metrics) in South Africa. But with these new literacies and methods of data collection come new ethical considerations. Gachago and Scheepers address these new conside-rations head-on in their case study of the Cape Peninsula University of Techno-logy's digital storytelling programmes. In Chapter 10 they provide us with an analytical framework through which ethical considerations of digital storytelling in research projects may be managed by using Tronto and Fisher's "ethics of care."

Themes of collaboration, active citizenship and addressing socio-economic challenges are drawn together in Part Four. Shabalala and Bezerra's case study in Chapter 11 illustrates how various government departments can collaborate with volunteer organisations in the Kruger National Park to improve the socio-economic conditions of surrounding communities through ecotourism and eco-education, while Davy *et al.*, address a more specific problem in Chapter 12: that of everyday resilience amongst cardboard collectors in Durban's informal economy. In a collaboration between Rhodes University's Department of Human Kinetics and Ergonomics, Asiye e'Tafuleni (who works with informal traders at

Warwick Junction in Durban) and Women in Informal Employment: Globalising and Organising (WIEGO), Davy *et al.*, reflect on their experiences of working together to design and produce an innovative trolley design which might solve some of the problems encountered by informal cardboard collectors in the course of their daily work. Nel and Govender, in Chapter 13, offer an evaluation process of such programmes, which might enhance societal inclusion through the adoption of socially innovative systems. They do so by offering insights into Employee Assistance Programmes in South Africa. This study looks at another vital element of the kinds of work covered in Chapters 11 and 12, that is, how might a researcher assess the efficacy of a project in terms which relate to the broader goals of community-based, participatory and social innovation orientated research.

To conclude the volume, Van Rooyen and Venter offer an explicit framing of the academic process aligned to the goals outlined here. In Chapter 14, they argue that the central processes of scholarly work already contain the elements with which to reach the goals of a developmental university. A clear commitment to a radical interpretation of the processes of "discovery, integration, knowledge sharing and application" leads scholars to a participatory and engaged research. In effect, a commitment to the academic process in itself, rather than baseline expectations of the academy, brings scholars directly into the research space outlined in this book. They argue this through a discussion of their experiences with the Common Good First programme at the University of the Free State, but leave us with a call to action in doing so: we needn't change the foundation of our endeavour, but we must make a clear commitment to our research process. In doing so, we can alter the way in which knowledge is produced, assist in breaking the apartheids of knowledge, and move towards the realisation of a higher education sector which works directly for the betterment of society and consequently acts as a positive and effective force in bringing about social justice.

References

Akpan, W., Minkley, G. & Thakrar, J. 2012. In search of a developmental university: Community engagement in theory and practice. *South African Review of Sociology*, 43:1-4.https://doi.org/10.1080/21528586.2012.694239.

Bernal, D.D. & Villalpando, O. 2002. An apartheid of knowledge in academia: The struggle over the "legitimate" knowledge of faculty of color. *Equity and Excellence in Education*, 35:169-180. https://doi.org/10.1080/713845282.

Brandt, C. 2004. A thirst for justice in the Arid Southwest: The role of epistemology and place in higher education. *Educational Studies*, 36. https://doi.org/10.1207/s15326993es3601_8.

Council on Higher Education. 2013. Council on Higher Education. *Higher Education Data*.

Davies, C.J. 2016. Whose knowledge counts? Exploring cognitive justice in community-university collaborations. Doctoral Dissertation: University of Brighton.

Department of Education. 1997. *Education White paper 3. A programme for the transformation of higher education*. Pretoria.

Erasmus, M. 2014. The political unconscious of higher education community engagement in South Africa. In: M. Erasmus & R. Albertyn (eds). *Knowledge as enablement: Engagement between higher education and the third sector in South Africa*, 100-118. Bloemfontein: Sun Press.

Fine, M. & Torre, M. 2008. Theorizing audience, products and provocation. In: P. Reason & H. Bradbury (eds). *The SAGE handbook of action research*. London: Sage Publications.

Fondacaro, M.R. & Weinberg, D. 2002. Concepts of social justice in community psychology: Toward a social–ecological epistemology. *American Journal of Community Psychology* 30:473-492.https://doi.org/10.1023/A:1015803817117.

Fricker, M. 2007. *Epistemic injustice: Power and the ethics of knowing*. Oxford: Oxford Scholarship Online.http://doi.org//10.1093/acprof:oso/9780198237907.001.0001.

Glass, R.D. & Newman, A. 2015. Ethical and epistemic dilemmas in knowledge production: Addressing their intersection in collaborative, community-based research. *Theory and Research in Education*, 13:23-37.https://doi.org/10.1177/1477878515571178.

Haas, P.M. 1990. Obtaining international environmental protection through epistemic consensus. *Millennium - Journal of International Studies*. 19:347-363.https://doi.org/10.1177/03058298900190030401.

Haas, P.M. 1992. Introduction: Epistemic communities and international policy coordination. *International Organization,* 46:1-35. https://doi.org/10.1017/S0020818300001442.

Hazelkorn, E. 2009. Community engagement as social innovation. In L. Weber & J. Duderstadt (eds). *The Role of the Research University in an innovation-Driven Global Society,* 63-76. London: Economica.

Karnilowicz, W., Ali, L & Phillimore, J. 2014. Community research within a social constructionist epistemology: implications for "Scientific Rigor." *Community Development,* 45. Routledge: 353-367.https://doi.org/10.1080/15575330.2014.936479.

Leblanc, S. & Kinsella, E.A. 2016. Toward epistemic justice: A critically reflexive examination of "sanism" and implications for knowledge generation. *Studies in Social Justice,* 10:59-78.https://doi.org/10.26522/ssj.v10i1.1324.

Medina, J. 2012. Hermeneutical injustice and polyphonic contextualism: Social silences and shared hermeneutical responsibilities. *Social Epistemology: A Journal on Knowledge, Culture and Policy,* 26:201-220.

Metz, T. 2014. Africanising institutional culture: What is possible and plausible. In S. Mathews and P. Tabensky (eds). *Being at "home": Race, institutional culture and transformation at South African higher education institutions,* 242-272. Durban: UKZN Press.

Moore, M.L., Westley, F.R. & Nicholls, A. 2012. The social finance and social innovation nexus 1. *Journal of Social Entrepreneurship,* 3:115-132. https://doi.org/10.1080/19420676.2012.725824.

Mulgan, G. 2006. The process of social innovation. *Innovations: technology, governance, globalization,* 1:145-162.https://doi.org/10.1162/itgg.2006.1.2.145.

Newman, A. & Glass, R.D. 2015. Ethical and epistemic dilemmas in empirically-engaged philosophy of education. *Studies in Philosophy and Education,* 34:217-228. https://doi.org/10.1007/s11217-014-9418-3.

Pizarro, M. 1998. "Chicana/o Power!"1 Epistemology and methodology for social justice and empowerment in Chicana/o communities. *International Journal of Qualitative Studies in Education,* 11:57-80. https://doi.org/10.1080/095183998236890.

Pol, E. & Ville, S. 2009. Social innovation : Buzz word or enduring term? *The Journal of Socio-Economics,* 38:878-885. https://doi.org/10.1016/j.socec.2009.02.011.

Potts, K. & Brown, L. 2005. Becoming an anti-oppressive researcher. In L. Brown & S. Strega (eds). *Research as Resistance: Critical, Indigenous, & Anti-Oppressive Approaches,* 255-286. Toronto: Canandian Scholars' Press.

Sohng, S. 1996. Participatory research and community organizing. *Strategic Perspectives on Planning Practice*, 23:123-137.

Soudien, C. 2010. Some issues in affirmative action in higher education in South Africa. *The South African Journal of Higher Education*, 24:224-237.

Sugden, J. 2006. Security sector reform: The role of epistemic communities in the UK. *Journal of security sector management*, 4:1-20.

Wood, F. 2018. *Universities and the occult rituals of the corporate world: Higher education and metaphorical parallels with myth and magic.* 1st edition. New York: Routledge.

Chapter 1

How to determine the role of community engagement in student development: Formulating a research project proposal to answer this question

Benita Bobo

RHODES UNIVERSITY
COMMUNITY ENGAGEMENT DIVISION

b.bobo@ru.ac.za

1. Context and introduction

Although anecdotal evidence is easily found, little research has been done on the role of CE in student development in the context of the Eastern Cape, South Africa, with a particular focus on the role of student volunteerism. This chapter presents a research project proposal developed by the coordinator of the volunteering programme (the Engaged Citizen Programme) at an HEI in the Eastern Cape in an attempt to answer important questions and to document the journey that culminated in this project proposal. Taking into consideration that this volunteering programme takes place at an HEI, Rhodes University, the relationship between CE and higher education is the starting point of this discussion.

HEIs play an important intellectual role in, and are important economic resources to, their communities. In line with the growing recognition of the importance of investing in community building (Gugerty & Swezey, 1996), the White Paper of Higher Education Transformation (1997) saw fit to make CE part of the

HEIs' agenda (Bengu, 1997). This has led to HEIs moving away from the concept of an 'ivory tower' and becoming more socially responsive and involved in their communities. The communities that HEIs exist in provide a rich learning environment for students, as well as an opportunity to contribute to community development (Gugerty & Swezey, 1996). CE in South African HE has shifted from being defined as one of the three pillars alongside teaching and research, to being seen as integrated within the broader projects of teaching and research (Lazarus, Erasmus, Hendricks, Nduna & Slamat, 2008). This shift has allowed for "a deeper sense of context, locality and application" (Lazarus, *et al.*, 2008, p. 62). D. Hornby, the Director of the Community Engagement Division of Rhodes University, notes that the aim at Rhodes University is to infuse CE across the university (personal communication, January 5, 2016), supporting the recommendation that it should be "institutionally embedded and cross cutting with teaching and research" (Preece, 2013a, p. 270).

CE can be defined as the process of using teaching, learning and research to build and exchange knowledge, skills, resources and expertise in "mutually beneficial relationships with communities" (Petersen & Osman, 2013, p. 4). It is typically expressed in a variety of forms, ranging from credit bearing service-learning academic programmes to non-credit bearing volunteer activities. Service-learning, as a form of CE, combines academic studies with service in communities, while volunteerism is the process of student engagement in community activities that are of a social and educational nature (Petersen & Osman, 2013). CE can also be defined as a process of bringing together different and often multiple stakeholders to build relationships in collaborative ways, with the ultimate goal of improving the collective wellbeing of all (Maurrasse, 2010).

Globally, in the past decade, there has been a paradigm shift in the way in which universities are positioning their work with communities. Whereas CE activities were formerly seen as extra-curricular activities, there has been a growing recognition that they should form a core part of institutional goals. UNESCO (2009, as cited in Preece, 2013a, p. 266) states that HE "should create mutually beneficial partnerships with communities and civil societies to facilitate the sharing and transmission of appropriate knowledge". These activities have shifted from a perspective of philanthropy to one of collaboration (Preece, 2013b).

A university that is engaged is described as one that is committed to producing graduates who are critically involved and are able to "link knowledge to the public good through engaged scholarship" (Netshandama, 2010, p. 354). This emphasises civic responsibility and the enhancement of students' learning. Graduating students need to be equipped to excel in a diverse, unequal and complex society. Being involved in CE activities gives students an experience that promotes their learning and personal development and helps them to engage in critical reflective thinking that enhances their social responsibility (Phelps & Dostilio, 2008). CE heightens students' knowledge and understanding of their local communities. It also develops students' "skills, disposition, and habits to work with others in a democratic way towards the common good" (Bringle & Hatcher, 2010, p. 413). Students develop the capacity to be global citizens who contribute to the common good (Carolissen et al., 2010). Outcomes for students who participate in CE include self-reported gains in civic respon- sibility, life skills and academic development (Bringle & Hatcher, 2010). Gugerty and Swezey (1996) propose that CE activities, as learning opportunities for students, should be as follows:

1. The location of the activities should be based in the local community.
2. Students' interactions with community partners must be based on mutual goals and democratic processes, forming reciprocal relationships.
3. The activities should include structured reflection sessions.

The ECP has been designed to include these three elements in the following ways. First, the majority of the CE activities at Rhodes University are based in the broader Makhanda community. In particular, this programme is based in diverse parts of the local community. Second, within the programme, an annual strategic planning session is held with all community partners, where the goals for the year are set and outlined. There is an emphasis on the building of mutually beneficial relationships between community partners and student volunteers. Third, each quarter all student volunteers and community partners who are part of the ECP engage in reflection sessions. For CE to be educational for students, students should be challenged to continuously reflect on their engagement. Asking community partners to facilitate and/or participate in these reflection sessions legitimises their role as educators in the learning process (Gugerty & Swezey, 1996).

There are four critical elements that lend themselves to thoughtful CE. These are:

- Orientation and training: They are important first steps in CE for both community partners and students. It is important to provide sufficient information from the onset about the terms of engagement.
- Community voice: The incorporation of the community's perspective is essential in building bridges, making changes, solving problems and combating exploitation or differing expectations, etc.

- Meaningful action: All engagement needs to be necessary and of value to both the community partner and the students.
- Reflection: This is a crucial component of CE, as it places the experiences into a broader context (Mintz & Hesser, 1996).

These four critical elements are evident in CE activities at Rhodes University, as outlined in the programme details discussed in the following sections.

2. The Engaged Citizen Programme (ECP)

The ECP is the biggest volunteerism programme currently running at Rhodes University, with over 300 students registered as active volunteers at 27 community partner organisations in Makhanda. Community partner organisations are grouped into the following categories:

1. Arts and alternative education: Students in these organisations engage in extra-curricular education-related activities, including (but not limited to) art, drama, music and computer literacy projects. These projects require creative engagement with extra-curricular activities, bridging academic and creative skills.
2. High school tutoring and mentoring: Students work with high school learners, providing academic tutoring and/or mentoring. Students who sign up to be academic tutors need to attend a mandatory course on tutoring at the beginning of the year. This is a certified National Qualifications Framework (NQF) level 4 short course that is offered through the Rhodes University Education Faculty.
3. Literacy and homework: Students in these organisations typically work with learners who are in primary school. They engage in literacy programmes such as homework clubs and reading clubs. Students who sign up to volunteer in reading clubs need to attend a mandatory course on reading club orientation at the beginning of the year. This is a certified NQF level 5 short course that is offered through the Rhodes University Department of Literary Studies in English.
4. Support: Students volunteer in organisations such as old age homes, shelters and orphanages.

Community partner organisations register as part of the ECP with the Rhodes University Community Engagement (RUCE) Division each year by signing a Memorandum of Understanding (MOU). This MOU outlines what the rights and responsibilities of both RUCE and the community partner are. Community partner organisations appoint a volunteer manager each year who works closely with RUCE in coordinating the programme in what RUCE terms a co-management process. This co-management process entails RUCE working closely with the volunteer manager in jointly planning, executing and evaluating any CE activities in which they are jointly involved as part of this programme. Whereas RUCE assumes the overall responsibility for training all student volunteers each year before they commence with their volunteer activities, volunteer managers are invited to form part of the training by facilitating some of the sessions. Additionally, volunteer managers, as part of the training, run a community partner fair where they recruit potential volunteers, informing them about their organisations and what they would be expected to do at the organisations should they choose to volunteer there. The volunteer manager is also responsible for orientating student volunteers and facilitating volunteer activities at their organisations. Additionally, they assume the responsibility of organising any additional organisation-specific training that they feel will be beneficial for their student volunteers.

Mandatory annual training is provided to all students who wish to participate in the programme. All students, regardless of whether they have volunteered previously, attend the training should they wish to participate in the programme in that given year. The training is an orientation towards the principles of CE at Rhodes University, as outlined below, and includes theoretical concepts. First time volunteers receive different training to that offered to repeat volunteers. Student leaders (senior volunteers who take on leadership roles within the pro-gramme) receive further practical training in leadership skills. Additionally, RUCE has partnered with faculties and departments at Rhodes University to run short courses for certain groups of volunteers. The Education Faculty runs a tutoring short course for all students who wish to tutor, whereas the Departments of Education and Literary Studies in English run a reading club orientation short course for all students who wish to volunteer in reading clubs. Both of these short courses are accredited by Rhodes University and are pitched at NQF level 4 and NQF level 5 respectively. They are mandatory for all volunteers who wish to work in these respective fields and are completed annually, once-off. The School of Languages and Literatures also offers a short course on basic isiXhosa conversational skills for all student volunteers who wish to learn the language. This short course is South African Qualifications Authority (SAQA) registered at the Adult Basic Education and Training Level 1. While this course is not mandatory, many student volunteers register for it and have found it beneficial for their volunteer activities.

After the signing of the MOU each year, volunteer managers attend an annual strategic planning session with RUCE where the goals for the year are set. Halfway through the year, a mid-year review is held where RUCE and volunteer managers jointly assess progress on set goals. An end of year review is also held annually. Additionally, at the end of each quarter volunteer managers co-facilitate, with their student leaders, team meetings with their groups of student volunteers where they reflect on progress and tackle problems that might have arisen. Student leaders are experienced student volunteers who have previous volunteer experience and have demonstrated leadership abilities. They are selected annually to work closely with volunteer managers and the coordinator of the ECP in managing small teams of student volunteers. RUCE has appointed two dedicated staff members who coordinate the programme, a coordinator of the ECP, as well as a Community Partner Liaison. Whereas the coordinator of the ECP works closely with student volunteers and manages the small team of student leaders, the Community Partner Liaison works closely with the volunteer managers throughout the year.

An asset-based approach to CE recognises that all communities have assets, whether they may be "natural environment resources, or human skills and knowledge" (Preece, 2013a, p. 990). The principles and the approach used by RUCE include:

- mutuality, which means that all CE activities are mutually beneficial for all parties involved;
- working from a strategic model of engagement, which entails recognising your own assets as well as that of others; and
- joint learning, action and reflection.

The goal of CE is thus "to build on existing assets in order to construct a resource-led foundation for development which is controlled by the community rather than external agents" (Preece, 2013b, p. 990). Effective engagement with com-munities leads to relationships that are mutually beneficial in nature, and shared responsibility develops amongst all stakeholders (Netshanadama, 2010).

All student volunteers and volunteer managers who have actively participated in the programme annually receive a certificate of participation at an award ceremony. Active participation entails attending a minimum of 80% of volunteer activities throughout the year. These volunteer activities include attending the mandatory training at the beginning of the year, volunteering weekly for a mini-mum of an hour during term time and attending the quarterly reflection team meetings. Additionally, for student leaders and volunteer managers this includes submitting the quarterly written reports.

There are also special awards that are given at the award ceremony, and while a majority of the award recipients are part of the ECP, a few of them are also involved in other CE activities at Rhodes University. One is either nominated to receive an award or must apply for it. These award categories include:

- Student volunteer of the year: This is a student who does exceptionally well in their volunteering, going over and above the minimum requirements. They devote an immense amount of energy to creating sustainable relationships with their community partner organisation. This student demonstrates a deep understanding of the principles of CE at Rhodes University. They show dedication, creativity and leadership initiative.
- Community partner of the year: This is a community partner who builds mutually beneficial and sustainable relationships with all their student volunteers. They collaborate well with student volunteers and RUCE. This partner makes a notable impact on their target community through using CE principles.
- Society/sports group of the year: This award goes to a student society group or a sports club that has made a valuable contribution in the Makhanda community through the use of the CE principles. They partner with an organisation in the local community to make a notable impact.
- Hall/residence of the year: This award goes to a hall or residence that has built a solid partnership with a community partner. They must demonstrate collegiality and collaboration, working on well-focused, organised CE activities with their community partner.
- Student researcher of the year: The recipient of this award is a student or a group of students who bridge the gap between academia and community development. Their research is mutually beneficial and contributes to the body of knowledge that informs CE practices.

It is hoped that student volunteers who actively participate in the ECP are able to demonstrate that they meet the following three goals by the end of their volunteer activities:

1. understand the socio-economic context and how it limits or advances life opportunities;
2. become socially active, contributing to community development in Makhanda; and
3. build meaningful relationships with a diverse range of people.

Having outlined in detail what the ECP is and how it presents a robust and structured volunteerism programme, the next section moves to the research question at the heart of the proposal I have developed to better understand the developmental role of the ECP. In sharing this proposal, I hope to outline how my thinking has been influenced by my practice and context and to provide guidelines on how to build these type of proposals.

3.   Research questions

In an interview about CE, Dr Sizwe Mabizela, Vice-Chancellor of Rhodes University, stated: "Every student who has had the opportunity to participate in community engagement is very, very grateful for the opportunity. And, you can really see young people who have participated in these activities, they are qualitatively different" (S. Mabizela personal communication, July 2015). This prompted me to question what it actually means for one to be 'qualitatively different'. What developmental process in the CE learning context would lead to a qualitative difference in persons?

I was struck by anecdotal evidence from past students who have been actively involved in the programme and feel that it has made a difference in their lives. One particular example involving a former student volunteer and student leader, Esihle Matshaya, stood out to me. She said: "Because you took a chance on me and made me a student leader way back then I found my true love. I am doing quite a bit in the CSI sphere (won't go into detail because God deserves the credit not me), my thesis will involve the love you introduced me to and I have come to the realisation that I am actually a developmental journalist. Guys, this woman works *pha kwi* [there at] community engagement offices. Please sign up and volunteer, the structures they have in place are phenomenal. I literally survived depression in third year and managed to pass because [of] RUCE office and Benita's hard work!" (E. Matshaya personal communication, June 1, 2018).

What both Dr Mabizela and Esihle say is that being actively involved in CE activities can make a difference in one's life. I decided to continue my studies and narrow in on the following research questions: "What do students understand the role of CE to be, and does this understanding change over time as students engage in community engagement activities?" Further research questions are: "What are students' understanding of 'engagement', a 'community' and their role in society?" and "What skills and knowledge do students gain from participating in community engagement activities?" The main aim of these research questions are to provide a space to reflect on the impact active involvement in CE activities makes on student development, and in particular, how the structure of the ECP provides an enabling space for this development to occur.

4. Methodology

4.1 Data collection

In order to answer my questions, the three goals of the ECP will be measured in various ways. Firstly, a pre- and post-test, in the form of a questionnaire, are used to find out what the students know about the principles of CE before they undergo training. This questionnaire is also used to check if there is any new learning at the end of the student's volunteering activities and is thus re-administered at the end of the student's volunteer activities. The questionnaire asks questions in relation to what the student is doing in their volunteer space, as well as what they understand the CE principles to be. The following four questions are included in this questionnaire:

1. What do you understand community engagement to be? What principles underpin it?
2. What role, if any, do you believe you have to play in community engagement?
3. What do you hope to gain from participating in community engagement activities? OR: What have you gained from participating in community engagement activities?
4. What role, if any, do you feel community partners have to play in your development? OR: Do you believe community partners have played a role in your development? Explain your answer.

Secondly, the student's attendance record will be tracked to check whether they are complying with the requirements of the programme. An assumption is made that if students participate fully in the programme, they learn more. Thus, a correlation will be made between participation and learning.

Thirdly, at the end of each quarter students will be asked to engage in a variety of reflection tasks, in addition to attending reflection team meetings with their community partners and student leaders. In the first and last quarter students will be asked to engage with the "Wedding Ring" model (**Figure 1**) (Talbot, 2016). In the second quarter they will answer a series of questions from a guided reflection task, and in the third quarter they will engage in a group reflection task. I outline what each of these entail below.

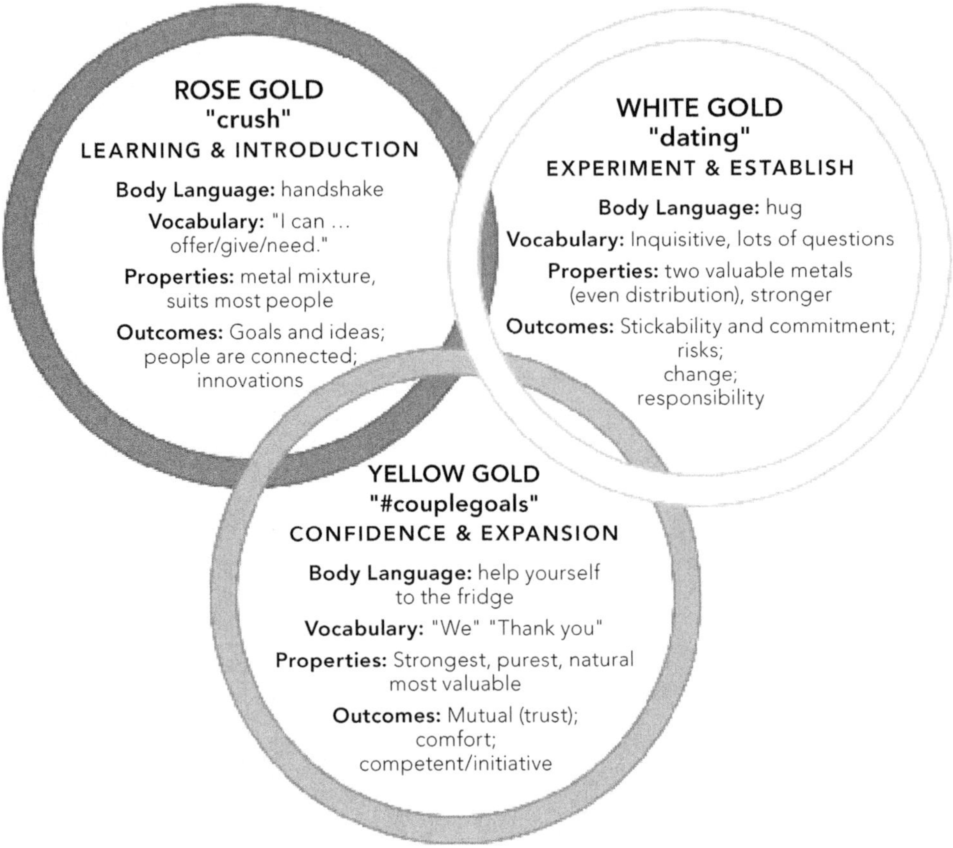

Figure 1: The "Wedding Ring" model

This model is based on the Russian wedding rings, which are made up of three different bands of gold that are bound together. Talbot (2016) proposed using this as a way of understanding CE, particularly at Rhodes University, as CE is centred around relationships. Talbot (2016) explains that while this reflects her own experience as a volunteer in CE, many students and community partners go through the same motions in developing their relationships. Thus, this model is used as a metaphor to express the experience and learning that occurs as one engages in volunteer activities. Each experience is built on from the previous experience, thus demonstrating that learning takes place. The three different bands represent the three different stages of the relationship-building process. The first band, the rose gold band, is regarded as the first stage, while the second band, the white gold band, is regarded as the second stage. The third band, the yellow gold band, is regarded as the third and final stage and also the ultimate goal. Moving through the various stages is not a linear process, as it is influenced by many factors. It is also important to note that as students move through the various stages, so do partners. Sometimes one might stay at one stage for a very long time; it is all part of a process (Talbot, 2016).

Stage one, the rose gold band, is the introduction of the relationship. This is where students visit the community partner organisation for the first time and are excited to learn about what the partner does, orientation occurs and there is goal setting between the community partner and the student volunteer. Usually there is a lot of emphasis on what the individual can do and very minimal emphasis on joint learning at this stage. In stage two, the white gold band, the relationship between the student volunteer and the community partner is solidified. Usually, student leaders are involved in this stage, where responsibility between student volunteers and community partners is negotiated and shared and joint learning begins to occur. Insight into the overarching RUCE goals is still limited at this stage, however, with much emphasis being on that particular partner relationship. Stage three, the final stage, which is the yellow gold band, is the ultimate goal of CE. At this stage, community partners and student volunteers are completely comfortable with learning from each other and equally contribute to their jointly set goals. Student volunteers feel that they are a part of the community and/or organisation that they volunteer in, and community partners feel that they are equal partners in the CE process. There is a complete understanding of the principles and practice of CE, and successes of the partner relationship are attributed not to individual effort, but to team effort (Talbot, 2016).

Based on this understanding of the wedding ring model, students will be asked to reflect by answering the questions below. In term 1 they will be asked the following questions:

1. Which stage of the wedding band do you feel you are in?
2. What were you expected to do when you arrived at your community partner each week?
3. What new knowledge do you hope to gain about your community partner?
4. Do you have some goals for the year ahead?

In term 4 they will be asked the following questions:

1. Which stage of the wedding band do you feel you are in? Has this changed since term 1? If yes, please explain how.
2. Did you see what you expected to see when you arrived at your community partner each week?
3. Have you gained new knowledge about your community partner?
4. Have you been able to link your volunteer experience to your own reality?

5. Have you been able to realise your reason for doing the activities? OR: Do you feel there is purpose to your volunteering?
6. From what you have observed, have you been able to make judgements that will help you progress?
7. Do you feel your opinions/goals have changed now that you have more knowledge of the ECP experience?

4.1.1 Guided reflection task
These are the questions that student volunteers will be asked to engage with in term 2:
1. Expectations
   a. What did you expect to learn?
   b. What did you expect to experience?
   c. What were your preconceived ideas ...
      i. ... about your community partner?
      ii. ... about the other volunteers?
      iii. ... about what would happen?
2. Observation of activities
   a. What observations did you make about yourself?
      i. Your kind of interactions?
      ii. Your thoughts and feelings?
      iii. Your interactions with your peers?
      iv. Your interactions with your community partner?
      v. How were other people feeling? Why?
      vi. Any adjustments you wish to make/have made based on what has happened?
         1. How have these worked?
3. Reflecting on your learning
   a. What have you learned?
   b. What do you think your community partner has learned?
4. Relate this volunteer experience back to fundamental lessons from your training.

4.1.2 Interactive reflection
In the reflection to be done in term 3, each person will choose and cut out headlines or pictures from newspapers or magazines that relate to their current situation or plans at their community partner organisations. The collection can either be a collage or in a table format, such as a SWOT (Strengths, Weaknesses,

Opportunities, Threats) analysis. They need to share with the group why they chose it. Questions to guide image collections are:

1.1 What key strengths exist at your community partner site and within your group?

1.2 How might you use these strengths effectively?

2.1 What key challenges exist at your community partner site and within your group?

2.2 Using the asset-based approach to community development, how might you address these challenges?

What key opportunities exist at your community partner site and within your group?

1.1 How might you maximise on these opportunities effectively?

1.2 What key threats exist at your community partner site and within your group?

1.3 Using the asset-based approach to community development, how might you address these threats?

OR

Students will be asked to take one headline or photo that they are really drawn to or taken aback by. This headline will be as local as possible, although not necessarily recent, and relevant to issues being dealt with by volunteers. In small group, students must ask each other:

1. Why did you choose that headline (tell the story of how it links/is pertinent to your site)?

2. Is there a pressing issue at your site?

3. Do you think this is an isolated issue, or are other sites experiencing it?

4. Who is it affecting?

5. What opportunities/duty bearers/stakeholders are there to help overcome it?

6. Does the site/student volunteers/student leaders/volunteer managers have the capacity and resources to plan a way forward?

4.2 Data analysis

Thematic analysis will be used to analyse the transcribed data and to identify themes (Braun & Clark, 2006). This process "interprets various aspects of the research topic" (Braun & Clark, 2006, p. 79). The six steps described by Braun and

Clark (2006) will be followed. To summarise, these authors state that the process involves "familiarizing yourself with your data, generating initial codes, searching for themes, reviewing themes, defining and naming themes, and producing the report" (Braun & Clark, 2006, p. 87). NVivo, a qualitative data analysis software, will be used to arrange and track findings of this research and to manage the volume of the transcribed data and conceptualise it (Creswell, 2007).

5. Ethical considerations

This research will adhere to a code of ethics. Participants will give informed consent for participating in this research. This means that they will be made fully aware of what the entire research process entails and will be asked to sign a consent form before the data collection process starts. Should students not be willing to give consent, they will still be required to adhere to the programme specifications; however, their reflections will not form part of the research process. Students will be asked to include their student numbers on all their reflections in order to identify them when tracking their personal development during the analysis process. The student numbers will, however, be treated confidentially, with myself as the principal researcher being the only person who has access to them. Additionally, all students will be given pseudonyms in all publications. Participation in this research will be voluntary, with all participants being high functioning adults who are 18 years or older.

As the principal researcher, I will respect the autonomy and welfare of all participants. This means participants will have the right to withdraw from the research at any point. In the process of asking for informed consent, I have disclosed all potential risks to participants, which include distress caused by being triggered by a question during reflections. This, however, is unlikely. Should participants find themselves in distress, I will advise that they discontinue the research process and advise them to seek further professional assistance. I have also informed participants of the potential benefits of participating in the research, which include that they could be provided with a space for reflection and tracking their personal development through CE. As the principal researcher, I will endeavour to be transparent at all times with the participants, not only declaring what the research will be used for but also giving them access to the research findings. I will also use a process of reflexivity in order to guard against the influence of prior beliefs or assumptions that I might have as I have been involved in the programme for a number of years, first as a student volunteer and student leader, and subsequently as the coordinator of the programme (Neuman, 1997).

6.   Conclusion

While this research is still in its early stages and it may be too soon to share some results, anecdotal evidence does seem to suggest that students who participate in CE activities, such as the ECP, are, as Dr Mabizela says, "qualitatively different". It is hoped that this research will shed some light on the factors that enable student development in participants in CE. This will inform the future development of the programme, which could eventually serve as a model that other HEIs can use in their own contexts, with recommendations on how volunteer programmes can be structured in order to promote student learning and development. The aim is also to shed more light on the important role that community partners play in facilitating student learning and development, and how their role is promoted through the co-management model of CE activities that RUCE proposes.

References

Bengu, S.M.E. 1997. *Education White Paper 3 – a programme for Higher Education transformation* (Government Gazette No. 18207). South Africa: Department of Education.

Braun, V. & Clark, V. 2006. Using thematic analysis in Psychology. *Qualitative Research in Psychology, 3*(2), 77-101. doi:10.1191/1478088706qp063oa

Bringle, R.G. & Hatcher, J.A. 2010. Student engagement trends over time. In: H.E. Fitzgerald, C. Burack & S.D. Seifer (Eds.). *Engaged scholarship contemporary landscapes, future directions – Volume 2: Community-campus partnerships* (pp. 411-430). East Lansing: Michigan State University Press.

Carolissen, R., Rohleder, P., Bozalek, V., Swartz, L. & Leibowitz, B. 2010. "Community psychology is for poor, black people": pedagogy and teaching of community psychology in South Africa. *Equity & Excellence in Education, 43*(4), 495-510.

Creswell, J.W. 2007. *Qualitative inquiry & research design: Choosing among five approaches* (2nd ed.). Los Angeles: Sage Publications.

Department of Education, 1997, *Education White Paper 3: A programme for the transformation of higher education*, Government Gazette, vol. 390, no. 18515, Government Printers, Pretoria.

Gugerty, C.R. & Swezey, E.D. 1996. Developing campus-community relationships. In: B. Jacoby & Associates (Eds). *Service-learning in Higher Education: concepts and practices* (pp. 92-107). San Francisco: Jossey-Bass.

Lazarus, J., Erasmus, M., Hendricks, D. & Slamat, J. 2008. Embedding community engagement in South African higher education. *Sage Publications, 3*(1), 59-85.

Maurrasse, D.J. 2010. Standards of practice in community engagement. In: H.E. Fitzgerald, C. Burack & S.D. Seifer (Eds.). *Engaged scholarship contemporary landscapes, future directions – Volume 2: Community-campus partnerships* (pp. 223-234). East Lansing: Michigan State University Press.

Mintz, S.D. & Hesser, G.W. 1996. Principles of good practice in service-learning. In: B. Jacoby and Associates (eds). *Service-learning in Higher Education: concepts and practices* (pp. 26-50). San Francisco: Jossey-Bass.

Netshandama, V.O. 2010. Community development as an approach to community engagement in rural-based higher education institutions in South Africa. *South African Journal of Higher Education, 24*(3), 342-356.

Neuman, W. 1997. *Social research methods: qualitative and quantitative approaches.* Boston: Pearson.

Petersen, N. & Osman, R. 2013. An introduction to service learning in South Africa. In: N. Petersen, & R. Osman (Eds). *Service learning in South Africa* (pp. 2-32). South Africa: Oxford University Press.

Phelps, A.L. & Dostilio, L. 2008. Studying student benefits of assigning a service-learning project comparted to a traditional final project in a Business Statistics Class. *Journal of Statistics Education, 16*(3), 1-11. doi: 10.1080/10691898.2008.11889574

Preece, J. 2013a. Service learning and community engagement in South African universities: Towards an 'adaptive engagement' approach. *Alternation Special Edition,* 9, 265-291.

Preece, J. 2013b. Community engagement and service learning in a South African university: The challenges of adaptive leadership. *South African Journal of Higher Education, 27*(4), 986-1004. doi:10.20853/27-4-278

Talbot, A.L. 2016. *The wedding ring model.* Unpublished.

Chapter 2

Thinking incisively about and acting effectively in Makhanda/Grahamstown public schools

Ashley Westaway

GADRA EDUCATION

ashley@gadraed.co.za

1. Introduction

South Africa is in the midst of a schooling crisis (e.g. Bloch, 2009), and there is consensus amongst academics and commentators alike about the dimensions and causes of the deep-seated and wide-ranging problems besetting the schooling system. The main problem, as all agree, is that the system comprises two sub-systems, one of which is deemed to be dysfunctional (e.g. Taylor, 2011). The vast majority of the country's school fall into this dysfunctional sub-system, resulting in overall systemic crisis. In this chapter, I suggest that the Achilles heel of this dysfunctionality thesis is that it cannot account for the extent of the problems. If schooling was merely 'in crisis' and the reasons for the crisis were understood, then there would be no justifiable reason for the duration of the problems. Yet, they persist and show no sign of dissipating.

An initial purpose of this chapter, then, is to put together a feasible and sustainable argument that explains the persistence of the South African schooling crisis. My starting point is simple: systems are reproduced not because of what they fail to do, but because of what they produce, because of what they achieve. In this case, that approach requires a willingness to explore and understand the functional value of schools that are typecast as 'dysfunctional'. To kick-start this exploration, I present Bourdieu's analysis of schooling in France to illustrate the usefulness of the functionality or productiveness lens. I then develop a summary characterisation of the post-1994 South African state, drawing attention to the importance of patronage and welfare as techniques of power. This is the contextual basis upon which I make suggestions about the functional value and significance of so-called dysfunctional schools. It is this functionality, this productive contribution (rather than dysfunction) that accounts for the duration of the schooling crisis. If one adopts this kind of counter-hegemonic epistemic perspective, it is possible and necessary to posit some pointers and guidelines about how to frame interventions aimed at disrupting the educational status quo. Here the ideas of Gramsci are particularly useful.

Following this initial incisive analysis about public schooling and suggested resistance strategies, the chapter then describes and assesses a recent attempt to revitalise public education in the locality of Makhanda. This initiative was sparked by the installation of Sizwe Mabizela as Rhodes University's 6th Vice-Chancellor in 2015. On the occasion of his inauguration, he committed to re-positioning the university within the local context and specifically indicated that Rhodes would seek to play a much more deliberate and substantial role in public education in the city of Makhanda. The chapter concludes with an appraisal of the effectiveness of initiatives in the local war of position in the public education sector.

2.   Establishing the limitation of the 'dysfunctionality' thesis

All informed perspectives on South African schooling and all data sets on the topic point to the same conclusion, namely that this schooling system produces very poor educational outcomes. For example, South Africa performs very poorly in international studies[1] assessing numeracy and literacy competence, and data generated through domestic examination processes (principally the Grade 12 'matric' examinations and the Annual National Assessments or ANAs) indicate generally weak and highly differentiated educational performance across the system. More specifically, only about 20% of South African public schools produce acceptable educational outcomes (e.g. Spaull, 2013). This 20% is made up of former white schools (10%) and exceptional township and village schools (the other 10%). That is, only about one in nine township and village schools actually deliver their stated educational purpose. Whether or not South Africa's public schooling system is the very worst in the world or not is a moot point; that

---

1   Progress in International Reading Literacy Study (PIRLS), The Trends in International Mathematics and Science Study (TIMMS) and The Southern and Eastern Africa Consortium for Monitoring Educational Quality (SACMEQ)

it is amongst the worst is not contested. The poor educational outcomes include low levels of literacy and numeracy amongst South African youth, high levels of school drop-out and high failure rates. Long-term consequences of this include low throughput to universities and other quality tertiary institutions and high levels of unemployment amongst the youth.

The response of the academy and education commentators to the schooling situation is remarkably uniform. They agree that the system is in a state of crisis, or, in the words of Bloch, "a national disaster" (2009:58). Furthermore, they agree that one of its most important characteristics is deep division, fashioned along the lines of race and class. Fleisch (2007) dubs the system 'bi-modal', whereas others such as Taylor refer to it as comprising "two school sub-systems: one which is functional, wealthy and able to educate students; the other being poor, dysfunctional and unable to equip students with the necessary numeracy and literacy skills they should be acquiring" (2011:11).

The term dysfunction is telling; analysts argue that schools that are not producing acceptable education outcomes are defined by what they are doing wrong and by what they lack. Weak management, ill-equipped teachers, in-adequate teaching and under-utilisation of textbooks are some of the factors deemed to produce overall dysfunctionality. Herein lies the rub: these technical issues have been identified not only in academic work but also government policy documents such as the National Development Plan, and they should therefore be relatively easy to work on and resolve over time. Yet, there is no indication at all that the downward trend has been reversed, or even arrested.

Most recently, issues that have received academic and public attention include literacy levels, the 'real' matric pass rate and 'NEETs' (referring to those young people not employed and not in education or training). In late 2017, the findings of the 2016 Progress in International Reading Literacy Study (PIRLS) were released. Earlier PIRLS reports had estimated illiteracy at Grade 4 level at between 55% and 60%. This assertion is on par with other data such as drop-out/push-out rates (per grade cohort) hovering around 50% and a further 10 – 15% of each cohort failing the final matric examinations. In the light of these realities, estimates of literacy rates amongst Grade 4 learners sitting at between 40% and 45% seemed to be generous, since in all likelihood this would translate into lower drop-out and failure rates than that of the reality. This has been corrected in the 2016 PIRLS, which asserts that illiteracy rates amongst Grade 4 learners are as high as 78%. Turning attention to the real pass rate, when the South African government releases the matric results in early January, it calculates pass rates in relation to the number of registered full-time candidates and not according to the number of children who registered for Grade 1 12 years earlier or according to the number of teenagers who registered for Grade 10 two years earlier.

Because of the massive drop-out problem in South Africa, both opposition political parties and academic commentators have held that calculating the pass rate in terms of total cohort size (at either the Grade 1 or the Grade 10 stage) is a more accurate reflection of educational outcomes or performance, hence reference to this as the real matric pass rate. If one makes the Grade 1 calculation for 2017, the pass rate was 39%, while the Grade 10 calculation yields a pass rate of 37%. Gustafsson has criticised this approach, pointing out that it fails to take cognisance of factors such as grade repetition, supplementary examination performance and other second chance institutions (DBE, 2016a). On this basis he suggests a higher real pass rate, but by factoring in interventions that are in-dependent of government and the public education system, his approach un-avoidably has the effect of exaggerating its performance. Irrespective of exactly where analysts place the real matric pass rate, all are agreed that the drop-out and failure rates are very high and that this is the cause of the very high number of youth NEETs. Like much of the rest of Africa, South Africa is currently expe-riencing a youth bulge, but instead of this presenting in society as a 'demographic dividend' (opportunity), it is developing into a 'demographic time bomb' (threat). Because South African youth are generally undereducated, they cannot proceed to further or HE and they do not have the skills and capabilities required by the job market. In May 2018 Statistics South Africa (Statistics South Africa, 2018) reported that the country's NEETs comprised 3.3 million people aged between 15 and 24 years, out of a total national age cohort of 10.4 million people. This statistic underlines the fact that South Africa's considerable unemployment problem is best characterised as a youth unemployment crisis. Worryingly, but unsurprisingly, Stats SA earlier reported that the proportion of young black Africans (aged between 25 and 34 years of age) in skilled employment actually dropped between 1994 and 2014 (Statistics South Africa, 2014:5).

If the South African schooling system was a neutral space characterised by lack and malfunction and devoid of power relations, then its technical problems could readily be solved by technical solutions. But it is not – it is part of and derives from a context that is teeming with power relations which produce a host of effects and outcomes. The dysfunctionality thesis analyses South African schooling from the fanciful perspective of what it should do (the liberating school), rather than what it does do. I suggest that what schools actually do, militates against them doing what they supposedly should do. Furthermore, in order to understand what they do – their functional *raison d'être* – one needs to be willing to engage with underlying structural realities. From here the paper attempts to understand precisely these issues, namely the functional productivity of schools dismissed as dysfunctional and the context from which these schools emerge and are sustained.

3.   Bourdieu's France

Michel Foucault commented extensively on power. One of his key assertions in this regard was that instead of expecting the exercise of power to always suppress or oppress, one should rather understand that it generally produces and enables effects. "We must cease once and for all to describe the effects of power in negative terms: it 'excludes', it 'represses', it 'censors', it 'abstracts', it 'masks', it 'conceals'. In fact, power produces; it produces reality; it produces domains of objects and rituals of truth" (Foucault, 1977:194). This insight is useful in arriving at an understanding of why the educational system in South Africa is reproduced relentlessly, year-in and year-out. To smooth the way for my ela-boration of the South African education system, I first present Bourdieu's broad Foucauldian analysis of the role of education in contemporary French society. His starting point is that the structure of social space is the product of economic capital and cultural capital. He goes on to assert that the educational system "plays a critical role in the reproduction of the distribution of cultural capital and thus in the reproduction of the structure of social space" (Bourdieu, 2008:33). More specifically, the system functions to conserve and legitimise inequalities. It performs this role very effectively because it is technically accessible to all and treats everyone equally (2008:36).

The formal equality that the education system practices amounts to a pro-motion of the values and culture of 'the most favoured'. Because children of the rich are imbued with these values and culture from birth, they thrive in the system, while children of the poor flounder. For this reason Bourdieu claims that "the formal equity that governs the entire educational system is actually unjust, and, in any society that proclaims democratic ideals, it protects privileges all the better than would be their open and obvious transmission" (2008:36). Bourdieu asserts that justice in the system would necessarily involve giving "the disin-herited the real means for acquiring what others have inherited" (2008:36).

According to Bourdieu, the "ideology of 'gifts' is ... the cornerstone of the whole system" because it enables competences that have been acquired socially to be regarded as personal aptitudes, and on the other end of the spectrum it excuses teachers from giving the disfavoured the means of acquiring these competences (2008:37). In this way, the school "transforms inequalities of fact into inequalities of merit" (2008:38).

The operation of the schooling system gives rise to considerable 'mystification'. That is, it persuades those who it excludes that their social destiny is due to their own lack (of gifts), and thereby prevents them from understanding the structural mechanisms at play. The exceptional success of a handful of individuals who escape this destiny (who Bourdieu calls "the miraculously saved") both feeds into the ideology of gifts and accredits "the myth of the liberating school" (2008:38). The system similarly allows the privileged to perceive their success as a product of their own capability and application rather than as a predetermined outcome. In summary, the "educational system thus contributes to legitimising economic and social inequalities by giving a social order based on the transmission of economic and – still more so – cultural capital the appearance of an order based on merit and individual gifts" (2008:38).

In contemporary society, jobs and positions are increasingly tied to qualifications. As outlined above, educational qualifications are the preserve of the elite classes. Thus the educational system "makes a very major contribution to the rigidity of social structure" (2008:39). Finally, Bourdieu is critical of those who assess the educational system in relation to an aspired equalising function rather than in relation to what it actually does. These opinions have the effect of entrenching the myth that the system does offer equal opportunities to all, and in this way "they are complicit with the system that they denounce" (2008:34).

4. Brief characterisation of the post-1994 South African state

In order to put the building blocks in place to construct a Bourdieuian/Foucauldian argument about the productive functionality of the South African schooling system, it is necessary to briefly characterise the post-1994 state. Much has been written about the nature of the transition from apartheid to formal democracy. I concur with the likes of Mamdani (1996) and Southall (2016) who regard 1994 as only a partial break from the apartheid past. The reason for this was what I have described elsewhere as "elite co-option" of the ANC by global and national political and economic elites (Westaway, 2009:61). The much-heralded Constitution adopted and enacted in 1996 reflects the limited nature of the transition; specifically, it left the structure and ownership of the South African economy intact.

Southall's specific formulation in this regard contrasts state and corporate power. While the ANC government was able to take control of the former, the latter has remained in hands of white elite groupings. Consequently, the ANC's focus over the past two decades has been to reconfigure the state. Amongst other things, this has involved a massive change in the racial composition of government and the public service. Moreover, successive ANC governments have developed various strategies to exercise power, two of the most important of which are welfare and patronage. For the purpose of this paper, welfare refers to the government's attempts to mitigate poverty and sustain the lives of those without the material means to fend for themselves. Because of the exclusionary and exploitative core of apartheid, there were many million black South Africans in this situation in 1994. In terms of *realpolitik*, one should also recognise that these people constitute a sizeable proportion of the considerable mass of the ANC's voting bloc. Over the past twenty years, three basic forms of government grant were initially designed and then dispensed to greater and greater numbers of recipients. These are the state pension, the child-support grant and the disability grant. In addition, there are numerous other forms of state welfare that have been introduced over this period, including the provision of housing (so-called RDP housing) and low-paying menial jobs (through the Expanded Public Works and Community Works Programmes). All told, there are around thirty million South Africans (half of the population) who benefit from state welfare of one description or another.

Welfare has essentially been a mitigation strategy, a technique of power designed to avoid calamity and death; by contrast, patronage is more ambitious and transformative in its purpose. It seeks to empower and enrich; over the past twenty years it has been the key mechanism used to expand and build a black middle class. Key mechanisms through which patronage has been dispensed have been cadre deployment, employment equity (affirmative action) and black economic empowerment. Cadre deployment refers to the practice of installing people with political credentials into professional positions. Employment equity is legislated government policy that requires employers to implement affirmative action in order to a build a representative workforce, specifically in relation to race and gender. Black economic empowerment is also legislated; it is prescriptive in relation to the ownership and management levels of companies and to company practices such as procurement. Cadre deployment can only happen in those institutions that are themselves controlled by 'cadres'; invariably therefore this mechanism has been used in state institutions. Employment equity and black economic empowerment cover all significant institutions, in both the public and private sectors.

If one tracks the brief history of patronage in post-1994 South Africa, focusing on the two most long-lived presidencies, those of Mbeki and Zuma, one notices a clear shift of emphasis from the private to public sector. Mbeki came into the presidency focused on building a black middle class through deracialising the private sector. This is not to say that there were not significant changes brought about in the public sector during his presidency, but rather that he held that sustainable economic development had to be driven by the private sector. This, ultimately, is why he pushed through the Growth, Employment and Redistribution Plan (Gear) – an attempt to make South Africa a destination of choice for both foreign and local direct investment and to drive through a deracialisation of South African capitalism.

Zuma's presidency was significantly different from Mbeki's. He had little interest in engaging constructively with the established and entrenched corporate sector. Rather, he focused almost exclusively on the state and public sector. In the process, patronage degenerated into crony capitalism and corruption. The Gupta businesses are most notoriously linked to the former and the building of the Nkandla compound with the latter. During Zuma's ten years in office, economic growth slowed considerably and unemployment grew. His only counter to this was to increase the size of the public service and improve its conditions of employment. All the while, as the country's economic woes worsened, he had to manoeuvre to keep his grip on power. He did this by marginalising his allies-turned-foes, including Julius Malema (who later formed the opposition Economic Freedom Fighters or EEF), Zwelinzima Vavi (former General Secretary of COSATU) and Blade Nzimande (leader of the South African Communist Party). One of the consequences of these changes was that COSATU increasingly became a congress of public sector unions; the South African Democratic Teachers' Union (SADTU), with a membership of around 250 000 people, is now one of the most powerful affiliates of COSATU. As patronage increasingly emerged as the more important mechanism to consolidate his power, the state's ability to sustain the welfare system declined. This had repercussions throughout the South African society, not only for the millions of grant beneficiaries whose livelihoods were threatened in the first quarter of 2017.

5.   A characterisation of the functionality of so-called 'dysfunctional' schools

Having established the inability of the dysfunctionality argument to explain the persistence of the schooling system in South Africa, together with my summary of the inertia in the French education system and characterisation of the post-1994 South African state, I am now in a position to suggest an alternative to the dysfunctionality argument. For purposes of contrast, we can posit this as a 'functional' explanation of the persistence of South Africa's schooling crisis. The argument that follows pertains specifically to those schools that are characterised by educationists and the media alike as 'dysfunctional'.

The argument is built by explicitly considering these schools through the lenses of patronage and welfare. First, we look through the patronage lens. South African children lack academic skills and competencies because they are not taught effectively and they are not taught enough. Yet, the teachers who teach badly and who seldom teach are not held accountable by either school authorities or education bureaucrats. While this situation seems incorrigible and incredible if one assumes the liberating school, it becomes much more logical when one recognises cadre deployment as a pervasive mechanism of patronage that cuts across the institutional landscape of South Africa. In the no-fee schooling context, patronage is tightly controlled and dispensed by SADTU. The extent of this reality was laid bare in a 2015 government report authored by a Ministerial Task Team under the chairpersonship of John Volmink (currently the Chairperson of UMALUSI). The release of the report, now generally referred to as the 'Jobs for Cash' report, had been delayed for a protracted period because of its explosive content and findings. The report finds that "[t]he Department of Basic Education has retained semblances of managerial and administrative control in three of South Africa's nine Provinces … In all other Provinces, SADTU is in de facto control" (DBE, 2016b:119). As a result of its power and control in the education system, SADTU has what the Task Team calls 'undue influence' throughout, "in offices, in schools, Unions and everywhere else" (DBE, 2016b: 122). Unsurprisingly, this has led to certain instances of what can be regarded as extreme abuse, such the selling of posts. But more generically and endemically, cadre deployment has "weakened the education system because people without the requisite skills, abilities and commitment now serve in key areas" (DBE, 2016b:124). Put another way, many district officials, principals and teachers do not have the capacities required of them to be effective in their respective roles.

The combination of the rising political power of SADTU and rampant invoking of cadre deployment had positive financial and material consequences for teachers over the past decade. In 2008, their conditions of employment were significantly improved (Paton, 10 March 2014). To boot, their job security has increased apace, to the extent that it is virtually impossible to fire a SADTU member, whether for absence from work, non-performance or sexual harassment of children. Hence, Jansen is quite correct to refer to the teaching profession as "the biggest job protection racket in South Africa" (Jansen, 2014, not page numbered). And so we reach a first insight into what South African schools are – they are sites that enable the dispensing of state patronage by the membership of SADTU, to the membership of SADTU. Ndebele points out that it is little wonder that SADTU's determination to "maintain a political hegemony now emptied of visionary substance" inevitably involves or requires the subordination of professionalism (Ndebele, 2015, not page numbered).

Viewing no-fee public schools through the lens of welfare is equally insightful. How, if at all, does the South African state manage the welfare of its young citizens in these institutions? If one thinks of welfare in strict educational terms, then the above summary about the very poor learner outcomes would lead one, inexorably, to a conclusion that the state does not look after the welfare of its young people. In fact, during Zuma's presidency, the schooling system was stripped further of educational character. Amongst other things, the past ten years have seen the introduction of progression and modularisation policies. Together, these policies regulate the passage of 'learners' through the schooling system, such that their retention does not impact negatively on the matric results. Progression prescribes that learners are not permitted to repeat a grade more than once per phase (e.g. Foundation Phase, Further Education and Training Phase, etc.). In the event that a learner fails a second time in a band, then he/she is progressed to the next grade regardless. If this policy was implemented in isolation, then it could very well have resulted in a low matric pass rate because there would invariably have been large numbers and a large percentage of very weak students writing the final examinations. Hence the Department of Basic Education introduced modularisation for learners who have been progressed into Grade 12. Unless these learners pass their June and September Grade 12 examinations, they are not permitted to write their full set of examinations across all seven subjects. Instead, they can only write four subject examinations and have to delay writing examinations in the other subjects until the following year at the earliest. Government officials spuriously maintain that this approach gives weak learners a better chance at obtaining a National Senior Certificate. These claims are not backed up by compelling evidence. A more likely explanation for the introduction of modularisation is that it enables government to claim a relatively high pass rate, which underpins the legitimacy of the entire schooling system in public opinion.

While the educational substance of the schooling system was further hollowed out during Zuma's presidency, that system increasingly plays a key welfare role in relation to the material survival of millions of poverty-stricken South

African children. A useful starting point in understanding the system's material functionality is the ANC's 'Good Story' election message crafted for purposes of the 2014 general election. Some of the main assertions made by the ANC about its achievements in education over the past twenty years were as follows:

- It has improved access to schooling, to the extent that there is now almost 100% access at Grade 1 level.
- It has introduced and rolled out no-fee schooling, such that many parents do not have to pay for the basic education of their children.
- It has introduced and rolled out feeding schemes at no-fee schools. All children at these schools receive one free meal a day.

South African schools deemed to be dysfunctional, are best understood as day-time repositories or storehouses for working class black children. The fact that the massification of black education that began under apartheid (during the era of 'Bantu' education) has now been completed – resulting in universal access to schooling – means that all working class children can be accommodated in these repositories. Furthermore, they are by no means empty repositories; on the contrary, they are places where services are delivered and goods are dispensed. First, employees called 'teachers' offer child care or child-minding services. Levels of oversight are low and the actual amount of care that the professionals show for the children is negligible. Nevertheless, the children are kept behind lock and key (schools are generally fenced and gates are locked during school hours) and they are supervised by adults. The supervision responsibility shifts, according to a timetable, from employee to employee. Children move from room to room between allocated time slots called 'periods'. The significance of this day care service for the children's parents should not be underestimated because they are very busy trying to make household ends meet. They spend their entire day in a menial job or explore other ways of trying to put a plate of food on the family table each night. So, for the state to take their children off their hands for almost the entire day, in a relatively safe environment, is undoubtedly beneficial and valuable for them. And, lest we forget, with the significant recent expansion in the number of no-fee schools, this is (in most cases) a free service. Second, the state provides children with a free meal daily. Because money is scarce in many black working class families, the importance of this welfare benefit of schooling should not be down-played. The ANC government is doing what many fathers and mothers would not easily otherwise be able to do for their sons and daughters – they feed the children. (By way of contrast, it should be noted that the welfare processes outlined above do not pertain to former Model C schools: there, the middle class parents are required to pay fees and feed their children.) In summary, the so-called dysfunctional schools actually function very effectively as sites both where ANC state patronage is dispensed (to teachers) and where welfare is doled out en masse to working class black learners and their parents.

6. Thoughts about resisting hegemonic functionality

The epistemic approach to the South African public schooling system outlined above provides certain guidance in relation to fashioning and implementing interventions with transformative potential. In setting out the role of the intellectual, Foucault called for attention to the fissures and fault lines in the power configurations that make up the battlefield that is contemporary society (in our case, contemporary education in South Africa):

> What's effectively needed is a ramified, penetrative perception of the present, one that makes it possible to locate lines of weakness, strong points, positions where the instances of power have secured and implanted themselves … In other words, a topological and geological survey of the battlefield – that is the intellectual's role. (Foucault, 1980:62)

Broadly speaking, I would suggest that the beneficiaries of patronage (SADTU teachers and bureaucrats) exercise the most uncomplicated (least fraught) and banal domination within the prevailing education set-up, and therefore there is little disruption that can be effected through working with them. Further, it is clear that the ANC is too beholden to SADTU support for it to provide progressive leadership in the public education sector. That would be tantamount to the ANC shooting itself in the foot. And so the submission of policy proposals, participating in parliamentary hearings and the like, are unlikely to yield positive outcomes as stand-alone advocacy interventions. By contrast, parents and learners may be beneficiaries of educational welfare, but they simultaneously bear the brunt of a system that functions to fabricate them as loyal servants and dependent subjects. There is therefore scope to work deliberately and strategically with these groupings to be more effective in their exercise of resistance than is currently the case. But the key point is this: a necessary pre-condition for any improvement in the educational outcomes achieved in the 'dysfunctional' schools is a change in the prevailing power configurations that underpin and structure the schooling system.

In my experience of the development sector in South Africa, a nuanced and strategic blend of service delivery and advocacy work can be very effective in bringing about fundamental and far-reaching change. For example, in the land sector, the Border Rural Committee (which I managed from 1997 until 2009) advocated successfully for the settlement of the restitution claim of the Cata community in the former Ciskei. This breakthrough was then used both to advocate for the inclusion of all 'betterment' cases within the restitution process and to enable the implementation of an ambitious integrated local economic development in Cata itself. Therefore, when I was given responsibility to manage GADRA Education in late 2011, I set about trying to blend a suitable mix between service delivery and advocacy in the public education sector in Makhanda. I have written elsewhere about this approach; suffice it to say here that GADRA enjoyed more success with service provision than with advocacy over the period 2012 – 2015. For example, those learners whose applications to the GADRA Matric School (GMS) were accepted benefitted considerably, whereas there was no marked improvement in local no-fee schools over this period. The significance of the former should not be underestimated; whereas only approximately 10 GMS students per year gained access to Rhodes prior to 2012, by 2016 this number had increased fivefold to approximately 50 students. GMS is now the university's largest feeder school. But, in the bigger scheme of things, the size of a grade cohort in no-fee schools in Makhanda is 1 200 children.

Some of the specific reasons for the limited advocacy success were:
- None of the interventions disrupted the prevailing power configuration in the local schooling system, with SADTU remaining firmly in control.
- The interventions were unable to mobilise a critical mass of support amongst the constituencies with the most to gain from transformation, namely learners, parents and principals.
- The interventions failed to secure 'critical linkages' across the sector. That is to say, GADRA Education operated in relative isolation and did not therefore attempt to synchronise its work with the likes of Rhodes University and other education NGOs operating in the city.

While it is relatively easy to identify these issues as crucial in advocacy work, the question remains: how does one actualise a genuine alternative reality within the public schooling system itself? Is it at all possible to do this without provoking those beneficiaries of patronage who dominate the system into rear-guard action? I cannot answer these questions definitively. But there are certainly useful indications in critical theory about how to think through these questions. For example, Gramsci argues that societal status quo is maintained through a combination of force and consent (Strinati, 1995). Whereas the former is exercised in political society, the latter is forged through hegemony in civil society. One of the key institutions of civil society is the public education system. Above I have attempted to describe how the public education system in South Africa is integral to the exercise of two significant forms of power, namely patronage and welfare. Gramsci does not stop with a description of the maintenance of state power; he also explores strategies of resistance. Specifically, he contrasts resistance against force (a war of manoeuvre) with resistance against hegemony/consent (a war of position). The latter entails a consistent and persistent building of counter-hegemonic institutions, agencies and ideas within society. Below I consider the post-2015 attempts by a collective of Makhanda institutions to revitalise local public schools and assess the extent to which these attempts amount to an effective war of position.

7. Case study: The VC's initiative to revive public schooling in Makhanda

The installation of Sizwe Mabizela as Rhodes University's 6th Vice-Chancellor provided a new opportunity to test possibilities in the realm of civil society in Makhanda. In his inauguration speech in February 2015, he undertook to re-position the university, such that it would become more relevant and effective in operating in its geographic locality, namely Makhanda. Specifically, he highlighted three sectors in which the university would enhance its local impact, one of which was public education in general and schooling in particular. This gave rise to what is now referred to as 'The VC's Initiative to Revitalise Public Schooling in Makhanda'.

In the immediate aftermath of Mabizela's inauguration speech, there was considerable discussion within GADRA Education about how the organisation should position itself in relation to Rhodes. My personal view at the time was that the speech opened a window of opportunity for GADRA to address some of the weaknesses and limitations of its advocacy work, as outlined above. Specifically, I was enthused by the possibilities associated with the university's considerable institutional muscle as well as the 'massification' potential that resided within the student body. Much of the discussion was held with Ms Margie Keeton, and focused on a discussion document that she was drafting at the time to inform the thinking and decisions of a committee that had been assembled by Mabizela. A short document was distributed to committee members on 22 March 2015. It comprised four sub-sections, namely 'Common points of departure', 'Theory of change', 'Model' and 'Making it all happen'. Essentially, the document presented an inclusive and pragmatic framework within which a wide range of initiatives and interventions could be accommodated. Three key ideas were that students should be placed at the centre of the initiative, that it should focus resources on facilitating the emergence of schooling sites of educational excellence and that the building of a supportive environment was a critical success factor. The last-mentioned came to be re-framed over the following months as the building of communities of good practice across the public schooling sector in Makhanda. Mabizela's committee adopted the document, and in April 2015 GADRA Education agreed to a request from the university that it would manage the implementation of 'the VC's Initiative'.

It is informative and interesting to view the above framework through a Gramscian lens. This exercise yields a dual military strategy in this war of position: to take control of sites of strategic significance and to win over the hearts and minds of the civilian population. A few words on the logic and rationale of each of these elements are necessary. First, there are numerous benefits to establishing sites of educational excellence in the no-fee sector. These include the fact that one secures significant bases of control in the heart of 'enemy territory', from which one can build new supporters amongst both the learner and parent communities. The potential support emerges from improved learner outcomes and the long-term benefits thereof. This points to another major benefit: since one writes a new narrative, one in which black children thrive and excel academically, there can be significant propaganda advantages in the broader civilian population. It potentially becomes possible for this population to engage critically with the hegemonic narrative that black educational failure is inevitable and that blame in this regard can be ascribed to the learners themselves rather than the schooling system. At the level of the school microcosm itself, institutional transformation involves a changed configuration of power relations. The school governing body exercises effective oversight, the school principal and management committee ensure the delivery of effective education and teachers are required to teach (both enough and to a reasonable standard). In essence, the local transformation trumps national and provincial realities and constraints. These schools are restored as places of teaching and learning; the educational welfare of the learners is prioritised. Second, if a war of position were to be waged solely in select sites, it could easily be contained, countered and ultimately quashed. By contrast, if one's military strategy is widely dispersed and disseminated across society, then it is more difficult to rebut. In the case of the

VC's Initiative, it is recognised that there are communities of learners, parents, principals and teachers that exist over and above the level of individual schools, at the broader level of the city of Makhanda. It is also a foregone conclusion that there are good learners, parents, principals and teachers across the schooling system, not only at sites deemed to be emergent sites of schooling excellence. In order to transform a local schooling system, it is necessary to strengthen the communities of educational practice that inhabit that system, especially those capable of enhancing accountability, and thereby change power relations.

Having outlined an epistemic approach to South African schooling (which can be regarded as an application of the ideas of Foucault and Bourdieu) and presented the VC's Initiative through a Gramscian lens, I conclude the paper by reflecting critically on the implementation of the latter over the past few years. (I should disclose that I carry professional management responsibility for the initiative and thus a critical stance is imperative, however difficult it may be to achieve and sustain.) Understandably, one of Mabizela's primary concerns is that the university should be accessible to as many deserving disadvantaged local students as possible. Thus, the focus in 2016, the first year of implementation, was on high school. From 2017 primary schools enjoyed more attention and by 2018 the initiative was beginning to strategise about how to promote early childhood education (ECE). The discussion will be presented in this (chronological but apparently top-down) order.

In 2015 Ntsika and Mary Water High Schools were selected as the emergent sites of excellence. (Nombulelo High School was added as a third site at the end of the following year.) From the onset, the flagship intervention at high school level was a Grade 12 (matric) mentoring programme called 'nine-tenths' or 9/10ths. This programme sees approximately 170 Grade 12 learners from the participating schools being mentored in a structured fashion regularly through the year by trained Rhodes volunteers. The main topics covered are personal planning, study and summarising skills and tertiary applications. Programme impact is measured largely in terms of bachelor pass rates and throughput to university. Performance in relation to both these indicators has been impressive (when gauged in relation to the historic track record of the no-fee sector). It should also be noted that there is compelling evidence that Ntsika is emerging as a school of genuine excellence. If one looks at Grade 12 performance, all the important indicators at the school (number of learners, pass rates, quality of passes, bachelor passes and throughput to university) have been moving in the right direction since 2015.

At the urging of Mabizela himself, in 2017 the GMS introduced a bridging programme for select students who had already secured bachelor passes. Specifically, 10 GMS students were registered for Psychology 1 as Occasional Students, while simultaneously upgrading their results in two school subjects. Eight of the 10 passed their final examinations and all 10 are registered as full-time Rhodes students this year. On the back of the success of the pilot, the bridging programme has been institutionalised and upscaled. It is clear therefore that the VC's Initiative has made Rhodes University more accessible to deserving disadvantaged matric candidates.

The VC's Initiative has encompassed interventions in all high school grades. In July 2016 the management team analysed the Grade 8 mid-year results at Ntsika and Mary Waters, a process undertaken as part of monitoring the impact of an English-support project called Iinthetho zoBomi ('existential conversations'). The analysis revealed shockingly high failure rates in Mathematics and English (especially at one of the schools) and this drew attention to the realities that educational foundations are built during one's primary school years, and that, if these are lacking, there is little remediation that can be done at high school level. There have been two consequences of these realisations. First, the high school interventions have increasingly been conceptualised as an attempt to maximise top-end learner performance. To elaborate, at Grade 12 level, more attention is given to bachelor passes and throughput to university than to basic pass rates. Second, since mid-2016, the management team of the initiative has given considerably more attention to primary school education (than in the initial period).

Various institutions, inside and outside Rhodes University, had been engaged in primary school interventions prior to the VC's Initiative. Most significantly, from 2015 a Primary School Consortium (comprising GADRA Education, Rhodes University, the Lebone Centre, amongst others) was constituted in response to a resourcing opportunity provided by the Vestas Empowerment Trust. The key advance made through this arrangement was that critical linkages were made across and between the city's most significant non-state primary education institutions. The consortium took responsibility both to sustain existing pro-grammes (such as accredited teacher professional development or TPD) and to launch innovative new ventures. In relation to the latter, arguably the most important innovation was the re-imagination and reconfiguration of after-care facilities as education sites. The consortium comprised both in-school and out-of-school projects, but there was a growing cynicism amongst partners about the prospects of the former, unless strategically targeted and carefully implemented. An institutional reality in after-cares is that they are not subject to SADTU control and therefore present opportunities that no-fee schools do not. Given the foundational importance of literacy and numeracy, the Vestas Consortium resolved to set up and sustain effective reading and maths clubs in six selected after-care facilities. The administrative and management competence underpinning these sites varies considerably, but in theory they have the potential to emerge and function as counter-hegemonic educational institutions.

GADRA's primary school programme was birthed in the late 2000s as a mechanism to enable no-fee public schools to improve. Since then it has been through various renditions, but never departed from this fundamental objective. Despite the organisation's best efforts, there has been no evidence of improvement in the Makhanda's no-fee primary schools. On the contrary, the poor quality of their foundation phase teaching means that most children entering the Intermediate Phase are not literate. Similarly, their Intermediate Phase offerings are chaotic and unsystematic, to the extent that the vast majority of children entering high school are unprepared for the complexity and volume of the Senior Phase. In 2016 GADRA and the Development and Care Centre responded to this stubborn crisis by selling up a literacy remediation and enrichment school, called Whistle Stop School (WSS). It was piloted at St Mary's School in 2017. Initially it was carried out with Grade 3 and 6 learners, but the latter proved impractical. From July, therefore, WSS worked with Grade 4 learners in the Intermediate Phase. The pilot involved thorough testing. The remediation intervention at Grade 3 level has enabled learner participants to address literacy deficits. Many of those who were behind the age grade reading level caught up to where they should be. Others, who were closer to expected reading level, leap-frogged numerous age-grades. Three of the participants were reading at Grade 6 level by October. The duration of the Grade 4 intervention was only four months, yet it too enabled participant learners to make excellent literacy gains (three times the normal rate of literacy development for the English HL learners and double the rate for English FAL learners). Based on the success of the pilot, WSS was institutionalised in expanded form from 2018. There are many benefits that come with effective counter-hegemonic institutions, one of which is the narratives that they enable. Whereas no-fee schools fuel narratives where the central character is the lacking/inadequate black child, the WSS narrative revolves around resourceful and capable black children. Over time, it will become increasingly important to broadcast this narrative throughout Makhanda, particularly in Joza.

Right from 2015, Mabizela had spoken about the imperative need for the VC's Initiative to support ECE. However, there was limited institutional capacity to address this need. It was only from mid-2017 that the management team gave practical attention to ECE. Modest research pointed to inadequate access to ECE sites and Grade R, and to generally poor quality ECE and Grade R offerings respectively, meaning that most of the 1 000 children entering no-fee Grade 1 classrooms are not school ready. In 2018, a team from the Rhodes Education Faculty formulated plans that are informed by the two central Initiative strategies of facilitating the emergence of sites of educational excellence and building communities of good practice. Fundraising to enable implementation has commenced.

It is too early to offer a definitive appraisal of the VC's Initiative as a strategy in the war of position for public education in Makhanda. There is clear evidence that certain project components, especially 9/10ths mentoring and the two bridging opportunities, have assisted local disadvantaged students to access Rhodes University. There are more students from Joza and other Makhanda townships now registered at Rhodes than ever before. This certainly amounts to important progress for Rhodes in its bid to integrate itself more thoroughly into the local community. However, the initiative cannot yet claim to have brought about systemic change in no-fee public schooling. The closest that it comes in this regard is the stellar rise of Ntsika High School, but the situation at primary school level is uniformly depressing and demoralising.

The three most important lessons that have been learned over the past few years are: 1) different educational opportunities and constraints present themselves at different stages of the schooling trajectory; 2) institutional credibility is a prerequisite for sustaining an intervention into the public schooling system; and 3) the stronger the key interpersonal relationships, the more durable the interventions are likely to be. To elaborate, firstly it is clear that as children get older it becomes increasingly difficult to remediate fundamental educational problems such as literacy and numeracy. Arguably, a reason that 9/10ths mentoring has enjoyed such success is that it deliberately aims to work with the strongest matriculants to maximise the number and quality of bachelor passes from the participating schools. (By contrast, it does not attempt to assist progressed learners to avoid modularisation, knowing that such a mission is futile.) At primary school level, there is a much stronger emphasis on building children's literacy and numeracy skills. Secondly, Rhodes University and GADRA Education have considerable institutional credibility amongst the Makhanda population in general and in its education community in particular. This has given principals (together with their strategic management teams and governing bodies) the confidence to give a variety of initiative interventions access to their respective schools. Thirdly, very strong relationships amongst the leadership team of the VC's Initiative and between these people and school authorities underpin these progressive decisions (pertaining to access). Indeed, the strength of the relationships that have been built in the public education sector bodes well for the future of the initiative. Building relationships and networks are crucial in order to establish a firm foothold in civil society, which in turn is fundamental to winning any war of position.

8. Conclusion

While no-fee South African schools perform very poorly as educational institutions, they function very effectively as institutional sites at which the ANC state dispenses patronage to hundreds of thousands of SADTU cadres and social and material welfare to approximately twelve million black working class children. This functionality is fundamental to the reproduction of South Africa in general and of many of its distinctive characteristics in particular, including the political dominance of the ANC and the pervasive racial and class inequalities that cut so deeply through society. As a result, the educational status quo is so entrenched that it is seemingly immovable. There is no doubt that it is extremely difficult to penetrate this institutional space, let alone alter it. In this context, a Gramscian-inspired focus on making gains through engaging civil society seems to have more potential than any direct attempted manoeuvre on the state. The VC's Initiative to Revitalise Public Schooling in Makhanda demonstrates that a strategic war of position can win small-scale skirmishes, but it is already clear that big battles will only be won through persistent and relentless building of a substantial social movement in which conscientised parents will necessarily have to play a leading role.

References

Bloch, G. 2009. *The toxic mix: What's wrong with South Africa's schools and how to fix it.* Cape Town: Tafelberg.

Bourdieu, P. 2008. *Political interventions: Social science and political action.* London: Verso.

Department of Basic Education (DBE), 2016a. *Report on progress in the schooling sector against key learner performance and attainment indicators.* https://www.education.gov.za/Portals/0/Documents/Reports/Education%20Sector%20review%202015%20-%202016.pdf [Accessed 10 July 2018].

Department of Basic Education (DBE), 2016b. *Report of the Ministerial Task Team appointed by Minister Angie Motshekga to investigate allegations into the selling of posts of educators by members of teacher unions and departmental officials in provincial education departments.* https://nicspaull.files.wordpress.com/2016/05/dbe-2016-volmink-report.pdf [Accessed 15 January 2018].

Fleisch, B, 2007. *Primary Education in Crisis: Why South African schoolchildren underachieve in reading and mathematics.* Cape Town: Juta.

Foucault, M. 1977. *Discipline and punish: The birth of the prison.* London: Allen Lane.

Foucault, M. 1980. *Power/Knowledge: Selected Interviews and Other Writings 1972 – 1977.* New York: Prentice Hall.

Jansen, J. 2014. Another Brick in the Wall. *Times live.* https://www.timeslive.co.za/news/south-africa/2014-06-20-the-big-read-another-brick-in-the-wall/ [Accessed 16 August 2020].

Mamdani, M. 1996. *Citizen and subject: Contemporary Africa and the legacy of late colonialism.* Cape Town: David Philip.

Ndebele, N. 2015. Letter from South Africa: Life in the interregnum. *Mail and Guardian.* http://cdn.mg.co.za/content/documents/2015/01/28/Turning-Points-Low-Res.pdf [Accessed 20 February 2015].

Paton, C. 2014. Class divide splitting Cosatu will not be bridged easily. *Business Day.* http://www.bdlive.co.za/opinion/2014/03/10/class-divide-splitting-cosatu-will-not-be-bridged-easily [Accessed 10 February 2015].

Southall, R. 2016. *The new black middle class in South Africa.* Johannesburg: Jacana.

Spaull, N. 2013. South Africa's Education Crisis: The quality of education in South Africa 1994-2011. *Report Commissioned by Centre for development and enterprise.* http://www.section27.org.za/wp-content/uploads/2013/10/Spaull-2013-CDE-report-South-Africas-Education-Crisis.pdf [Accessed 30 June 2018].

Statistics South Africa, 2014. Youth employment, unemployment, skills and economic growth, 1994-2014. *Statistics South Africa*. Pretoria.

Statistics South Africa, 2018. *Media Release: Quarterly Labour Force Survey – QLFS Q1: 2018*. http://www.statssa.gov.za/?cat=45&paged=2 [Accessed 15 July 2018].

Strinati, D. 1995. An introduction to theories of popular culture. London: Routledge.

Taylor, N. 2011. Priorities for addressing South Africa's education and training crisis. https://www.jet.org.za/resources/Taylor%20NPC%20Synthesis%20report%20Nov%202011.pdf/view [Accessed 16 August 2020].

Westaway, A. 2009. Bare life in the Bantustans (of the Eastern Cape): Re-membering the centennial South African nation-state. PhD thesis. Fort Hare University Press: Fort Hare.

Chapter 3

The problem of power: The practical challenges of power dynamics and power distance in community engagement

Nicola Hayes

CENTRE FOR SOCIAL DEVELOPMENT,
RHODES UNIVERSITY

n.hayes@ru.ac.za

1. Introduction

The HE community engagement/volunteering sector space is continually looking for more equable models of engagement where power and value commitment are shared, moving away from old paradigms of receiver and giver.

This paper is an autoethnographic exploration, grounded in practical experience of my perspective as the school head of a quintile 3 school in the Eastern Cape, South Africa, where I am involved with community engagement in a number of forms. It interrogates the power dynamics that are intertwined in the process, with my own power and powerlessness as a starting point. My interest in this study was sparked by a revelation that, despite my theoretical positional authority, I feel largely powerless in the community engagement arena as regards our school. This comes despite a strong sense of personal confidence, proficiency in public speaking and having English (in which almost all meetings are conducted) as my home language.

This paper critiques the extent to which it is possible to move away from the 'old charity/deficit' model, to a grassroots-up but mutually beneficial developmental approach. In particular, it examines the practical barriers to such a new model, given the multi-layered power dynamics at play. Different engagement models are contrasted – those offered by various schools, organisations, businesses and the university – and the critical factors in creating a successful model with a sense of co-ownership are explored. Challenges that are faced in forming positive partnerships are highlighted, such as a lack of internal capacity; the multilingual environment in which we engage; the reality of high power distance in the secondary education milieu and the perceived gap between those with 'valued knowledge' (in particular those within the academy) and those without.

Possible solutions include the importance of a multi-layered approach both in the initial phases of project development, as well as during reflection. Possible solutions include the use of mini-meetings, questionnaires and informal discussions within the school in preparation for planning and reflection meetings. The importance of the inclusion of open questions, particularly in the planning phases, is also highlighted. Such techniques will hopefully mitigate against some of the factors which hinder honest interactions in these settings by decreasing power differentials both within the school and between the school and the partner organisations.

This study may have relevance not only to community engagements involving schools but to any engagement where there is an imbalance of power between the two partners, and specifically where there is a high power differential within one or more of the organisations.

By working towards planning and reflection processes in which strategies are engaged that actively work against the pre-existing hierarchies and power distances, open honest communication will be increased, and hopefully the time taken in setting up such processes will be repaid in smoother pilot programmes and greater chances of ongoing success.

2. Context

Two-and-a-half years ago, I was appointed as head of a non-fee-paying, quintile three school in Makhanda (formerly Grahamstown) in the Eastern Cape in South Africa. The area has a high level of unemployment (42,3% amongst the youth in the municipal district of Makana), and in the environment from which the school draws its learners, 13,2% of households have no income at all according to Statistics South Africa (StatsSA, 2011). Before I arrived at the school it had suffered a scourge of vandalism and neglect. Once a successful and proud school, it was now merely a skeleton of its former self with matric pass rates having plunged. Few classes had window panes, half the school had no electricity and there were three working toilets for girls and three for boys for approximately

1 000 learners. The effects of the absence of fire-fighting equipment was (and still is) evident in the top floor of the boys' toilets having been ravaged by a fire, leaving no roof or ceiling and gutters and the odd tile dangling precariously from charred pieces of timber. In both infrastructure and spirit of place, the school was depressed.

Luckily the city of Makhanda has the advantage of having many willing volunteers from all walks of life – from the retired to the unemployed, from past pupils to teachers in other schools. In addition, it has a number of organisations that are committed to education, including GADRA Education (Grahamstown Area District Relief Association), Rhodes University and a number of private and fee-paying public schools. Each of these institutions, along with countless individuals, has assisted in getting our school back on its feet. Their assistance has been much needed and is deeply appreciated, but this is not to say that such engagements have been without challenges. Thus, over the space of two-and-a-half years, I have had the opportunity to compare and contrast a number of engagement styles. This chapter will highlight some of the major challenges as well as some of the successes. Before delving into this comparison, however, I will sketch a picture of my position within the matrix of power and powerlessness as a 'receiver' in the community engagement arena.

(For details on the incidents that led me to consider my position and that of the school in terms of the power dynamics in community engagement, see Addendum A.)

3. Methodology

This study is autoethnographic in nature. Autoethnography holds that by merging the genre of autobiography with the discipline of ethnography, where the "narrator's lived experience is at the core of the story" (Raab, 2013:2), textured and nuanced facets of culture can be revealed. In combination with other similar or different stories, an accurate cultural picture can be painted. The story of the individual should shed light on the story of the culture as a whole.

Chang (2008) highlights the benefits of autoethnography as a methodology:

> Autoethnography is becoming a useful and powerful tool for researchers and practitioners who deal with human relations in multicultural settings: e.g., educators, social workers, medical professionals, clergy, and counsellors. Benefits of autoethnography lie in three areas: (1) it offers a research method friendly to researchers and readers; (2) it enhances cultural understanding of self and others; and (3) it has a potential to transform self and others toward the cross-cultural coalition building. (Chang 2008:11)

In the context of community engagement in our school, the issue of "human relations in a multicultural setting" is central to understanding the dynamics at work. It is hoped that through the interrogation of my specific experience in this field, some light will be shed on how best to engage in this multicultural, power-embedded space.

Drawing from ethnography, three categories of 'other' are distinguished. This classification assists in mapping relationships with stakeholders in community engagement projects:

> "others of similarity" (those with similar values and experiences to self), "others of difference" (those with different values and experiences from self), and "others of opposition" (those with values and experiences seemingly irreconcilable to self) (Ngunjiri, W., Hernandez, K.C. & Chang, H., 2010: unpaged).

It is likely that communication between oneself and others of similarity will be more honest and clear than with other 'others'. These are considerations that should affect the design of initial planning and reflection sessions.

4.   My position in the matrix of power

Hierarchy is a dominant feature in South African schools, and indeed throughout our society. In terms of this hierarchy, I should theoretically feel strongly empowered compared to many others. In the community engagement field, however, I have felt disempowered by multiple factors including self-censure, expectations of others and responses of others. The realisations of the extent to which I have felt silenced in this arena is what sparked my interest in writing this chapter. It occurred to me that, if I feel disempowered in this space despite my supposed positions of power, how much more must others feel silenced, at a disadvantage and unable to speak the truth of the needs of their organisations. What follows is a dissection of the factors that should contribute to my sense of being empowered, followed by an examination of what undermines this. I also attempt to compare my position to others from different cultures operating in the same milieu.

4.1 *Factors contributing to a sense of empowerment*
Theoretically, I have a position of power as a school head.

"The original French and Raven (1959) bases of power model posited six bases of power; reward, coercion, legitimate, expert, referent, and informational (or persuasion; Raven, 1965)" (Raven, 1993: 227). Raven (1993: 227) later developed a more complex and nuanced model, which adjudges the effectiveness of the power base in relation to multiple factors including the "implementation of the power strategies",

My professional power is, in theory, based on legitimate (as conferred by the position), expert (from qualifications) and coercive modes of power and on my ability, in general, to implement power strategies in the context of the school.

In addition to this, I have the advantages of white embodied privilege; I have English as my home language, and as English is used as the lingua franca in official meetings, this gives me an advantage over those for whom it is a second or third language. I have a Master's Degree in Education. Besides these extrinsic factors, as a Drama teacher, I have both innate and trained confidence, and have very little anxiety about speaking in public. Additionally, having been brought up by feminist parents, I was encouraged from a young age to speak my mind and fight for what I believed to be right.

This combination of factors should enable me to engage from a position of strength in most interactions.

Another factor that plays a role in engagements with others in a school context, however, is that of culture.

Hofstede, Hofstede and Minkov (n.d.) identify four dimensions of culture, where a culture positioned on each of these six spectra has a significant effect on the way that individuals within that culture will relate to others. The six dimensions are:

1. Power distance index (acceptance of hierarchy)
2. Collectivism versus individualism
3. Femininity versus masculinity
4. Uncertainty avoidance index (face saving)
5. Long-term orientation versus short-term normative orientation
6. Indulgence versus restraint

Of particular interest here are numbers one and four. Hofstede *et al.*'s power distance index measures "the extent to which *the less powerful members of organisations* and institutions (like the family) *accept and expect that power is distributed unequally*". This represents inequality (more versus less), but defined from below, not from above. It suggests that a society's level of inequality is endorsed by the followers as much as by the leaders.

Uncertainty avoidance, among other factors, indicates the extent to which members of a culture will seek to avoid public shame (both of themselves and others) (Hofstede, n.d.). For a culture that has a high Uncertainty Avoidance Index (UAI), shame will be more significant than guilt. "Countries exhibiting strong UAI maintain rigid codes of belief and behaviour, and are intolerant of unorthodox behaviour and ideas." **Figure 1** below indicates my positioning of myself relative to how I perceive my own culture in general as well as my perception of Afrikaans speaking white South Africans and isiXhosa speaking black South Africans with regard to four of Hofstede's cultural dimensions, completed as part of my master's research. Although I discussed these perceptions with learners in my English and Drama classes in the course of a different study, and they agreed with my perception of their cultures, the power differential between me as the teacher and them as the learners is too great for their validation to carry much weight, so this should be seen purely as my personal perspective.

Bearing in mind the caveat above, my power-base in interactions with others of different cultures is further strengthened theoretically by the fact that I have very little respect for hierarchy as a concept (low score for power distance); I have a very high sense of individualism, and my uncertainty avoidance is extremely low.

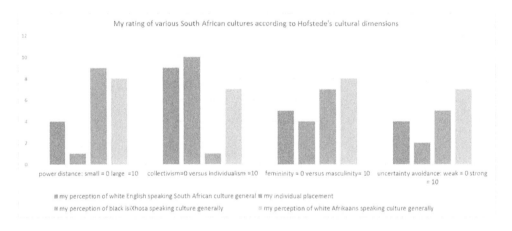

Figure 1: My rating of South African cultures according to Hofstede's cultural dimensions

All of these factors combined should result in me feeling powerful and in control in most circumstances. However, this is not the case in the community engagement environment for multiple complex reasons.

In his more recent power/interaction model of personal influence, Raven (1993) identifies several power preferences and inhibitions of which cost and efforts, norms and values, and relation to self-perception are of relevance here.

With reference to the assessment of the cost of utilising influence strategies, Raven comments:

The agent must also examine the costs of the influence attempt – it may be effective, but at what costs … The legitimacy of dependence ("I need your help") may lead to loss of respect and perhaps may imply an obligation to return the favour …" (Raven, 1993:13).

In terms of community engagement, the cost that must always be considered is the potential of the organisation or individual choosing not to support the school at all if one is not prepared to accept their offer or project exactly as they had envisioned it. Furthermore, in a community engagement consultation, the cultural norm that one should not 'look a gift horse in the mouth' creates a barrier to honesty.

Further factors contributing to my sense of powerlessness in community engagement settings will be discussed below.

5. Community engagement, gifts, donations and volunteering

As expressed by the authors of *Literacy and Power: The Latin American Battleground*:

> Before long [Paulo Freire] was made aware of the contradictions involved in charity work, in which the benevolent middle classes would do things for the poor but not with them. At the end of the day the caring bourgeois would return home to food and comfort, far away from those whom they sought to help (Archer & Costello, 1990: 197).

In some respects we have come a long way since those ideas of middleclass benevolence, although, at a practical level, until the poverty gap is narrowed, the realities of some returning to 'food and comfort' while others remain without it will persist. Certainly, however, the ideology behind community engagement has shifted from this deficit model to an asset-based model in which the assets of both parties are recognised and the potential gain for both sides acknowledged. It is my contention, however, that unless factors of power are deliberately and explicitly mitigated against at every level of engagement, the new theories will remain forever theoretical.

Below is a comparison of various types of donations and assistance that the school has received. Though not completely comprehensive (for example, solicited material gifts have not been included), I have attempted to give a clear and representative overview.

5.1. Gifts and donations

Although somewhat out of the range of discussion, I have included gifts and donations as I think that the examples give a clear picture of the potential problem with the old fashioned idea of charity. **Table 1** below itemises unsolicited gifts and donations that the school has received in a roughly two-year period. In particular, I would like to draw the reader's attention to column A. The R50 000 rand installation fee that the school funds had to cover could have been avoided if the donor had asked one simple question regarding the alternatives of this particular gift. This was a glaring example of a well-meaning institution making their own decisions about what would be best for the school, at great cost to the school. While we are obviously grateful for all contributions made, so often a smaller contribution with consultation can be much more meaningful than a larger gift given carelessly. The same is true of community engagement projects.

Table 1: Unsolicited gifs and donations received by the school

A	B	C	D	E
Gift of R80 000 worth of equipment, which cost to install R50 000 to install	Gift of 28 tablets, whiteboard with eBeam, server, Wi-Fi	Gift of two laptops	Gift of three projectors	Donations of books, speakers, clothing, soccer boots, soccer kit, water filters
Arrived three hours late, keeping the "welcoming party" of children that they had "ordered" waiting. Supposedly ongoing but have not been heard from since	No-one could use it, passwords did not work, no follow-up. Wi-Fi does not work			
Used sometimes	Never used	Used often	Used often	The more specific the better

Column E also provides a useful contrast. The soccer boots were donated for a specific, keen and talented soccer player, they were the right size for him and have greatly enhanced his game. The soccer kit was generic, not in the school colours and on the whole too small for our players, we are thus unable to use it.

5.2 Projects

5.2.1 COLLABORATIVE PROJECTS

As with community engagement projects, the success of any project is largely determined by the extent to which it is fit-to-purpose and the extent to which the project itself or the individuals within the project are willing to adapt to the circumstances of the school (see **Table 2** below).

Table 2: Success of collaborative projects

A	B	C	D
Existing project not working; substituted for another with consultation; then adapted with minimal consultation	Three existing projects from another school replicated	Internship project; governed, not managed	Individual volunteers willing to adapt to changing needs
Partially successful	Two successful with adaptation; one not	Successful	Highly successful

5.2.2. COMMUNITY-INITIATED PROJECTS

Ironically, although the literature puts community-initiated projects forward as ideal, our experience so far with projects initiated by the school was not good. Factors contributing to this are outlined in **Table 3**.

Table 3: Success of community-initiated projects

A	B
Academic support required	Infrastructural support required
Largely unsuccessful, mainly owing to insufficient coherence on the part of the school	Largely unsuccessful, mainly owing to insufficient input on the part of the community partners

5.3 Engagement with other schools

The engagement with schools has something in common with the engage-ment with other partners shown above in that School C offers a specific project (Table 4) that adapted over the years until a successful model was established, which then continues to roll out fairly seamlessly. Unlike any of the other projects, it requires no oversight or commitment from the staff at our school but generates commitment from the learners.

Table 4: Engagement with other schools

School A	School B	School C
Offers the world	Thoughtful, targeted offers in response to needs	Specific ongoing project
Does not deliver or takes months and months to deliver	Delivers instantaneously on what is promised	
Says "yes" but often does not deliver	Said "no" to the first two things I requested	
Much talk of mutual benefit but not much achieved	Little talk of mutual benefit, though there is quite a bit; it is not expected or required though	Quietly, efficiently, effective
Some growing relationships with individuals beginning to bear fruit	Established relationships; regular contact about OTHER things; no attitude of great "giving"	Sustained by the learners

6. Challenges to successful mutually beneficial engagements

Many of the challenges to successful community engagement activities revolve around practical issues and time is a particularly profound issue. Almost all projects, however amazing, come at the expense of time. Time constraints are real for any functioning teacher or school head. In a school context, whatever the community engagement project is, it is almost never our core business (it may assist massively with the core business but it is NOT the core business). This means that such projects will always be lower on the priority list than attending to the core business of the school. I would guess that many outside organisers of projects would consider that their project dovetails perfectly with the core business of the school because most project leaders are at pains to make explicit (especially to funders) the extent to which what they are working on is covered by the curriculum of one of the school subjects. However, it is often not as simple as that.

I will use a fictional example to illustrate this point to protect the anonymity of our partners. Teacher A is a Drama lecturer with a passion for Boal. She is excited to see that Boal is in the grade 10 syllabus. She thus offers to run three 2-hour workshops at the school. She decides that school time will be the best time to implement it in order for learners to take it seriously. She, however, fails to notice that the time allocation for Boal plus two other theorists is 30 minutes or that the school periods are 45 minutes and not two hours. She thus feels that she is offering a perfectly helpful solution to the teacher, but this teacher now has to make up an hour-and-a-half of tuition time and has to swop lessons with other teachers to accommodate her.

Even in the rare instance where an outside project does feed directly and neatly into the school's core business, it takes a lot of time and planning and coordination that would not have been needed if the teacher had just taught that section him- or herself. This is not by any means to say that such engagements are not worthwhile. Very often, the quality and enthusiasm of an outsider's input is greatly valued by learners and teachers alike. In addition, I believe that outside input gives a message to the learners that they are considered important by the community at large, and thus even if a lesson or activity by an outside individual or group is not strictly speaking successful, the mere fact that it has been offered contributes to the self-esteem of learners at a subconscious level. Nonetheless, time remains a precious resource which a good teacher must use optimally.

I believe that one of the reasons for the success of the school engagements in **Table 4** columns B and C relate to time. In column B, the school assisted with exactly what we asked for (senior learners from their school to assist junior learners from our school with Maths); however, I had the advantage of knowing both organisations well and was thus able to come up with a logistical solution that did not require much more work from teaching staff of either schools. Similarly, school C has created a system in which senior learners in their life skills programme recruit and mentor junior learners, which creates a self-perpetuating programme. I receive a report once a year and report on to our staff and community, and that is the full extent of my involvement. I think it needs stating that it is not at all that I, nor I am sure our teachers, resent the time spent on other projects – it is just that the juggling of responsibilities, people and projects within the limited time available is a real issue.

While it is clear that some projects are successful and some are not, causality is hard to prove. Nation *et al.,* (2011) discuss the issue of power with regard to projects designed to reduce violence amongst youth in Nashville. They identify 'community initiation' and 'community collaboration' as preferable approaches to equalise power. This matches my experience; however, even when utilising these approaches, there are challenges.

A few that I have noticed are:

- We (the school) do not necessarily always know what we need/want/can ask for. (An example that illustrates this is the occasion on which I asked a business if they would sponsor us with materials for a skills club when they wanted to offer a three-year internship programme for two interns!)
- Organisations and individuals in most need sometimes lack the organisational capacity to effectively utilise assistance. This is what I attribute the failure reference in **Table 4** column A to. In this instance, we were unable to cope as an organisation with the individual needs of our matric learners for academic support. Precisely this lack of organisational capacity, however, caused us to not manage optimally the support that was offered.
- The contrast between the 'desirable' and the 'desired' somehow needs to be managed. This distinction is highlighted by Hofstede (1991) who points out that often what we state as being desirable does not match with what we actually desire. I always think of this in terms of weight loss. While it is desirable for me to lose weight, I do not actually desire to be on a calorie restricted diet. We are most likely, in a consultation, especially with others whom we do not know well and who may well fall into the ethnographic realm of 'others of difference' or 'others of opposition', to state the desirable. However when it comes to implementation, the desired comes to the fore. Simply put: consultation does not necessarily mean buy-in even if everyone agrees.
- An organisation is not necessarily cohesive in term of what it desires. Community partners will almost always engage with the principal. Very often this engagement will then move on to consultation with the teaching staff concerned, but the consultation rarely involves learners. What I, as the principal, desire for the learners is not necessarily something that they will buy into with enthusiasm. This makes it very difficult if not impossible for community partners to know if collaboration and consultation has been successful.
- Lastly, and perhaps most significantly in terms of successful consultation, is the issue of power, even within the collaboration process. This will be explored in more detail below.

6.1 Power imbalances as a challenge to successful consultation and collaboration in community engagement settings

Kinchloe and McLaren assert that "... all thought is fundamentally mediated by power relations which are socially and historically constructed" (as cited by Carspecken, 1996:4). Despite the many changes in the concepts behind community engagement in recent years, the underlying feeling of being the 'receiver' of 'generosity' is hard to shake. This creates an immediate power imbalance from the beginning of engagement. Even with community-initiated projects, the community approaches their 'partners' to ask for 'help'.

Again, in terms of Hofstede's (1991) dimensions of culture (power distance – acceptance of hierarchy; collectivism vs individualism; uncertainty avoidance (face saving); and femininity vs masculinity), the power distance in the community engagement relationship between the giver and the receiver is traditionally very high. Add to this the fact that the power distance within schools is very high, and it makes it difficult for many teachers (let alone learners) to contradict the principal in a public forum, especially if any of the parties are also from a culture that has a particularly high power distance, and even more so if that culture also happens to have high uncertainty avoidance.

Casually stated, mix that all together and you get a meeting where teachers will look to HODs or heads or even the outside organisation to find out what their answer should be as to whether or not they are interested in participating in a project. This is where I feel that the project in **Table 3** Column A fell short – the teachers felt that I wanted them to want to be involved in the project. This point ties in with the broader question of: Who is silenced and who may speak?

It is generally acknowledged that those in power and those with privilege are able to speak, however, there is more complexity to it than meets the eye. As discussed earlier, as a principal I am theoretically empowered on many levels. However, there are many ways in which I feel silenced. I perceive myself to be:

- silenced as a woman;
- silenced by heteronormative expectations;
- silenced by religious norms;
- silenced by the fact that I am told that as someone representing white embodied privilege, it is time for me to keep quiet and listen;
- silenced by conversational conventions that are different from mine;
- silenced by the law which says I may not bring my employer into disrepute;

- silenced most surprisingly by my position in the hierarchy (as a principal you should not …); and
- silenced by my own desire to let others speak lest I quell their voice.

I highlight these silencings not in any way to paint myself as a picture of pathos, because on balance the ways in which I am empowered are far greater than the ways in which I am silenced. (Especially as the choice to be silent is ultimately self-inflicted regardless of the pressures of social mores). I point out these perceptions of silencing rather to highlight the extent to which others who do not share my feelings of empowerment must feel silenced.

Other factors that contribute to increased power differentials are the issues of valued knowledge, the language of engagement and the mode of engagement. Both personal and positional power are (often unwittingly) held by those initiating community engagements. In our setting, this applies particularly to engagements with richer schools and with the university. Related to this is the perceived gap between those with 'valued knowledge' (in particular those within the academy) and those without, which also contributes to the power differential.

In our setting, English is generally used as the language of consultation as it is the language that most stakeholders have in common; however, often the majority of people at a meeting speak English as a second language. This immediately puts those who speak English as their first language at an advantage. For most people working in business or within the university setting, email is a standard and easy mode of communication. Some of my teaching staff (and almost all of our learners) are left out of conversations by not having access to email.

6.2 Power in relation to reflection on community engagement projects

Whereas the importance of structured reflection as an integral part of any community engagement process is generally acknowledged, the complications of power in an open meeting, where individuals are asked to offer their perspectives, are often overlooked.

Uncertainty avoidance and power distance are again critical factors to consider in a reflection session. While we may all ostensibly value honest reflection, we are also constrained by cultural niceties that prohibit honesty when it may cause offence. In a community engagement arena, this is exacerbated by the desire not to seem ungrateful for what has been so generously offered.

This politeness, in my experience, causes a breakdown in honesty on both sides of the community engagement equation. An example of this is when university students offering assistance to our learners feel that it would be impolite to complain that the learners are not attending extra classes regularly.

All the factors mentioned with regard to collaboration also play a role in structured feedback sessions.

7.   Factors that contribute to a successful project

Much has been said of the challenges; however, many projects are highly successful and contribute in immeasurable ways to the lives of individual learners and hopefully also enrich the lives of those offering their time and expertise. Below are the factors that in my limited experience have contributed to successful engagements with schools:

- The project responds to a real rather than a perceived need whether conceptualised by the 'offerer' or the 'receiver'.
- At least one teacher, management, the social partner and preferably many of the learners see the value in the project (this avoids the danger of principal-driven projects that do not receive buy-in from learners).
- Regular two-way feedback is encouraged beyond structured feedback sessions. This is further enhanced if there is a sustained relationship between the two partners. The better the relationship, the less likely that one of the partners will take offence when confronted with honest feedback and the more likely it is that the relationship will bounce back from any temporary offence caused.
- Context specific rules of engagement are important. For example, in a school like ours which is in recovery from a period of 'depression' as discussed in the context section, compulsory sessions work better than voluntary ones because voluntary activities have not habitually been linked with commitment. It is pointless to replicate a structure from a school that has a different history or ethos and expect that it will work in the same way.
- Much of the ground work is done on site. This gives the partners a clearer idea of logistics, atmosphere and ethos.

8. Suggestions for creating a sense of co-ownership

8.1 Suggestions for creating a sense of co-ownership: Don'ts

- Do not be too specific when starting off in collaborative discussions – this allows for solutions to be more emergent and context based.
- Try to avoid discourse that reinforces power dynamics (the examples listed below come from real conversations between me and community partners):

  "As long as all the schools understand clearly up front that if we don't get cooperation from the participating schools, we will suspend [the project]."

  "The faculty and I have decided …" (in response to a request that we renegotiate an idea and involve the relevant teachers in the discussion)

  "The following meetings are MANDATORY"

8.2 Suggestions for creating a sense of co-ownership: Do's

- Both partners should, with as much as possible equal power, be engaged in planning (consider: time-equalising techniques in discussion, number imbalance to counterweigh power balance, language factors and flexible starting points); explicitly ask about the 'price' that the school will need to pay in order for this intervention to be successful and whether that is a reasonable price to pay. This price may be the time a specific teacher needs to put into the project, it may be altering the school's schedule or timetable or may be other factors. There will almost always be some 'price' and foregrounding this in planning phases makes it more likely that teachers will consider and be able to be honest about this factor.
- Think of structures that enforce equality in meetings. Some examples might include the use of structures adopted from Kagan (n.d) cooperative learning techniques such as timed pair shares which ensure that partners (or group members) get equal airtime, or jot down thoughts which ensures that everyone has the opportunity to get their most important ideas on the table (literally).
- Those in theoretical power (partner, principal, etc.) should give explicit permission for those with less power (e.g. teachers and learners) to object/reject/refine the proposals and programmes in progress.
- Include learners in initial discussions where possible.
- Before entering into structured reflection sessions, encourage schools to hold micro- meetings to discuss the issues that the teachers and learners

wish to bring up. This technique ensures thoughtful reflection but also boosts the confidence of those unaccustomed to sharing their views and mitigates against language factors for those who will be speaking in their second language, enabling them to consider working before the time. It also allows those from high uncertainty avoidance, communalist cultures to feel secure in knowing that they do not speak alone nor will they bring shame on their peers when responding.

• The Rhodes University Engaged Citizens project requires schools (and other organisations) to request assistance with projects that do not rely entirely on the assistance – it is supplemental rather than absolutely necessary. Despite the fact that we have had challenges in utilising the assistance offered by this programme to its full potential because of various internal factors, I believe that this is an excellent model for community engagement organisations to replicate.

9. Conclusion

This autoethnographic exploration of my experiences as a secondary school principal in dealing with multiple stakeholders with regard to community engagement will hopefully highlight the problems of unequal power in such partnerships, while at the same time adding to the conversation about ways of mitigating against the existing hierarchies.

By working towards planning and reflection processes in which strategies that actively work against the pre-existing power dynamics are used, open honest communication will be increased. Hopefully the time taken in setting up such processes will result in smoother pilot programmes and greater chances of ongoing success.

References

Archer, D. & Castello, P. 1990. *Literacy and Power: The Latin American Battleground.* London: Earthscan Publications Ltd.

Carspecken, P.F. 1996. *Critical Ethnography in Educational Research.* New York and London: Routeledge.

Chang, H. 2008. *Autoethnography as method.* Walnut Creek: Left Coast Press Inc.

Hofstede, G. 1991. *Cultures and organizations.* Berkshire: McGraw-Hill Book Company Europe.

French, J., & Raven, B. 1959. The bases of power. Michigan: University of Michigan Press.

Hofstede, G., Hofstede, G.J., & Minkov, M. n.d. Clearly cultural. Making Sense of Cross Cultural Communication [online]. Available from:

http://www.clearlycultural.com/geert-hofstede-cultural-dimensions/power-distance-index [Accessed 10 March 2018].

Hofstede, G. n.d. National culture [online]. Available from: https://www.hofstede-insights.com/models/national-culture/ [Accessed on 5 August 2018].

Kagan [online]. Available from: https://www.google.com/search?q=kagan+cooperative+learning&ie=utf-8&oe=utf-8&client=firefox-b-ab [Accessed on 5 August 2018].

Nation, M., Bess, K., Voight, A., Perkins, D.D. & Juarez, P. 2011. American Journal of Community Psychology, 48:89. https://doi.org/10.1007/s10464-010-9414-x

Ngunjiri, F.W., Hernandez, K.C. & Chang, H. 2010. Living autoethnography: Connecting life and research [Editorial]. *Journal of Research Practice*, 6(1), Article E1. http://jrp.icaap.org/index.php/jrp/article/view/241/186 [Accessed on 5 August 2018].

Raab, D. 2013. Transpersonal approaches to autoethnographic research and writing. *The Qualitative Report 2013*, 18(42):1-18. http://www.nova.edu/ssss/QR/QR18/raab42.pdf [Accessed on 11 August 2015].

Raven, B.H. 1993. The Bases of power: Origins and recent developments. *Journal of Social Issues*, 49:227-251. doi:10.1111/j.1540-4560.1993.tb01191.x

Statistics South Africa. http://www.statssa.gov.za/?page_id=4286&id=554 [Accessed on 5 August 2018].

Wall, S. 2008. Easier said than done: Writing an autoethnography. *International Journal of Qualitative Methods*, 7(1):38-53. [Accessed on 4 August 2018].

Addendum A

Critical incidents that led to my reflections on issues of power around community engagement:

1. Receiving a gift of R80 000 worth of equipment which arrived three hours late – meaning I had to miss another appointment, and learners who should have been at home learning for exams had been standing around for three hours waiting to be part of the reception party that was insisted upon by the donors. The donors made no apology but rather had a "here we are, aren't you lucky, come for a photoshoot" attitude. This gift then necessitated a R50 000 gas installation because nobody bothered to wonder if we would have preferred version A (R0 installation) or version B (R50 000 installation). They came with promises of continued support but none has been forthcoming.

2. Sitting at a meeting in Kirkwood with a partner who was expecting me to solve an insoluble clash – some staff members were required to be at the partner's training and at an Education Department meeting at the same time, both of which had been postponed from previous dates. I then received the following text after my suggestion that the three teachers split themselves between the two meetings:

   > "As long as all the schools understand clearly up front that if we don't get cooperation from the participating schools, we will suspend [the project]."

3. Following these two incidents, I found the courage to tell someone who was offering a project that I thought it would be better if he first discussed his ideas with the teachers concerned. I then received the following response:

   > "The faculty and I have decided …"

Chapter 4

A community-based water monitoring programme in Makhanda/Grahamstown using the improved hydrogen sulphide test kit

Thandiswa Nqowana,
Sharli Paphitis, Roman Tandlich
and Sukhmani Mantel

COMMUNITY ENGAGEMENT, ENVIRONMENTAL
HEALTH AND BIOTECHNOLOGY
RESEARCH GROUP, FACULTY OF PHARMACY

t.nqowana@ru.ac.za

1. Introduction

HEIs have been largely focused on a prejudicial system that focuses on the idea of there being a correct way of generating and interpreting knowledge about the world (Altbach *et al.*, 2009). Most of these institutions follow strict disciplinary approaches, despite decades of attempts to encourage transdisciplinarity (Davies, 2016). Davies describes the legitimacy and value of knowledge as being dependent on the lay and expert knowledge (Davies, 2016). According to Miller *et al.*, (2008), a concept that has the ability to breach this gap is epistemological pluralism. Epistemological pluralism suggests that there may be several ways of generating knowledge and that accommodating this plurality can lead to a more successful, integrated generation of knowledge (Miller *et al.*, 2008). This approach is particularly useful in the study and management of social–ecological systems.

The legitimacy of knowledge has been known to be affected by the stereo-types associated with particular persons based on unconscious or implicit biases (Fricker, 2007). These prejudicial stereotypes, as Fricker describes, give rise to epistemic injustice within society (Fricker, 2007; Glass & Newman, 2015). Injus-tices that are epistemic in nature seek to discredit people of various groups as 'knowers', either in the eyes of society or the academy (Fricker, 2007). In the pursuit of correcting this injustice, community engagement over the past two decades has been used worldwide in HE institutes to promote epistemic justice. Community-Based Participatory Research (CBPR) engages the multiple stake-holders, including the researchers, the public and community providers, who affect and are affected by local challenges (Israel *et al.*, 1998). Each partner of the CBPR contributes unique strengths and knowledge, with the aim of improving the health and wellbeing of community members concerned (Israel *et al.*, 1998). CBPR begins with a research topic of importance to the community and aims to combine knowledge with taking actions, including social innovation, to solve the problem at hand.

Rhodes University is one of the HEIs in South Africa that has been applying CBPR in different disciplines of the university. The application of CBPR at this university, although applied by a small sector of the academic departments, has been aimed at including the community of Makhanda (a small town in the Eastern Cape under the Makana Local municipality) in solving various problems faced by the town in innovative ways with the local community as agents in the process (Makana revision draft, 2017). One of the major problems faced by Makhanda has been its microbial water quality, which is lower than what is recommended by the Department of Water Affairs (DWA) (DWAF, 1996). Typically, water quality is determined by comparing the physical, biological and chemical characteristics of a water sample with water quality guidelines or standards. These standards are usually based on scientifically assessed and acceptable levels of toxicity to either humans or aquatic organisms (Luyt *et al.*, 2012).

Access to clean water across Makhanda has increased since 2004; however, the increasing demand for water is concerning as it may lead to more frequent drought conditions (DWA, 2016; Ashbolt, Grabow & Snozzi, 2001). Droughts are due to insufficient rain or an increase in the population of an area that has insufficient infrastructure (Tempelhoff, Gouws & Botha, 2009). For example, the drought in Makhanda, which started around February of 2008, is considered severe. This drought has led to the declaration of Makhanda as a water disaster area. This has left citizens of Makhanda in a difficult position where there is a shortage of water, and when the water is available, the water quality is questionable. In this context, community-based water quality monitoring programmes are important as they equip the community with tools and knowledge of how to treat the water if the water is contaminated and consequently put their minds to rest. These programmes can include the community in the knowledge-building process, creating awareness about the danger of consuming contaminated water. For example, running workshops about the dangers of consuming poor quality water and getting the community involved in monitoring and purifying their water can help prevent outbreaks of diseases or illness.

Over the last couple of years, the Environmental Health and Biotechnology Research (EHBR) group at Rhodes University has been involved in studies of water quality monitoring and treatment strategies of tap and rainwater in Makhanda, as well as disaster management strategies. The purpose of introducing new ways of monitoring water quality to the community is to increase awareness and understanding about water quality in the community to avoid outbreaks of waterborne diseases. In geographically isolated areas such as Makhanda, alternative water monitoring tests can be used to ascertain the microbial water quality, introducing a socially innovative way to address local challenges (Tandlich, Luyt & Ngqwala, 2014). One such test is the improved hydrogen sulphide (H_2S) test kit, which has been used for monitoring microbial water quality in Makhanda for several years (Tandlich *et al.*, 2014; Luyt *et al.*, 2012). In previous studies conducted by the EHBR group at Rhodes University, it was shown that the test kit was 64% as reliable as standard indicator microorganism tests when the indicator microorganism concentration is around the regulatory detection limit for drinking water quality (Luyt *et al.*, 2012). Rates of false positive for the Colilert\u00ae18-derived concentrations have been reported to range from 7.4% to 36.4%. At the same time, rates of false negative results vary from 3.5% to 12.5%; and the Colilert medium has been reported to provide for cultivation of only 56.8% of relevant strains. Identification of unknown sources of faecal contamination   is not currently feasible. Based on literature review, calibration of the antibiotic-resistance spectra of Escherichia coli or the bifidobacterial tracking ratio should be investigated locally for potential implementation into the existing monitoring system. The current system could be too costly to implement in certain areas of South Africa where the modified H_2S. Therefore, the improved testing protocol involves the use of five test kits per sampling site. In the analysis of the results yielded from the five-test-kit protocol, the water sample is considered positive for faecal coliforms if all five test kits turn black within 72 hours of incubation at room temperatures. Water samples are considered negative if all five test kits are negative after 72 hours of incubation. Reliability of the test kit results using this modified protocol is 99.4% compared to the original testing protocol which gave a reliability score of 64% (Nhokodi *et al.*, 2016).

2. Community-based participatory research (CBPR)

In 2014, Tandlich *et al.* worked on the introduction of the H_2S test kit to a small part of the community of Makhanda for monitoring of rainwater (Tandlich *et al.*, 2014). This study led to the improved method of using the H_2S test kit used by Nhokodi *et al.* in 2016 to monitor tap water in the Eastern part of Makhanda and rainwater at Rhodes University (Nhokodi *et al.*, 2016). The results from these studies led to the development of the current extensive transdisciplinary research between the community engagement division and EHBR, where the H_2S test kit is to be introduced to a larger community basis of Makhanda using the public schooling system.

2.1 *Engagement with a community partner*

In 2014, the EHBR group conducted a study using a community-based monitoring and treatment programme which was based on the introduction of the H_2S test to the community (Tandlich *et al.*, 2014). A pamphlet about the sources of faecal contamination and the treatment of rainwater tanks was drafted to inform the community. Volunteers were recruited through collaboration with the non-governmental organisation Kowie Catchment Campaign (KCC)(Tandlich *et al.*, 2014). The recruitment of the volunteers with rainwater tanks was completed through contact with the KCC chairperson (Tandlich *et al.*, 2014). It was stipulated that forming a partnership with members from KCC would allow easier access to sampling sites and aid the authors in gathering information about health threats related to rainwater in Makhanda, since the authors and the KCC members had previously held discussions about microbial-related issues in water (Tandlich *et al.*, 2014). A total of eight volunteers from the KCC took part in the study, which supplied the authors with eight sampling sites. The method of engagement used in the study involved an initial meeting, where the principles of the H_2S test kit and sampling procedure using one H_2S test kit was demonstrated to the volunteers by the authors (Tandlich *et al.*, 2014). Occasional visits to the volunteers' households were also planned by the authors, with the aim of acquiring feedback from the volunteers on the use of the test kits and their experiences with their rainwater. These occasional visits would also afford the authors the chance to advise the volunteers on observed problems during the monitoring of the rainwater (Tandlich *et al.*, 2014). Four out of the eight rainwater tanks were positive for faecal contamination on one or two occasions. The owners of these four tanks were advised by the authors on how to dose bleach into the rainwater tank according to the pamphlets provided to the volunteers. According to one-on-one interviews with the volunteers, they found the H_2S test kit easy to use.

The overall monitoring programme delivered the desired results, even though only 87.5% of the original volunteers completed the sampling. The programme could reach only seven volunteers out of total of 80 390 people in the Makhanda population. This means that not even one percent of the population was reached by the civic engagement programme launched in the study. The water quality results from the study were also not released to the public; instead, they were written in a thesis, which was printed out and displayed at the Rhodes University Library. Analysing the impact the study had on raising awareness about water quality, it can be concluded that even though it involved scientific engagement with community members, a big gap between the water quality knowledge of the community versus that of the university remained.

2.2 Civic engagement and environmental sustainability in student projects

In 2016, the EHBR group conducted a civic engagement and environmental sus-tainability project through teaching and learning (Nhokodi *et al.*, 2016). In this CBPR strategy, the research group did not involve a community partner as it did on the previous occasion. Instead, teaching and learning strategies in an academic course were used to conduct water quality monitoring. The researchers in this water monitoring project were a Bachelor of Pharmacy student and a student enrolled for Honours in Biotechnology (Nhokodi *et al.*, 2016). Both students' projects were focused on the monitoring of microbial quality of rainwater at Rhodes University campus and the Makhanda Local Municipal bulk drinking water supply. The main aims of these two projects were to use sound scientific strategies to develop a water monitoring approach where the results could be communicated easily to the Makhanda public and could benefit them (Nhokodi *et al.*, 2016)

Nhokodi *et al.*, (2016) sampled three rainwater tanks at the Rhodes University campus. The tanks were situated in various parts of campus. Permission for sampling of all rainwater tanks was obtained from the relevant Rhodes University officials (Infrastructure Division) and the results of the analyses were provided to them (Nhokodi *et al.*, 2016). Another section of the study by (Nhokodi *et al.*, 2016) involved the sampling of municipal drinking water taps in Makhanda by Nqowana. This author chose all three sampling sites based on her scientific understanding of public health and water microbiology. She also chose the sites based on her knowledge and understanding of the water supply in the area and her concerns about possible implications of inferior microbial drinking water in her community (Nhokodi *et al.*, 2016). The author sampled all the sites herself, without involving any volunteering bodies from the community. This researcher's initiatives demonstrated a combination of scientific expertise and civic engagement, where she could introduce the H_2S test kit through interaction with the community. This interaction was prompted by the curiosity of the community when they saw the researcher sampling the communal tap (Nhokodi *et al.*, 2016). The analysis of the water using conventional methods showed that there was bacterial contamination in the water that could not be detected by these methods, therefore the author proceeded to conduct more tests on the water (Nqowana, Dube & Tandlich, 2017). These tests showed that the water in Makhanda might contain bacteria that is introduced into the water via the water distribution system (Nqowana, Dube & Tandlich, 2017).

This form of community engagement could involve a few community members, making them aware of the existence of the water quality testing kit but was not able to engage a large section of the community. This led to a partnership between the EHBR researchers with the Community Engagement Division at Rhodes University, with the vision of formulating a carefully planned CBPR water monitoring programme. The collaboration of these researchers:

- established a community-based programme with Grade 9 students at three Makhanda high schools to determine the quality of water in Makhanda through the community-based programme using the H_2S test kit;
- closed the knowledge-gap about water quality in the community using communication tools written in English, IsiXhosa and Afrikaans; and
- resulted in the distribution of water quality results acquired from the community-based programme using communication channels.

The implementation of these aims and objectives has given rise to a successful and efficient science engagement programme that can be adapted and used by local municipalities across South Africa to raise awareness about any issue at hand. The community-based programme has also lead to access to a broad spectrum of sampling sites around Makhanda, which gives an accurate representation of the water quality across Makhanda.

3. Methods

The project development process of water quality monitoring in Makhanda was investigated and described as set out below.

3.1 Training of volunteers and Grade 9 learners

During the process of volunteer recruitment, six volunteers were recruited from Rhodes University's third-year Pharmacy class. Each volunteer facilitated at an introductory workshop session for the three schools. There was one introductory workshop per school, and this meant that two volunteers needed to facilitate at one workshop each. The six volunteers were trained in a lab at the Rhodes University Pharmacy Department to demonstrate the use of the H_2S test kit to the Grade 9 learners. They were also educated on the safety precautions of the kit and were asked to impart this knowledge to the Grade 9 learners.

3.2 Piloting of manuals, surveys and workshop material

The PowerPoint presentation on the manuals, surveys and workshop was piloted to five randomly selected Grade 9 learners from a different school to those in the study, with the aim of seeing if the material is clear and understandable. The pilot study allowed for the capturing of the time it takes to answer the surveys and could determine whether the questions on the surveys were capturing what was required.

3.3 Preparation of the H2S sampling kits

A modified version of the Venkobachar et al., (1994) H_2S water testing kit was used. This contained peptone (40 g), dipotassium hydrogen phosphate (3 g), ferric ammonium citrate (1.5 g); sodium thiosulphate anhydrous (2 g); Teepol (2 mL), L-cysteine (25 mg); distilled water (100 mL) (Venkobachar et al., 1994). It was modified by the addition of deoxycholate (0.5% w/v) (Sobsey & Pfaender, 2002; Luyt et al., 2011a). Deoxycholate has been suggested to inhibit non-faecal bacterial growth, decreasing false positive result occurrence (Sobsey & Pfaender, 2002).

The kit's preparation method was modified from Genthe and Franck's method (1999). The medium was mixed with a magnetic stirrer for 30 minutes and then left to stand for 15 minutes, forming a coffee brown solution. A one millilitre aliquot of the medium was absorbed into a 5 x 10 cm piece of filter paper which had been folded and placed into a sterile urine jar (Spellbound Labs, Port Elizabeth, South Africa). The jars with the filter paper were placed into the UFE 700 oven (Memmert, Schwabach, Germany) overnight at 54°C . The sterility of the sterilised kits was checked periodically with 20 mL of sterile deionised water and incubation to identify positive a H_2S result due to contamination.

3.4 Sampling procedure

During the introductory workshop, the H_2S sampling procedure was explained to the learners verbally, while also referring to the distributed manuals which were available in English, IsiXhosa and Afrikaans. Each Grade 9 learner then received 30 H_2S test kits to collect water samples on a weekly basis for three weeks. Each learner used five kits for control purposes by adding deionised water, while the other five kits were used for sampling the source of water they use at their homes, making it a total of 10 kits per sampling occasion. Each learner conducted on-site sampling by sampling the source of water they use at their residence, be it tap or rain water. The H_2S water testing kits had approximately 20 mL of sampling water placed aseptically into the bottles. These were sealed and hand shaken to suspend the media, before being incubated at room temperature (18 – 25°C) for 72 hours. Samples were checked for the presence of a black precipitate, which was recorded as a positive result, every 12 hours. Tests remaining the initial yellow colour or which turned grey without going black within the 72 hour time limit were recorded as negative.

3.5 Detection of faecal coliforms

The method used in this study to assess faecal coliform concentrations was the membrane filtration method (m-FC) (MERCK) described in *Standard Methods* (APHA 1995). This method was used as a control in the study of the H_2S test kit vs conventional means of testing for presence of faecal contamination and also to calculate the correspondence rate (C_r). The correspondence was calculated with the following formula:

$$C_r = \frac{\textbf{(total number of corresponding H2S and mFC results)}}{\textbf{(total number of campured results)}} \times 100$$

100 mL of each water sample were filtered through a 0.45 μm pore membrane (Metricel Membrane Disc filters, Spellbound, Port Elizabeth, South Africa) and the filter was transferred to the medium slowly to avoid air bubble formation using sterile technique. Each sample was analysed in triplicate for independent

sampling results. The agar was incubated at 44.5°C for 24 hours and the results were captured in the form of colony forming units (CFU)/100 mℓ.

4. Results and discussion

4.1 Water quality monitoring, traffic light system and GIS mapping analysis

In Makhanda, water from the dams is treated in the treatment plants and then released into the pipe distribution system. But the condition of the water at the tap depends on the condition of the pipes, as well as factors like the concentration of the residual chlorine (Heibati, *et al.*, 2017). Brown coloured water from particles and sediment in the distribution system due to pipe breaks has increased an already sceptical Makhanda population's mistrust of the safety of its water (Richards & Daniel, 2008). Makhanda's community is very water conscious due to newspaper reports (Maher, 2006; Naketi, 2009; MacGregor, 2010; Mini, 2010; Mmango, 2010; Mngcambe, 2010) about unsafe drinking water and other reports around town. So many people are left wondering if the water is indeed safe. Thus, the aim of this project was to identify the microbial condition of tap water through science engagement using the H_2S water testing kit and identifying water quality problem areas using GIS mapping. The use of GIS maps to pin-point where drinking water is not of satisfactory microbial quality helps identify the extent of the problem as well as the size of the area affected.

Science workshops were run at three Makhanda high schools namely, School 1, School 2 and School 3. Each Grade 9 learner received 10 H_2S test kits to collect water samples on a weekly basis for a duration of three weeks. Of the 10 H_2S kits that were distributed to each leaner, five kits were used for control purposes by adding sterile deionised water, while the other five were used for sampling the source of water they use at their homes. Each learner conducted on-site testing by sampling the source of water they use at their residence and recorded the results on a supplied booklet. The results from each learner were transcribed and translated into a newly developed traffic light system as shown in **Table 1**. The traffic light system was developed with the aim of using it to communicate the results obtained from the H_2S kits in a manner that can be understood by the public. This traffic light system works on the basis that green stands for clean and safe water to drink, Yellow is a warning that the water might contain faecal contamination and may need further treatment i.e. boiling the water, and red suggests that the water is not safe to drink (Nhokodi *et al.*, 2016).

No. of kits positive	Colour representation	Interpretation of water quality
0	Green	Safe to drink
1-4	Yellow	Water requires further treatment (boiling) before consumption
5	Red	Do not drink! Report to councillor/Municipality

Adapted from **Nhokodi** *et al.*, (2016)

Table 1 was used to translate the water quality results from the learners. The data was first arranged according to the area of residence for each learner so that common area water quality results could be combined into one area, even if the learners were not from the same school. The water quality results for each area were then analysed and converted into their respective traffic light colour based on the number of positive H_2S water testing kits in that area for each week. The representative percentage for each traffic light colour at each area was then calculated and used as a point on a GIS map to depict the water quality at that area. For example, from the 90 learners who took part in the study, there were seven learners who came from a street called Daniels Street (Daniels Street is situated in Joza Location, Makhanda East). The number of positive kits from Daniels Street for the three weeks of sampling ranged from 1 – 4, meaning that on the traffic light system they were represented by a yellow colour. Therefore, Daniels Street had 100% yellow representation on the traffic light system. This 100% yellow representation meant that the water from Daniels Street required further boiling before use. This analysis was done for all the areas and a GIS map was created, as seen in Figures 1 and 2. The GIS maps were drawn for all Makhanda sampling points, **Figure 1** shows the sampling points according to GPS coordinates on the street layout of Makhanda, while **Figure 2** shows an enlarged region from **Figure 1** and the microbial water quality for each region.

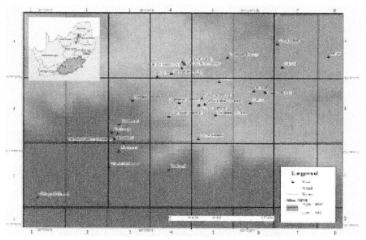

Figure 1: GIS map of the sampling during testing of water quality. The improvement of sampling results if resilience will repair the work when the sources of GIS sampling points. A 10 m digital elevation model (DEM) was obtained from the Shuttle Radar Topography Mission (SRTM) was used as the background.

The use of GIS also allows the identification of the different areas and levels which may be affected. Results from the different sampling rounds varied due to changing conditions of the water quality, which is the result of treatment efficiency and the number of pipe breaks within the area sampled.

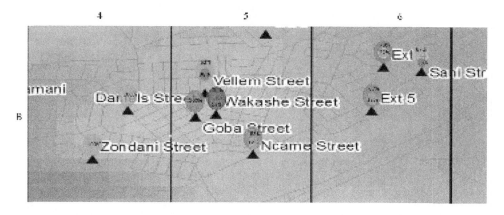

Figure 2: GIS map of contamination sampling rounds B4, B5 and B5 from Figure 1. This report is Ngqeleni township. Extensions 4 and 5 as well as Sani Street. The water quality was then represented using the Traffic Light system with the colour codes as follows: ● = Life positive, ● = Low positive, ● = Not positive. The percentage list of the lines has good sample points represents the number of occurrences for line where quality of line are indicated on the points on the GIS map represents the water quality indicator on for the 3 rounds of sampling.

Results in **Figure 2** above show varying microbial water quality, with Daniels Street and Zondani Street having 100% of the colour yellow on the traffic light system. This meant that the water at Zondani Street and Daniels Street needed to be treated further by boiling before consumption. As can be seen in **Figure 2**,

Vellem Street and Sani Street had similar water quality (approximately 38% being safe to drink (green) and approximately 62% requiring further treatment before use (yellow). On the other hand, Extension 4 (Ext 4), Extension 5 (Ext 5) and Ncame Street had 78%, 88% and 67% respectively of water quality that was safe to drink (green) within the three weeks of sampling, while the remaining percentage for Ext 4, Ext 5 and Ncame Street showed the colour yellow on the traffic light system, which means that the water requires further treatment before use. Goba Street had 100% green which suggests that the water quality was good, while Wakashe Street had a mixture of good and bad water quality. In Wakashe, week 1 and 2 both had 5 H_2S water testing kits that were positive, showing a red colour on the traffic light system. This means that the water during those 2 weeks had to be reported to the local officials as it was not safe to drink. Further engagement with learners from Wakashe Street showed that there was concern about brown water due to a pipe break in that street, and through the engagement with the learners they were made aware that officials were working on the pipe.

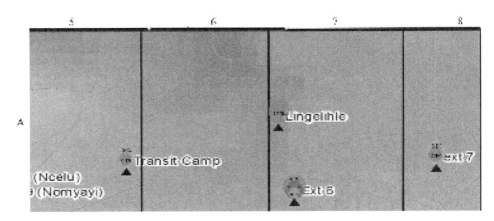

Figure 3: Screenshot of Google map showing streets A5 – A8 (here: Streets 5 to 8). The streets are Lingelihle 5, Transit Camp, Lingelihle 7, the water quality results are represented using the traffic light system, with each colour representing ● = 0 kits positive, ● = 1–4 kits positive, ● = 5 kits positive. The percentage for each traffic light colour at each point represents the number of occurrences of that water quality at that one point is used to show how the results change over time over time and representative for the 3 weeks of sampling.

Figure 3 also had a mixed water quality results, ranging from 100% green in Lingelihle (A7), to points of red colour in Extension 6 (Ext 6). The water quality in Ext 6 varied greatly within the three weeks of sampling, which could be the result of many reasons. There was no pipe burst in the area, but the poor water quality could have been caused by issues with treatment during those three weeks of sampling. Transit Camp and Ext 7 had similar water quality over the three weeks of sampling, with approximately 56% and 51 % of the water quality results showing an yellow colour of the traffic light system respectively. The yellow colour representation of these samples on the traffic light system meant that the water required further treatment as there were 1 – 4 H_2S water testing kits positive in those cases.

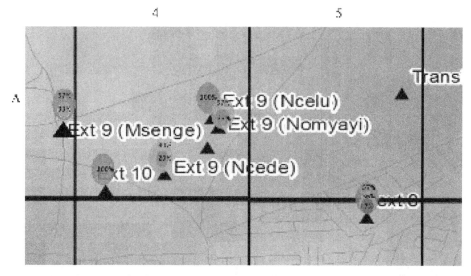

Figure 4: GIS map of Grahamstown showing section A4 and A5 from Figure 1 - this region is Extension 8 and 9. The water quality results are represented using the Traffic light system, with each colour representing, ● - 0 kits positive, ● - 1- 4 kits positive, ● - 5 kits positive. The percentage for each traffic light colour at each point represents the number of occurrences for that water quality at that location and is used as a point on the GIS map to depict the water quality in that area for the 5 weeks of sampling.

In **Figure 4** above, Extension 10 (Ext 10) and a street in Extension 9 (Ext 9) called Ncelu Street showed the colour green on the traffic light system. Msenge Street, a street in Ext 9, had 67% of its water samples represented by green in the traffic light system, which means that the water was safe to drink, while Ncede and Nomyayi Street, also in Ext 9, only had 20% and 33% respectively of its samples labelled as green on the traffic light system. Ext 8, however, had occasions where the water that was sampled resulted in five positive H_2S water testing kits and was represented by red on the traffic light system.

Most of the areas in **Figure 5** had the representation of green in the traffic light system, excluding Victoria Road and Vukani. In fact, Victoria Road had 17% of its water samples as red.

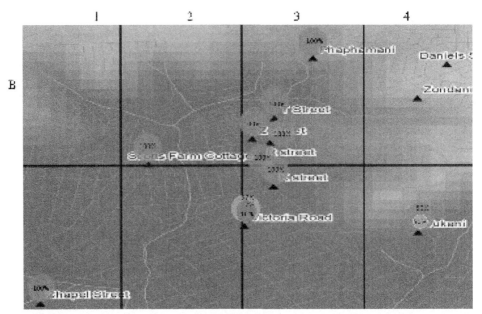

Figure 5. GIS map of Grahamstown showing section B1, B2, B3, B4, C1, C3 and C4 from Figure 1. The water quality results are represented using the traffic light system, with each colour representing: ● = colony positive, ● = test kit positive, ● = less reactive. The percentage for each traffic light colour at each point represents the number of occurrences for that water quality at that area and is used as a point on the GIS map to depict the water quality at that area for ease of sampling.

Water quality seemed to deteriorate significantly after pipe breaks or treatment failure. The most surprising results were for samples collected in Makhanda East, where water quality seemed to be better in some parts than others. Makhanda East is left without water more frequently and for longer periods of time than the rest of Makhanda. Positive H_2S water testing kit results were correlated with pipe breaks in the area and, on resampling, were negative, which means that the pipe breaks were fixed. This is a distinct contrast to the situation arising from the lack of chlorination in 2018, May. This has also been reported in other countries (Allen et al., 2004). Pipe breaks can lead to an increased likelihood of diarrhoeal diseases (Nygård et al., 2007). Using Faecal Coliform (FC) concentration as an indicator of treatment failure and distribution network issues is well-established (Carter et al., 2000; Sartory, 2004; Chowdhury, 2012). A good correlation between the modified H_2S water testing kit and FC concentration values shows that it is a good alert system even under chlorinated water conditions. This is not surprising as the original H_2S water testing kit was used for tap water tests amongst others (Genthe & Jagals, 2003). Opportunistic samplings were run in middle income houses in Makhanda for three weeks and all produced positive results on week 1 with the H_2S water testing kit and FC (Luyt et al., 2011a). This was due to lack of chlorination of the Makhanda water, as was published in the local Grocott's newspaper by Sue Maclannan:

> A notice dated Monday 21 May from the directorate of engineering and Infrastructure Services and signed by acting municipal manager Ted Pillay is headed 'Public notice: Water quality'. It warns residents of Makhaanda and Alicedale of a high concentration of *E. coli* – a bacterium found in the faeces of animals and humans – in municipal water.
>
> 'The municipality therefore request the residents, as a precautionary measure to … boil the water before drinking,' the notice, issued Monday afternoon, reads. However, the high turbidity in water, while it may cause stains on clothing, does not pose a health hazard, the notice says. The problem is the result of Makana running out of supplies of the correct chemicals – a problem managers said was caused by supply chain delays (Grocotts' mail, 2014).

4.2 Learners as citizen scientists

The question of reliability arises from including school learners as volunteers in a water quality monitoring programme, or as citizen scientists. The Water Watch Group in America showed that volunteers can do many simple tests as reliably as experts if they are properly trained. Volunteers, such as the learners that were involved in this water quality monitoring project, provide man power which is often in short supply. Although their skills and equipment constraints limit the variety of tests they can do, they can access a large number of sites, providing more data for decision-making. The data indicates that the learners were successfully able to monitor the microbial water quality for their homes for a period of three weeks using the kit. Based on the GIS maps supplied above, the learners were also successful at recording and understanding the water results that came from the water quality monitoring programme.

As result of the water quality monitoring by the learners and their involvement in broader training and education components as part of the project, the learners gained better understanding of the term 'water conservation' and why it is important. We are unable to go into details about this broader educational and engagement project (which included workshops and poster designing competitions at the schools) in this chapter – that would provide material for another chapter in itself – but will briefly discuss some of the learnings from the qualitative studies undertaken to evaluate these aspects of the project. Through the science engagement, learners were able to understand more about water quality and learned about the risks associated with consuming water contaminated with faecal coliforms like *E. coli*. There was wide agreement amongst learners on the risks associated with consuming water of poor quality and its links to illness/disease. The qualitative evaluations showed that before the learners were exposed to the kit, their method of water quality monitoring included appearance of the water, taste of the water and reporting it to someone who has access to testing materials. After the learners were exposed to the H_2S water testing kit, they were more accustomed to using the kit or reporting the water to the lab. After the engagement with the learners, more learners acquired some form of agency where they decided to boil the water first before reporting it to municipality. During the time of the engagement, the learners were having more conversations about water, specifically about water quality, with their families, and the learners got the chance to learn more about the H_2S kit and also tell their community about the kit during their presentations. Learner attitudes towards science as a subject and a career changed significantly from the time they were introduced to the programme to after they completed their individual projects of monitoring water at their homes.

5.   Conclusion

The large-scale citizen-driven science project described in this chapter would not have been possible without challenging the boundaries of the traditional knowledge creation paradigm or the epistemic prejudices which underly it. While those traditionally deemed to be non-specialised scientists have fre-quently been excluded from participation in research in the role of scientist, citizen science projects assume epistemic credibility in citizens and include them as collaborators in the knowledge-making project. Learners were trusted as knowers and co-investigators in the research, as well as in coming to under-stand and address their own community challenges. Learners were allowed to take up active roles as scientists, thereby the testing of water quality in Makhanda were placed in the hands of the community. The learners collected and tested water samples from a large geographic area which allowed for the thorough microbial quality analysis of Makhanda water in a broad area. Through involving learners and their families in the project, science was presented as accessible. The application of science in the daily lives of community members and participants transformed these people, who are more in tune with their space and resources, into agents of change in their communities. The community-based water quality monitoring programme described in this article can be used as a template from which to draft an efficient tool for establishing involvement of citizens in science at a community level and narrowing the knowledge-gap about water quality and water treatment options. As a result, the outbreak of waterborne diseases at the local government level, not only in Makhanda, but also in South Africa as a whole, can be prevented.

References

Allen, M. J., Edberg, S. C. & Reasoner, D. J. 2004. Heterotrophic Plate Count Bacteria – What is Their Significance in Drinking Water? International Journal of Food Microbiology, 92, 265274.

Altbach, P. G., Reisberg L., Rumbley, L. E. 2009, Trends in Global Higher Education: Tracking an Academic Revolution, Report prepared for the UNESCO 2009 World Conference on Higher Education, UNESCO Publishing, Paris. http://unesdoc.unesco.org/images/0018/001831/183168e.pdf.

APHA (1995) Standard Methods for the Examination of Water and Wastewater. 19th Edition, American Public Health Association Inc., New York.

Ashbolt, N.J., Grabow, W.O.K., Snozzi, M., 2001. Indicators of microbial water quality. In: L. Fewtrell & J. Bartram (eds). Water Quality: Guidelines, Standards and Health. Risk assessment and management for water-related infectious disease. IWA Publishing, London (Chapter 13): 289-315.

Carter, J. T., Rice, E. W., Buchberger, S. G. & Lee, Y. 2000. Relationships between Levels of heterotrophic Bacteria and Water Quality Parameters in a Drinking Water Distribution System. Water Research, 34, 1495-1502.

Chowdhury, S. 2012. Heterotrophic Bacteria in Drinking Water Distribution System: a Review. Environmental Monitoring and Assessment, 184, 6087-6137.

Davies, C.J. 2016. Whose knowledge counts? Exploring cognitive justice in community-university collaborations.

Department of Water Affairs 1996. South African Water Quality Guidelines. [online]. Available at: https://www.iwa-network.org/filemanager-uploads/WQ_Compendium/Database/Selected_guidelines/041.pdf [Accessed 8 October 2018].

Department of Water Affairs 2016. Guide to National Water act. [online]. Available at: https://www.dwa.gov.za/documents/publications/NWAguide.pdf [Accessed 6 October 2018].

Fricker, M. 2007. Epistemic injustice: power and the ethics of knowing. Oxford scholarship online 6.

Genthe, B. & Jagals, P. 2003. Application of an H2S Strip as a Field Test Kit for Microbial Water Quality Assessment. Division of Water, Environment and Forestry Technology, CSIR, Stellenbosch, RSA; Centre for Health and Environment Research and Development, Free State Technikon, Bloemfontein, RSA.: Water Research Commission.

Genthe, B. & Franck, M. 1999. A tool for Assessing Microbial Quality in Small Community Water Supplies: an H2S Strip Test. WRC Report, 33.

Glass, R. D. & Newman, A. 2015. Ethical and epistemic dilemmas in knowledge production: Addressing their intersection in collaborative, community-based research. *Theory and Research in Education,* 13:23-37.

Groccotts. (2014). Makana water quality better. Retrieved November 15, 2018, from https://www.grocotts.co.za/2014/02/06/makana-water-quality-better/

Heibati, M, Stedmon, C. A., Stenroth. K., Rauch, S., Toljander, J., Säve-Söderbergh, M. & Murphy, K. R.2017. Assessment of drinking water quality at the tap using fluorescence spectroscopy. *Water Res.*;125:1-10. doi:10.1016/j.watres.2017.08.020

Israel, B. A., Schulz, A. J., Parker, E. A. & Becker, A. B. 1998. Review of community-based research: assessing partnership approaches to improve public health. *Annual Revision of Public Health,* 19:173-202.

Luyt, C. D., Muller, W. J., & Tandlich, R. (2011a). Low-cost tools for microbial quality assessment of drinking water in South Africa. HealthMed, 5(6), Supplement 1, 1868-1877.

Luyt, C.D., Tandlich, R., Muller, W.J. & Wilhelmi, B.S. 2012. Microbial monitoring of surface water in South Africa: An overview. *International Journal of Environmental Research and Public Health,* 9:2669-2693.

MAHER, V. (2006). Water Update: No Threat to Humans. Grocotts Mail, 2 November 2006.

Makana Revision Draft. 2017. Makana Municipality Integrated Development Plan Revision IV Draft 2016- 2017. Accessed on 20 March 2017 from: http://www.makana.gov.za/wp-content/uploads/2013/06/Draft-IDP-2016-2017.pdf

MACGREGOR, D. 2010. Grahamstown Water Debate Continues. Daily Dispatch, 10 March 2010. Page 248

Manager, A. M. 2017. *Grahamstown Municipality Revision Draft 2016- 2017.*

Miller, T.R., Bair, T. D., Littlefield, C. M., Kofinas, G. & Chapin III, F. S. 2008. Epistemological pluralism: Reorganizing interdisciplinary research. *Ecology and Society,* 13(2): 46. [online].

Mini, P. 2010. Experts Question Water Quality Claims. Grocotts Mail, 24 August 2010. Mintz, E. D., Reiff, F. M. & Tauxe, R. V. 1995. Safe Water Treatment and Water-Storage in the Home: A Practical New Strategy to Prevent Waterborne Disease. JAMA-Journal of the American Medical Association, 273 948-953.

Mmango, M. 2010. Water Crisis Continues in the Townships. Grocotts Mail, 7 September 2010.

Mngcambe, N. 2010. Locals Say Why They Don't Drink Tap Water Grocotts Mail, 29 June 2010.

Naketi, A. 2009. High Levels of *E. coli* in Water Under Question. Grocotts Mail, 20 November 2009.

Nhokodi, T., Nqowana, T. & Collings, D. 2016. Civic engagement and environmental sustainability in teaching and learning at higher education institution in South Africa. *Acta Technology*, 6:66-82.

Nqowana, T., Dube, C.S. & Tandlich, R. 2017. Monitoring of potable water quality in Grahamstown Local Municipality, South Africa. Paper presented at the 9th Air and Water Components of the Environment conference, held in Cluj-Napoca, Romania from 17th until 19th March 2017, pp. 345-350 (ISSN: 2067-743).

Nygård, K., Wahl, E., Krogh, T., Tveit, O. A., Bøhleng, E., Tverdal, A. & Aavitsland, P. 2007. Breaks and Maintenance Work in the Water Distribution Systems and Gastrointestinal Illness: A Cohort Study. International Journal of Epidemiology, 36, 873-880.

Richards, E. & Daniel, P. 2008. Grahamstown's Other Drinking Problem. Activate, 3 March 2008.

Sartory, D. P. 2004. Heterotrophic Plate Count Monitoring of Treated Drinking Water in the UK: A Useful Operational Tool. International Journal of Food Microbiology, 92, 297-306.

Sobsey, M. D. & Pfaender, F. K. 2002. Evaluation of the H2S Method for Detection of Fecal Contamination of Drinking Water. Geneva: University of North Carolina.

Tandlich, R., Luyt, C.D. & Ngqwala, N.P.A. 2014. Community-based rainwater monitoring and treatment programme in Grahamstown, South Africa. *Journal of Hydrocarbons, Mines and Environmental Research,* 5:46-51.

Tempelhoff, J., Gouws, I. & Botha, K. 2009. The December 2004-January 2005 floods in the Garden Route region of the Southern Cape, South Africa. *Jàmbá Journal of Disaster Risk Studies,* 2:93-112.

Venkobachar, C., Kumar, D., Talreja, K., Kumar, A. & Lyengar, L. J. 1994. Assessment of Bacteriological Water Quality Using Modified H2S Strip Test. Water SRT Aqua, 43, 311-314.

Chapter 5

Translanguaging online: A case study of a bilingual online mathematics programme for Grade 7 learners in Diepsloot, Johannesburg

Nathalia Lourenço

SCHOOL OF LANGUAGES,
RHODES UNIVERSITY

nvonwitt5@gmail.com

1. Introduction

South Africa has an education system that was crippled by apartheid and is still not adequately developed to meet the needs of the South African people. Despite recognising 11 official languages, a prevailing form of unequal access to education is the use of English as the dominant language of learning and teaching (LoLT), which is a second language (L2) for 90.4% of South Africa's population (Statistics South Africa, 2012). With English becoming the LoLT after only three years of schooling, learners who are not raised in an English-medium environment will not yet have developed adequate proficiency in English (Heugh in Howie et al., 2006) making it difficult for them to have meaningful engagement with the curriculum context. These language deficiencies are then exacerbated as learners progress to higher grades where content becomes more abstract and complex. With this being a lived reality for so many South African learners, it is imperative that this inequality is addressed.

2. Motivation: Language in education in South Africa

South Africa's education system is often considered to be in crisis, and mathematics and literacy are two areas which are at the forefront of the problem. For example, in the 2014 Annual National Assessments (ANAs), learners scored on average 43% for mathematics in Grade 6, but only 11% for mathematics in Grade 9 (Department of Basic Education, 2014). At Grade 6 level, 35% of learners achieved more than 50% in the ANA, while only 3% of Grade 9s achieved more than 50% (Department of Basic Education, 2014). This suggests that learners increasingly struggle with mathematics as the content becomes more complex and abstract and as their deficiencies in their foundational understandings become increasingly apparent.

The South African Language in Education Policy (LiEP) alludes to fostering additive bilingualism, that is, the learning of a L2 while maintaining the first language (L1) (Heugh & Luckett in Probyn, 2009). Additive bilingualism tends to foster higher language proficiencies in both languages and validates the learners' identities, supporting learners' pride in their identities (De Mejía, 2002). However, the L1 is used as LoLT only until Grade 3, and from Grade 4 onwards English is used as the LoLT (Howie *et al.*, 2006). This shift occurs too early, creating a language learning environment of subtractive bilingualism, wherein the L2 is learned at the expense of the L1 and gradually replaces it (Heugh in Howie *et al.*, 2006). The result of this is that learners often do not become fully proficient in either language, and have their self-confidence and feelings of self-worth diminished (De Mejía, 2002). This insufficient language proficiency then also limits learners' access to what is taught in all of their L2 subjects, making learners struggle throughout school (Wababa, 2009).

Even though many teachers are apprehensive about the use of L1 in classes where the L2 is the target language, codeswitching still occurs in classrooms (Moore, 2002). Setati and Adler (2000) found that the teachers in their study experienced the "dilemma of codeswitching" (Adler in Setati & Adler, 2000:255). Teachers need to use the learners' L1 in order to ensure their understanding of a concept, or to encourage discussion of the concept; however, teachers also need to use as much English as possible so that learners can become familiar with and competent in mathematical English (Setati & Adler, 2000). This dilemma is extended to the teacher's encouragement and allowance for their learners to use codeswitching (Setati *et al.*, 2002). While codeswitching is in some cases beneficial, codeswitching paired with the premature introduction of English as LoLT often results in 'semilingual' learners who have an inadequate grasp of the languages or the curriculum. While the use of codeswitching in the classroom is important both pedagogically and politically, it is also a complex matter (Setati & Adler, 2000). Although the LiEP encourages codeswitching in the classroom (Setati, 2002), very little guidance is given on how to do so, and there are no readily-available resources for teachers to guide their codeswitching. This project undertook to create a replicable codeswitching model which could be implemented in addition to existing policies, in this way attempting to solve a social or educational problem by combining new and existing practices.

3.   Context
3.1   *Diepsloot, Johannesburg*

This research was undertaken in Diepsloot, a township in northern Johannesburg, South Africa. Diepsloot was planned and created by the apartheid government in the early 1990s (Bénit, 2002), and has grown rapidly, with an estimated current population of around 200 000 (Cross, 2014). The great majority of Diepsloot's population are black Africans (97%), and almost 20% of Diepsloot residents are foreign nationals (Mahajan, 2014). Many people live in or move to Diepsloot because of its proximity to work opportunities in relation to other townships (Mahajan, 2014). As a result of people moving to Diepsloot in search of economic opportunity, the mix of language and cultures is extremely diverse, making Diepsloot a reflection of the multilingual country in which it is situated. Many of the schools in Diepsloot teach in Sesotho, Sepedi, Setswana or isiZulu for the Foundation Phase (after which English becomes the LoLT), and these languages are offered as the home language. While very few school children speak English at home, they are exposed to written English on the posters, signs and flyers found in Diepsloot and, for those who have access, on the radio and television.

3.2   *OLICO Maths Education*

For this project I worked with OLICO Maths Education, a not-for profit non-governmental organisation that runs an after-school academic support pro-gramme in Diepsloot. OLICO Maths Education was created with the vision of living "in an inclusive, just and humane society without poverty" (OLICO Founda-tion NPC, 2015).

OLICO Maths Education's learners are required to attend two mathematics sessions a week, and they can elect to attend literacy sessions, Lego clubs and human rights workshops in addition to this. The mathematics course started out by opening up the computer lab for Grade 9 learners to improve their mathe-matics through Khan Academy (which can be found at www.khanacademy.org)

videos and practice activities. It was found, however, that this online platform was too flexible and that learners would often end up doing copious repetitions of the same exercise, or mistakenly doing very difficult work due to incorrectly navigating through the site. It was also found that the videos were often not appropriate to the South African context in terms of language, mathematical processes and writing conventions and culture. In response to this, OLICO Maths Education created its own online mathematics videos using Explain Everything, as part of OLICO Maths Educations' own online mathematics course, created with the Moodle platform. This course takes into account the expected level of learners' mathematical proficiency as informed by Spaull and Kotze (2015), which suggests that Grade 7 learners in Diepsloot are three to four grade levels behind in mathematics. Diagnostic mathematics assessments conducted with all Grade 7s at OLICO Maths Education found that the projection was true for the OLICO Maths Education learners, as these learners were roughly three grades behind grade level. The course is also based on the premise that foundational concepts need to be solidified in order for them to be built upon and for new knowledge to be created, and so, for these reasons, core foundational concepts from previous grades are re-taught and, where applicable, linked with grade-level, Curriculum Assessment Policy Statements (CAPS)-aligned work. In line with OLICO Maths Education's vision of using education to ultimately create a more equal society, the content produced by OLICO Maths Education is open-source, meaning that it is freely available to be shared and distributed and can be found at learn.olico.org.

4. Socio-cultural considerations

In any language intervention one must take into account the socio-cultural considerations which may influence it. The main tension existing within the socio-political sphere is the tension between the utility and prestige of the language on the one hand and the heritage or cultural importance of the language on the other.

The economic, political and social utility of English tends to outweigh the value of the development of true additive bilingualism in parents' convictions (Webb, Lafon & Pare, 2010). Furthermore, mother-tongue education (MTE) is a rather taboo topic among many South Africans. It is a reminder of the deliberately oppressive use of MTE during Bantu Education which limited learners' access to English (Plüddemann et al., 2004). South Africa's current LiEP reflects this aversion to MTE, as learners learn through their L1 only from Grades 1 to 3 before switching to English as LoLT. This policy also reflects the "maximum exposure fallacy" (Brock-Utne in Plüddemann *et al.,* 2004), which is the belief that L2 proficiency is best attained through more exposure to it, albeit at the expense of the L1. As a result, many parents choose to have their children learn through English from as early an age as possible, irrespective of their English proficiency (NEPI in Setati *et al.,* 2002).

As such, resistance from parents and learners to this project was anticipated. At the beginning of the school year, I informed the learners' parents that I would be implementing an optional bilingual mathematics course. The parents believe that it is important to learn English because it is a medium of instruction and because it allows people to communicate everywhere. They also believe that it is important to learn in English, because school subjects are taught in English and school textbooks are in English. However, the parents also believe that it is important to learn African languages because it "is our culture, and our roots". This led to the question of whether it was important or useful to learn in African languages. The first parent to offer an opinion stated that it was not useful because the medium of instruction at school was English. Several parents showed their agreement with this. Following this, another parent suggested that the learners be taught in English, and that the word is then repeated or explained in the L1 to help the learners understand. Several more parents then expressed their agreement with this suggestion. This then served as an opportunity to share with the parents our hopes to create an experimental course where their children would have the opportunity to learn in a similar manner to this, of which the parents were largely supportive. It is worth noting that the good organisational reputation held by OLICO Maths Education, as well as my personal history of working at OLICO Maths Education for the year prior to this intervention, may have positively contributed to the trust and support the parents showed towards this experimental intervention.

Despite the parents' support of the use of translanguaging, most of the learners initially stated they would prefer to learn through English: 70% of learners stated they would prefer to watch the OLICO videos in English, and only 30% would have preferred to watch the videos in their home language. Learners gave various reasons for their answers. The trends in their answers are represented in Tables 1 and 2 below, after which selected reasons from the learners are given.

Table 1: Reasons for No

Reasons for No				
Understand English better than L1	Importance of English	Undecipherable	Multilingual context	Like English (no reason given)
52%	20%	12%	8%	8%

Some of the reasons given for this include:
- It will make it more difficult than it is because I understand English better than my home language.
- Because some of the children they don't understand English they only understand their home language so they must understand English.
- No, because there are some of my language words I don't know like maths in Setswana and Nathalia won't be able to help me.
- I choose 'no', because in the room we speak a lot of languages and watching the videos in English helps a lot when coming to exams.
- Because I only like learning maths in English.

Table 2: Reasons for Yes

Reasons for Yes	
Understand L1 better than English	Translanguaging suggested
90%	10%

Some of the reasons given for this include:
- Because I will be able to know the steps they show, which means I can be able to understand and how to get an answer.
- Because some of the videos we sometimes don't understand them so it is better to watch them in our home language so that we can understand them more.
- Because we can't understand some of the words that are spoken in English but we can have a mix language.

5. Linguistic considerations

Second language acquisition is an integral component of South African education, as the vast majority of learners are required to acquire a second language (usually English) in order to access the curriculum beyond the first three years. However, English is introduced after only three years of schooling, meaning that learners' basic interpersonal communicative skills are still developing, and most of the time they have certainly not developed the cognitive academic language proficiency needed to use English as a language of learning. It is therefore problematic that the South African education system formally assesses understanding through English.

Cognitive processes and social development are facilitated through language (Webb, Lafon & Pare, 2010). As such, the higher one's language competence, the better one's ability is to access and understand information (Webb, Lafon & Pare, 2010). This is especially true in the education context, within which learners' linguistic competence directly affects their ability to grapple with the content and concepts they encounter.

The Department of Basic Education recognises that many learners in South Africa are learning through their L2 (Department of Basic Education, 2011). The CAPS curriculum sets out to equip learners with basic interpersonal communication skills (BICS) in the Foundation Phase (Grades 1 to 3) (Department of Basic Education, 2011) and to build cognitive academic language proficiency (CALP) in the Intermediate (Grades 4 to 6) and Senior (Grades 7 to 9) Phases (Department of Basic Education, 2011). However, it is noted by the Department of Basic Education (2011) that it is unlikely that learners will have CALP from the time they are learning through their L2, as it is stated: "By the end of Grade 9, these learners should be able to use their home language and first additional language effectively and with confidence for a variety of purposes, including learning" (Department of Basic Education, 2011: 8). However, while BICS can be attained within three to five years, CALP can take from four to seven years to attain (Hakuta *et al.* in Valdés, 2004) and up to 10 years or even longer to attain L1-level CALP (Cummins *et al.*, 1998). Clearly this would put any L2 speaker of the LoLT at an immediate academic disadvantage and they would need many years to catch up to their English-L1 peers.

It is therefore of critical importance that high-quality L2 instruction is provided while CALP is developed in the L1, as many CALP skills can be transferred to the L2 once developed (Wababa, 2009). This is illustrated through Cummins' Common Underlying Proficiency (CUP) model and Development Interdependence Hypothesis. This model argues that different languages share the same faculties in the brain, for example reading strategies, higher-order thinking skills and subject and conceptual knowledge (Cummins in Fitzgerald, 1995). As these faculties are shared among different languages, the CUP model argues that these linguistic skills are transferrable across languages. As L1 knowledge is transferrable to the L2, it is important that learners have solid conceptual knowledge in their L1 (Wababa, 2009). It is, however, also important to note that certain concepts may differ when they are reinterpreted from one language to another (Wales, 1990). Language and culture are deeply intertwined as culture often influences the interpretation of language, and so it is important that these cultural and linguistic matches and mismatches are taken into account when considering the transference of concepts across languages.

6.   Mathematical considerations
6.1   The language of mathematics
It is often thought that mathematics is one of the easier subjects to learn through an L2 because it is perceived that mathematics is less language-dependent than other subjects. This assumption is, however, incorrect and problematic. Newman (in Wales, 1990) found that Grade 6 learners' mathematical errors often arose from misunderstanding the language used, rather than simply applying incorrect mathematical processes.

A mathematical register does not consist solely of words, but also of a particular way of communicating (Halliday in Pimm, 1991). Furthermore, mathematical English differs from everyday English as words hold different meanings or functions (Pimm, 1991). While there are some words unique to mathematical English, other words are borrowed from ordinary English and altered (Shuard, 1982). Everyday English and ordinary English may cause confusion when words have altered meanings, with the more formal grammar and the actual mathematical symbols (Pimm, 1981). When learners are able to communicate in formal and informal mathematical language, they are able to synthesise spontaneous and technical concepts, and in this way they are able to build mathematical knowledge (Mphunyane in Setati & Adler, 2000).

While mathematics has a certain vocabulary and register associated with it, it is not a language in itself. As such, mathematics needs to be communicated through another language (for example English or isiZulu) (Setati, 2002). It then follows that the learning of mathematics is complicated by learning it through a language in which one is not fluent. An additional complication to mathematical language is that learners may confuse mathematical language with everyday language where the two overlap; for example the words "'and', 'or', 'if ...

then', 'some', 'any', and so on" (Rowland in Setati, 2002:10) seem simple in conversational English, yet they have a very specific and slightly different meaning in mathematical English (Setati, 2002:10). Setati (2002:9) suggests that learners in South African mathematics classrooms encounter many types of languages: conversational English and mathematical English, "formal and informal mathematics language", conversations about procedure and conversations about concepts, and 'leaners' L1s and the LoLT.

When learners are learning in an L2, it is not always possible to differentiate between errors made due to conceptual misunderstanding vs errors due to language proficiency (Moschkovich, 1999). In order to understand and communicate mathematics, learners need the necessary vocabulary and understanding of the written mathematical language (including the signs and symbols), and this mathematical language proficiency is best developed through extensive opportunities for reading, writing and speaking about mathematics (Sfard *et al.*, 1998). Learners process thoughts by communicating and synthesising them into more cohesive ideas (Sfard *et al.*, 1998). As such, talking about mathematics not only provides learners with opportunities to grow their language proficiencies but also to refine and expand their mathematical understanding (Sfard *et al.*, 1998).

6.2 Learning fractions

The mathematics topic used in this project was fractions. This is of particular significance because fractions are renowned for being one of the more complex concepts in primary school mathematics. Learners often struggle with fractions because they do not represent set numbers, as for example natural numbers do, but rather represent relations between different quantities (TLRP, 2006). This is confusing because fractions that look the same could represent different quantities (for example ½ of 4 is different to ½ of 6) and fractions that look different may represent equal quantities (for example ½ and ²⁄₄) (TLRP, 2006). When learners begin to learn mathematics, they are taught to reject fractions as numbers, because they are not whole numbers (Charalambos & Pitta-Pantazi, 2007), and so this fundamental understanding needs to be overhauled in order for learners to successfully grapple with fractions. Fractions are also seen as particularly difficult because each fraction can be understood in five different ways: as part of a whole, as a ratio, as a quotient, as a measure or as an operator (Pantziara & Philippou, 2012).

7.   Methodology

Conducting studies about how people learn requires contextual observations and experiments, and a methodological framework is needed in order to do this effectively (Barab & Squire, 2004). Design-based research (DBR) was selected as the most fitting methodology for this research, because, even though it is context-embedded research, the aim of the findings from the data collected through this methodology is to create educational interventions that are applicable and replicable beyond the context in which they were studied (Barab & Squire, 2004). It is this focus on the real-life context and application that sets DBR apart from methodologies such as laboratory experiments.

Each time the design is altered (even though this is central to DBR), the implementation of the design becomes more synthetic (Barab & Squire, 2004), which could lead to what Brown and Campione refer to as "lethal mutations" (in Collins, Joseph & Bielaczyc, 2004) – where the design is changed in unintended ways through its implementation, thus detracting from the underlying principles of the design. In order to ensure the most important elements were adhered to, the critical elements of implementation (Collins *et al.*, 2004) for this research project were drawn up as follows:

Table 3: Critical elements of implementation

Critical element	How it was implemented
The translanguaging model should be used for all the bilingual videos.	The bilingual resource creator and I worked closely to adapt the videos.
The isiZulu used should be familiar to the learners.	This was done at the discretion of the bilingual resource creator and was evaluated by the external evaluator.
The mathematical meanings conveyed in the English-medium videos should be reflected in the bilingual-medium videos.	This was done at the discretion of the bilingual resource creator and was evaluated by the external evaluator and myself.
Learners must have freedom to choose which course to do.	I spoke to each learner individually to ask them which course they would like to do, placing no pressure on them to choose one course over another.
All learners must do a pre-quiz, and, if they score less than 80%, they must then watch the video and complete a post-quiz.	This was automated on the computers.
Learners must watch the videos in the correct order.	This was automated on the computers.

Critical element	How it was implemented
Learners must know how to use the glossary.	The facilitators and I showed the learners how to use it and checked that they understood the process.

8. Implementation

In an effort to make the OLICO Maths Education course more linguistically acces-sible to its users (while also ensuring learners acquire the necessary English required for doing mathematics at school), a bilingual mathematics course was run as a pilot. This was for the Grade 7 fractions course, which was started by all Grade 7s at the beginning of the third term, 2015. The course was created in English and isiZulu. IsiZulu was chosen as it is one of the languages spoken by the majority of the OLICO Maths Education learners and for logistical reasons such as staffing and intelligibility to the researcher.

To implement the design, I created a translanguaging model informed by the literature. I then worked closely with the OLICO Maths Education team to jointly create English-isiZulu bilingual videos using the translanguaging model and a bilingual online glossary of mathematics terms. We created the videos using Explain Everything, a video-making application similar to Microsoft PowerPoint, but adapted to online teaching, and we used Moodle as a platform for the online course. The team of people involved in this project include: the mathematics coordinator Dr Lynn Bowie, who has extensive experience working in mathe-matics education and creates OLICO Maths Educations' mathematics content; the bilingual resource creator Thabiso Simelane, a facilitator at OLICO Maths Education whose L1 is isiZulu; and the project co-founder Andrew Barrett who manages the technological elements and the monitoring and evaluation of the OLICO Maths Education online course. The rest of the OLICO Maths Education team also showed an interest in the project and provided feedback throughout the project.

This research project was discussed with all learners and their parents at the beginning of the year. Before the experiment was begun, permission letters were sent to learners' parents, as the learners were 11 – 14 years old and as such required permission from a parent or guardian. All permission letters were signed and returned. Parents could give permission for learners to participate in the study and to participate in the experimental course. All parents gave permission for their children to participate in the study, but two parents did not give per-mission for their children to take part in the experimental course. A further level of agency and autonomy was granted to learners, as learners whose parents had given permission for them to participate in the experimental course could then self-select to participate in the experimental course. All verbal feedback from the learners was voluntary.

When the fractions course began, I spoke to each learner individually to find out whether they would sign up for the English-medium or English-isiZulu bilingual fractions course. I explained the differences between the courses, clarified that informal isiZulu would be used and asked learners which course they would like to do and if they would like to share their reason for their choice with me. At the beginning of the term, learners self-selected to enrol in either the English-medium fractions course or the English and isiZulu bilingual fractions course. Learners then all did the same course, but those doing the bilingual course watched the bilingual videos, had access to the hyperlinked glossary and received a glossary insert to keep in their homework books.

Throughout the course, I had regular discussions with the Grade 7 mathematics facilitators and the learners about how learners were experiencing the bilingual fractions course. As the learners already knew me as a member of the OLICO Maths Education team, my presence as a researcher was less invasive. They also felt comfortable with giving uninhibited feedback and commenting on and evaluating elements of the course at OLICO Maths Education.

The bilingual nature of the course is outlined in the following sections.

8.1 English-isiZulu bilingual hyperlinked glossary

This glossary was only made available to learners who enrolled in the bilingual online mathematics course. There was a bilingual glossary available as hyperlinks in all of the fractions pre-quizzes, skills practice quizzes and mixed practice quizzes. Glossary terms that appeared in the bilingual online mathematics course were indicated in blue. Learners could choose to click on any of the hyperlinked glossary terms at any time they came across them in the course. When learners clicked on the term, a pop-up box would open with the English and isiZulu definitions of the term, illustrated by Figure 1:

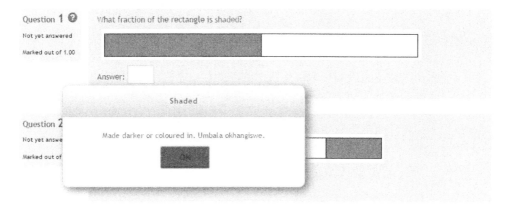

Figure 1: Hyperlinked glossary

The glossary was created as follows:

1. I selected terms from the mathematics course and homework books based on and informed by observations I had made of learners' understanding of the fractions course in the previous year.

2. I wrote short definitions in English, similar to an explanation I would give to a learner in class, which would be informed by my experience in the subject. Learners were also instructed to read textbooks, watch videos, attend classes, etc.

3. I then passed this list on to the bilingual resource creator, who wrote short definitions in isiZulu, also similar to an explanation he would give to a learner in class. 'Borrowing' (Mawonga, Maseko & Nkomo, 2014), that is, using English terms within isiZulu, and 'paraphrasing' (Mawonga *et al.*, 2014), that is, creating descriptions of the term, were used in the creation of the glossary and the videos. This process was rather basic as the intention was to find a method that is replicable by other teachers with similar linguistic proficiencies and mathematics backgrounds.

4. The project co-founder then uploaded this glossary onto the online bilingual fractions course so that whenever learners encountered one of the words from the glossary they could simply click on it and the short explanations in both English and isiZulu would pop up.

8.2 Homework book: English-isiZulu bilingual glossary

The glossary (see **Figure 2**) used in the course was also printed in the learners' homework books. It was in the form of an additional page stapled into the homework books. It appeared as such:

English-isiZulu Maths glossary

Convert
Change it to something.
Kushinye kulenombolo eyiyo ukwenze
ighezumbulu.

Diagram
A picture that explains something.
Umdwebo o chaza okuthize.

Equivalent
The same as something else.
Okune nani elifinayo kunaleli
elighathaniswayo.

Illustrate
Show something using a picture.
Khombisa ngokucacile usebenzise isithombe.

Represent
Show something using words or a picture.
Khombisa umfanikiso omele amagama noma
isithombe.

Revise
Look at your work and practice it again.
Buyekeza Umsebenzi wakho.

Shaded
Made darker or coloured in.
Umbala okhangiswe.

Share fairly
So that everyone gets the same amount.
Kuhlukwaniswe ngokulinganayo.

Simplest form
With the easiest or smallest numbers.
Kukhobise ngendlela elula kahulu.

Figure 2: Printed glossary

8.3 Bilingual videos

Through careful review of the literature it was possible to create a translanguaging model that synthesises key elements of second language acquisition (SLA) theory. The first premise on which this theoretical framework is based is that we conceptualise in our L1 (Cummins, 1979). This means that when we learn new things or create ideas, we do this in our L1 (where L1 refers to the language in which one is most proficient). This links to Vygotsky's theory (Lantolf & Appel, 1994) that thought is dependent on language and that we need language to facilitate what is commonly called in layman's terms 'the voice inside your head'. In order to facilitate conceptualisation in one's L1, two main factors need to be considered: the input, or how one gains conceptual knowledge, and the output, or how one expresses this knowledge.

Secondly, in receiving information one needs to take into consideration the learner's language proficiency and whether the language being used is context-embedded or context-reduced. As explained by Baker (1993), when one is learning through a L2 one depends on the context to make sense of the content, for example, when meeting someone, one is able to deduce meaning from greetings because those greetings are the expected language practices in that context. In order to understand language that is more abstract or not directly related to the context, as is the case in much of the mathematics curriculum, one needs to have stronger language proficiency in the language being used in order to understand the meaning without relying on the context (Baker, 1993). Therefore in SLA theory it is common to use context-embedded language while learners are developing their L2 and to then move toward context-reduced language as their proficiency improves (Cummins & Swain, 1986). However, it is important to note that in the South African context, where learners are often not proficient in the LoLT, learners are often required to make sense of context-reduced language when school content is more abstract and does not relate to clearly identifiable context. Only once a learner is able to make sense of the language is it possible for conceptualisation to fully take place. Even if the language used in conveying the information is not the learner's L1, the learner is likely to build a fuller mental understanding through their L1.

Third, once conceptualisation has taken place, it is necessary in the context of learning and teaching for this conceptualisation and understanding to be articulated. However, simply because one conceptualises in one's L1 does not necessarily mean one is unable to express these conceptualisations in another language. Indeed, many people express intricate conceptualisations in their L2 on a daily basis. In order to do this, these people make use of what Cummins calls the developmental interdependence hypothesis. This hypothesis states that a person's L2 competence is greatly influenced by their existing L1 competence (Cummins, 1979) and that certain linguistic skills and conceptual knowledge can be transferred from the L1 to the L2 (Cummins, 1979). By extension, this means that if the L1 is already well developed, the L2 will also become well developed at no expense to the L1 (Cummins, 1979). However, if the L1 is underdeveloped there will not be adequate linguistic skills to transfer and aid the development of the L2, resulting in "semilingualism", or poor proficiency in both the L1 and the L2 (Cummins, 1979:231).

When considering how these three theories inform one another, it is clear that different languages can be used in the process of stimulating cognitive activity. While the term 'codeswitching' is used as a broad term for mixing more than one language, 'translanguaging' is a more apt term in this context. Translanguaging presupposes the use of more than one language, but also goes further to ensure that the languages are conscientiously used to best facilitate the cognition process. This is illustrated in the theoretical framework below (**Figure 3**), where input is received through the L2 (which is the LoLT), made sense of in the L1, and reproduced in the L2 (LoLT). This theoretical framework informs the creation and analysis of the experiment of this research project.

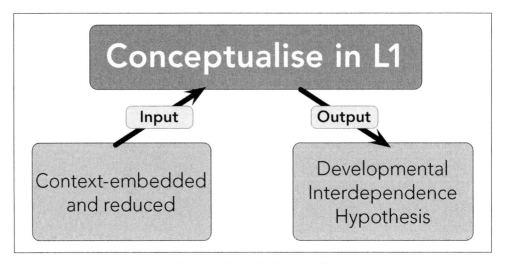

Figure 3: Theoretical framework

This translanguaging model was to be implemented as such: First, the concept is introduced in isiZulu. The use of the L1 here provides a context for the subsequent input the learner will receive. Once the concept has been clarified, it is expanded on in English. Because isiZulu has been used to introduce the concept and provide some context, the expansion of the concept is context-embedded and easier for the learners to understand. After this, isiZulu is used to introduce the next concept, similarly setting the context. Again, English is then used to expand on this concept. This pattern is repeated throughout the video and finally recapped in English at the end. The aim of this model is to allow the learners to grapple with new ideas and conceptualise the information in their L1, while also giving them the English tools they need in order to be able to recognise, understand and reproduce the concepts in English, as this is necessary at school.

9. Challenges

Because design experiments aim to improve learning, if it is seen that it is not doing so in the desired manner, design experiments can be revised during the process of implementation (Collins *et al.*, 2004). However, to ensure that they still provide valid research from which others may learn and upon which further research can be built, it is important that if something is not working as intended, the reason for it not working is analysed and this reason – along with the measures taken to improve it – are recorded (Collins *et al.*, 2004). In doing so, one does not only provide an accurate and honest account of the experiment, but one also provides valuable information about failures (Collins *et al.*, 2004).

After making the first three videos, the mathematics coordinator put me in touch with a quality assessor, Thulelah Takane, a PhD candidate with isiZulu L1 proficiency whose research focus was language and mathematics. The mathematics facilitator and quality assessor pointed out that the fractions drawn in the video were not divided into equal parts[1] and so the bilingual resource creator edited the video so that fractions were always represented equally (i.e. if one divided a whole into four quarters, each quarter would be of equal size). After the creation of fractions Video 5, the project co-founder pointed out that the English-isiZulu bilingual video was considerably longer than the English-medium video. The bilingual video was about 17 minutes while the English-medium one was around six minutes. The project co-founder suggested that we should try to keep videos below 10 minutes, as he and the mathematics coordinator had found that learners lose concentration when videos exceed this length. The bilingual resource creator and I then discussed why the video was so long. It was initially predicted that the English-isiZulu bilingual videos would be slightly longer than their English-medium counterparts, particularly because much academic vocabulary has not been standardised in African languages (Webb, 2004) and the isiZulu adaptations tend to be slightly longer than the English terms. However, we had not anticipated that the English-isiZulu bilingual videos would be that much longer. In discussion with the bilingual resource creator, we realised that he was speaking slightly slower than the mathematics coordinator spoke in her videos because he wanted to ensure he was fully audible and understandable in the videos. He also explained to me that there were different ways in which to explain certain things in isiZulu and he would sometimes explain something more than once, using different ways of explaining it each time, with the hope that if learners did not understand the first explanation, they would

---

1   It is important for representations of fractions to be equal so that learners can grasp the idea of equivalent fractions.

then understand a subsequent explanation. In our discussion we spoke about how the mathematics coordinator explains things in one way and that, if learners did not understand the explanation given in the videos, they were aware that they had the opportunity to ask the facilitators to explain it in a different way to them, which they often did. We then decided that the bilingual resource creator would choose an explanation he felt learners were most likely to understand and only use that one. He also decided to look at the time spent on each slide in the mathematics coordinator's videos and align the time he spent on those slides as closely as possible. He then redid Video 5 (again, after a few learners who were ahead had watched it) and implemented the decisions from our discussion in the subsequent videos. As a result, all the subsequent videos were much closer in length to the English-medium videos.

The quality assessor's feedback about the ambiguity of using the term *izikhathi* to reflect fractions speaks to Pimm's (1981) point that translating mathematical language directly into ordinary language is a commonly used technique; however, confusion may arise from its use as mathematical terms often do not have direct and constant equivalent terms in English (or the LoLT). The feedback given by the mathematics coordinator and the quality assessor regarded ambiguities of the language used and the correct explanation of core tenets of the subject as vital in this process and suggested that, if this model of codeswitching were to be applied elsewhere, it would require the creator of the videos to have a sound understanding of the language and the subject, ideally more than any layperson. This would need to be a consideration if one were to scale such a project.

As is seemingly inevitable with many interventions, the technology component also posed a difficulty in the video creation. The bilingual resource creator and I set aside a week in the school holidays to create all the videos, but that week happened to coincide with the re-networking of the computer lab and we were not able to create the videos in that week. As such, we were working on the videos while the course was running. This resulted in us rushing to get the videos up in time, giving us less time to review the videos in more detail before rolling them out in the experiment. Furthermore, several videos consisted of mostly isiZulu audio and did not use as much English as suggested in the translanguaging model. As such, the results of this design experiment are more indicative of the success of a bilingual language model than the specific translanguaging model outlined in this paper. This is an example of the 'messiness' of real-world applications that DBR accounts for and illustrates the importance of the adaptability of the DBR methodology, as we had to adapt the experiment according to these constraints.

10. Data presentation and analysis

A total of 40 learners participated in the design experiment, with 18 learners in the experimental group (i.e. the group that enrolled in the English-isiZulu bilingual online mathematics course) and 22 learners in the control group (i.e. the group that enrolled in the English-medium online mathematics course). These learners were Grade 7 learners aged 11 to 13. The learners were from four different schools in Diepsloot. The linguistic biography of the learners who enrolled in the English-isiZulu bilingual group is as follows: six learners whose L1 is isiZulu; six learners whose L1 is a Sotho-based language; five learners whose L1 is isiXhosa; and one learner whose home language is Xitsonga. The linguistic biography of the learners who enrolled in the English-medium group is as follows: 17 learners whose L1 is a Sotho-based language; three learners whose L1 is isiZulu; one learner whose L1 is isiNdebele; and one learner whose L1 is Xitsonga.

10.1 Pre-quiz to post-quiz improvement

The pre-quiz is an online short quiz of roughly six questions on the lesson topic and determines whether or not the learner has sufficient understanding of the topic. Learners who attained less than 80% for the pre-quiz, indicating that they do not have sufficient understanding of the topic, would then watch the video. Those who attained 80% or more, indicating that they understood the topic, automatically progressed to the next level. Learners who attained less than 80% and watched the video then attempted the post-quiz after the video. The post-quiz checks whether the learner has understood the lesson as explained in the video. To illustrate that they have understood the lesson, learners should attain at least 80%, after which they progress to the next level. In determining the improvement learners showed after watching the video, only the results of the learners who achieved less than 80% for the pre-quiz (and thus wrote the post-quiz) were included.

Effect size was used to ascertain the quantitative differences in this evaluation. This is done by finding the difference in achievement between the experimental and control groups, as well as the standard deviation within these groups, thus illustrating the overall improvement (Coe, 2002).

Ultimately, the quantitative difference in improvement between the experimental and control groups was inconclusive, with the bilingual group showing more overall improvement of an effect size of only 0.01 – which is too small to be meaningful.

These inconclusive results are attributed to the very short space of time over which the experiment was conducted. The minimal quantitative improvement does not, however, indicate a failure of this intervention. Contrarily, it illustrates that learners were able to perform with at least as much improvement as their peers while learning through the language of their choice, which also enhanced learners' motivation and sense of self-worth. A group of four learners commented that sometimes they found it difficult to understand in English and so it was easier for them to understand in isiZulu. They noted that the isiZulu used in the videos made it easier because "it's not that deep Zulu". However, since learners were not familiar with learning through isiZulu, this may also be an aspect in which further improvement may be seen as they are familiarised. And a very important quantitative note to be made is that the project improved learners' enthusiasm about and pride in their home languages. At the beginning of the year, many learners were adamant that they needed to learn in English, but this attitude changed dramatically with the introduction of the bilingual course. I once asked a group of learners in passing conversation what the best part of the term had been and one quickly replied: "We get to learn maths in isiZulu!"

10.2 Glossary use and understanding

The bilingual glossary was available to the learners throughout the quizzes. To measure the efficacy of the glossary I examined the number of clicks per glossary item and tested the learners afterwards to measure their retention of the meaning (**Figure 4**).

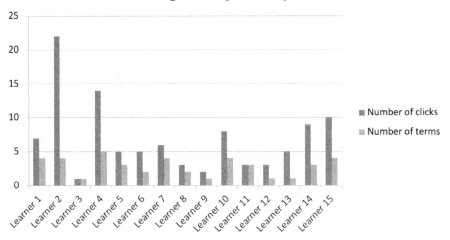

Figure 4: Number of glossary clicks per learner

The above diagram shows how many times each learner clicked on the glossary and also gives a breakdown of how many terms each learner clicked on. While Learner 3 and Learner 11 clicked once each on one and three terms respectively, most learners clicked on one to five terms a number of times each. A noteworthy case is Learner 2, who clicked on *shaded* once, *diagram* twice, *convert* three times and *simplest form* 16 times.

Figure 5 illustrates how many times each glossary was clicked on in total. There are clear differences here, with *equivalent* receiving very few clicks, *convert*, *diagram* and *shaded* receiving a similar number of clicks, and *simplest form* receiving substantially more clicks than any of the other terms.

Clicks per glossary item

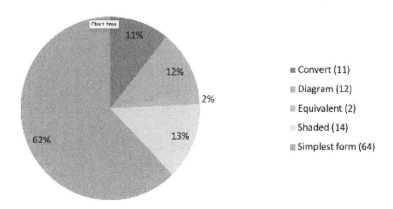

Figure 5: Number of glossary clicks per term

Figure 6 illustrates the results of the glossary quiz the learners completed after the completion of the experimental course.

Number of correct answers per term

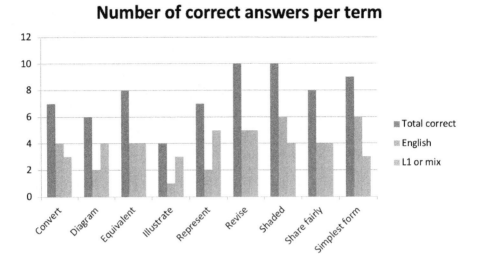

Figure 6: Number of correct answers per term

Fourteen of the learners who participated in the experimental course participated in this quiz and are represented above illustrating learners' understanding and retention of the terms learned through the glossary. The findings suggest that the words that were not clicked on were already known by the learners, that the term *equivalent* was already known by most of the learners, that *convert, diagram* and *shaded* were unknown to several learners, and that most learners did not understand the meaning of *simplest form.* The fact that most learners who used the glossary clicked on one to five terms several times each could indicate that either the learner did not understand the definition, or that they forgot it. The reason for the term *simplest form* receiving so many clicks could be because of an inadequate revision of the term; because putting an answer into *simplest form* makes the difference between an answer being correct or incorrect; or because the term *simplest form* occurred significantly more often throughout the course than the other glossary items. The word *illustrate* was not known by the learners, despite this being a general language term that is not limited to the mathematics context. The fact that it was not clicked on suggests either that the learners did not deem understanding it to be important or relevant to the work they were doing, or they lacked the meta-cognitive awareness of which words they did and did not understand.

The experimental glossary improved learners' language proficiencies as they recalled many of the terms they had clicked on. The glossary furthermore facilitated a change in their attitude towards using their L1 in the mathematical context, as several learners chose to use their home language to explain the English terms. It is interesting to note that isiZulu and isiXhosa speaking learners wrote in their L1s more readily than had ever been noted in a written task at OLICO Maths Education. The fact that learners successfully used their L1s to explain terms illustrates that learners believe their languages are suitable for use in mathematics. This is contrary to the commonly held belief, noted by Probyn (2009) and evidenced by the learners prior to the experiment, that African languages have insufficient terminology to be used in mathematics. The learners' use of their L1s to explain the glossary terms also illustrates their (albeit perhaps surface-level) understanding of the use of language for cognitive activity, which Titone (1978) cites as an important role of multilingual education. This also indicates that learners can benefit greatly from the use of multilingual teaching resources such as this glossary, as these resources equip learners with the linguistic knowledge needed to facilitate conceptual development.

Learners' positive feedback and evident enthusiasm throughout the experiment contrasted sharply with the attitudes expressed in the pre-course surveys. This positive attitude towards their L1 appeared, however, to be short-lived as learners only actively advocated using their L1 in learning mathematics when this was available to them as an option. After the experiment, when learners returned to learning in English, most learners once again argued that they should be learning through the medium of English. This illustrates that learners' motivation for their choice of LoLT is not necessarily influenced by knowledge of the relation between language and cognition, but rather by hegemonic language in education practices.

11. Recommendations and conclusion

This research has detailed the impetus, creation and evaluation of a bilingual education intervention in Diepsloot, Johannesburg, South Africa. While the period in which this research was conducted was too short to yield a large number of quantitative results, the qualitative results illustrated learners' improved motivation to learn and take pride in their L1s. The multilingual resources detailed in this research project were successful and are replicable, and it would be beneficial to replicate the videos, glossary and translanguaging model (as illustrated in the theoretical framework) throughout the different South African contexts. South Africa has very different language environments, from linguistically homogenous rural areas where only one language is spoken, to highly multilingual environments such as Diepsloot. These contexts naturally impact the results. Furthermore, DBR is an iterative process that requires further iterations of the design to be carried out and analysed, such that in this case the translanguaging model could be refined.

As argued by Cummins and Swain (1986), the use of the learners' L1 asserts their pride in their identity, and as argued by Benson (2004), it promotes the status of the language. This was clearly illustrated by learners' positive reactions to learning in isiZulu and also later by learners requesting a similar experiment using their various L1s. Learners' enthusiastic lobbying for the experiment to be conducted again in all languages, and not only their own L1s, illustrates Lindholm's (in Lindholm-Leary, 2001) point that additive bilingualism also fosters learners' embrace of other cultures. Several learners who had elected to do the English-medium course later said they would like to do a course through the medium of isiZulu or their home language after seeing the experimental course. This is encouraging and could indicate that learners felt motivated by seeing their friends doing the experimental course, or that their preconceptions about the type of language that would be used differed to the actual language use. That learners then said they would prefer to watch the videos in English in the post-video surveys suggests that learners got excited about it in the moment but lost enthusiasm when it was not a current or tangible event. This may illustrate that, while the experimental course did improve learners' enthusiasm, this enthusiasm may not be sustainable as for some learners it is extrinsic and dependent on external factors such as the novelty and newness of the course rather than intrinsic motivation and desire to learn in their L1.

By incorporating learners' L1 into teaching and learning, South Africa's education system could provide learners with a better understanding of classroom content, while simultaneously affirming learners' linguistic and cultural identities and opening a space for intercultural understanding. Learners' improved understanding of classwork would not only lead to improved test results and pass rates, but would also lead to improved life prospects as new opportunities become available to these learners in both the educational and socio-economic spaces. This in turn would allow for greater socio-economic mobility and greater equality of opportunity for all of South Africa's learners.

12. Acknowledgements

Thank you to everyone who helped and supported me with this research project. My sincere and heartfelt gratitude is extended to the following people for their support and contributions:

- Andrew Barrett for supporting my research, for his advice and for setting up the technology needed for this project to be possible;
- Dr Lynn Bowie for helping me to believe in my research, for her insight into the complexities of mathematics education and for her feedback throughout this research;
- Carol Leff for inspiring me and providing guidance and support;
- Verena Lourenço for being by my side throughout this journey and providing constant emotional and practical support;
- OLICO Maths Education and the OLICO Maths Education team and learners for hosting this research project;
- Thabiso Simelane for the vast amount of time and thought he put into making the videos and glossary and for his assistance in their implementation;
- Thulelah Takane for sharing her knowledge and insight and providing valuable feedback on the videos; and
- The volunteers from the OLICO Maths Education Winter School for their assistance with the data collection.

The financial assistance from the National Research Foundation, through the Rhodes National Research Foundation (NRF) SARChI Chair: Intellectualisation of African Languages, Multilingualism and Education, is acknowledged. The views and opinions expressed here are, however, those of the author and should not be attributed to the NRF.

The financial assistance of the National Institute of Humanities and Social Sciences towards this research is hereby acknowledged. Opinions, findings and conclusions or recommendations expressed here are those of authors and none of the above sponsors accepts any liability whatsoever in this regard.

References

Baker, C. 1993. *Foundations of Bilingual Education and Bilingualism*. Bristol, Great Britain: Multilingual Matters Ltd.

Barab, S. & Squire, K. 2004. Design-based research: Putting a stake in the ground. *The journal of the learning sciences*, 13(1):1-14.

Bénit, C. 2002. The rise or fall of the 'community'? Post-apartheid housing policy in Diepsloot, Johannesburg. *Urban Forum*, 13(2): 47-66.

Benson, C. 2004. Do we expect too much of bilingual teachers? Bilingual teaching in developing countries. In J. Brutt-Griffler & M. Varghese (eds). *Bilingualism and Language Pedagogy*, 112-129. Bristol, Great Britain: Multilingual Matters Ltd.

Charalambos, Y. & Pitta-Pantazi, D. 2007. *Education Studies in Mathematics*, 64:293-316.

Coe, R. 2002. It's the effect size, stupid: What effect size is and why it's important. [online] *Annual Conference of the British Educational Research Association*. University of Exeter, England, 12–14 September 2002. http://www.leeds.ac.uk/educol/documents/00002182.htm [Accessed 30 September 2015].

Collins, A., Joseph, D. & Bielaczyc, K. 2004. Design research: Theoretical and methodological issues. *The Journal of the Learning Sciences*, 13(1):15-42.

Cross, C. 2014. Qualitative assessment of the Diepsloot economy. In S. Mahajan (ed). *Economics of South African Townships: Special Focus on Diepsloot* (143-178). Washington, D.C.: World Bank Group.

Cummins, J. 1979. Linguistic interdependence and the educational development of bilingual children. *Review of Educational Research*, 49(2):222-251.

Cummins, J. & Swain, M. 1986. *Bilingualism in education: Aspects of theory, research and practice*, 86. London: Longman.

De Mejia, A.M. 2002. *Power, prestige and bilingualism: International perspectives on elite bilingual education*, 35. Bristol, Great Britain: Multilingual Matters Ltd.

Department of Basic Education. 2011. *Curriculum and Assessment Policy Statement Grades 7–9: English First Additional Language*. [online] Department of Basic Education. < https://www.education.gov.za/Portals/0/CD/National%20Curriculum%20Statements%20and%20Vocational/CAPS%20SP%20%20FAL%20%20ENGLISH%20GR%207-9%20%20WEB.pdf?ver=2015-01-27-155732-820> [Accessed 31 August 2020].

Department of Basic Education. 2014. *Report on the Annual National Assessment of 2014: Grades 1 to 6 & 9*. [online] Department of Basic Education. < https://www.saqa.org.za/docs/rep_annual/2014/REPORT%20ON%20THE%20ANA%20OF%202014.pdf>[Accessed 31 August 2020].

Fitzgerald, J. 1995. English-as-a-second-language learners' cognitive reading process: A review of research in the United States. *Review of Educational Research*, 65(2):145-190.

Howie, S., Venter, E., Van Staden, S., Zimmerman, L., Long, C., Du Toit, C., Scherman, V., & Archer, E. 2006. *PIRLS [Progress in International Reading Literacy Study] 2006 Summary Report: South African Children's Reading Achievement*. Pretoria: Centre for Evaluation and Assessment.

Lantolf, J. P. & Appel, G. (Eds.) 1994. *Vygotskian approaches to second language research*. Boston, MA: Greenwood Publishing Group.

Lindholm-Leary, K.J. 2001. *Dual Language Education*. Bristol, Great Britain: Multilingual Matters Ltd.

Mahajan, S. 2014. Overview. In S. Mahajan (ed). *Economics of South African townships: Special focus on Diepsloot* (143-178). Washington, D.C.: World Bank Group.

Mawonga, S., Maseko, P. & Nkomo, D. 2014. The Centrality of translation in the development of African languages for use in South African Higher Education Institutions: A case study of a political science English-isiXhosa glossary in a South African university. *Alternation Special Edition*, 13:55-79.

Moore, D. 2002. Code-switching and learning in the classroom. *International Journal of Bilingual Education and Bilingualism*, 5(5):279-293.

Moschkovich, J. 1999. Supporting the participation of English language learners in mathematical discussions. *For the Learning of Mathematics*, 19(1):11-19.

OLICO Foundation NPC. 2015. *Why OLICO?* [online] http://olico.org/about/why [Accessed 7 December 2015].

Ovando, C.J. & Collier, V.P. 1998. *Bilingual and ESL Classrooms: Teaching in multicultural contexts*. New York City, NY: McGraw-Hill.

Pantziara, M. & Philippou, G. 2012. Levels of students' "conception" of fractions. *Educational Studies in mathematics*, 79:61-83.

Pimm, D. 1981. Mathematics? I speak it fluently. In A. Floyd (ed). *Developing Mathematical Thinking* (139-150). Wokingham: Addison Wesley.

Pimm, D. 1991. Communicating mathematically. In K. Durkin and B Shire (eds). *Language in Mathematical Education* (17-23). London: Milton Keynes.

Plüddeman, P., Braam, D., Broeder, P., Extra, G. & October, M. 2004. *Language policy implementation and language vitality in Western Cape primary schools*. Cape Town: PRAESA.

Probyn, M. 2009. 'Smuggling the vernacular into the classroom': Conflicts and tensions in classroom codeswitching in township/rural schools in South Africa. *International Journal of Bilingual Education and Bilingualism*, 12(2):123-136.

Setati, M. 2002. Researching mathematics education and language in multilingual South Africa. In A.J. Hackenberg (ed). *The Mathematics Educator*, 12(2):6-20.

Setati, M. & Adler, J. 2000. Between languages and discourse: Language practices in primary multilingual Mathematics classes in South Africa. *Educational Studies in Mathematics*, 43: 243-269.

Setati, M., Adler, J., Reed, Y. & Bapoo, A. 2002. Incomplete journeys: Code-switching and other language practices in Mathematics, Science and English language classrooms in South Africa. *Language and Education*, 16(2):128-149.

Sfard, A., Nesher, P., Streefland, L., Cobb, P. & Mason, J. 1998. Learning Mathematics through conversation: Is it as good as they say? *For the Learning of Mathematics*, 18(1):41-51.

Shuard, H. 1982. Reading and learning in mathematics. *Language teaching and learning: Mathematics*. London, England: Ward Lock Educational.

Spaull, N. & Kotze, J. 2015. Starting behind and staying behind in South Africa: The case of insurmountable learning deficits in mathematics. *International Journal of Educational Development*, 41:13-24.

Statistics South Africa 2012. *Census 2011: Census in brief*. [online] http://www.statssa.gov.za/census/census_2011/census_products/Census_2011_Census_in_brief.pdf [Accessed 18 October 2015].

TLRP (Teaching and Learning Research Programme). 2006. *Fractions: difficult but crucial in mathematics learning*. [online] Teaching and Learning Research Programme. http://www.tlrp.org/pub/documents/no13_nunes.pdf [Accessed 10 November 2015].

Titone, R. 1978. Some psychological aspects of multilingual education. *International Review of Education. Internationale Zeitschrift fur Erziehungswissenschaft/Revue Internationale de l'Education*, 24(3):283-293.

Valdés, G. 2004. Between support and marginalisation: The development of academic language in linguistic minority children. In J. Brutt-Griffler & M. Varghese (eds). *Bilingualism and Language Pedagogy* (10-40). Bristol, Great Britain: Multilingual Matters Ltd.

Wababa, Z. 2009. *How scientific terms are taught and learnt in the Intermediate Phase* (Master's thesis). Stellenbosch University, Stellenbosch, South Africa.

Wales, L. 1990. Literacy for learners of English as a second language. In F. Christie (Ed.) 1990. *Literacy for a changing world.* Australia: The Australian Council for Educational Research. pp. 167–186.

Webb, V. 2004. African languages as media of instruction in South Africa: Stating the case. *Language Problems & Language Planning,* 28(2):147-173.

Webb, V., Lafon, M. & Pare, P. 2010. Bantu languages in education in South Africa: An overview. Ongekho akekho! – the absentee owner. *The Language Learning Journal,* 28(3):273-292.

Chapter 6

Legitimate knowledge: At the border between learning and perceived learning for students in service-learning

Joana Bezerra and Sharli Paphitis

COMMUNITY ENGAGEMENT, RHODES UNIVERSITY

j.bezerra@ru.ac.za; s.paphitis@ru.ac.za

1. Introduction

In this chapter we analyse a year-long service-learning course at the honours level at a South African university. We investigate specifically how the course triggered personal growth in students and contributed to their academic learning. Interestingly, in the assessment surveys we used, students reported learning very little in relation to what they themselves expected to learn. Our analysis of students' reflective journals, however, brought these reports into question. The reports showed evidence of both academic learning and personal development in students. This suggests that there is a remarkable discrepancy between learning evidenced through the student reflections and what the students recognised as 'legitimate' knowledge gained through community-based service-learning as reported by themselves in their assessment surveys. In this chapter we suggest that these findings raise important questions about what knowledge students see as 'legitimate' or 'academic' and the challenge this poses in terms of the institutionalisation of service-learning and the transformation of HE as a whole.

Service-learning is often understood as both a teaching philosophy and a pedagogy (Osman & Petersen, 2013), though the roots of service-learning as a pedagogical approach stem from the North American tradition (Taylor, Butterwick, Raykov, Glick, Peikazadi & Mehrabi, 2015). Within this tradition, service-learning activities are undertaken by students to address the needs of communities in the context of disciplinary learning (Bringle & Hatcher, 1996). Increasingly, service-learning is gaining momentum as both a philosophy and a pedagogy in different disciplines at universities across the globe (Butin, 2006; Jackson, 2008; Gearan & Hollister, 2013; Taylor, 2017). The increased uptake and popularity of service-learning is potentially explained by the belief that service-learning makes positive contributions to all stakeholders involved: students grow as citizens, communities benefit from an active and eager-to-learn group working within their organisations and universities enhance their social responsibility (Chambers & Lavery, 2018).

Service-learning, however, is not merely the addition of service to a traditional academic 'learning' course; it is the integration of both service and academic components within the learning of a course (Howard, 1998). The service must be relevant to the academic goals so that it enhances students' learning, and it must be also relevant to the community partner in order for the relationship to be mutually beneficial (Butin, 2005; Deeley, 2010). It is the unique ability of service-learning that situates service in a context that is familiar to students' own lifeworld that provides a space for their personal growth and enhanced meaning-making. By bringing together the cognitive and the affective learning in academic and service activities, service-learning courses support the personal development of students (Eyler, 2002; Butin, 2005).

As a pedagogy, service-learning courses challenge students, lecturers and community partners to take on a new role in the learning space, but these experiences are not necessarily beneficial. Students do not always see the value of such courses, and lecturers are not always prepared for challenges that they will face (Jones, 2002). These challenges are heightened when courses are poorly planned, designed and prepared, but even the most well-designed courses will present challenges to students and staff. Nonetheless, service-learning courses' potential to combine learning goals with practical service activities – a process that can benefit community partners and enhance students' civic and universities' social responsibility – has great appeal and can justify the increased attention such courses have received in both the HE and secondary schooling sectors.

South Africa in particular has seen a rapid uptake of service-learning in the HE sector (Preece, 2016). HE institutions in post-apartheid South Africa are increasingly concerned with developing graduates who understand and contribute to the development of a more just society, using their acquired knowledge to do so (Osman & Petersen, 2013). This is partly attributable to the increasing prominence given to The Education White Paper 3 (Department of Education, 1997), which brought forward a national programme for the transformation of HE. This programme has both national and institutional goals and identifies community service initiatives as catalysts of change. The transformation of HE is also aligned with the development of the South African Critical Cross-Field Outcomes (CCFOs)[1], which set out the qualities that should be the goal of all qualifications (National Qualifications Framework). These skills go beyond disciplinary boundaries and are associated with how one relates to other people and skills that will be useful throughout people's lives (SAQA, 2000; Carmichael & Stacey, 2006). Service-learning has been seen as a pedagogical approach which allows the CCFOs to be embedded within course goals, contributing to the growing popularity of service-learning courses.

An important dimension of service-learning is the personal growth of students during the course (Eyler & Giles Jr., 1999; Taylor, 2017). The personal growth of students seen in service-learning is thought to underlie the transformative potential of the pedagogy (Butin, 2005). This transformative quality could develop citizens who are aware of the social and local issues and are able to use their knowledge to tackle real problems (Eyler, 2002). Furthermore, the skills learned serve a deeper purpose in society by building social cohesion, which is important in relation to the broader transformation of HE in South Africa.

What is particularly interesting about service-learning is that it raises critical questions about the type of knowledge that is recognised and prioritised in HE settings. Service-learning challenges the priority of declarative knowledge over procedural knowledge; stresses the relationship between knowledge and behavioural change; and expands the boundaries of the traditional knowledge economy.

---

1   SAQA defined seven outcomes to be pursued: identify and solve problems; team work; organisation skills; collect and critically evaluate information; communication skills; use science and technology effectively and critically; demonstrate an understanding of the world as a set of systems within a context (South African Qualifications Authority SAQA 2000). SAQA also laid out five developmental outcomes, which speak to the growth of students as citizens and their awareness of: the importance of reflecting on how to learn more effectively; the key role they play as citizens in local, national and global communities; the importance of being culturally and aesthetically sensitive in a variety of social contexts; the key role of exploring education and career opportunities; the importance of developing entrepreneurial opportunities (South African Qualifications Authority SAQA 2000).

A traditional theory of knowledge bases knowledge claims on empirical evidence (Liu, 2000). To claim to have knowledge is to be able to justify it and its accuracy. This would suggest that declarative knowledge – explained as 'know-what' (Hong, Pi & Yang, 2018) – holds a key place in HE. Declarative knowledge involves understanding and remembering what was learned. In contrast, procedural knowledge, the 'know-how', implies learning the declarative knowledge related to the subject and understanding how to use or apply what was learned (Hong *et al.*, 2018). Declarative knowledge demands less cognitive skills than procedural knowledge (Anderson, 1995), yet commands less attention in formal learning due to the difficulty involved in assessment. Service-learning courses provide a space for students to not only learn from real-life problems, but also to apply the knowledge that they already have to resolve such problems – working as a bridge between the 'knowledge' and the 'real world'.

Service-learning thus calls for a pedagogy that is essentially relational, bringing together the theory and the practice (Liu, 2000). In so doing, service-learning challenges the priority of declarative knowledge in student learning.

Service-learning courses challenge students' "inert" knowledge (Eyler & Giles Jr., 1999), the knowledge that students possess but which is dormant unless it is accessed through reflection. The concrete examples with which students are faced in service-learning give them an opportunity to relate abstract concepts with their experience, thereby promoting deeper learning (Eyler, 2002). This is crucial in triggering students' critical thinking about their understandings of the world, challenging their assumptions, and, most importantly, promoting a change in behaviour (Mezirow, 1991; Mezirow, 1994; Lynch, 1996).

By bringing a community partner into the learning space, service-learning also pushes the traditional boundaries of who has knowledge and where knowledge is produced (Osman & Petersen, 2013). Students learn not only from their lecturers but also from their peers and from the community partners. The knowledge is then constructed through the experience (Eyler, 2002) and with the partners. This process of knowledge co-production integrates different sources of knowledge and ways of knowing (Davies, 2016), and, in doing this, recognises the legitimacy of other sources of knowledge.

The service-learning pedagogy mirrors the broader South African HE framework, but there is a lot of unexplored territory regarding the implementation of such courses. Many questions can be asked, such as: Is the partnerships truly beneficial? How prepared are the lecturers to handle the challenges that will be faced? The objectives of service-learning courses might be well-defined and known; however, the extent to which these courses actually achieve these goals is yet to be established.

The aim of this chapter is to investigate the impact of a year-long service-learning project at the honours level at a university in South Africa looking at how, if at all, the service-learning triggered changes at the personal and at the academic levels of the students. On a personal level, the paper seeks to uncover if the service-learning course had an impact on students' behaviour in relation to their social context and their role as citizens. On an academic level, the aim is to assess students' learning in relation to their discipline in practice.

On the strength of the above, the chapter argues that the course did in fact reach both academic and personal growth goals. However, the students did not recognise the learning process, which raises questions about the type of knowledge that they were most used to. The chapter will also discuss the role of time and consistency as key in the learning process.

2. The Environmental Science service-learning course

Service-learning is an integral component of the honours programme of the Environmental Science Department at Rhodes University. The honours year is a one-year postgraduate course offered to students who have completed a three-year undergraduate degree majoring in Environmental Science. A year-long service-learning course is a compulsory module which honours students must take along with other modules offered throughout the year. The department sees the course as providing students with the opportunity to apply the academic knowledge on environmental issues to real-world cases and contexts. It is also seen as providing students with the opportunity to share the knowledge gained through the classroom-based components of the degree as they work with local communities to address challenges.

During the academic year of 2017, the Environmental Science Department partnered with the Amakhala Foundation for their service-learning course. Through this partnership, the course aimed to successfully establish an Eco-Schools[2] Project at the Sandisulwazi High School in Paterson[3], Eastern Cape.

---

2   The Eco-Schools Project is an education programme that has been implemented in over 52 countries. In South Africa, Eco-Schools are managed by WESSA (Wildlife and Environment Society of South Africa) and it has the support of Nampak (Wildlife and Environment Society of South Africa, 2013).

3   Paterson is a small town the Eastern Cape, South Africa, part of the Sundays River Valley municipality. One of the poorest provinces in South Africa, the Eastern Cape is faced with issues regarding inequality and access to education.

The Sandisulwazi High School formed an Eco-School committee with learners from Grade 9 to 12. Learners had to submit an essay outlining why they wanted to be a part of the Eco-School Committee. These essays were used to assess the level of commitment learners were willing to make to the Eco-School Project. Thirteen students submitted an essay and were all selected to participate as they had all written eloquently about their desire to improve their school environment.

The 2017 Environmental Science Honours class consisted of 21 students. The class was divided in two working groups in order to have appropriate ratios of students to learners in the Eco-School activities, as well as for logistical reasons, owing to the need to transport students by bus to the school. The honours students divided themselves up, making sure they had an equal number of isiXhosa speakers (the home language of Sandisulwazi learners) in each group (two isiXhosa speakers in each group). Group 1 comprised 10 students who went on four trips to carry out Eco-School activities in the first semester of the year. Group 2 had 11 students who went on two trips to carry out Eco-School activities in the second semester. The whole group had two trips together, one in July and one in October. The July meeting served as a symbolic handing over between Group 1 and Group 2, as it was the last meeting Group 1 would attend before the end of the year October meeting. In July and in October both groups worked with the learners on Eco-School activities. In total there were eight trips to Sandisulwazi High School for joint student-learner Eco-School activities.

3. Methods

The project utilised two means of data collection: assessment surveys and student reflections. An initial assessment survey was administered before the start of the service-learning course. The survey contained eight open-ended questions related to: what the students' expectations about the experience were; what the students thought they would learn through the course; and what the students thought the partners would learn (**Table 1**). The survey contained 11 Likert-scale questions related to the extent to which students thought the project would provide a space for them to improve particular skills, such as: analytical skills, organisation skills, personal growth and knowledge about local issues (**Table 2**). Answers to the Likert-scale questions had a four-point distribution: 1) not at all, 2) minimally, 3) moderately, and 4) extensively. After the completion of the course, each student answered a second assessment survey with the same questions, but with reference to what they believed they had learned on completion of the course.

Table 1: Open-ended questions on the before and after surveys

Question number	Before survey	After survey
1.1	What do you understand by the term service-learning?	What do you understand by the term service-learning?
1.2	Describe your expectations in relation to the service-learning project you are about to embark on.	Describe your experience in relation to the service-learning project you have been involved in.
1.3	What do you think you are going to learn personally and academically?	What do you think you have learned personally and academically?
1.4	What do you expect to learn from working with your community partners?	What do you think you have learned from working with your community partners?
1.5	Do you think the service-learning will help you to gain specific skills or knowledge that you might not learn otherwise? If so, which ones?	Do you think the service-learning has helped you to gain specific skills or knowledge that you might not have learned otherwise? If so, which ones?
1.6	In what ways do you think your community partners will benefit from this service activity?	In what ways do you think your community partners have benefitted from this service activity?
1.7	What do you think your community partners will be able to learn from you?	What do you think your community partners have learned from you?
1.8	Why do you think service-learning activities might be worthwhile activities for university students to participate in, and do you think that such activities can contribute to the broader transformation agenda of universities?	Why do you think service-learning activities might be worthwhile activities for university students to participate in, and do you think that such activities can contribute to the broader transformation agenda of universities?

Table 2: Likert-scale questions on the before and after surveys

BEFORE: I expect my participation in the service-learning activity to:				
	Not at all	Minimally	Moderately	Extensively
2.1 Strengthen my **analytical skills**				
2.2 Improve my **research skills**				
2.3 Enhance my understanding of **academic content**				
2.4 Enhance my understanding of **local issues**				
2.5 Enhance my understanding of **social issues**				
2.6 Enhance the likelihood that I will **participate in civic activities**				
2.7 Improve my **ability to listen** to others				
2.8 Improve my ability to **work as part of a team**				
2.9 Deepen my **understanding of myself**				
2.10 Improve my **understanding of how environmental issues affect communities**				
2.11 Improve my **organisational skills**				

AFTER: My participation in the service-learning activity has:				
	Not at all	Minimally	Moderately	Extensively
2.1 Strengthened my **analytical skills**				
2.2 Improved my **research skills**				
2.3 Enhanced my understanding of **academic content**				
2.4 Enhanced my understanding of **local issues**				
2.5 Enhanced my understanding of **social issues**				
2.6 Enhanced the likelihood that I will **participate in civic activities**				
2.7 Improved my **ability to listen** to others				
2.8 Improved my ability to **work as part of a team**				
2.9 Deepened my **understanding of myself**				
2.10 Improved my **understanding of how environmental issues affect communities**				
2.11 Improved my **organisational skills**				

Students were also asked to, as part of the service-learning course, write down their experiences in a reflective journal after each trip to the school. Critical reflection is a key step in the learning process of a service-learning course (Mezirow 1991; Mezirow, 1998). According to Cress, Collier and Reitenauer (2005), reflective practice helps students to grapple with the multiple knowledges being taught in service-learning: content, process and social knowledge. Reflective journals have been used extensively in transformative and experiential learning and have subsequently become popular tools for teaching, learning and assessment within service-learning courses. Experiential learning takes place in a continuous process of action and reflection on that action, which will change one's understanding of past experiences and way of thinking and will inform future experiences (Mezirow 1991; Mezirow 1998).

Students are asked to integrate course materials (such as reading and lecture notes) and thoughts about their experiences through service activities into a written piece when completing their reflective journal. In constructing the written narrative, students are asked to critically analyse their knowledge, together with their thoughts, experiences, beliefs and assumptions. Through reflective journals, students are thus able to critically bring together their learning in relation to both course materials and their experiences throughout service activities over time. Students can revise unfounded assumptions in their beliefs and derive meaning from their experiences and so concretise and showcase their learnings and plan for future actions (Hubbs & Brand, 2005). At the beginning of the academic course of 2017, the honours class went on an honours year introductory excursion during which, amongst other things, they learned about reflection and reflective practice. They were each given a reflection journal. During the week-long excursion, they wrote reflections about their daily activities. Most of the students used the same journal for their service-learning reflections. To reiterate the importance and the process of reflection, there was a two-hour session dedicated to reflection before the start of the service-learning course.

Student reflections were first coded following an inductive pattern finding method, and, from this, a set of themes of was identified. The reflections were then re-coded accordingly (Boyatzis, 1998). The codes were then manually counted and added to a spreadsheet, where after they were divided into groups 1 and 2 from which descriptive statistics were derived. The open-ended questions from the survey were handled in the same way. The Likert-scale questions were added to a spreadsheet that led to descriptive statistics.

The project received ethical clearance from Rhodes University Centre for Teaching and Learning in Higher Education.

4.   Results

4.1   Open-ended survey responses

Table 3 (below) shows a summary of the themes which emerged in the open-ended responses given by students across the before and after surveys. With regards to their expectations about personal transformation in the service-learning course, prominent themes in student responses suggest that they: believed that the experience would challenge their perceptions about life; thought that they would learn about themselves; and believed that they would become more aware of social and local issues. In terms of the academic learning, prominent themes in student responses suggest that they felt they would gain by: learning specific skills; learning new methods; and by being able to link what they have learned in class with their lived experiences through service.

Table 3: A comparison of themes and their prominences across open-ended questions in before and after surveys

Question	Before survey		After survey	
	Theme	Prominence	Theme	Prominence
What do you understand by the term service-learning?	Learning from service	31.25%	Teaching and learning approach	20%
Describe your expectations/ experiences in relation to the service-learning project.	Learn about social networking	21.42%	Help translate know-ledge to practice; great potential	16.66%
What do you think you are going to learn/have learned personally?	Calm, patience	20%	Patience	27.27%
What do you think you are going to learn/have learned academically?	Mutual learning; direct space inhabitants	20%	Not much	25%
What do you expect to learn/think you have learned from working with your community partners?	Be more creative	20%	Organisa-tional skills (team work, the value of communi-cation, time management, planning)	44.44%
Do you think the service-learning will help/has helped you to gain specific skills or knowledge that you might not learn otherwise? If so, which ones?	People skills	25%	Organisa-tional skills	15.38%
In what ways do you think your community partners will benefit/ have benefitted from this service activity?	Partners will learn	50%	Knowledge about environ-mental issues	25%

Question	Before survey		After survey	
	Theme	Prominence	Theme	Prominence
What do you think your community partners will be able to learn/have learned from you?	Environmental awareness; different angle	27.27%	Confidence about their knowledge	22.22%
Why do you think service-learning activities might be worthwhile activities for university students to participate in, and do you think that such activities can contribute to the broader transformation agenda of universities?	Broader horizon	21.42%	Applied and engaged learning	45%

When asked about what they thought they had achieved at the end of the course in a second survey, students believed that they had learned: to be patient in relation to situations that are out of their control; to facilitate; to relate to people/people's skills; and to communicate and engage using different methods. When asked which skills, if any, they thought they had acquired throughout the year, students mentioned: organisation skills; facilitation skills; and new methods of engagement.

Looking at what students thought they were going to learn and what they say they have learned, it is evident that students have indeed learned some of the skills they believed they would and also acquired many skills they had not expected to. Most importantly for this paper, in the after survey students reported that they felt they had not learned much academically from the course when responding directly to the question of what they felt they had learned academically. However, students reported in the same after survey, just two questions before, that they felt they had learned to translate their knowledge into practice. This highlights students' association of declarative knowledge with academic learning and clear lack of association between procedural knowledge and academic learning.

4.2. Likert-scale survey responses

Likert-scale questions were analysed in two thematic groups:

1. *Academic Learning*, comprising questions 2.1; 2.2; 2.3; 2.4; 2.5; and 2.10.
   Figure 1 shows the answers before the start of the course as well as the
   results after completion of the course.
2. *Personal Growth*, comprising questions 2.6; 2.7; 2.8; 2.9; and 2.11.
   Figure 2 shows the answers to both the before and after survey.

Again, when asked directly, students reported that they thought they had not learned as much as they expected to from the course. Yet, both academically and particularly in terms of personal growth, students believe that they have learned from and grown through their participation in the course.

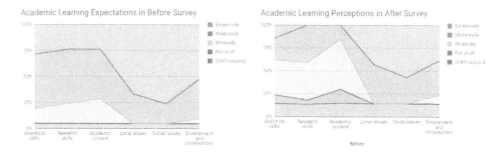

Figure 1 and Figure 2: Academic learning expectations and perceptions Before (1) and After (2)

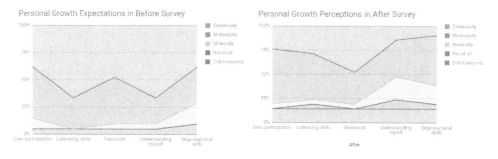

Figure 3 and 4: Personal growth expectations and perceptions Before (3) and After (4)

4.3. Reflective journals

From the reflections, three main themes emerged: methods; group dynamics; and process, which speak to the themes that emerged throughout the service-learning course. These will be presented separately and according to groups. 'Methods' refers to any methods or techniques that the honours students mentioned in their reflections, such as games and forming small groups, as well as facilitation insights, participatory approaches or techniques. These methods speak directly to the academic goals. **Figure 3** presents the methods mentioned by group.

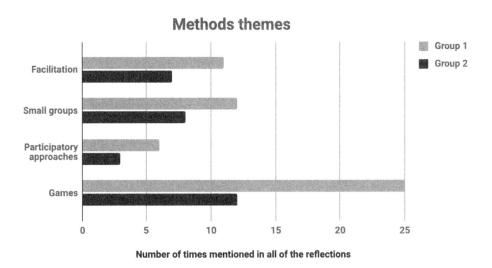

Figure 3: 'Methods' themes

On improving his/her facilitation skills, one student pointed out:

> "The process requires us as facilitators of this initiative to be attentive and allow the learners to equal contribution information on how they plan to achieve sustainable development at their school. This whole process is improving my listening skills."

'Process' refers to the analysis the honours students made of the process, if they were able to relate it to their academic learning and/or the social and political context, and their acknowledgement that this was a learning experience. This is intimately related to both academic and personal growth goals. **Figure 4** illustrates these sub-themes.

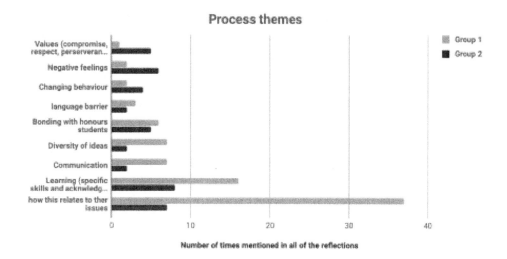

Process themes

Group 1
Group 2

- Values (compromise, respect, perserveran...
- Negative feelings
- Changing behaviour
- language barrier
- Bonding with honours students
- Diversity of ideas
- Communication
- Learning (specific skills and acknwledg...
- how this relates to ther issues

Number of times mentioned in all of the reflections

Figure 4: Process

Students recognised the importance of the service-learning component in providing a space for them to witness some of the issues they had learned in the classroom, as illustrated in the quotes below:

> "This theme ties in with the module I am currently learning; it was interesting for me to see it being demonstrated as I have only learned about it through academic readings and conversations."

> "Interesting to note is how if not dealt with especially water problems these can serve as barriers to pupils' learning experience. Although some studies have documented this, this programme gave me a chance to witness this first-hand."

One journal entry demonstrates how the course triggered students to reflect upon their own experience:

> "My school had many tools for recycling and using resources efficiently in place; however, the values of the children did not match these as they did not care. In contrast to this, the children that we visited did not have access to recycling systems or resources as well as having very little access to information regarding environmental issues. They, however, seem interested in learning and broadening their horizons in this regard. I was reminded of my privilege."

Under group dynamics, both honours groups stressed similar issues but on different scales. The lower level of participation of female learners in comparison to the male learners was more noticeable to Group 1, as was the will of learners to learn, illustrated in **Figure 5**. On the other hand, the presence of disruptive learners in the meetings stood out more for Group 2 students, as did the careless attitudes of learners and the school itself. This suggests that the group that went less often, Group 2, focused on the negative aspects of the challenges they faced.

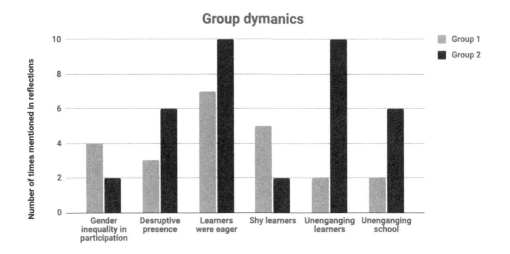

Figure 5: Group dynamics

One student pointed out the low level of female participants in the group participation:

> "I was surprised at how female students [learners] were significantly more quiet than the males and contributed very little. I am interested to see the contribution/ initiative of female participants throughout the programme and how this may or may not increase."

Results of this case study reveal that the honours students did in fact gain academic knowledge during the year-long course and experienced personal growth. **Figure 4** shows that students were able to relate their experience to subjects they learned at their university, a career or to broader contexts 44 times, and **Figure 3** illustrates how the students opened their minds to other ways of engaging with people. Learning of skills was mentioned 24 times, which would imply that learning did take place.

5. Discussion

Results suggest that students have actually learned and grown as citizens, thus these goals were achieved. However, two issues require more attention: the difference between what students think they have learned and what they have actually learned; and the process of achieving these goals, which speaks to the role of the lecturer and implementing aspects of such courses that, at least in this case, played a crucial role in reaching those goals.

5.1 Perception versus reality

The results from the reflections and from the surveys reveal different pictures of the same course. If one were to only look at the answers in the questionnaire and reflections throughout the year, one would conclude that the project did reach its academic goals. Upon a closer look, however, it is evident that the honours' students have not realised exactly what kind of learning took place.

The disparity between the responses from the questionnaires and the reflection journals brings into question the type of knowledge that students are exposed to and their ability to realise that learning took place effectively. The questionnaire, a more quantitative and superficial method with its Likert-scale, revealed that the students felt that they did not learn as much as they would hoped for in the beginning of the year. In other words, their perception was that they did not learn much from the experience. The reflection journal entries, on the other hand, revealed that they did in fact acquire precisely the skills they claimed they did not have, as outlined by them in the questionnaires: organisational skills, analytical skills and methods.

The contrast between what they think they learned and what they showed they have learned through their reflections, we would argue, speaks to different types of knowledge. Students are more familiar with declarative knowledge, which is how traditionally knowledge is 'acquired' in classroom set-ups. Procedural knowledge, which is closely related to experiences, is acquired without people necessarily realising that they are learning and that they have acquired knowledge. There are two issues that emerge from this situation. The first is that students are not equipped to recognise the full extent of procedural knowledge, which highlights the importance of the role of the lecturer. The changing role of the learners in their learning (from individual to collective, from private to public) and the different stages (which include resistance) that students can go through in these spaces demand patience and perseverance from the lecturer (Howard, 1998). The change from a 'traditional' course to a service-learning course also affects the lecturer, who is no longer the sole expert (Howard, 1998;

Osman & Petersen, 2013). This change in role, coupled with the difficult and complex discussions that emerge in service-learning courses, precisely because of their counternormative and transformational stance, begs the question of how prepared the lecturers are to respond to that (Jones, 2002).

The second issue, more closely related to the conceptual discussion about tertiary education, is the type of learning that takes place at universities. Service-learning strives for the learning that takes place when students derive meaning from what they learn, in other words, it strives for engaged learning (Mayaba, Ralarala & Angu, 2018). This, however, is not necessarily the case throughout HE institutions. The standard approach is the 'banking model', in which students are passive and faculty members are the experts (Butin, 2006).

This also brings into question what type of knowledge is more present and valued by academia in general and what is being taught to the students – tensions that are at the surface of service-learning courses (Howard, 1998). One important aspect of this discussion is how students are going to use their knowledge in the real world. This discussion speaks to the dormant knowledge that students acquire in the classroom that can only be accessed through cues, the 'inert' knowledge (Eyler & Giles Jr., 1999). With this type of knowledge, students are unable to relate and apply their learning to the real world without these cues.

Thus, although learning happened, the ability of the students to recognise it opens up different discussions about knowledge, knowledge recognition, accepted and recognised ways of learning as well as students' role in their own learning.

5.2   *The service-learning process*

The difference between personal and academic goals is also a difficult subject for students. The subjective nature of personal growth makes it even more difficult for students to recognise any change in this area themselves. Difficulty in identifying knowledge that is acquired through a different process, as well as the difficulty in differentiating between academic and personal goals, highlight the key role of the lecturer in guiding the process. Moving from a 'traditional' to a service-learning course implies a change in the role of the lecturer and in the role of the student. Rather than preparing lecture notes, the lecturer will build on the readings and the experiences of the service to guide discussions (Howard, 1998), which means that the role of the lecturer is that of a facilitator rather than an expert. Led by the lecturer, the student moves from a passive role in his/her learning to a more active one. This change is likely to be uncomfortable for the student and it will require patience from the lecturer (Howard, 1998).

Interesting to see is that what students thought they were going to learn – and what they in fact did learn – is part of the critical cross-field learning outcomes in the South Africa National Education Strategy. The goals identified by SAQA are part of the skills that the students did not realise that they had learned, which also raises the question of how to teach such skills in a manner that students will recognise that they have learned.

Students from Group 1, who took the trip more often than the students in Group 2, showed to be more aware of the social and local issues, and the learning of cross-cutting outcomes was very obvious in their reflections. This highlights the importance of the time spent at the community sight as well as the con-sistency of the trips. This statement indicates that, in order to reach their goals, service-learning courses should run for longer, regular periods and require that more time is spent at a community site. This means that lecturers and departments where such courses are run would need to invest a great amount of time on this, since they would have to prepare for longer and more time-consuming courses, which in turn would impact the department's organisations and division of courses through semesters/terms. Furthermore, consistent visits to community sites also result in increased transport costs (if needed) and the need for more resources. An advantage of consistent visits, however, is that it confirms commitment and helps build/strengthen relationships with community members.

The bottom line is that this is really about how invested lecturers and their departments are in offering service-learning courses that will yield the desired goals. Given the challenges of service-learning, this is no simple question and one that requires much thought from lecturers, departments and their institutions.

6.   Conclusion

The aim of this chapter was to investigate the impact of a service-learning course on honours level at a university in South Africa, focusing on the learning as well as personal growth aspects of the course. Pre- and post-course surveys and reflection journal entries indicate that students did reflect on their discipline and its applicability and on social injustices in their country and reached cross-cutting outcomes. What this case study also reveals is a need to discuss the type of knowledge that students are used to, as well as their ability to recognise learning. Service-learning courses challenge the students, the lecturers and the institutions, and, while reaching academic and service goals is important, it is not the only determinant of success of such courses.

References

Anderson, J.R. 1995. *Cognitive psychology and its implications*. 4th edition. New York: WH Freeman.

Boyatzis, R.E. 1998. *Transforming qualitative information: Thematic analysis and code development*. Thousand Oaks, CA: Sage Publications.

Bringle, R.G., & Hatcher, J.A. 1996. Implementing service learning in higher education. *The Journal of Higher Education*, 67:221. https://doi.org/10.1080/00221546.1996.11780257

Butin, D.W. 2005. Service-learning as a postmodern pedagogy. In: Dan W. Butin (ed). *Service-learning in higher education: critical issues and directions*, 89-104. New York: Palgrave.

Butin, D.W. 2006. The limits of service-learning in higher education. *The Review of Higher Education*, 29:473-498. doi:10.1353/rhe.2006.0025

Carmichael, T. & Stacey, A. 2006. Perceptions of SAQA's critical cross-field outcomes as key management meta-competencies. *South African Journal of Business Management*, 37:1-15.

Chambers, D. & Lavery, S. 2018. Service-learning: enhancing inclusive education. *International Perspectives on Inclusive Education*, 12:3-19.

Cress, C.M., Collier, P.J. & Reitenauer, V.L. 2005. *Learning through service: a student guidebook for service-learning and civic engagement across academic disciplines and cultural communities*. Sterling, VA: Stylus Publishing.

Davies, C.J. 2016. Whose knowledge counts? Exploring cognitive justice in community-university collaborations (PhD Thesis). University of Brighton.

Deeley, S.J. 2010. Service-learning: Thinking outside the box. *Active Learning in Higher Education*, 11:43-53. doi:10.1177/1469787409355870

Department of Education. 1997. *Education White paper 3. A Programme for the Transformation of Higher Education*. Pretoria: Government Printing Works.

Eyler, J. 2002. Refection: Linking service and learning – linking students and communities. *Journal of Social Issues*, 58:517-534. doi:10.1111/1540-4560.00274

Eyler, J. & Giles Jr, D.E. 1999. *Where's the learning in service-learning?* First edition. San Francisco: Jossey-Bass.

Gearan, M. & Hollister, R. 2013. *Moving beyond the ivory tower – a growing global movement*. Forum European Association for International Education.

Hong, J., Pi, Z. & Yang, J. 2018. Learning declarative and procedural knowledge via video lectures: cognitive load and learning effectiveness. *Innovations in Education and Teaching International*, 55:74-81. doi:10.1080/14703297.2016.1237371

Howard, J.P.F. 1998. Academic service learning a counternormative pedagogy. *New Directions for Teaching and Learning*, 21-29. doi:10.1002/tl.7303

Hubbs, D.L. & Brand, C.F. 2005. The paper mirror : Understanding theories behind the paper mirror. *Journal of Experiential Education*, 28:60-71.

Jackson, E. 2008. The CUE Factor: Community-University Engagement for Social Innovation. *Open Source Business Resource*, (September 2008). http://timreview.ca/article/189

Jones, S. 2002. The underside of service learning. *About Campus*, 10-16.

Liu, G. 2000. Knowledge, foundations and discourse: Philosophical support for service-learning. In: D. Lisman & I. Harvey (eds). *Beyond the Tower: Concepts and Models for Service-Learning in Philosophy*. Washingotn D.C.: American Association for Higher Education.

Lynch, C.L. 1996. Facilitating and assessing unstructured problem solving. *Journal of College Reading and Learning,* 27:42-47.

Mayaba, N.N., Ralarala, M. & Angu, P. 2018. Educational research for social change (ERSC) student voice: Perspectives on language and critical pedagogy in South African higher education. *Educational Research for Social Change*, 7:1-12. doi:http://dx.doi.org/10.17159/2221-4070/2018/v7i1a1

Mezirow, J. 1991. *Transformative Dimensions of Adult Learning*. San Francisco: Jossey-Bass.

Mezirow, J. 1994. Understanding transformation theory. *Adult Education Quarterly*, 44:222-232. doi:https://doi.org/10.1177/074171369404400403

Mezirow, J. 1998. On critical reflection. *Adult Education Quarterly*, 48:185-198.

Osman, R. & Petersen, N. 2013. *Service-learning in South Africa*. Cape Town: Oxford University Press Southern Africa.

Preece, J. 2016. Negotiating service learning through community engagement: Adaptive leadership, knowledge, dialogue and power. *Education as Change*, 20:1-22. doi:10.17159/1947-9417/2016/562

South African Qualifications Authority (SAQA). 2000. *The National Qualifications Framework and curriculum development. The National Qualifications Framework and Curriculum Development*. (Pretoria, SAQA).

Taylor, A. 2017. Service-learning programs and the knowledge economy: Exploring the tensions. *Vocations and Learning*, 10:253-273. doi:10.1007/s12186-016-9170-7

Taylor, A., Butterwick, S., Raykov, M., Glick,S., Peikazadi, N. & Mehrabi, S. 2015. *Community Service-Learning in Canadian Higher Education*. Knowledge Synthesis

Report for the Social Sciences and Humanities Research Council. URL: https://open.library.ubc.ca/cIRcle/collections/facultyre

Wildlife and Environment Society of South Africa. 2013. *WESSA Eco – Schools South Africa Handbook*. WESSA Report. https://wessa.org.za/news-media/publications/

Chapter 7

Challenging mainstream 'psychologies' through community-based service-learning at master's level: Critical reflections at the interface of theory and practice

Jacqui Akhurst

DEPARTMENT OF PSYCHOLOGY, RHODES UNIVERSITY

j.akhurst@ru.ac.za

1.   Introduction

A key aspect of the widespread HE students' protests during 2015 – 2016 in South Africa (SA) was students' dissatisfaction with the limited curricular transformation since the inception of democratic rule (Molefe, 2016), including the predominance of theoretical perspectives that privilege certain academic discourses (Mbembe, 2016). In mainstream psychologies, curricula have remained largely Eurocentric, reinforcing the dominance of knowledge systems in service of neoliberal and technocratic systems of governance that eschew critique (Painter et al., 2013). Here, I purposely use the term 'psychologies' (as in Fryer & Laing, 2008) rather than the singular 'psychology' to indicate that the discipline is neither unified nor adequately globalised, with no universally accepted theoretical frameworks. This raises questions about the perspectives that have dominated what has been taught in university psychology curricula, as well as which have been subjugated because they raise critical questions. Central questions are about the utility of the dominant theories in the SA context; how various psychologies have been constructed, including particularly whose purpose they have served and continue to serve.

In HE in SA, a patriarchal view of knowledge has continued to predominate, vesting authority in the knowledge of the expert. There has been limited progress in tackling injustice and gross inequalities during the two past decades and into the current transition period (Mbembe, 2016), highlighting the need to transform educational practice. Teaching methodologies are still persistently reliant on the 'transmission' mode (Freire, 1970), where the authority figure appears to know better or have all the 'answers', resulting in the still widespread use of rote learning. Students find it difficult to question educators or to explore other possible ways of understanding. This leads to entrenched power differentials, with students being fearful of expressing themselves and struggling to formulate or ask questions about the relevance of their learning to their experiences. They thus become passive recipients of what is presented, rather than actively constructing their learning; leading to a dependency on authoritative texts and decontextualised 'facts', rather than independent learning (Nyamupangedengu, 2017). Students find it difficult to learn the skills needed to become autonomous practitioners, to construct meaning relevant to their lives and to apply their knowledge and capabilities or interrogate their beliefs and values.

In contrast to the above, in the Community Psychology module of the Master's Degrees in Clinical and Counselling Psychology, which forms the basis of this chapter, I favour an organic approach to knowledge construction. Initially, trainees are provided with examples of the applications of more subjugated theoretical frameworks that I have found to be helpful; then they are encouraged to draw from their own experiences and knowledges in participatory engagement and the central activity of the module, Community-Based Service-Learning (CBSL). In this learning, pairs of students actively build a partnership with a community organisation, aiming to meet the identified needs of their community partners. In the USA 'service-learning' has a well-established literature base, but much of the writing tends to be somewhat acritical (Mitchell, 2008) and not linked to specific postgraduate training in psychology. I prefer to use CBSL as a term, to foreground the importance of the community-based partners who contribute to trainees' learning. Students are encouraged to actively construct their learning – drawing from their engagements in reflective activities and learning collaboratively with their partners and peers – to produce a portfolio that illustrates how they have worked at the theory-practice interface.

In this chapter, I explore the module that has unfolded over the past three years (2015 – 2017), describing the basis of some of the less widespread theoretical frameworks that students have found useful. I outline concepts from Vygotsky (1962) that inform the provision of reflective spaces and describe the influences of Freire (1970) and Martin-Baró (Aron & Corne, 1996) on Critical Community Psychologies (CCP), critiquing a more dominant mode of practice in Community Psychology (the 'Mental Health' model). I then illustrate the application of some of these perspectives in CBSL, drawing from students' writing and reflections. The insights gained from this work then lead to suggestions for curricular amendments in SA, to move towards more relevant psychologies and to promote interdisciplinary working across various settings.

2. Vygotskian challenges to current training models in psychology

Vygotsky's research occurred in a period of momentous political and societal change in Russia a century ago, strongly influencing the resultant theorising. Learning and cognitive development were viewed as embedded in the socio-historical and socio-cultural processes of the learner, "social rather than individual … a communicative process, whereby knowledge is shared and understandings are constructed in culturally-formed settings" (Mercer, 1994:92-93). The resultant socio-cultural frameworks that were developed by Vygotsky and his collaborators (e.g. Luria) conceptualise key aspects of learning contexts; however, this work was suppressed by the authorities after Vygotsky's untimely death in 1934 and was only gradually translated and made accessible decades later, by which time 'western' psychologies had institutionalised other much more individually-focused models of learning. Such models do not adequately emphasise the co-construction of cognitive contents and processes, nor do they foreground the profound influence of the context on this content and processes. Some of the key ideas will be summarised below.

The first of Vygotsky's (1962:125) books to be translated emphasised the "continual movement back and forth from thought to word and from word to thought", highlighting the importance of 'thinking and speaking' in socio-cultural experiences, as tools for development and action. Vygotsky preferred the active terms 'speaking' and 'thinking', rather than the more abstract forms 'language' and 'thought', emphasising the dynamic interconnectedness of thinking and speaking. External speech is crucial in developing thoughts, which are then represented by inner speech. In turn, the interactions that lead to thinking (which tend to be associative, using condensed words and forms) being expanded into external speaking are very important in enabling thoughts to be verbalised as linear grammatical forms, thus elaborating meaning. So 'talking through our thoughts' can create links from the specifics of one example to more generalised applications and future actions. The 'tools' of words and symbols are used both in talking about actions and translating these actions into mental functions to guide future action. All of this occurs during interactions with others – those who are providing assistance to the learner (being more experienced in the tasks) or those to whom the learner is conveying meaning.

Vygotsky (1962) distinguished between everyday 'spontaneous' concepts, which emerge from processing the actions of self and others, and 'scientific' (or 'scholarly') concepts, derived from the systematic knowledge conveyed in formal educational contexts, beyond the learner's experience. In 1934, Vygotsky noted that theoretical knowledge is abstract, "... mediated through other concepts with their internal, hierarchical system of relationships" (Wertsch, 1985:103). Thus, scientific concepts do not originate in the learner's mental processing of reality, leading to a gap between theory and experiences that needs to be bridged during instruction. Scholarly concepts need to be translated into more concrete terms, with links made to spontaneous concepts which are known by the learner, and the learner's experiences need to be discussed in relation to theory. These ideas point to the importance of reflective discussions to enable students to theorise their practice and internalise these ideas. Vygotsky (1934, in Wertsch, 1985:112) stated "it is in argumentation, in discussion, that the functional moments appear that will give rise to the development of reflection". Vygotsky (1962) also emphasises the need for time to process reflections, to enable new meanings to be formed through others' words becoming "half-ours and half-someone else's" (Bakhtin, in Wertsch, 1991:79). Such internalisation of speaking enhances reflections on one's activities, stimulating the ability to feel greater control and mastery (Moll, 1990).

Two further important functions of speech were acknowledged by Vygotsky (Wertsch, 1985): those of 'emotional release' and 'social contact'. These two functions are also socio-cultural, and spaces for these functions need to be made in HE settings. The iterative and continually interactive nature of speaking and thinking is both social and individual, reflecting embedded historical and contextual influences. The important challenge is to find ways of encouraging students to be far more active in speaking about their thinking and reactions, i.e. speaking about their processing of ideas and reflection on them.

Tharp and Gallimore (1988) suggest that, over time, the above processes move from social regulation of activities to internalised self-regulation. Learners may need more support or assistance earlier, when ideas and techniques are new, and then develop greater autonomy gradually. The assistance that is provided may take various forms, with 'instructional conversations' that include modelling, feedback, questioning and cognitive structuring. The term 'conversation' points to interactive contexts of equality and responsiveness, including the above four elements (which are less common in formal HE settings). These ideas thus support collaborative learning conversations, where peers verbalise their thoughts and feeling to convey their understandings to each other. Opportunities need to be provided so that peers, who are closer in cognitive development and more at ease to explore with and question each other, can discuss and rehearse the application of ideas.

The ideas explored above challenge the more 'authoritative' models of teaching and supervision that are commonly found in training settings. Wertsch (1991:78) notes the inhibitory effect of the authoritative voice, which is more 'univocal' than other voices, allowing "no interanimation with other voices". A Vygotskian approach thus proposes pedagogies that are as interactive as possible to encourage speaking about thinking – active discussions of the students' applications of scholarly concepts and their theorising of their everyday experiences of work, with each other.

3.   Developments in CCP

As in other countries, where community psychologies evolved in response to repressive regimes or inequalities that oppressed groups of people (Fryer & Laing, 2008), forms of community psychology emerged during the 1980s in SA. Groups of psychologists linked to certain universities promoted a psychology that was more socially relevant than the dominant individually-focused approaches (Yen, 2008). They criticised organised psychology for its silence and seeming collusion with the policies and violent actions of the apartheid state and for not protesting strongly against the state-perpetrated violence and its deleterious effects on people's mental health. These groups struggled for services and became involved in providing psycho-emotional support for people who had been detained, tortured and persecuted by the state (Hayes, 2000). Community psychology was thus well positioned to be influential post-1994 (Pillay, 2003), holding great promise as a foundation for SA psychology to develop approaches much more responsive to the needs of the majority (Foster, 2004).

Sadly, however, community psychology has not had as widespread an influence on practice as it promised (Carolissen, 2006). Applications of the subdiscipline have often been theoretical rather than practical (Pillay, 2003) and there has been a lack of a unitary voice in community psychologies due to the political positioning of some of its proponents, whether conservative, progressive or radical (Yen, 2008). In SA, clinical psychology has been central to influencing the profession, working closely with psychiatry and predominantly associated with individual pathology and treatment, even though there have been regular calls for shifts in focus (e.g. Ahmed & Pillay, 2004; Seedat, 2014). It is important to challenge the pathologising of individuals, typical of much of mainstream psychology (Cromby, Harper & Reavey, 2013), since community psychologists locate much aetiology firmly in the unequal social structures that promote inequalities in access to resources and discrimination against and systemic oppression of certain people (Naidoo, 2000).

Apolitical approaches to community psychology that have emerged from the United States, which have had extensive influences on the field globally (Fryer & Laing, 2008), have led to community psychologies that have not challenged the prevailing political, social and economic conditions, limiting the impact of interventions. In some contexts, as a result, forms of CCP that strive for systemic change have gained ground. The emphasis drawn from critical approaches relates to the impact of power and challenges to societal structures, politically and socio-economically, which promote inequality and a lack of social justice (Painter et al., 2013; Seedat & Lazarus, 2011).

Some of CCP's ideas originate from the Latin American 'popular education' movement as espoused in Brazil by Freire (1970), drawing from theories more likely to be taught in education than in psychology departments. It has also been strongly influenced by Latin American Liberation Psychology, such as that formulated by Martín-Baró in El Salvador, with academic workers standing in solidarity with people experiencing oppression (Aron & Corne, 1996). Freire's (1970) work encourages participatory psycho-educational approaches in which people are provided with material that stimulates discussions of the impacts of societal inequality on their conditions of living and working through such techniques as 'conscientisation'. Another important, though not dominant, approach in the teaching of methodologies of psychology is Action Research, which gained great importance in Liberation Psychology, particularly in its participatory form, working for social justice (Fals Borda, 2001). These influences promote collaborative work with groups of people, valuing the attributes everyone brings and their everyday knowledges, striving to work in solidarity and cooperatively, with a focus that promotes systemic activism and working towards social justice.

The term 'community' also must be considered. In apartheid psychology, it was often used to describe the settlements used to separate people and oppress the majority (Carolissen, 2006). To move away from ideas of 'community' as a euphemism for an area that is impoverished and disadvantaged by lack of access to resources, Kagan et al., (2011) use the term 'community' rather as a verb and a key element of CCP. In this way the term promotes engagement that is prosocial, drawing individuals together, whether formally or informally (and not necessarily in proximity, since online communities have grown drama- tically over recent times). Kagan et al., (2011) also emphasise social justice, mentioned earlier, and then add as a third key element the need for inherent respect of people and the planet, formulated into the concept of 'stewardship'. I give more detail of the overlaps between the principles of CCP and CBSL in Akhurst (2017).

All of the above ideas resonate in the unequal and socially divided context of SA, where the imprints of the oppression and racial discrimination of the apartheid era are still very evident more than twenty years after the dawn of democracy. CCP has the potential to encourage asset-based and more inclusive participatory approaches, and through these approaches conscientise trainees to the very evident social asymmetries in SA, which in turn will impact limited educational opportunities, increased poverty and inadequate healthcare pro- vision (Carolissen et al., 2010). It is important to provide opportunities for critically reflective discussions (as in CBSL) on the impacts of the neoliberal policies of recent years and ways in which psychologists' practice could become more transformative in relation to societal structures and service delivery, rather than reinforcing the status quo (Foster, 2004).

3.1 The mental health model of community psychology

Although forms of community psychology in the United States evolved from the Civil Rights Movement of the 1960s, a 'community mental health' approach has predominated in practice there. Naidoo (2000) notes the apolitical form of this approach because it developed within the political system in which structural discrimination is embedded, rather than challenging it. One of the core aspects of an approach that strives to promote improved mental health is to challenge work that is ameliorative, with the emphasis moving to work that is focused on prevention (Nelson & Prilleltensky, 2010), although this has been focused in particular geographic locations, rather than becoming influential at policy and resource levels. The mental health model thus retains strong interconnections with the medical and social care systems, and so it may unintentionally reinforce existing systems of power because they are not critically analysed.

Naidoo *et al.,* (2007) outline the applications of community psychology in South Africa, with Ahmed and Suffla (2007) discussing the limitations of the mental health approach to community psychology, which still emphasises the 'top-down' expertise of the psychologist, the pathologising of distress and the focus on individual behaviour change. The challenge is to move towards more transformative approaches that might have a wider impact, such as those espoused by the 'social action' or 'psycho-political liberation' models (as described in Arumugam, 2001). The social action model more actively focuses on the self-determination of people through cooperative social support and self-help groups. It encourages groups to claim their rights and to put pressure on those in power to be more responsive, with advocacy being a core role for the psychologists involved (Naidoo *et al.,* 2007). The psycho-political liberation model is more radical in its aims, working towards systemic change through building the social capital of participants and encouraging collective action through intersectional campaigning. The goal of this model is to lead to policy changes and shifts in resource allocation towards greater social justice.

Trainees need to be exposed to the different ways of working as psychologists (as outlined in Naidoo *et al.,* 2007), and a central question of this chapter is whether and how trainees might use such ideas in their CBSL settings.

4. The role of CBSL in linking theory and practice

This article explores an approach to CBSL that is integrated into the curriculum in a module that is a core element of counselling and clinical trainee psychologists' coursework at master's level in one SA university. At an early stage in their module, trainees are informed of the potential projects with which they can become involved via presentations by the previous year's cohort and being given information about any new requests for assistance that have come from community-based organisations (since there is a natural evolution of the work, with some completed during the previous year). Pairs of students then volunteer for the projects with which they would like to work, and once the allocation has been agreed upon, trainees contact their respective community partners to negotiate the nature of the work to be planned. For new projects, this may involve some form of needs analysis (Kagan *et al.,* 2011).

The annual cohort is made up of 12 master's level counselling and clinical psychology trainees who pair up by category. This enables six projects to be worked on during the course of the module (that spans from May to the end of October). The trainees worked in the following community placements during 2017:

- With staff members of a local secondary school, where the principal was concerned about the conflict between two groups;
- In a day centre for people discharged from the local psychiatric hospital, where participants engage in craft-work and psychosocial skills development, with the trainees providing group therapeutic support;
- With Grade 11 learners in a career development programme for the children of employees on campus (the learners attended various previously disadvantaged schools lacking in resources);
- In a school for learners who had been excluded from mainstream schools due to their intellectual and socio-emotional needs, with trainees providing group psychoeducation;
- Providing lifeskills workshops with boys (ages 6 – 18) housed in a local childcare shelter;
- Facilitating regular peer support groups for the volunteer counsellors who provide a peer counselling programme based at a local youth centre.

As the work unfolds, the students plan and work together in their pairs, but also in larger groups of six, to promote regular critical conversations and reflection. Gilbert and Sliep (2009) outline the ways in which critical reflection with peers is essential in enhancing students' learning. The two groups of six meet weekly for structured peer group supervision (see Akhurst & Kelly, 2006), and at points of decision-making the pairs also seek supervision from a tutor (Langa & Graham, 2011). These opportunities for critical reflection encourage trainees to ask deeper questions about both the theoretical frameworks that inform their work, but also about social justice and how their work might promote working in solidarity with their partners to challenge inequalities. CBSL therefore encourages meta-reflections on engagements to promote more active citizenship (Akhurst, Solomon, Mitchell & Van der Riet, 2016). Since CBSL is designed to be mutually beneficial to both trainees and community partners, trainees are encouraged to consider how they position themselves as trainee psychologists. Nguyen (2016:7) proposes five core values for CBSL, namely "rigour, reflection, relationship, reciprocity, and real life", and one of the purposes of this chapter is to consider the evidence of these values in the trainees' accounts of their project work.

5. Methodology

This research has ethical clearance (PSY2016/03) and participants all signed consent forms. The data collection was participatory, with me facilitating the events involving trainees. The data were collected from two focus groups of six trainees each on completion of their community projects. The prompts for the focus group were open-ended. In addition, I collected the same trainees' contributions to a day-long reflective colloquium where they met with another regional university's trainees. On this occasion, each pair of trainees led the discussions about their projects, focusing on their learnings. Finally, in order not to influence the data collection from some community partners, a research assistant interviewed three representatives of the partner organisations and subsequently transcribed and analysed these data, using thematic analysis (Braun & Clarke, 2006). A summary of this phase of data collection is presented first.

Verbatim transcriptions of the two focus group discussions (2 x n = 6) were done by a research assistant, and I summarised the colloquium presentations and key points of the emerging discussions. This summary was circulated to all present for their additional comment/suggestions. The findings that follow draw from these data using template analysis (King, 2012) to identify themes of relevance to this chapter.

6. Findings

A brief summary of the main themes to emerge from community partners' accounts follows (a perspective often neglected in the service-learning literature), with a somewhat more detailed focus on trainees' experiences thereafter. The research to collect data from community partners is continuing and will be reported more fully in a subsequent publication.

6.1 Benefits to partners

1. In relation to the establishment and maintenance of the partnership, participants made comments about the ways in which this had been an organic process. They reported that negotiations had been based on 'community' needs and that they were consulted at every step of the unfolding process. They had felt a sense of agency in these processes, constructing their roles as contextual mediators for the students. In order to maintain the contact, they appreciated the regular communication with trainees, as well as trainees' flexibility in adjusting and accommodating plans when the situation changed from week to week.

2. Without the partners being 'led' in the interviews, they gave examples of what they valued about the approaches taken to partnership building. These examples included collaborative decision-making, i.e. their sense of influencing the evolving processes and being co-determinants of the nature of the interventions. They were impressed by the trainees' preparedness

for the work that was done and also appreciated the passion and energy of the trainees, as well as the professionalism shown (which they contrasted to their experiences of other students who had not been trainee psychologists).

3. Partners reported multiple gains for their organisations as a result of collaborating with the trainees. These gains included referrals to appropriate agencies for individuals needing further assistance; building strong and reliable bonds with the trainees who had shown care in their engagements; learning together, where they were key informants assisting trainees to work in culturally sensitive ways; gaining greater insight into psychological work; and an enhancement of their own work as a result of support.

4. Few project difficulties were reported by partners, even though they were encouraged to be open about any they had experienced. Some of the challenges were the shifting needs of the context as the processes unfolded, some sense of dependency on the trainees' input since this could not be substituted by other resources and, related to this, the time limitations of having at most six months together.

5. Their comments about their future needs for cooperative work were that they wished for: more psycho-educational workshops; the development of more interdisciplinary linkages and three-way partnerships which include service providers in the area; and working more on building resources and connections to referral agencies and strengthening these bonds.

6.2. Benefits to trainees

In the analysis below, the trainees' identities are anonymised, with their words shown in italics. The participant code after the quotations links to a key: F1 – F4 and M1 – M2 are used for the counselling group; and F7 – F10 and M3 – M4 are used for the clinical trainees (with F and M indicating male or female). The themes to emerge from the data (and noted in bold in what follows) include: learning from the experiences (building on relationships); learning about/applying community psychology and the role of theory; the value of supporting each other and reflecting with peers informally and in a group; and limitations of the work in relation to influencing systems.

Trainees noted the value of *learning from the experiences* that CBSL had provided: *"… so you're going into community and we experience it then first-hand, but until we engage with community work and actually do it, … then, only then I think, I feel that we can really learn."* (F10)

Planning was described as important in allaying anxieties, but they often needed to respond to what was unexpected and needed to be flexible to accommodate the situation: "... *we actually had to experience the feeling of being uncertain, the anxiety that comes with that ... we actually had to sit with this uncertainty ... 'cause it doesn't always turn out the way you hope, or that we expect that things would turn out. ... I think with every community project that's going to be different ... you can't really pre-plan the skills I'm going to need for this community project, because depending on the community, depending on the needs of the community ...*" (F7)

They noted ways in which learning came from the speaking and thinking embedded in the *relational approach* that informed their engagements. They reported this as being very different from their clinic-based work: here they were "*trying to understand our community from a point of not being an expert*" (F7). They needed to remain open-minded in their approach and listening:"*... feeling like this uncomfortability actually opens me up to experience a bit more ... and to new things, that I wouldn't have, I think experienced.*" (F8)

This comment highlights the sense that the work is imbued with uncertainties, but if trainees can find ways to cope with them, there is the potential for creative interaction with their partners (both the other trainee and community participants). Trainees thus used their counselling skills to connect with people, recognising that "*people wanted to be heard*" (M1) and to communicate more clearly with each other. This was "*initially very challenging*" (M2), but they saw the value of participants being "*provided a safe space that you could see where the problems were*" (M2). This illustrates the exploratory co-creation and elaboration on thinking that become possible in conversational spaces.

The importance of the relations that were built is also evident in: "*feeling that connection with, with them as a group but also with some of them individually*" (F2), and their sense that their partners gave them the freedom to make plans but "*they gave us the feeling that they also supported us*" (F1). At times they felt some relief due to the nature of participatory work: "*... like one wasn't under too much pressure to sort of change things, or to come up with solutions*" (F7). Thus trainees found that it was best to work in a way that was not "*pre-scripted*" (F1) and were rather responsive to what they encountered and were "*thinking on our feet*" (M1).

They gave some examples of the assistance they provided, which was different from the predominance of instruction or advice in didactic settings. In work with youth, one noted that what worked best was "*creating activities with things that stimulate them, that are engaging for them*" (F1). Another trainee commented on the ways in which they interacted with each other, "*modelling the open and honest struggles"* (M1) in exchanging ideas, and a further trainee commented on the usefulness of *"role play"* (M2) for participants to experiment with different possible responses to events. Trainees emphasised how they encouraged participants to express their needs, thoughts and opinions in order to enhance mutual understanding.

They discussed *learning about and applying principles and ideas from community psychology.* Some described their lack of knowledge at the beginning of the projects and that their learning progressed through engagement. Examples are:

"Starting with community psychology, I felt very unsure, as if I didn't know anything ... there's this initial sense of anxiety and not knowing and being unsure, going into the unknown ..." (F8) *"Initially ... I'm not known and how are they going to receive me as a psychology student ... So it was very important I think, ... for us to create rapport and ... collaborate ... so it shifted from just being unknown people to becoming part of the community."* (F10)

As noted earlier, a number of trainees felt unsure or anxious early on, but once they had initially engaged, they realised that their people skills could be usefully applied and that taking a non-expert position was helpful. Further examples are:

"We formed connections with people, real authentic meaningful connections ... bringing our own personhood to the work." (F8)

"The community that we went into was sort of receptive of us, so that helped. I was less anxious going there rather than if they were not accommodating ... so if I think if the community wants people to come from the outside, ... it helped with whatever anxieties ... and the fears I might have had." (M3)

The trainees saw the value of doing a needs and assets evaluation in a collaborative way that enhanced participation:

"... we can only work out what people need when one builds the relationship ..." (M4) *"... we focused more on strengths and what was positive ..."* (F9)

A key aspect they noted was the role of theory at the intersection between 'everyday' and 'scholarly' concepts. Trainees reflected upon theoretical ideas they had used in a practical way to inform their workshop planning as one pair noted *"giving psychology away"* (F10) and using *"different resources and participatory approaches"* (M3) that were distinct from teachers' didactic positions. They also saw the *"value of coming from the outside to address some of the tricky issues"* (F10) that teachers struggled to manage with learners and being able to initiate more conversational spaces with learners. Theory was used to provide "very loose scaffolding" (M1) for the interventions and one trainee noted that "theory helped keep us grounded when things chopped and changed" (F3).

Drawing from a number of different sources provided a framework or principles for the work, "giving direction" (F3), with models being "protective factors for facilitators" (F4). It thus appeared that the theoretical lenses that they used gave them some security as they worked in evolving processes. Theory thus played a formative role and also seemed to be a resource to draw from in practice. The trainees also used theory to inform their evaluations after the interventions.

A number of trainees contrasted CBSL to both their clinic-based work and to having previously only read about community psychology in practice.

"… it's different to therapeutic work, it can be administrative … organisational management, like managing people and meeting times and paper work" (M4). They mentioned some community psychology-specific resources such as ecological systems theory, as well as drawing ideas from psychology more broadly. For example:

"We used the CBT [Cognitive Behaviour Therapy] model of substance abuse as a basis for psychoeducation, role plays, making resources available, … pictures … cards …" (F10)

"… the use of breathing exercises, mindfulness techniques, playing with clay, group members interviewing each other …" (F8)

Trainees noted the value of supporting each other and reflecting with peers. A number agreed that working in pairs was beneficial because "you have that person to bounce ideas off" (F4) and with whom to discuss the links between theory and practice. In addition, they could take turns in facilitating, debrief immediately with a peer and give each other feedback. This promoted greater autonomy. Having peers as partners was furthermore valuable because the discussion could be "more relaxed" (F10) and they could "practice" (F10) voicing ideas.

Commenting on the peer supervision group in which they participated, they said "humour is an aspect that features outside of authoritative supervision" (F3) and that there was a "degree of openness and authenticity" (F2) that they appreciated. The group furthermore provided opportunities for "venting … whereas with individual supervision you need to be more contained (all laugh) " (F4).

The peer group discussions led to "group generation of ideas" (M4) and "peers could also provide critique" (F2). One noted "I think it was very helpful … for all of us" because "people came with different previous experiences" (M2), for example those who had been teachers could reflect on their work experiences. The group could assist weekly with "processing frustrations" (F10) when a project was not progressing according to plan. They appreciated being *"accountable"* to each other and working collaboratively enabled *"shared responsibility"* and helped them to *"take decisions"* (M2).

Trainees also experienced first-hand *the limitations in relation to influencing systems*. They became far more sensitised to people's struggles, enabling them to feel compassion for and an appreciation of what their community partners encountered. For example, trainees described their experiences of the struggles of a group of school teachers who had a*"lack of funds, the school kids coming from, you know ... disadvantaged homes, they brought their own problems in which then affect the teachers ... with these various pressures ... really brought home how all these different levels impact on these teachers and how difficult it makes their lives."* (M1)

The above excerpt illustrates the structural and systemic challenges faced by people. A further example is:

"The environment around the school is not conducive for learners and gives a message to them about being placed on the margins." (F10)

They showed greater awareness of their positioning and lack of power, mentioning their frustrations at not being able to influence the system:

"Even us as trainee psychologists, there are very limited things that we could do ... especially getting to be advocate and things like that." (F8)

This was summarised by one trainee in relation to their aspirations to move beyond a mental health model, but feeling unable to shift their practice:

"While we worked from a mental health model, coming from a preventative approach, we would have liked to take a social action model approach that would lead us to mobilising and activism with the Department of Education to make a broader impact ... but with only two of us, we're not sure what our contributions could assist in making a difference." (M3)

7. Discussion

The findings reported above are not an exhaustive account, but illustrate a number of features of the CBSL. Firstly, it is useful to consider the overlaps between the community-based partners' experiences and those of the trainees. Then, while the explicit references to theory were not extensive, the influences of the theoretical frameworks they applied may be seen implicitly in the evidence. Finally, I make some suggestions for curricular amendments and note the limitations of this research.

Considering the summary of the partners' experiences alongside those of the trainees highlights the foundations that are built relationally, and it is these relational foundations upon which the work is then based. Both parties reported on their respective learnings from working together while building a sense of agency and being flexible. Also important were mutual respect and an acknowledgement of strengths. Partners appreciated that they influenced decision-making and also noted trainees' preparedness, commitment and professionalism (contrasting this to their experiences of less experienced students). The trainees in turn felt supported by their partners. The partners reported on organisational gains from the trainees' inputs, while the trainees valued their experiential learning. Trainees also reported gaining support and direction from their peers; however, this was a forum that did not include community partners, which might be viewed as inhibiting fully participatory collaboration.

Researchers have found that participation in service-learning could have a transformational impact on trainees (e.g. Deeley, 2015; Eyler & Giles, 1999). In adjusting to their CBSL, the trainees demonstrated some aspects of Mezirow's (2000) model of transformational learning. They reported initial disorienting dilemmas (in their noting of uncertainties and anxiety), where they realised that the work would be different from the therapeutic mode that their training has prepared them for. The resulting dissonance, resulting from the realisation that they need to work differently, motivated them to learn more through grappling with ideas with their peers. This disorienting experience then lead to some re-evaluation of their ways of working, resulting in new learning and potential changes in practice. However, trainees may also resist the process of critically assessing their worldviews, highlighting the importance of a dialogical reflective processes.

With regard to the specific theoretical frameworks described earlier in the chapter, it is clear that the findings show the utility of Vygotskian ideas, where learning is embedded in the relational and interactive conversations. The trainees highlighted the importance of opportunities for reflections on their work to assist in their learning. Theoretical frameworks need to be flexible rather than overly determinative in order to be useful. Then, the CCP concept of the building of 'community' (as in Kagan *et al.*, 2011) in various ways was central to much of the data. When they moved beyond community psychology ideas, the trainees did not make any reference to theories they had learned in undergraduate curricula but rather referred to those theories derived from therapeutic practice.

This research has provided rich evidence of the value of CBSL to trainees, with clear support for four of Nguyen's (2016) core values: reflection, relationship, reciprocity and real life. The fifth value, rigour, evolves from a developmental learning process – I would have liked to see trainees being more adept at talking about theory than was evident in the focus groups. However, future analysis of trainees' written portfolios might provide such evidence. In terms of curriculum transformation, seeing the benefits of CBSL raises questions of ways in which such material and experiences might be integrated and expanded upon earlier in psychology curricula, along with the associated theoretical frameworks (to take the place of some of the current dominant theories). The trainees' comments and disappointment about their limited impact systemically need further interrogation, and ways in which they might be able to work for more advocacy and support partners' activism (where appropriate) in order to promote greater social justice, should be considered. Ways to promote more interdisciplinarity (as noted by partners) and to enhance the sustainability of the CBSL also need consideration.

8.   Concluding remarks

CBSL provides the possibility of developing (community) psychologies that are more relevant and responsive to the realities of life in SA. This chapter has illustrated in a small way how taking an alternative approach to trainees' learning through CBSL has such potential. However, to expand on this work will require systemic investment that is currently not in evidence, either in many HE institutions (where there is increasing pressure of student numbers) or in the policies that the professional body influences. The development of psychologies that are more appropriate to and evolve organically from the SA context depends on shifts in theory and practice to enable greater integration of CBSL as a social innovation and to work towards social justice.

9.   Acknowledgements

I would like to thank the M1 students who contributed their reflections to this research. I also appreciate the work of the research assistants who helped me with the analysis of aspects of the data, funded by a research grant that I was awarded by the university (for which I am also grateful).

References

Ahmed, R. & Pillay, A.L. 2004. Reviewing clinical psychology training in the post-apartheid period: Have we made any progress? *South African Journal of Psychology*, 34:630-656.

Ahmed, R., & Suffla, S. 2007. The mental health model: Preventing illness or social inequality? In: N. Duncan, B. Bowman, A. Naidoo, J. Pillay, & V. Roos (eds). *Community psychology: Analysis, context and action*, 84-101. Cape Town: UCT Press.

Akhurst, J. 2017. Student experiences of community-based service learning during Masters' level training, as related to critical community psychology practice. *Journal of New Generation Sciences*, 15(1):1-20.

Akhurst, J.E., & Kelly, K. 2006. Peer group supervision as an adjunct to individual supervision: Optimising learning processes during psychologists' training. *Psychology Teaching Review*, 12(1):3-15.

Akhurst, J. Solomon, V. Mitchell, C. & van der Riet, M. 2016. Embedding community-based learning into psychology degrees at UKZN, South Africa. *Educational Research for Social Change*, 5, 2, 136-150.

Aron, A. & Corne, S. (eds). 1996. *Ignacio Martín-Baró: Writings for a Liberation Psychology*. New York: Harvard University Press.

Arumugam, S. 2001. A discussion of the Ecological, Indigenous, Organisational, Mental Health, Social Action and Liberatory Models of Community Psychology. Unpublished manuscript, University of Zululand, KwaDlangezwa.

Braun, V. & Clarke, V. 2006. Using thematic analysis in psychology. *Qualitative Research in Psychology*, 3, 2, 77-101.

Carolissen, R. 2006. Teaching community psychology into obscurity: A reflection on community psychology in South Africa. *Journal of Psychology in Africa*, 16:177-182.

Carolissen, R., Rohleder, P., Bozalek, V., Swartz, L., & Leibowitz, B. 2010. "Community Psychology is for poor, Black people": Pedagogy and teaching of Community Psychology in South Africa. *Equity and Excellence in Education*, 43(4):495-510.

Cromby, J., Harper, D., & Reavey, P. (eds) 2013. *Mental health and distress*. London: Palgrave Macmillan.

Deeley, S. 2015. *Critical perspectives on service learning in Higher Education*. Basingstoke, UK: Palgrave Macmillan.

Eyler, J., & Giles, D.E. Jr. 1999. *Where's the learning in service-learning?* San Francisco: Jossey-Bass.

Fals Borda, O. 2001. Participatory (Action) Research in social theory: Origins and challenges. In: P. Reason & H. Bradbury (eds). *Handbook of Action Research: Participative Inquiry and Practice*, 27-37. London: Sage.

Foster, D. 2004. Liberation psychology. In: K. Ratele, N. Duncan, D. Hook, N. Mkhize, P. Kiguwa & A. Collins (eds). *Self, community and Psychology*, 1-44. Cape Town: UCT Press.

Freire, P. 1970. *Pedagogy of the oppressed*. Harmondsworth, Middlesex: Penguin.

Fryer, D. & Laing, A. 2008. Community Psychologies: What are they? What could they be? Why does it matter? A Critical Community Psychology Approach. *The Australian Community Psychologist*, 20(2):7-15.

Gilbert, A. & Sliep, Y. 2009. Reflexivity in the practice of social action: From self- to inter- relational reflexivity. *South African Journal of Psychology*, 39(4):468-479.

Hayes, G. 2000. The struggle for mental health in South Africa: Psychologists, apartheid, and the story of Durban OASSSA. *Journal of Community and Applied Social Psychology*, 10:327-342.

Kagan, C., Burton, M., Duckett, P., Lawthom, R. & Siddiquee, A. 2011. *Critical community psychology*. Chichester: BPS Blackwell.

King, N. 2012. Doing template analysis. In: G. Symon, & C. Cassell (eds). *Qualitative organizational research*, 426-50. London: Sage.

Langa, M., & Graham, T. 2011. Experiences of supervising postgraduate community psychology students at Wits University, South Africa. *Journal of Community & Applied Social Psychology*, 21(2), 178-191.

Mbembe, A. 2016. Decolonising the university: New directions. *Arts & Humanities in Higher Education*, 15(1):29-45.

Mercer, N. 1994. Neo-Vygotskian theory and classroom education. In: B. Steirer & J. Maybin (eds). *Language, literacy and learning in educational practice*, 92-110. Clevedon, Avon: Multilingual Matters and Open University Press.

Mezirow, J. 2000. Learning to think like an adult: Core concepts of Transformation Theory. In: J. Mezirow & Associates (eds). *Learning as Transformation. Critical Perspectives on a Theory in Progress*, 3-33. San Francisco: Jossey-Bass.

Molefe, T.O. 2016. Oppression must fall: South Africa's revolution in theory. *World Policy Journal*, 33(1):30-37.

Moll, L.C. (ed). 1990. Vygotsky and education: Instructional implications of socio-historical psychology. New York: Cambridge University Press.

Mitchell, T. 2008. Traditional vs. critical service-learning: Engaging the literature to differentiate two models. *Michigan Journal of Community Service Learning*, 14(2):50-65.

Naidoo, A.V. 2000. Community psychology: Constructing community, reconstructing psychology in South Africa. Inaugural lecture. Stellenbosch: University of Stellenbosch.

Naidoo, A., Duncan, N., Roos, V., Pillay, J. & Bowman, B. 2007. Analysis, context and action: An introduction to community psychology. In: N. Duncan, B. Bowman, A. Naidoo, J. Pillay & V. Roos (eds). *Community psychology: Analysis, context and action*, 9-23. Cape Town: UCT Press.

Nguyen, C.H. 2016. Partners for success. *Journal for Service-Learning, Leadership, and Social Change*, 5(2), Art 3.

Nelson, G. & Prilleltensky, I. (eds). 2010. *Community psychology: In pursuit of wellness and liberation (second edition)*. London: MacMillan/Palgrave.

Nyamupangedengu, E. 2017. Investigating factors that impact the success of students in a Higher Education classroom: A case study. *Journal of Education*, 68, 113-130.

Painter, D., Kiguwa, P. & Bohmke, W. 2013. Contexts and continuities of critique: Reflections on the current state of Critical Psychology in South Africa. *Annual Review of Critical Psychology*, 13, 849-869.

Pillay, J. 2003. "Community psychology is all theory and no practice": Training educational psychologists in community practice within the South African context. *South African Journal of Psychology*, 33(4):261-268.

Seedat, M. 2014. Mobilising compassionate critical citizenship and psychologies in the service of humanity. In: S. Cooper & K. Ratele (eds). *Psychology Serving Humanity: Proceedings of the 30th International Congress of Psychology: Volume 1: Majority World Psychology*, 1-17. London: Psychology Press.

Seedat, M. & Lazarus, S. 2011. Community psychology in South Africa: Origins, developments and manifestations. *Journal of Community Psychology*, 39(3):241-257.

Vygotsky, L.S. 1962. *Thought and language*. New York: MIT Press.

Tharp, R. & Gallimore, R. 1988. *Rousing minds to life: Teaching, learning and schooling in social context*. Cambridge: Cambridge University Press.

Wertsch J.V. 1985. *Vygotsky and the social formation of mind*. Cambridge, MA: Harvard University Press.

Wertsch, J.V. 1991. *Voices of the mind: A sociocultural approach to mediated action*. London: Harvester Wheatsheaf.

Yen, J. 2008. A history of community psychology in South Africa. In: C. van Ommen & D. Painter (eds). *Interiors: A history of Psychology in Southern Africa*, 381-408. Cape Town, South Africa: UCT Press.

Chapter 8

Chasing significance in sports science research – a human factors and ergonomics approach to social innovation

Bennet Ryan and Andrew Todd

HUMAN KINETICS AND ERGONOMICS,
RHODES UNIVERSITY

g08r5157@campus.ru.ac.za; a.todd@ru.ac.za

1. Background

Academe is at a crossroad where there is a growing realisation that research can no longer be conducted in ivory towers for the sake of enquiry. Academic institutions are now under increasing pressure to align research with both teaching and community engagement endeavours, with tangible practical implications for society. Nowhere is this more pertinent and important than in South African academic institutions which are required to undertake social redress as a cornerstone of research and teaching. For example, the Rhodes University Vice Chancellor argues for "producing graduates who are knowledgeable intellectuals, skilled professionals, and critical, caring and compassionate citizens who can contribute to economic and social development and an equitable, just and democratic society." (Mabizela, 2018). In order to produce such graduates, it may be necessary for a paradigm shift amongst the South African academic community. The purpose of the current chapter is therefore to illustrate our own journey from ivory tower to engaged research focused on social innovation. To do this, it is first necessary to provide some background to our discipline and areas of research interest.

A key component of the work done in the Rhodes University Human Kinetics and Ergonomics (HKE) Department is the promotion of participation in physical activity and sport through the disciplines of sports science and human factors. Numerous studies have shown that involvement in physical activity can result in many advantages including physical, psycho-social and educational benefits. From a physical perspective, the benefits include improved body composition, cardiovascular fitness and long-term health (Humphreys, McLeod & Ruseski, 2014), while, from a psycho-social view, well-designed programmes are associated with improved self-esteem and self-concept as well as confidence (Lubans *et al.*, 2016). Other positive effects include improved life skills and peer relationships. Lastly, those involved in physical activity have been shown to have better academic achievements and higher pass rates (Donnelly *et al.*, 2016). It is therefore clear that participation in well-designed physical activity programmes is a vitally important component of youth development and healthy living in general.

As the importance of physical activity and sport have become apparent, there has been a concurrent professionalisation of sport, resulting in the proliferation of talent identification and development (TID) programmes. Rongen, McKenna, Cobley and Till (2018) recently contended that, due to the resource intensive nature (in particular the financial resources required) of such programmes, they are under pressure to translate investment into elite athletes. This pressure often results in an unbalanced focus on high level performance rather than holistic development. Consequently, researchers have started to question the effectiveness of talent identification programmes and the wellbeing of participating athletes in terms of both psychological impact and injury risk (Rongen *et al.*, 2018). They conclude by advocating for a shift away from development of elite athletes to a broader objective of supporting participation in sport and the important benefits thereof already highlighted in this chapter. We would go one step further and suggest that the focus should shift from identification and development to broad based participation of youth in a variety of physical and sporting activities. The identification of talent would be a latent benefit at a later stage in the life cycle of the programme (i.e. talented athletes will naturally emerge from within the system).

2. Towards systems thinking in sports science

Recent researchers have argued that sports science has traditionally taken a reductionist approach (Balagué *et al.*, 2017; Salmon, 2017; Toohey *et al.*, 2018) to understanding and optimising sporting performance. The reductionist approach often oversimplifies integration amongst organisational levels of living systems and further limits integration of biological and social sciences (Loland, 2013). This author further stresses the need to shift from not only the reductionist approach but also from the disciplinary specificity to a transdisciplinary view. For example, Toohey *et al.*, (2018) argues that transdisciplinarity is an important research outlook through which to investigate complex real-life matters. We would concur, and within the context of the current chapter, there have been several important developments that have come out of the challenge to sports science to shift its perspective. One of the key shifts has been towards an athlete-centred approach. For example, Rongen *et al.*, (2018) proposed a model for the design, implementation and management of TID programmes. In this athlete-centred approach, there is a dual focus on personal and performance development. We have adapted this model to focus more broadly on mass participation within sporting organisations. The details of the key factors that should be considered within this approach are outlined in **Figure 1**.

Figure 1: Adaptation of Rongen et al.*'s model for an athlete-centred approach for optimisation of sporting organisations*

The model has a dual focus on resources and values important for successful sporting organisations. There is firstly an emphasis on high-quality in terms of staff and facilities, along with support services. Secondly, there is also a clear notion of authenticity and transparency to ensure responsible autonomy and caring relationships. It is important that none of these focus areas are looked at in isolation but are rather seen as an interconnected whole. Optimisation of each of these focus areas and their interactions will lead to successful sporting organisations.

A second shift has been the adaptation of the iceberg model to a sports science context. In particular, this view has been advocated amongst those interested in reducing injury risk in sport (Hulme & Finch, 2015). These authors unpack underlying factors that contribute to injury, considering both the physical and social environment in building an understanding of latent failures. This model moves the focus away from the individual (active failure) to consideration of the role that society, community and organisations (latent failures) play in the development of injuries (Ivarsson *et al.*, 2017). It is our stance that this could and should be extended beyond injury to mass involvement in sport. The lack of participation of an individual could be seen as the active failure, while the complex societal and social factors could be seen as the latent failure. The model presented in **Figure 2** is one adapted from Hanson *et al.*, (2005) and Hulme and Finch (2015) to illustrate latent and active failures for effective mass participation. To create the type of organisation as outlined in the sporting organisation model, it is necessary to understand both physical and social environments at the various levels within the system. For example, beliefs and attitudes at society, community and organisation levels are imperative for defining clear values and expectations and developing caring and authentic relationships. Additionally, economic and educational factors impact the ability to provide high-quality staff and infrastructure. All of these factors interact to either promote participation in sport or act as barriers, blocking easy and effective participation.

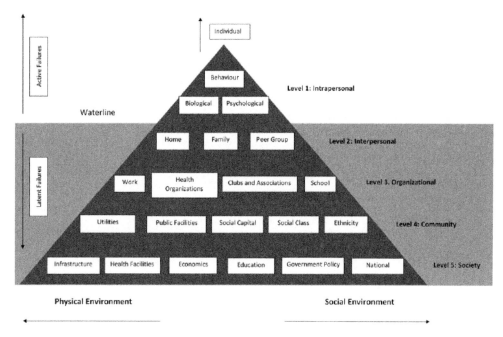

Figure 2: Iceberg model adapted to participation in sport (adapted from Hulme & Finch, 2015)

From these models, it is clear WHAT is needed; however, the more practical component of HOW is not apparent. For example, in financially constrained contexts, the provision of high-quality facilities, expert support services and highly trained people represents a significant challenge. The reality is that research and social innovation in South Africa requires adequate methodologies to guide sporting organisation application, analysis and design. To understand these realties, it is necessary to unpack both active and latent factors within the system, which requires a broader systems thinking perspective (Salmon *et al.*, 2017). It is these factors that are likely to be key hindrances to the identification and development of youth with a passion for involvement in sport.

3. Towards a multidisciplinary approach

The HKE department promotes both a sports science and a human factors and ergonomics (HFE) approach to understanding human performance. This allows for tools and methods from different disciplines to be integrated in efforts to optimise performance and human wellbeing. This is consistent with international calls to apply systems ergonomics to sports science (Salmon, 2017; Hulme *et al.*, 2018). The utility of this approach is in acknowledging the systemic nature of performance. For example, Hulme *et al.*, (2018) recently argued that "adverse events ... are emergent properties that arise from the many decisions, actions and interactions between actors and agents across the entire system [pp. 223]". Acknowledging these emergent characteristics is important in research focused on building strong participation in sport and on long-term sustainability.

A further reason for the appeal of the HFE approach for our research group was the values underpinning the theoretical models (known as sociotechnical systems theory). Read *et al.,* (2018) characterise these values as:

- Humans as assets
- Technology as a tool to assist humans
- Promote quality of life
- Respect for individual differences
- Responsibility to all stakeholders

According to the community engagement and social innovation symposium's (from which this chapter stems) call for papers, "social innovation encompasses creative, community-centred transformations that address societal issues and challenges. The relationships and collaborations which emerge through the processes and products of social innovation all rest, fundamentally, on the level and nature of engagement between and among the different stakeholder groups." It is clear that there are many similarities between sociotechnical systems theory of HFE and social innovation values.

Within a TID context, it is evident that it is inherently multidimensional in nature, with numerous physical, technical, tactical and psychological factors (to name but a few) interacting with each other. The result is a complex and dynamic situation that requires methods that can bring these complexities to light. Systems theory contends that such complex systems cannot be understood by studying components in isolation (Ottino, 2003). Rather, the focus should be on the interactions between the various system elements and on building webs of interacting interventions at all levels in the system. Acknowledging and understanding these characteristics therefore becomes the cornerstone of any attempt to build sustainable and resilient TID programmes.

Beyond the values of HFE and sociotechnical systems theory is the manner in which this approach can be successfully applied. In 2014, Wilson proposed six fundamental notions that promote the optimisation of HFE approaches to system design (**Table 1**). The first two notions emphasise the need to take a holistic systems approach to understanding the next three notions of context, interactions and emergence, while the 6th notion of embedding is the manner through which the first five notions are elucidated.

Notion	Characteristics of the notion
Systems focus	Recognition of the area of focus as a system and providing clear boundaries.
Holism	Recognition that systems should be seen as a whole.
Context	Recognition that performance happens and should be understood in context, typically within a complex sociotechnical context.
Interactions	Recognition of interactions between system parts (human-machine, sociotechnical, joint cognitive systems, etc.). Recognises the interactions between human, technical, information, social, political, economic and organisational components.
Emergence	Recognition of the emergent properties of systems, including those of the human component.
Embedding	Importance of true engagement with the context.

Effective systems analysis requires reliable data on the various components and interactions within the system. While access to documentation may allow for some measure of understanding, it only provides insight into work as imagined, as opposed to completed work. Furthermore, considering the vast networks of stakeholders involved with social innovation initiatives, combined with traditional models of research which encompass short involvement with community partners, it is clear that developing an understanding of the nature of the system is highly challenging. Embedding describes an effective method to engage with people and stakeholders and to develop an understanding of the complex interactions (Wilson, 2014).

We have used concepts from across the two disciplines to interrogate the functioning of talent identification and development programmes within our local community. To do this, it has been necessary to adopt several systems theory tools and methodologies, as highlighted in the next section.

4. Systems theory tools and methodologies

An important component of systems methodology is the use of mental models to build an abstraction of the system being researched. In order to develop a holistic understanding of complex interactions between individuals, social networks and their environments, representations of such systems are necessary. Fundamentally, all models are limited in their abstraction as "[a]ll models are wrong, while some are useful" (Box, 1976, pp. 792). We have used several tools for building a mental model of talent identification and development programmes that have been useful both from a research and practical application perspective. The most versatile and flexible low-cost tool, as indicated by Salmon and colleagues (2017), is that of Cognitive Work Analysis (CWA), which provides a useful methodology for conceptualising and performing system mapping.

4.1   Cognitive Work Analysis (CWA)

CWA is a systems analysis and design framework that has been used extensively within human factors across a number of domains. It has been employed within aviation (Naikar & Sanderson, 2001), road transport (Birrell, Young, Jenkins & Stanton, 2012), health care (Miller, 2004), manufacturing (Higgins, 1998) and football (McLean *et al.*, 2017). The diversity of these areas points to the versatility of the tool, with the formative nature of the method allowing for the analysis of systems from different paradigms. It originates from the RISO National Laboratory in Denmark in the 1970's and 80's, with its primary application within the nuclear power industry. The structured framework allows for the analysis and redesign of complex sociotechnical systems (McLean *et al.*, 2017; Salmon, 2017). In coping with complexity, CWA aims to establish why the system exists, what activities are performed to meet this purpose, how this can be achieved and who can perform these activities. A fundamental feature of the framework is that it is used to determine the constraints imposed on behaviour within the system (McLean *et al.*, 2017). For example, a footballer's movement on the pitch is constrained by the line markings, the physical presence of other players, the rules of the game and the tactics set by the coach. By determining the barriers and affordance present within the system, resulting design recommendations can be explored. Potential benefits of making constraints more explicit to users, removing constraints on behaviour or better exploiting existing constraints to support behaviour allow for increased resilience within the system.

CWA is comprised of five phases, namely 1) work domain analysis (WDA); 2) control task analysis (ConTA); 3) strategies analysis (StrA); 4) social organisation and cooperation analysis (SOCA); and 5) worker competencies analysis (WCA). The purpose of each step is to identify the unique constraints and affordances that exist within the system. The WDA serves to model the system, including the general functions that are performed, while the ConTA models activities and decision-making processes that speak to these functions. StrA describes how activities are and could be performed. The SOCA defines the agents that can perform the various activities, while the WCA notes the cognitive skills required for each task. In essence, each step aims to bring order to the complexity inherent within human related systems. The framework leads the analyst to consider different sets of constraints influencing the way work can be conducted, with a constraint defined as something that limits or controls what you do. Through effective analysis, practitioners can gain insight into the unique characteristics of the systems itself, the tasks that are required, and how workers go about achieving these tasks.

Salmon *et al.*, (2017) notes that during CWA application, it is fundamental that all analyses include a WDA. Additional steps can be included, depending on resources available and the nature of the question posed. For the purposes of this chapter, we will focus on WDA, a vital part of effective system mapping. For further information regarding the additional steps, please see the book entitled "Cognitive Work Analysis: Coping with Complexity" by Jenkins and Colleagues.

4.2   *Work domain analysis (WDA)*

WDA provides an event- and actor-independent description of the system under analysis. As previously mentioned, this is a formative tool, allowing for relevant subject matter experts (SMEs) to engage with the system of which they are a part. The fact that this phase is stakeholder-independent is crucial, since it allows for a certain measure of objectivity, removing personal justifications for work-related tasks under review. The WDA describes the purposes of the system and the constraints imposed on the actions of any actor performing activities within that system. Furthermore, it describes all resources available and their affordances, along with the related functions required to achieve the overall purpose of the system. Through this method, effective system mapping can be achieved, enabling a better understanding of the unique context of the system under review.

To make sense of the systems, the method of an abstraction hierarchy is used. This method provides a platform for conceptualising the various components of the systems and for gaining tangible insight into the affordance of and barriers to performance. The abstraction hierarchy includes five stages, with each level defining different characteristics of the system. These stages include: 1) functional purpose; 2) values and priority measures; 3) purpose-related functions, 4) object-related processes; and 5) physical objects or resources. WDA is typically done using two data collection techniques to develop the map of a system. This includes document review and interviews or work groups with SMEs. When interacting with SMEs, it is vital to view them as what they are: the experts. They are the experts for their systems, and so the role of the practitioner is that of a facilitator, to assist SMEs to develop comprehensive system maps utilising the abstraction hierarchy. Mclean *et al.,* (2017) notes the characteristic of each step within the application area of football:

1. Functional purpose – the overall purposes of the system and the external constraints imposed on its operation. For example, in a football match, these would include achieving the desired result and/or implementing the game plan.

2. Values and priority measures – the criteria that are used for measuring progress towards the functional purposes. For example, in relation to football, this level would include values and measures that a football team uses to determine whether or not it is achieving the functional purposes of a particular match. Example values and measures would include the match score, amount of possession and attempts on goal.

3. Purpose-related functions – the general functions of the system that are necessary for achieving the functional purposes. For example, to attack, defend, transition and maintain possession. These are more generalised in order to categorise the unique system involved.

4. Object-related processes – the functional capabilities and limitations of the physical objects within the system that enable the generalised functions. For example, a player can kick and head the ball, run, communicate and tackle, etc.

5. Physical objects – the physical objects within the system that are used to undertake the generalised functions. For example, the players, the ball, pitch, crowd, referees and coach.

The output from an effective WDA is a detailed description of the system of interest in terms of the constraints influencing behaviour and how the physical objects and the functions they support enable the system to achieve its functional purpose. Importantly, the abstraction hierarchy model uses means-ends relationships to link nodes across the five levels of abstraction. The means-end links show the why-what-how relationship between each of the nodes at different levels (McLean *et al.,* 2017). This method allows for the justification of the inclusion of each node and its relation to the rest of the system. Fundamentally, each system map will be different due to the unique characteristics of the system. However, below (**Figure 3**) is the WDA produced by McLean *et al.,* (2017) of the game of football. This should provide an effective example for how the abstraction hierarchy is utilised, the categorisation of each component and the links between that generate the complex system.

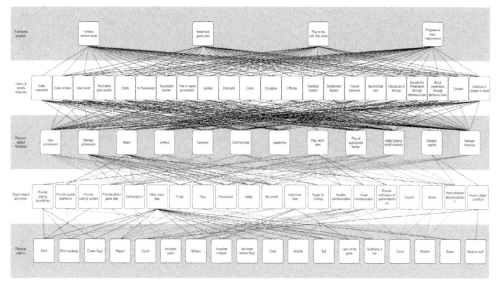

Figure 3: A completed WDA for soccer match play performance, adopted from McLean et al., (2017)

4.3   Tools for successful WDA application

The SMEs are a very important component of WDA as they provide contextual knowledge of the system and therefore provide access to reliable data. Therefore, access to SMEs is vital, again justifying the importance of embedding within systems of interest. Embedding within the system provides two important opportunities for researchers. Firstly, it allows for the identification of key SMEs, and secondly, it enables the building of trust between the researcher and the SME. Within an HFE perspective, this is important as it sheds light on the four archetypes of human work: work as done, work as prescribed, work as imagined and work as disclosed (Shorrock & Williams, 2016). Understanding the differences between these archetypes is vital in building a model of the dynamic interactions within a system.

Following identification of relevant SMEs, the formative process of generating a system map is complex. It is vital to first define system boundaries. A clear and definitive purpose of the analysis is fundamental to successful systems application. Are you analysing the system as it is, or how it could be? Are you identifying the work as prescribed by broader organisational structures, or as is done by workers on the ground? Essentially, defining the scope and system of interest is paramount. With regards to the generation of the WDA, time is a vital constraint. System maps are complex and require a number of iterations and discussion to reach consensus. Thus, numerous sessions are often required to dissect the various components. Furthermore, once the system boundaries are well defined, it is crucial to involve all relevant stakeholders. Multiple perspectives inform a more comprehensive conceptual model, which is important in meeting the fundamental goal of analysis. An understanding of the constraints placed on those within the system allows for the generation of interventions that seek to increase the autonomy and resilience of the system.

5.　Case study: Making an impact – Our journey to community-engaged research

Systems thinking in talent identification and development is particularly important in a country like South Africa with its complex and unjust socio-political history. Such legacies have resulted in significant inequality and poverty gaps, while divides across racial and socioeconomic lines have further impacted social cohesion within our communities. Although infrastructure and financial resources are scarce, it is important to note that we are rich in social capital. Our research experiences have led us to realise that there is distinct passion and enthusiasm within South African communities, where there is a desire to combat the status quo. In order to optimise such social networks and stakeholders, researchers and practitioners must acknowledge and engage with complexity. As noted by Hulme and Finch (2015), performance is impacted by the decisions and actions of all actors across the system, not just athletes at the sharp end. Furthermore, threats to performance are caused by multiple contributing factors, not just a single poor decision or action. Particularly within participation in sport, threats to performance result from a lack of communication and feedback across levels of the system, not just from deficiencies at one level alone.

As the nurturing of sporting talent is inherently multidimensional, and influenced by numerous factors (Till *et al.*, 2015), it is vital that TID is viewed as a complex adaptive system (Johnston *et al.*, 2018). Few studies have met these aims of conceptualising the interactions relevant to the development of elite sporting talent. Furthermore, in a country such as South Africa there have been limited efforts to take such an approach to talent identification and development. Many South African systems are failing and not producing the quality required from TID or actively looking how such programmes should be reimagined to suit the needs of the local context. It is our contention that this is at least partially due to a lack of a systematic approach to athlete development in which TID should see development as an ongoing and never-ending process. This is both consistent with recent developments in literature and our experiences working at a grass roots level.

5.1 Shifting philosophy from journal impact factors to impactful research

The traditional approach taken to research within our department was to strive for high-quality laboratory-based research. Furthermore, our initial focus within the context of talent identification and development was on improving our understanding of soccer performance within a South African context. This involved the identification of gaps in the academic literature, which resulted in research project identification. Through this process, an initial area of interest was in hamstring injuries during intermittent soccer performance. These laboratory-based studies were well received and have been published internationally (Jones, Ryan & Todd, 2015). Key findings were also important, illustrating how ethnicity may be an important consideration in understanding hamstring injury causation and suggesting that using guidelines and training practices developed for European soccer players may be questionable in our own context. This was the start of an important journey for the group into trying to understand the local context in more detail, including working more closely with soccer teams in the Makhanda region.

Although the research was successful according to traditional academic metrics (journal publications in high impact journals), there were several events that occurred around the same time that made us question our traditional wisdom and the approach:

5.1.1. THE CHANGING LANDSCAPE OF SOUTH AFRICAN UNIVERSITIES

There are well documented changes relating to universities' higher echelons promoting the integration of research and community engagement. Furthermore, the Fees Must Fall movement, with a focus on bringing the social injustices of the past to the forefront and questioning the role of academic institutions, had an impact on the mindset of our research group.

5.1.2. INTERNATIONAL TRAVEL

At the same time as the aforementioned changes were happening in the South African academic landscape, we were fortunate enough to be involved with the International Ergonomics Association as part of the executive committee. This resulted in numerous international trips to regions of the world requiring support for development of the profession of ergonomics. Many of these trips were to Latin America and included countries such as Uruguay, Peru, Panama, Colombia and Brazil. Working with academic institutions was an eye-opening experience. For example, in Uruguay the academic institutions have satellites within the poorest communities which are responsible for co-constructing research focus areas based on the problems identified within these communities. This information is fed back to the funding bodies and then promoted as a national research priority. In this manner, the communities that are most vulnerable and in need are supported as a priority for problem solving. This approach was in significant contrast to the manner in which we as a research group had identified problems to research.

5.1.3. WILSON'S NOTIONS OF HFE

The notions published by Wilson (2014) also influenced our thinking, particularly where he poses a fundamental question to the philosophy of research. "It is tempting to be hard-nosed and suggest that any study, investigation, analysis or development which does not take a systems view is, in fact, not E/HF at all. Rather such an initiative should be seen as a sub-set of E/HF, a biomechanical, cognitive psychology or physiology study, and possibly of limited practical value … My own view is that systems ergonomics should be carried out 'in the wild' … That is, laboratory research has its place but not a primary one. [pp.6]"

Considering these factors, when questioning the actual impact of our research at a local level, we were left to reflect uneasily on whether our research was transformative in nature. It was concluded that we had adopted an approach that was too narrow and focused on problems pertinent to the international publishing community, with minimal local relevance. A key realisation for us was the need to 'look outside the ivory tower', and to acknowledge the agency of the community in which we live. Through a series of discussions, meetings and deeper reading of HFE literature we came to a vastly different approach and philosophy to research – entrenched in understanding systemic barriers to performance. It was our view that, to contribute in a meaningful way, it was necessary to shift our research out of the laboratory and into our community, to build relationships focused on co-constructing research needs. Through this process our new aim was: to build towards equity of opportunity for all South Africans, starting with capacity building in our area of expertise in talent identification and development.

5.2 Our journey

After the completion of our laboratory studies and the realisation that we needed to understand more about the local context, we undertook a study to investigate hamstring injury reduction strategies in local players. Many lessons were learnt from this experience in terms of barriers to not only community members but also to research. Although we had already realised the importance of investigating responses of South Africans and that these responses are likely to be different to those of European athletes, we had underestimated the importance of the broader context and its influence on the efficacy of interventions within a sports science framework. The South African context places significant burdens on the local population in terms of access to sufficient housing, employment opportunities, health care, nutrition, education and access to basic utilities. Without engaging the local community in problem identification, the researcher failed to truly 'help' the community. In other words, the reduction of hamstring injuries simply did not feature on the list of priorities for local soccer players. As such there is little invested interest in the research from participants and no long-term benefits were derived out of the intervention.

This resulted in a significant paradigm shift, which is best summarised by the following quote by Lilla Watson: "If you have come here to help me you are wasting your time, but if you have come because your liberation is bound up with mine, then let us work together." It was evident that the participatory approach, a truly engaged mutually beneficial model to community-engaged research, was needed.

5.3 *Embedding to liberate*

Engaging with the local context is a vital part of successful systems theory application. This is done through the process of embedding, as outlined by Wilson (2014). Traditionally, embedding has been viewed as the placement of human factors experts within the organisation that you are working with. However, due to the challenges previously discussed and the lack of organisational design and infrastructure of community-related systems (in our context here we are referring specifically to talent identification and development within soccer), a new paradigm is needed. It is clear that embedding strategies are needed in the unique South African context. Fundamentally, sustainable social innovation involves integrating and building trust with stakeholders.

There were a couple of key lessons that we needed to learn to be able to effectively embed within our community. Firstly, it was imperative to identify all the stakeholders for talent identification and development and then to engage with them to understand their attitudes and motivations. This process allows for the development of areas of common interest and builds trust and sustainable relationships. Secondly, we needed to take a participatory approach as it allows for sharing of knowledge (and the duality thereof) and the building of capacity.

A vital component of this step was acknowledging that the capacity of all stakeholders could and should be developed through the process of engagement. Researchers, students and community partners, through the sharing of knowledge, benefited in having their potential and understanding (i.e. capacity) enhanced. Considering the power dynamics that traditionally exist between tertiary institutions and their communities, the building of trust was fundamental to our approach. Thus, it was necessary to become a component within the system in order to demonstrate dedication to building platforms for effective mass participation in sport.

Growing and developing relationships with community sport stakeholders was crucial. Fortunately, an opportunity presented itself through a community request. A local club, Sakhulutsha FC, was looking for assistance with the training of their players. The researcher initially performed this consultancy individually, travelling to the local club and conducting training three times a week. As new football researchers joined the group, the aim and direction of the research group were discussed with these students who were then integrated into the strength and conditioning programme of the Sakhulutsha senior team. This involved assessment of players, periodisation of training programmes and tactical and technical coaching. In return, related research would be focused on Sakhulutsha players, developing physical profiles in order to better understand the development of youth players. The Sakhulutsha Community Engagement programme was born, with more recent developments being the integration of undergraduate students into the programme, with service-learning strategies the next phase.

Although very positive, an issue with this programme was that it focused on a single team and did not speak to the broader football playing community. The most obvious avenue was the shift towards understanding the organisational side of grassroots football development in Makana. The platform of sporting participation, in this case football, is significantly influenced by those responsible for its governance. Through contacts at Sakhulutsha FC, the original researcher was then nominated to the position of Treasurer of the Makana Local Football Association following support from community partners involved with the Sakhulutsha programme. Additionally, the researcher became involved with the Competitions Committee as secretary.

Engaging with the administrative aspects of local football provided a fantastic opportunity to gain insight into the barriers to effective grassroots football development. Constant interactions with various stakeholders, from club administrators, coaches, players, referees, funders, as well as local government offices such as the Department of Sports, Recreation, Arts and Culture (DSRAC), indicated the complexity of football development and general mass participation in sport. This led researchers to engage with complex systems theory related literature in order to identify appropriate strategies such as those previously discussed. Such analysis methods allow for effective problem identification, as well as system mapping, which are crucial elements to developing an understanding of the various components and making attempts to engage with the emergent properties. Multiple studies within the research group are now aimed at investigating the vast number of factors affecting mass participation in sport. The impact of local organisations such as DSRAC requires broader analysis to understand the system of sport development in Makana. Some of the relevant stakeholders and the related research partnerships have been listed in **Table 2** below. These stakeholders have been categorised according to the framework laid out by Dul, Bruder, Buckle, Carayon, Falzon, Marras, Wilson & van der Doelen (2012), describing system actors, decision makers, influencers and experts.

Table 2: Stakeholders and partnerships associated with the complex systems in the Sport Research Group

Stakeholder	Partnerships
System actors Members of sports clubs, etc.	Players in sports clubs, etc.
System decision makers	Local Football Association administrators and coaches,
System influencers	Department of Sport Recreation and Culture Makana Municipality Eastern Cape Academy of Sport
System experts	HKE department

In order for the talent identification and development programmes within Makana to function effectively, it is necessary that all of the aforementioned stakeholders are engaged. From an HFE perspective we are interested in understanding the interactions between the different elements of the system. TID requires the optimisation of the relationship between all of these stakeholders and the development of common, shared objectives. Currently, we are using the tools of CWA to develop this understanding and to identify constraints and affordances within the system. A crucial component of this process has been the recognition of our community partners as SMEs; as such we become mere facilitators of capacity building.

5.4 Capacity building

Through our experiences, it has become evident that the most significant demand from the local community is assistance with capacity building. Furthermore, we have also seen the tremendous benefit the building of partnerships can have on developing the capacity of students and researchers. Firstly, we gained important practical experience and knowledge of how to do applied participatory research. Secondly, our preconceived ideas about the relationship between science, research and community were challenged. These interactions, and through them a growing understanding and appreciation of diversity, have often resulted in the liberation of students' minds about what it means to be a South African. We believe that this approach is an effective way of producing both students and academics that meet the criteria of being the critical, caring and compassionate citizens Dr Mabizela referred to earlier in this chapter.

We are currently using the model outlined in **Figure 4** to integrate teaching and learning, research and community engagement within our programme.

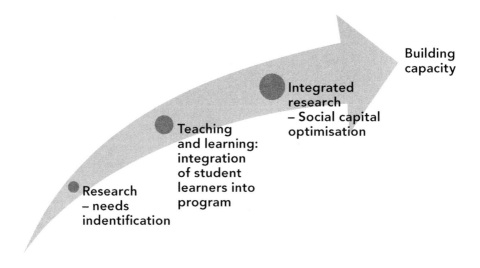

Figure 4: Model of the complex systems in sport research group – the integration of the pillars of academe

The initial focus of the model is on the identification of needs through the participatory approach that identifies both constraints and affordances within the system. Student learners are then integrated into the system to address these needs at both undergraduate and postgraduate levels as part of the service learning structures within the HKE department. Once students have been integrated into the system and trust between the stakeholders has been built, research projects that address the needs are developed. For example, through this approach we are now running several research projects with the local football association that are focused on developing coaching skills and new administration structures to improve the ability of the association to provide local soccer players with high-quality coaching and administrative support

6.   Conclusion

It is clear that tertiary institutions in South Africa must engage with their local communities. To enhance sustainability of such community-engaged initiatives, the systems approach, as described in this chapter, is advocated as an appropriate method with which to develop an understanding of the complex nature of human-centred systems. A fundamental notion is that of embedding, noted as a crucial tool for establishing trust with communities and gaining access to the unique perspectives of SMEs, the community members themselves. Through effective systems analysis utilising CWA, researchers can effectively identity problems through the participatory approach and develop sustainable solutions. The application of systems theory to TID in soccer, as the noted case study, further engages with the complex journey of a research group and the implications for tertiary institutions. A core component is that of liberation for students, researchers and community partners alike through the unification of the pillars of academe.

7.   Acknowledgements

This research has been made possible by the National Research Foundation of South Africa. We also acknowledge the fundamental role of the Human Kinetics and Ergonomics Department, and Rhodes University.

References

Balagué, N., Torrents, C., Hristovski, R. & Kelso, J.A.S. 2017. Sport science integration: An evolutionary synthesis. *European Journal of Sport Science*, 17(1):51-62.

Birrell, S.A., Young, M.S., Jenkins, D.P. & Stanton, N.A. 2012. Cognitive Work Analysis for safe and efficient driving. *Theoretical Issues in Ergonomics Science*, 13(4):430-449.

Box, G.E. 1976. Science and statistics. *Journal of the American Statistical Association*, 71(356):791-799.

Donnelly, J.E., Hillman, C.H., Castelli, D., Etnier, J.L., Lee, S., Tomporowski, P., Lambourne, K., & Szabo-Reed, A.N. 2016. Physical activity, fitness, cognitive function, and academic achievement in children: a systematic review. *Medicine and science in sports and exercise*, 48(6):1197.

Dul, J., Bruder, R., Buckle, P., Carayon, P., Falzon, P., Marras, W.S., Wilson, J.R., & Van der Doelen, B. 2012. A strategy for human factors/ergonomics: developing the discipline and profession. *Ergonomics*, 55(4):377-395.

Hanson, D., Hanson, J., Vardon, P., McFarlane, K., Lloyd, J., Muller, R. & Durrheim, D. 2005. The injury iceberg: An ecological approach to planning sustainable community safety interventions. *Health Promotion Journal of Australia*, 16(1):5-10.

Higgins, P.G. 1998. Extending cognitive work analysis to manufacturing scheduling. In: *Computer Human Interaction* [Conference proceedings]. *Australasian*. IEEE. 236-243.

Hulme, A. & Finch, C.F. 2015. From monocausality to systems thinking: a complementary and alternative conceptual approach for better understanding the development and prevention of sports injury. *Injury epidemiology*, 2(1):31.

Hulme, A., Thompson, J., Plant, K.L., Read, G.J., Mclean, S., Clacy, A., & Salmon, P.M. 2018. Applying systems ergonomics methods in sport: A systematic review. *Applied ergonomics*, 80:214-225.

Humphreys, B.R., McLeod, L., & Ruseski, J.E. 2014. Physical activity and health outcomes: Evidence from Canada. *Health economics*, 23(1):33-54.

Ivarsson, A., Johnson, U., Andersen, M.B., Tranaeus, U., Stenling, A. & Lindwall, M. 2017. Psychosocial factors and sport injuries: Meta-analyses for prediction and prevention. *Sports medicine*, 47(2):353-365.

Jenkins, D.P., Stanton, N.A., Salmon, P.M. & Walker, G.H. 2009. *Cognitive work analysis: coping with complexity.* Surrey: Ashgate Publishing, Ltd.

Johnston, K., Wattie, N., Schorer, J. & Baker, J. 2018. Talent identification in sport: a systematic review. *Sports Medicine*, 48(1): 1-13.

Jones, R. I., Ryan, B. & Todd, A. I. 2015. Muscle fatigue induced by a soccer match-play simulation in amateur Black South African players. *Journal of sports sciences*, 33(12):1305-1311.

Loland, S., 2013. Sport Sciences and ECSS: Approaches and Challenges. Apunts Educación Física y Deportes, 111: 7-14.

Lubans, D., Richards, J., Hillman, C., Faulkner, G., Beauchamp, M., Nilsson, M., Kelly, P., Smith, J., Raine, L., & Biddle, S. 2016. Physical activity for cognitive and mental health in youth: A systematic review of mechanisms. *Pediatrics*, e20161642.

Mabizela, S. 2018, 25 January. Vice Chancellor's Welcome. Available at: https://www.ru.ac.za/admissiongateway/whyrhodes/introducingrhodes/ [Accessed 27 Aug. 2020].

McLean, S., Salmon, P.M., Gorman, A.D., Read, G.J. & Solomon, C. 2017. What's in a game? A systems approach to enhancing performance analysis in football. *PloS one*, 12(2): e0172565.

Miller, A. 2004. A work domain analysis framework for modelling intensive care unit patients. *Cognition, Technology & Work*, 6(4):207-222.

Naikar, N. & Sanderson, P.M. 2001. Evaluating design proposals for complex systems with work domain analysis. *Human Factors*, 43(4):529-542.

Ottino, J.M. 2003. Complex systems. *AIChE Journal*, 49(2):292-299.

Read, G.J., Salmon, P.M., Goode, N. & Lenné, M.G.A. 2018. Sociotechnical design toolkit for bridging the gap between systems-based analyses and system design. *Human Factors and Ergonomics in Manufacturing & Service Industries*, 28(6): 327-341.

Rongen, F., McKenna, J., Cobley, S. & Till, K. 2018. Are youth sport talent identification and development systems necessary and healthy? *Sports medicine-open*, 4(1):18.

Salmon, P.M. 2017. Ergonomics issues in sport and outdoor recreation. *Theoretical Issues in Ergonomics Science*, 18(4): 299-305.

Salmon, P.M., Walker, G.H., M. Read, G.J., Goode, N. & Stanton, N.A. 2017. Fitting methods to paradigms: Are ergonomics methods fit for systems thinking? *Ergonomics*, 60(2):194-205.

Shorrock, S. & Williams, C. 2016. *Human Factors and Ergonomics in Practice: Improving System Performance and Human Well-Being in the Real World*. New York: CRC Press.

Till, K., Cobley, S., O'Hara, J., Morley, D., Chapman, C. & Cooke, C. 2015. Retrospective analysis of anthropometric and fitness characteristics associated with long-term career progression in Rugby League. *Journal of Science and Medicine in Sport*, 18(3):310-314.

Toohey, K., MacMahon, C., Weissensteiner, J., Thomson, A., Auld, C., Beaton, A., Burke, M. and Woolcock, G., 2018. Using transdisciplinary research to examine talent identification and development in sport. *Sport in Society*, 21(2): 356-375.

Watson, L. 1985. 1985 United Nations Decade for Women Conference in Nairobi. Available at: https://en.wikipedia.org/wiki/Lilla_Watson [Accessed 27 Aug. 2020].

Wilson, J.R. 2014. Fundamentals of systems ergonomics/human factors. *Applied ergonomics*, 45(1):5-13.

Chapter 9

Wordless picturebooks and moolas: A case study of a collaborative community engagement project

Adrie Haese, Elmien Claassens, Abigail Mzayidume and Elmarie Costandius

GRAPHIC DESIGN, UNIVERSITY OF JOHANNESBURG; SOCIAL WORK & CRIMINOLOGY, UNIVERSITY OF PRETORIA; FUNANANI TRUST; VISUAL ARTS, STELLENBOSCH UNIVERSITY

ahaese@uj.ac.za;elmien.claassens@up.ac.za; abigail@funanani.com; elmarie@sun.ac.za

1. Introduction

In 2017, the *Dithakga tša Gobala* (Reading Champions) project was launched and hosted at the Funanani Trust Centre in Mamelodi, Tshwane. This community engagement project sought to work with members of the local community to create a series of community-authored wordless picturebooks. The methodology for this project was initially developed as part of a doctoral study. However, the doctorial study was characterised by low participant retention, especially at the Mamelodi research site. As a means to encourage participation, it was decided to link the *Dithakga tša Gobala* project to another community development project started by social workers at the Funanani Trust: the Moola Project.

This chapter describes the development of the *Dithakga tša Gobala* community engagement project from its inception as a doctorial study hosted at Funanani in 2015 to its implementation as a community engagement project linked to the Moola Project. We hope to demonstrate how partnerships and co-production can create sustainable and reciprocal community engagement projects that speak to the more specific needs of the wider community. In particular, we examine a strengths-based perspective to community engagement and emphasise the importance of choice and ownership during the development and implementation of such projects. Further, we aim to highlight the benefits of collaborations between academics and non-governmental organisations (NGOs) and the role that postgraduate courses can play in mobilising community engagement projects.

We start by outlining the background and context of both the inception and the development of the *Dithakga tša Gobala* project, first as a postgraduate study at Stellenbosch University and later as a community development project linked to the Moola Project. The challenges identified in each of these separate projects are discussed with reference to their specific contexts. This is followed by a description of the implementation of the 2017 *Dithakga tša Gobala* project as linked to the Moola Project. Initial findings and a subsequent discussion follow.

2. *Dithakga tša Gobala:* From study to community engagement project

The methodology used for the *Dithakga tša Gabola* project was initially conceptualised as part of a postgraduate study. Below is a brief overview of the doctoral study that led to the development and implementation of the 2017 project. The scope of this chapter does not allow for a detailed discussion of the study, but its development, methodology and main findings are outlined.

2.1 The PhD study

Le Roux's (2017) doctoral study followed from her MPhil study, which investigated the use of wordless picturebooks in joint parent–child reading in a controlled setting at a local pre-primary school in the Kayamandi township, Stellenbosch, South Africa. The study suggested that wordless picturebooks could be used in reading activities that could easily be practiced independently by the participants in their own homes, but that further research was needed to establish this (Le Roux & Costandius, 2013).

South Africa faces the challenge of providing appropriate reading materials to a culturally and linguistically diverse population. The result of the 2016

Progress in International Reading Literacy Study (PIRLS), which indicated that 78% of South African Grade 4 children cannot read for meaning in any language (Spaull, 2017), is indicative of what researchers are referring to as a "national crisis of reading" (Spaull, Van der Berg, Wills, Gustafsson, & Kotz, 2016:24), in terms of which literacy development in South Africa has come under increased scrutiny.

The role of the parent as a child's first educator cannot be underestimated in this regard. Children who are read to often have better cognitive and language skills and do better at reading comprehension when they reach school-going age than children who are not read to (Martorell, Papallia & Feldman, 2014). Yet, the 2016 national survey into the reading and book reading behaviour of adult South Africans (South African Book Development Council, 2016:35) reports that "agreement about reading to children is very low – even amongst households with children". The survey noted that parents need to be empowered to create a reading culture at home. Consequently, joint reading and other cognitively stimulating activities are receiving increased attention.

Reading is a complex and multidimensional activity. The term 'literacy' has broadened from being print-centric, focusing on written text to create meaning, to one that is multimodal and focused on how meaning can be made using multiple modes, of which pictures is one (Mantei & Kervin, 2015). Because they do not contain words, the books can be enjoyed by readers of different literacy levels, from different contexts and in different languages. In a multilingual country such as South Africa, wordless picturebooks can be used by a diversity of readers because they are not dependent on text as a specific language. Only a few academic studies have dealt with the potential of this genre to address the multilingual context of South Africa or its use in parent–child reading locally, specifically in South African families where social and economic challenges exist.

Wordless picturebooks allow for a story to be read by interpreting the images (Beckett, 2012), using speech and language to express thoughts and ideas about the story (Nodelman, 1988) and gestures to point to images. They require very little in terms of translation, as only the title and publisher's peritext is written language and parents are able to tailor their interpretation of the story to be relevant to their child's daily life and context (Le Roux, 2017). Further, it can be argued that wordless picturebooks provide children who have not yet learned to decode written text with an opportunity to experience the enjoyment of reading and storytelling through an accessible medium.

It is from this context that Le Roux's (2017) doctoral studies, with funding from the NRF, focused on the use and creation of wordless picturebooks to foster a love of reading in South African homes. The study shifted the research site from the controlled setting of a preschool centre to participant homes and focused predominantly on participant experience of joint reading activities using wordless picturebooks in the home. The study received ethical clearance from Stellenbosch University's Ethics Committee: Human Research (HUMANIORA).

In addition to the reading programme, the study piloted a methodology for creating wordless picturebooks from content sourced from local communities. The aim was to discover what themes would arise from stories collected from participants if an economically viable model of book creation could be developed using this approach. At the time the study was conducted, very few local wordless picturebooks were available.

Both reading and book creation components of the study were hosted at two of the Funanani Trust's Early Childhood Development (ECD) centres in Mamelodi and Soshanguve. This allowed for the then student researcher to receive support and guidance not only from her supervisor, but also from experts within the organisation and allowed a safe and private meeting area where primary data could be collected.

In addition to data collected on the reading experiences of the participants, the study facilitated the creation of 18 wordless picturebooks that were authored by parents and their children who took part in the project. Parents and children were invited to tell a story in a manner with which they were comfortable (writing, drawing, singing, voice recording, dancing, etc.). The participants chose to illustrate their books and used emergent reading strategies to co-create a story. The parents documented this story, and with the child's original illustrations, this was given to illustrators to interpret and to illustrate into a 12-page wordless picturebook. These prototype wordless picturebooks functioned as a means to investigate how content gathered from local communities could be used in the production of South African wordless picturebooks. These prototype books were by no means completed products, but served as a means to test the proposed methodology for running book creation projects.

The data indicated that the majority of the participants responded positively to the wordless picturebooks. The adult participants' perception of reading as an activity, and of their child as a reader, changed noticeably after the introduction of the wordless picturebooks in their homes. Reading went from being an activity that would often frustrate parents to one that they could enjoy with their children at home, and where both adult and child could participate in the creation of a story. The adult participants reported feeling that their children could understand and actively take part in the reading activity using the wordless picturebooks, as opposed to having to read to their children (Le Roux, 2017).

Themes that emerged from the participant-authored picturebooks dealt predominantly with the children's immediate environments. Very few of the parents added more details to their children's stories, and as such, the illustrated books were very basic, containing little detail. Consequently, the illustrators found it difficult to create an engaging narrative. Illustrators needed to elaborate on the stories by adding visual elements or deciding on key events using the drawings and story provided by the participants as a starting point. The children were also very young, aged between 3 and 6 years old; they could not be expected to produce a narrative that could be used as is, and as such, the narratives were very basic. The findings indicated that story collection workshops may subsequently need to consider including older children and their parents to have more engaging narratives emerge through the process and to allow more time for narrative development. The workshops were described by all participants as being a positive experience and they enjoyed having access to art and craft materials (Le Roux, 2017).

A small number of participants found these books "too easy" compared to the other books used during the reading programme, but all participants expressed a sense of pride when discussing their own books and were impressed that their names appeared on the front cover and that they were the authors of the story. One participant said "We were excited! Am I actually reading a book that my child wrote? It was very exciting!" The pride experienced by participants when receiving a copy of their book was an important aspect of the research. Confidence in reading can be linked with self-confidence and motivation, and the creation of participant-authored books consequently fulfilled another aim: to give people confidence in their own ability to tell stories and create books.

The prototype books were pilot-tested at a third, unrelated research site. Feedback again indicated that the books were very easy to use, but that they were enjoyed by both adult and child readers.

2.2 Problem identification: Participant retention

Although data was collected from 39 participants in total, the reading programme and book creation project were characterised by low participant retention, especially at the Mamelodi research site. Twelve participant pairs, consisting of a parent/primary caregiver and a three- to six-year-old child, volunteered for the project (i.e. a total of 24 participants). Of the 12, six participant pairs attended only the initial focus group discussion and consequently did not take part in the complete reading programme or book creation part of the project. Only two participant pairs attended every session. Participants who missed one session would often make plans to attend the next one and continue with the programme.

However, some of them did not return after missing one session and only returned to collect the printed versions of their own wordless picturebooks. Reasons for non-attendance varied and included illness and work opportunities or responsibilities. In some instances, no reason for non-attendance was volunteered. Only five books were created at the Mamelodi site, compared to 13 at the Soshanguve site.

Lack of parental involvement in projects such as this is a common phenomenon in South Africa. Wessels, Lester and Ward (2016:1) report that structural barriers are often the main reasons for low parent involvement in parenting programmes, reporting that "[w]hile being a parent can be demanding in any context, parents in South Africa typically face a great number of challenges. These challenges relate especially to poverty, which can make parenting in a positive way much more difficult." All research sites included in the doctoral study were based in areas characterised by poverty and high unemployment. It is therefore increasingly important that researchers and community engagement facilitators who work with parents and children understand the context in which participants live and support parents in their role as caregivers.

In terms of understanding the context of non-participation, other underlying issues (such as issues of power, race, class and economic relations) which could play a role in projects like this also need to be considered. The student researcher acknowledged her position as a white woman and the contextual differences that needed to be acknowledged alongside this. Harvey (2013) encourages reflecting on one's own identity as integral to any research. Positions of power are also emphasised by Das (2010), as social science research is based on human interaction. Gottfried (in Das, 2010:5) explains that: "The process of conducting enquiry based on relationships introduces issues of power where the researcher-researched relationship is also guided by larger social structures." South Africa is still troubled by the legacy of apartheid, and, as such, the student researcher's identity as a white person working with black participants needed to be both acknowledged and carefully negotiated. This was another reason why no prescriptions were given to the participants in terms of how or when to use the books, just as no prescriptions were given regarding the stories collected during the workshops.

Respect was the guiding principle for the research, and therefore the creation of the prototype books, which relied wholly on the participants, was an attempt to remove any preconceived ideas about what books to provide in reading programmes. Further, the reliance on research participants to be actively involved in the creation of stories and content is one of the aspects of this study that sought to empower communities through their participation in this project, but the risk of the participants responding in ways that 'please' the researcher, rather than reporting on their true experience, still existed due to the aforementioned contextual factors. Throughout the research, the participants were encouraged to be honest about how they experienced using the wordless picturebooks. Interpreters were made available at all times and the participants' preference in terms of how the project was managed and what language they preferred to speak was respected above anything else.

3. The Moola Project

3.1 The Funanani Trust

The Funanani Trust was founded as a community-based NGO in 1998. Today, the trust operates three centres in the greater Tshwane district of South Africa, through which it sources and coordinates the distribution of resources and programmes that are run from its centres.

The social welfare sector's response to South Africa's transformation to a genuine democracy is embedded in the White Paper for Social Welfare, which was adopted in 1997. The Board of Trustees at the Funanani Trust used the guiding principles outlined in this white paper as a foundation for the activities of each of its centres. These included principles such as people-centred policies, investment in human capital, accessibility and appropriateness of programmes. Through their offering, the trust aims to address the structural inequality that was established by the apartheid history of South Africa.

The trust mobilises volunteers to become involved at grassroots level with children, families and communities in need. The programmes hosted on site are predominantly focused on young children, the youth, their families and the surrounding community. The organisation is guided by the principle belief that by focusing on the child and the family, the community can benefit from these programmes. As such, the organisation centres most of its efforts on programmes that assist, develop and benefit children.

Funanani's Soshanguve and Mamelodi centres are located in impoverished communities in and around Tshwane and focus on orphaned and vulnerable children and their families. Both locations have an ECD centre which provides preschool education to these children at no cost. Children are also provided with a healthy breakfast and lunch every day as well as a morning and afternoon snack. The centre is committed to providing a physically and emotionally safe environment where learners can develop, grow and learn while having fun in order to prepare them to successfully navigate through their primary school years. Further, the trust provides family support services to the families of the children in the programmes (Funanani, 2018).

All the children enrolled at the centres are from homes where one or sometimes both biological parents are absent, deceased or unemployed. A condition of enrolment is that the child is from a 'vulnerable' family that does not have the means to provide preschool education (King, personal communication, May 3, 2016). The families' vulnerability also extends to their financial situation. Their income is generally in the form of grants received from government (Holtzhausen, personal communication, May 3, 2016).

In addition to offering educational programmes, the Funanani Trust also assisted struggling families by providing them with pre-packed food parcels, mainly consisting of donated products such as non-perishable food products, on a monthly basis. Although the products met the basic needs of the service users, there was no room for meeting the individual needs of the community. This well-meant assistance unintentionally gave rise to high levels of dependency and passivity among recipients of the food parcels. As a means to address these unintended consequences, and in line with a developmental approach to social work, the social workers at the organisation developed the Moola Project (Claassens, Holtzhauzen, & Mzayidume, personal communication, March 30, 2016).

3.2   Moola Project: Approach and initial findings

The Moola Project uses developmental social work theories as guiding principles. Although no standard definition of developmental social work exists, Midgley (2010) outlines several common themes that function as the foundation for a systematic conceptual perspective of developmental social work. These are outlined as including "agreements about the importance of facilitating change, the use of strengths, empowerment and capacity enhancement, the notion of self-determination and client participation, and a commitment to equality and social justice" (Midgley, 2010:13). Through a focus on the above-mentioned themes, developmental social work seeks to encourage social change through a focus on the individual, the environment and the interaction between them (Patel, 2015).

Patel (2015:127) further describes the aim of social work in addition to seeking social change as follows:

> ... social work from a developmental perspective aims to balance needs with resources and promotes the optimal use of opportunities presented by the wider social environment and through tapping the assets, strengths and inner resources

within the client groups themselves and the environment. It is concerned less with what people cannot do, but with what they can do.

The Moola Project demonstrates the above-mentioned themes by moving away from deficit centredness and focusing on the inherent strengths of community members, making a shift from 'giving' people resources to empowering them to use their own inherent capacities to meet their needs.

In summary, the Moola Project works on a points-based system. Service users are awarded points, referred to as 'moolas', for participating in activities hosted by Funanani at either of its centres. Activities include, but are not limited to, the following:

- Volunteering at the Funanani ECD centre in Soshanguve and Mamelodi
- Attending group work facilitated by Funanani care workers and student social workers
- Attending any training opportunities provided by Funanani (depending on availability of opportunities)
- Participating in competitions, such as gardening competitions, launched by Funanani care workers, who visit the homes of participants weekly
- Daily attendance of the Funanani ECD centre in Soshanguve and Mamelodi (for participants' children)
- Attending parent meetings at either ECD centre.

To date, some of the training opportunities have included parenting groups with social workers and social work students; financial skills development, including a focus on creating savings; and practical life skills workshops that help partici-pants build the capacity to deal with stressful situations.

The points earned by service users can then be used at the Moola Shop as currency to purchase goods of their choice. Commodities available at the shop include basic non-perishable food items, baby food, toiletries, cleaning materials, clothing, furniture, appliances and so forth. These commodities are all allocated predetermined Moola points, and service users are provided with a printout of all available items in the shop. The system also allows for service users to order any item that is not available on the list or that is too big to be stored at the physical Moola Shop (e.g. furniture and appliances). Service users are also en-couraged to ask Funanani staff about any specific products that they need. Service users who are not able to visit the shop due to medical conditions, dis-tance or frailty are not excluded from this service. They can order according to their needs and the care workers will deliver the order at home.

The Moola Project was implemented in Soshanguve in 2016 and in Mamelodi in 2017. The two communities differ vastly, and, as a result, the two Moola Shops contain different items, which are curated based on input from the service users who help identify their specific needs.

Interviews conducted with service users after the implementation of the Moola Project indicate that it has brought about several evident changes in the community, including a sense of own decision-making power being restored, choices given back to people and the restoration of the worth and dignity of the participants.

Before its implementation, care workers delivered the pre-packed food parcels to service users' homes. This handout system could be seen as disempowering, especially as the recipients had no choice regarding what household items they received. The social workers noticed that there was very little parental involvement at the centres. Very few parents attended parent meetings with the ECD centre staff or took part in group work sessions with social workers or social work students.

Interviews with service users indicated that they preferred being able to choose what products they received, with one service user saying: "I prefer the Moola, because then you can choose what you want. With the Moola it helps us because we come out of the home and meet other people."

The Moola Project allowed for more contact between Funanani staff and community members, which previously mostly took place when food parcels were being delivered. Consequently, parents became more involved at the ECD centres, which also allowed staff and care workers to learn more about the parents and the community and to identify more specific needs with which they could help. One participant noted that it also strengthened her ties with other community members, saying: "I like to volunteer because I meet other women at the centre and we get to share life experiences and encourage each other." Midgley (2010) states that social justice in development social work should reflect the belief that those who receive services from social workers not only have the right to make their own decisions, but also need to benefit from the support and the services received. This approach also recognises the inherent worth and dignity of all people.

The importance of parental involvement at the ECD centres extends beyond the contact with Funanani staff to include fostering feelings of support in their children. Children can see their parents speaking to teachers and staff at the Funanani ECD centres and this may lead to them feeling supported and encouraged at school. Hornby (2011) refers to extensive international research that supports the role that parental involvement may have on improving both academic performance and social outcomes for children.

From this perspective, the Moola Project tries to break down some of the barriers that often lead to lack of parental involvement within school environments. Barriers – including parents' current context, their beliefs in terms of parental involvement and class, race or gender (Hornby, 2011) – can be broken down by creating accessible programmes that parents could choose from, learn skills from and also benefit from in terms of being able to use the moolas earned to provide for their families. One service user said: "The Moola Project has made me feel valuable in my family as I can also contribute."

As an example, service users who took part in a group work session stated that they struggled to feed their children during the school holidays when they did not receive breakfast or lunch from the ECD centre. Together, the service users shared ideas and came up with a menu that each household could use to cook meals for their families, using their Moola points, items available from the Moola Shop and their social grants.

The training opportunities, group work and projects offered by the Funanani Trust as part of the Moola Project aim to forge partnerships with parents that go beyond simply meeting the statutory requirements set out by government policies. They also aim to provide parents with training and skills development opportunities that will allow them to be more involved in their children's education, to build self-confidence and self-esteem and to generate coping mechanisms to deal with the contextual problems that they face on a daily basis. They furthermore aspire to foster economic inclusion by giving service users a means to purchase goods and services of their choice and to have confidence in their earning capabilities after their children leave the ECD centre for primary school.

4.   Implementation of the *Dithakga tša Gobala* project

In 2017, the *Dithakga tša Gobala* project was launched with the aim of working with members of the Mamelodi community to create six community-authored wordless picturebooks. Due to the relationship that had been developed during the doctorial study, Funanani was again approached as a site from which to run the community engagement project. However, based on the previous project run at the site, there were obvious concerns about participant retention at the Mamelodi centre, where the project would be based. Project sponsors were aware that contextual factors often play a role in the outcomes of community engagement projects, but as community participation formed an integral part of the project, participant retention became a major part of the project planning.

Although the project involved the creation of a product in the form of a wordless picturebook that would be given to the participants at the end of the project, it could not be assumed that that alone would be enough to motivate the participants to complete the project. Initial interviews with volunteers indicated that the majority neither read often at home nor owned any books. The majority indicated that their parents did not read with them when they were growing up. The Bible and magazines were the only reading materials that were consistently available in their homes, and the volunteers reported that they generally did not have reading materials for their children in their homes unless an older, school-going child brought books home from school. Many of the volunteers did not read with their preschool children, and those who did stated that it was difficult to get their younger children to concentrate on reading, one stating that they would not read: "[u]nless you [the parent] promise them something. If you promise them, then they will do it". Another said: "I have to be serious, take her, put her, and be serious about reading. It makes it difficult – you have to tell her, 'now we need to read.'"

For one participant in particular, reading had not been a positive experience growing up. She explained as follows:

> It was difficult for me, when like the teachers would say, come and stand in front and read for us. So when, I enjoyed to take a book … but it was difficult for me to say some words and I was afraid. … It was very painful. And so I try to read with my child because I don't want him to [go through the same thing].

When considering the reading history and context of the volunteers, it can be argued that it might have been difficult for them to imagine what their own books would look like, and it could not be assumed that the production of a book was necessarily a motivating factor in itself.

As a means to encourage participant retention, the *Dithakga tša Gobala* project was positioned as a programme offering linked to the Moola Project, which, as previously explained, had been implemented at the Mamelodi centre in the beginning of 2017, as shown in **Figure 1**. Parents who volunteered for the project would receive Moola points for each session that they attended. The project ran from April to November 2017.

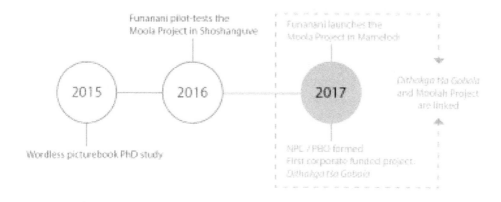

Figure 1: A timeline of the development of each project before the collaboration in 2017

4.1 Methodology

Instead of circulating existing wordless picturebooks, of which there are very few available, the project aimed to give communities ownership of the reading materials that would be circulated in their community. This was done by sourcing the content for the books from the community itself. The collaboration between the Moola and book creation projects aimed to engage service users as partners in the development of reading material that could be enjoyed at home by the service users and other parents with their children. In this way, the service users would be active decision makers in terms of the books they made.

An introduction served to inform the community members of the project and to recruit volunteers. It was explained that project participation was linked to the Moola Project and that participants would receive Moola points for every session attended. Six community members volunteered for the project and together decided on *Dithakga tša Gobala*, which is Sepedi for Reading Champions, as a project name. The main aims of the project were identified as fostering a culture of reading in their community and sharing stories so that other parents could enjoy reading with their children. The project made of use of a participatory design approach. According to Collin and Swist (2016), Participatory Design [PD] underlines stakeholders' knowledge, rights to representation and determination over what is designed. Importantly, the stakeholders they refer to can include the future users of an intervention, rather than only researchers or designers. Knowledge in PD is produced through a process of mutual learning that takes place between all participants. Kolko (2012:104) defines PD as: "… a broad label for creative activities that are done with end users—where designers act as facilitators or visual translators …"

This type of approach allowed the volunteers to direct the project and to give feedback and input regarding the development of the final product. The approach also created a space for the volunteers to share stories in a manner with which they were comfortable. In this way, the project aimed to harness the volunteers' strengths, knowledge and skills in the creation of books that could be used in their immediate community. The participants actively decided on the days they would meet and on the format the meetings would take.

The *Dithakga tša Gobala* did not go through any formal ethical clearance procedures, as it was implemented outside of the university context as a follow-up of the PhD study. However, the same ethical principles that governed Le Roux's PhD study were followed, and all forms were developed with the assistance of social workers based at Funanani. Participation in this project was voluntary, and the participants were free to withdraw from the project at any time, with no negative consequences. Informed consent was given by all the participants, and children and their parents were required to sign assent forms. Because the books were made available publicly, the participants could choose to have their names appear on the cover and copyright information of the book, or they could choose to remain anonymous authors.

Where participant names would appear on the books, responses in any reports were coded to keep individual answers, opinions and feedback confidential. The participants were all aware that reports on the project would be written and gave consent for their responses to be used. Prior to the project, the participants all signed contributor agreement forms, which allowed the books to be licensed under a Creative Commons Attribution 4.0 Licence (Creative Commons, 2018). This allows anyone to share the books in any format and to adapt the content of the books for any purpose. All participants were made aware of the implications of this, and agreed that their stories, concepts and illustrations may be used in this manner.

In order to collect stories from the participants, two story collection workshops were hosted on site at Funanani. These workshops allowed the six participants to work with their children, younger siblings or nephews/nieces to create and document a story. The children were between the ages of three and six years old and enrolled at the Funanani ECD centre. Participants could choose how they wanted to document their story, and a variety of materials was provided for them to do so. All participants used drawing and writing as a primary means of documentation (**Figure 2**), while voice recordings, photographs and video recordings were used as secondary means of documentation, depending on participant preference.

Data collected from the workshops were scanned and transcribed and sent to six South African illustrators. They used this data as the starting point for the illustration of 16-page wordless picturebooks. Three final-year illustration students and three working illustrators illustrated the books for the project. Data from the workshops ranged from being very specific about the details of the story and its representation to being very open to interpretation.

Figure 2: An example of visual reference material sent to illustrators

In order to ensure that the participants felt that they could give their honest opinion on the visual interpretation of their story, they provided feedback on the illustrations through the facilitators (the project manager and the social worker on site). The participants were given the opportunity to provide feedback on the illustration drafts (**Figure 3**) and the final illustrations before the books went to print.

Figure 3: Example of participant drawing and the illustrator's interpretation in the draft, followed by the final illustration

By the end of the project, six community-authored wordless picturebooks were produced. All books were given an ISBN for the printed and e-book versions, which were registered with the National Library of South Africa. In this way, the ownership of the books (and the project) remains with the participants.

4.2 Distribution

The project participants were each given a set of 10 copies of each book (60 books in total) to distribute in their communities in a manner that they preferred. They reported giving their set of books to under-resourced crèches and day care centres in Mamelodi, or donating them to the school that their older children attended. Over 3 000 printed copies of the books were circulated to the concept authors, the ECD centre and Grade R classes at Funanani and to other reading organisations, schools and not-for-profit organisations that work with children. Positive reaction to the material was received from the majority of the beneficiaries, and data on how the books have been used will be collected throughout 2018.

The licensing of the books allowed for the books to be used beyond the scope of the project. Print files were made available to several organisations, who have started creating their own content using the illustrations. Two of the books were used as newspaper or magazine 'pull-out books' which readers can cut out and assemble by themselves. Illustrations were also appropriated by the South Africa Sign Language Material Development Unit in the Department of General Linguistics at Stellenbosch University.

5. Findings and discussion

It should be noted that findings discussed in this section pertain only to the *Dithakga tša Gobala* project and not to the earlier mentioned PhD study. The initial findings indicate that the collaboration with the Moola Project made a diffe-rence in participation, attendance and motivation in the book creation project. All six participants who volunteered for the project as well as their children attended the majority of the sessions. In cases where a participant could not attend, other arrangements were made, for example sending the rough illustration work home with the child participant and then conducting feedback sessions telephonically.

This was an important distinction between the PhD study and the *Dithakga tša Gobala* project. Whereas some participants in the PhD study simply did not arrive for a session, *Dithakga tša Gobala* participants who were unable to attend a session informed the facilitator, social worker or another participant as such, rather than simply not attending.

The participants took ownership of the project, deciding on the name, out-comes and organisation of the project. Feedback from interviews conducted after the completion of the project indicated that the project provided the partici-pants with a sense of empowerment and raised their sense of self-worth. Quotes such as: "It gave me an opportunity to show to other people that I have a potential to do something which I didn't know that I can do", "I experienced something that I did not know I can do" and "I am proud of myself now, I can tell people that I have a book and that I can do something" are evidence of the positive impact that the project had on the participants' self-concept.

The methodology used allowed for the participants to actively decide on the days they would meet and what format the meetings would take, which may have allowed for the participants to have more control and power over the project. The context in which the participants live is complex, characterised by difficulties that extend beyond their economic status to include underlying issues of power, race, class and economic relations, and may play a bigger role than is often antici-pated. The reasons for high or low participant retention could be very straight-forward, such as employment opportunities and responsibilities or transport, but could also extend to include feelings of, for instance, disempowerment or incapa-citation. By focusing on active participation in decision-making processes during the project, it was hoped that we would discourage feelings of disempower-ment that can be caused when participants are passive recipients of a process or product. We aimed to engage with the community as partners and active decision makers in both product and process.

Dithakga tša Gobala project participants reported that they felt as if they could make decisions about their own books. During feedback sessions, some participants added personal touches to their story, for example adding their child's favourite toy to a scene, or requesting that something from their immediate context be included. One parent described her involvement in the illustrations in the book:

> I changed a few things before [the book] went to final print, I had a chance to go through what was there already – I got a chance to say "Why can't we do things this way?" … I had a chance to say something about how I think the book should be like.

One participant made major changes to the illustrations, indicating that she felt the illustrations were not relevant to her community or could be misunder-stood. She explained that she did not feel she would be able to tell her children enough about a scene depicting space travel, and that she would prefer to see illustrations that were more relevant to her context and that she could talk to her children about.

The collaboration with illustrators proved to be successful, and the parents were able to follow the progression of their book during feedback sessions. After receiving printed copies of their completed books (**Figure 4**), one parent said: "[The illustrations are] too much [nice]! It was nice, even though I didn't know I can make something like that, but the illustrators, they make it perfect." Another said that the illustrations and the books as a whole were: "even more than I expected". The feedback sessions proved to be valuable to both participants and illustrators, both parties noting that it was a learning experience for them. This is typical of the participation design process, which emphasises mutual learning between designers and users (Simonsen & Robertson, 2013).

All participants felt that the project should be continued, and the feedback suggested that they had a vested interest in seeing it continue. This is also evident in the participation of 2018's project, with four of the six participants acting as project mentors to new project participants, even though their children are no longer enrolled in the Funanani ECD centre.

Figure 4: Example of a completed wordless picturebook from the project, Serepana

Feedback was collected from the wider community by sending a set of books and a questionnaire with open-ended questions home with children from the ECD centre who reside in the Mamelodi community. The forms included questions pertaining to the experience of reading the books at home. Although only 13 of the 38 forms were returned, feedback from these indicated that the books were well received and enjoyed. Most of the positive feedback on the books were linked to educational outcomes. Quotes such as: "to teach my baby to learn more" and "they are educating our kids" were frequent. The opportunity for children to use their imagination was also emphasised, with one respondent noting that she liked that fact that "children can use their imagination without being told that they are wrong, because the books have no words". The books offered a safe, enjoyable and non-threatening reading experience for participants of different literacy levels and diverse language groups.

The feedback forms also indicated that parents who had children in the ECD class but did not take part in the project felt that the concept authors needed to be supported and the book creation project continued. Future feedback is planned and will take place in the form of interviews conducted by care workers from the Funanani Trust.

6. Conclusion

The *Dithakga tša Gobala* project continued in 2018. Participants from the previous year have taken up roles as mentors to new project volunteers and have decided on ways in which to carry the project forward. The project is again linked with the Moola Project, and to date (30 July 2018), the project has resulted in four new books created at the Mamelodi centre. More data on continuing participation and the medium- and long-term effects of the intervention, in terms of the project itself and the books created, will need to be collected before it can be established whether the projects, on their own and as a collaboration, have a lasting impact on service users at the Funanani Trust. Both the product of this project (the wordless picturebooks) and the process should undergo continued scrutiny and investigation with the community as active participants in decisions made on project structure and implementation.

We believe that the development of the *Dithakga tša Gobala* project demonstrates how public universities can mobilise the development of ongoing community engagement projects by encouraging responsible research within local communities. The methodologies encouraged specifically by the supervisors at Stellenbosch University required that, even after the study was completed, the student researcher followed up on the findings and responded to the feedback and findings of her doctoral study. In this way, the practical component of the degree served to foster a relationship between the institution, the student and the NGO (Funanani), and it can be argued that relationships such as these enable stakeholders to create interventions and devise projects that include and benefit the community. Perhaps the Moola Project could investigate how they, by giving service users a choice of projects in which to participate, might allow for the community to develop projects and interventions that address their direct needs, rather than interventions coming from outside the community.

The methodology developed through this cooperation also allows for its continuing contribution in the space of higher education, specifically with the inclusion of student illustrators in the project. The methodology is also currently being used and adapted by an MA Art Education student at Stellenbosch University, with the project scope being extended to include members of the Kayamandi community. This allows for stories to be sourced and books to be created beyond the scope of what the *Dithakga tša Gobala* project and its associated not-for-profit company could achieve on their own. The project as such also demonstrates how studies conducted with the support of NGOs and universities can collaborate in the development of resources and methodologies for university students.

The project has benefitted the immediate community through making resources for reading available to families that make use of services at the Funanani Trust, other day care centres in the area and other, unrelated projects.

The authors believe that this collaborative project demonstrates how partnership and co-production between not-for-profit organisations, HEIs and local communities can create sustainable and reciprocal community engagement that functions to the benefit of more specific needs of the wider community. The learning that took place for the student researcher during the development of the *Dithakga tša Gobala* project was valuable because it emphasised reflection on the role of the researcher and, later, on the facilitator of community engagement projects. The study, which encouraged the student to consider and reflect on input and feedback from the research participants and their community, the research supervisors and experts and professionals in NGOs, allowed for the development of a collaborative approach not only to research, but also to the further development and implementation of the methodology in collaboration with others. This learning shaped the central approach used for the *Dithakga tša Gobala* project.

7.   Acknowledgements

The authors gratefully acknowledge funding for the PhD study received from the NRF and funding for the *Dithakga tša Gobala* project received from corporate sponsors Vodacom, the Vodacom Blue Bulls, Puma, AFGRI and United Litho Printing.

References

Beckett, S.L. 2012. *Crossover Picturebooks: A genre for all ages.* London: Routledge.

Claassens, E., Holtzhauzen, M. & Mzayidume, A. Personal communication, March 30, 2016.

Collin, P. & Swist, T. 2016. From products to publics? The potential of participatory design for research on youth, safety and well-being. *Journal of Youth Studies,* 19(3):305-318. doi:10.1080/13676261.2015.1098774

Creative Commons. 2018. *Attribution 4.0 International (CC BY 4.0).* https://creativecommons.org/licenses/by/4.0/. [Accessed 23 July 2018].

Das, C. 2010. *Considering ethics and power relations in a qualitative study exploring experiences of divorce among British-Indian adult children.* COMCAD working paper no. 76. Bielefeld: COMCAD.

Funanani. 2018. www.funanani.com [Accessed July 23 2018].

Harvey, J. 2013. Footprints in the field: Researcher identity in social research. *Methodological Innovations Online,* 8(1):86-98. doi:10.4256/mio.2013.0006

Holtzhausen, M. 2016. Personal communication. 3 May, Pretoria.

Hornby, G. 2011. *Parental involvement in childhood education: Building effective school-family partnerships.* New York, NY: Springer.

King, M. 2016. Personal communication. 3 May, Pretoria.

Kolko, J. 2012. *Wicked problems: Problems worth solving.* Austin, TX: AC4D.

Le Roux, A. 2017. *An exploration of the potential of wordless picturebooks to encourage parent-child reading in the South African context* (Doctoral thesis). Stellenbosch University, Stellenbosch. http://hdl.handle.net/10907/1282 [Accessed 20 June 2018].

Le Roux, A. & Costandius, E. 2013. Wordless picture books in parent-child reading in a South African context. *Acta Academica,* 45(2):27-58.

Mantei, J. & Kervin, L. 2015. Examining the interpretations children share from their reading of an almost wordless picture book during independent reading time. *Australian Journal of Language and Literacy,* 38(3):183-192.

Midgley, J. 2010. The theory and practice of developmental social work. In: J. Midgley & A. Conley (eds). *Social work and social development: Theories and skills for developmental social work,* 3-29. New York, NY: Oxford University Press.

Martorell, G., Papallia, D.E. & Feldman, R.D. 2014. *A child's world: Infancy through adolescence* (13th edition). Dubuque, IA: McGraw-Hill.

Nodelman, P. 1988. *Words about pictures: The narrative art of children's picture books.* Georgia: University of Georgia Press.

Patel, L. 2015. *Social welfare and social development* (second edition). Midrand: Oxford University Press.

Simonsen, J. & Robertson T. 2013. Participatory design: An introduction. In: T. Robertson & J. Simonsen (eds). *Routledge international handbook of participatory design,* 1-17. New York: Routledge.

South African Book Development Council. 2016. *National survey into the reading and book reading behaviour of adult South Africans.* http://sabookcouncil.co.za/wp-content/uploads/Final-Report-NRS-2016.pdf [Accessed 23 July 2018].

Spaull, N. 2017. *The unfolding reading crisis: The new PIRLS 2016 results.* https://nicspaull.com/2017/12/05/the-unfolding-reading-crisis-the-new-pirls-2016-results/ [Accessed 9 July 2018].

Spaull, N., Van der Berg, S., Wills, G., Gustafsson, M, & Kotz, J. 2016. *Laying firm foundations: Getting reading right.* Final report to the ZENEX Foundation on Poor Student Performance in Foundation Phase Literacy and Numeracy. Stellenbosch: ZENEX Foundation.

Wessels, I., Lester, S. & Ward, C.L. 2016. *Engagement in parenting programmes: Exploring facilitators of and barriers to participation. Institute for security studies policy brief 82.* [PDF]. https://www.issafrica.org/uploads/PolicyBrief82.pdf [Accessed 27 July 2018].

Chapter 10

Telling stories about stories: Towards ethical guidelines for HE in digital storytelling

Daniela Gachago, Jacqui Scheepers and Candice Livingston

CAPE PENINSULA UNIVERSITY OF TECHNOLOGY

gachagod@gmail.com; scheepersj@cput.ac.za;
livingstonc@cput.ac.za

1.   Introduction

Originating from community work, digital storytelling (DST) has been embraced in educational settings because of its potential to empower students through personal reflection, growth and the development of new literacies. The founding father of DST, Joe Lambert, states that this genre has made it "into every corner of higher education" (2017:vi). Digital storytelling has also carved a niche for itself as a qualitative research methodology (Haigh, 2017), mostly in health sciences/ health education (Haigh, 2017; Gubrium, Hill & Flicker, 2014; Hill, 2014; Hardy, 2017). Increasingly other disciplines are adopting DST research methodologies as well, such as teacher education, where our own research resides (Condy, Chigona, Gachago & Ivala, 2012; Gachago, Ivala, Condy & Chigona, 2013; Gachago, 2015; Stewart & Ivala, 2017; Thomson Long & Hall, 2017; Livingston, 2014).

Digital storytelling is rooted in the rich history of oral narratives. Storytelling, a genre that transcends all disciplines, can be used to engage participants from all walks of life and often relies on a personal history story that is shared orally. The universalising nature of storytelling allows for the understanding of many different contexts (Van Luyn, 2011). Jessee (2011) notes that oral storytelling has the potential to humanise history and that the narratives of ordinary people have generally been absent from the tomes of history. The StoryCenter[1] (former Center for Digital Story) set out do exactly that: to help make stories that are usually not heard accessible to a wider audience. Introducing DST at our institution has improved digital literacies and student engagement, provided a space for critical reflection and enhanced multicultural learning and an engagement across difference.

Through digital media and a carefully facilitated storytelling and production process, the telling of these unheard stories empower ordinary people to share what is important to them (Lambert, 2013). Their focus on usually unheard/unshared stories means that many of these stories have sensitive content that can render the storyteller vulnerable. Although literature agrees that the positive aspects of collecting these previously marginalised/misrepresented (digital) stories can only be of benefit to the greater population, there are inherent ethical dangers in collecting these stories, especially if they depict trauma. Adopting this emotional and process-orientated practice into an educational context, with its constraints of course objectives, assessment regimes, timetables and large classes, raises ethical concerns. What support and follow-up mechanisms exist to help students cope with an emotional fallout? Is it ethical to assign marks to these stories? How well equipped are educators to handle strong emotions and difficult dialogues in the classroom? How would one go about writing about the digital stories collected? How would it be possible to follow the rigid ethical guidelines as stipulated in "research with sentient beings" (Mandal, Acharya & Parija, 2011:n.p.) in a process that is designed to elicit discomfort? How is it possible to adhere to the stringent rules regarding the anonymisation of data in a practice that is inherently transparent?

This chapter addresses these questions under a broader discussion of our experiences working with DST within the three different prongs of HE. Building on previous work done at our institution (Livingston, 2014; Gachago, 2015; Gachago & Sykes, 2017; Stewart & Ivala, 2017), we will reflect on our own DST practices in teaching and learning, research and community engagement. Through our own stories of ethical dilemmas we have encountered in our practice, we will show the complexities academics, researchers and practitioners adopting DST will have to face and negotiate in teaching and learning, research and community engagement. We write to invite practitioners to consider DST and the ethical dilemmas confronted in its practice, hoping that this chapter will initiate a wider discussion on their ethics of practice. As such, it, like much of this volume, considers, but

---

1   www.storycentre.org

does not necessarily conclusively provide, answers to the questions it raises. Answers, in such early phases of exploration into a field, must come from the discussions it stimulates.

There is a growing interest in these issues, and the urgency to move towards an ethical practice of DST in HE is felt. Some of us were also part of the 2017 Untold[2] conference, which featured a stream on ethics across various DST contexts, including HE, and influenced much of our thinking in this chapter. Although the StoryCenter and their close collaborators such as Silence Speaks[3], PatientVoices[4] or The Silver Stories Partnership[5] (an EU lifelong learning programme) have put together guidelines for ethics in digital storytelling, this is an area that is currently under-researched, specifically in HE. Some universities internationally, like the University of Wollongong[6] (Australia), the University of Toronto[7] (Canada) and the University of Brighton[8] (United Kingdom) have placed caveats on their websites regarding ethical behaviour in digital storytelling. There is not much evidence, however, that other universities are actively seeking to publish specific guidelines in this arena. A recently published anthology on DST in higher education features only one chapter on the ethics of DST in HE, although some chapters do refer to ethical challenges when introducing DST into teaching, research or community engagement (Jamissen, Hardy, Nordkvelle & Pleasants, 2017).

2.   HE institutions engagement with the ethics of digital storytelling

The StoryCenter,[9] under the leadership of Joe Lambert, is dedicated to the telling and collecting of stories and propagates the use of DST in particular. This organisation has been instrumental in rethinking the generalised ethics that have been transferred from the realm of historical oral storytelling and participatory media production, in order to create guidelines for DST. The change of name from the Center for Digital Storytelling to StoryCenter also indicates a heightened awareness of the sensitivity of engaging with personal stories and aims to be more inclusive and ethical in its dealings with participants. The

2   https://www.uel.ac.uk/events/2017/07/unconference-digital-storytelling
3   https://www.storycenter.org/silence-speaks/
4   https://www.patientvoices.org.uk/
5   http://arts.brighton.ac.uk/projects/silver-stories/silver-stories-home
6   https://uow.libguides.com/c.php?g=622444&p=4335982
7   http://www.newcollege.utoronto.ca/event/new-media-digital-storytelling-in-the-classroom/
8   http://arts.brighton.ac.uk/__data/assets/pdf_file/0005/196448/SS-Guide-2015.pdf
9   https://www.storycenter.org/

StoryCenter places the wellbeing of the storyteller at the heart of its ethical processes and stresses the importance of ongoing consent (StoryCenter, 2018). One of the unique ethical issues, related to storytelling, that is addressed by the StoryCenter relates to the issues of ethical knowledge production and owner- ship and the concerns related to the ethical dissemination of digital stories[10]. This is of particular interest to the DST arena, as the idea of "digital afterlife" (Ban & Nagy, 2016:57) may raise moral and ethical questions as to whether or not a researcher may or may not use 'the other's' story, in an ongoing research cycle, so organisations often negotiate 'right of use agreements' rather than copyright agreements (Concordia University, 2018). A further ethical aspect that is high- lighted by the StoryCenter is that of cultural sensitivity and the need for con- textual awareness, not only in the recruitment of storytellers, but in the manner in which they are treated. An additional stress is placed on the fact that ethical engagement is an ongoing process and cannot be seen as a 'once-off' pheno- mena of gaining consent.[11]

An arena which has seen a flood of work related to situated ethical practice is that of the public health sector, particularly in relation to DST. This is highlighted by the work of Gubrium, Hill and Flicker (2014: 1606) who conducted a meta- analysis of several DST projects in public health and highlight what they call "moments of ethical debate and tension" specific to the public health sector, which were encapsulated in the ethical conundrums of fuzzy boundaries, recruit- ment and consent to participate, power of shaping, representation and harm, confidentiality and release of materials; issues which have also been identified by the StoryCenter. Amy Hill (2014), also working in the public health sector, slightly amended the StoryCenter's bill of rights to reflect the even more sensitive context in which she and her organisation, Silence Speaks, operates.[12]

With DST being embraced across HE, institutional committees, mostly from the US, UK and Australia, have been formed to draw up guidelines on an ethical practice of DST. However, from our literature review, we have learned that these ethical guidelines often draw from two specific disciplines, i.e. oral history or photography, tend to engage only certain ethical aspects of DST and are not as holistically concerned about the wellbeing of the storyteller, as for example the StoryCenter.

---

10 https://static1.squarespace.com/static/55368c08e4b0d419e1c011f7/t/579134a05016e13d
    de264720/1469133984611/Ethics.pdf
11 For a full list of principles of an ethical DST practice and the storytellers' bill of rights see
    https://static1.squarespace.com/static/55368c08e4b0d419e1c011f7/t/
    579134a05016e13dde264720/1469133984611/Ethics.pdf
12 https://www.storycenter.org/silence-speaks/

Universities like Concordia University and the University of Cambridge[13] and organisations like the Oral History Society[14] that collect oral histories have long known about the ethical dilemmas and dangers inherent in collecting personal stories, and were the first to put situated ethical practices in place. The predominant ethical guidelines related to storytelling, in both the oral and digital forms, have grown from the lessons learned in history departments at universities. Concordia University (2018:n.p.), for one, acknowledges that ethics lie at the "heart of oral history theory". At the heart of ethical behaviour in collecting oral histories is informed consent, mitigation of harm and the right to withdrawal (Concordia University, 2018). Specific interviewer behaviours, such as dealing with cultural sensitivities and responding to emotional reactions by storytellers, have also been targeted for ethical discussions.

DST has diverged from oral histories' concerns around ethical issues regarding the images used in digital stories. Universities concerned with these issues follow the guidelines of organisations such as the National Press Photographers Association[15] around the ethical use and taking of photographs. Images are powerful, and part of the ethical practice needed in DST is to acknowledge that visuals are not 'neutral', and inherent power dynamics between the 'photographer' and the 'photographed' need to be addressed. It is also important that ethical behaviour is adhered to with regards to the use of downloaded images from the internet. Prager (2017) has compiled a guide to navigating the sensitive arena of copyright with regard to the use of internet images. These guidelines include explanations of copyright and fair use and outline when you can use an image that has been downloaded from the internet. There are also suggestions on how to create your own images and how to use free images.

Other unique aspects in the genre of DST that make an additional engagement with ethical processes necessary, concern the sharing of digital stories online and the potential trauma that DST can cause. With the introduction of participatory storytelling projects and the online dissemination of stories on platforms like YouTube, the situated practice of ethical DST has to be modified to fit the demands of these forums. The generalised ideas of consent, harm and the right of withdrawal have remained as pillars of good ethical practice, but issues regarding the dissemination of stories, copyright and the potential risk for participants are concerns that have come to the fore and need to be properly

13 https://www.hist.cam.ac.uk/graduate-students/phd-years-2-4-handbook/oral-history-guidelines
14 http://www.ohs.org.uk/journal/
15 https://nppa.org/code-ethics

addressed. The following section discusses some of the assumptions on which the StoryCenter DST model is based, and this center's guidelines of ethical practice, which are not necessarily applicable to a HE context. Furthermore, we will address gaps we recognise in the current guidelines for ethical practice in HE. This section is split into three parts (1. teaching and learning; 2. research; and 3. community engagement), and each part is preceded by an example of an ethical dilemma from our own practice – although some of the issues highlighted cut across all three areas of practice.

3. General assumptions about DST and how practices differ in HE

3.1 DST in teaching and learning in HE

Snapshot 1 (Daniela): I sit in a story circle with five students. We have heard a number of painful stories. Students have opened up, surprising me with their honesty and willingness to share. There were tears; we had to stop at various points to allow students to compose themselves. Students have hugged, shared tissues and listened intently. So far, the group has managed to support each other, to contain the pain. The last student is a young white woman. Her story stays on the surface. I try and push her, ask probing questions, trying to help her dig deeper. Still she resists. Suddenly she bursts out in tears and leaves the classroom. I don't know where she has gone. She doesn't come back to any of the workshops. Through the grapevine I hear that she has complained to the department head, arguing that such personal projects shouldn't be part of the curriculum. I worry about her. What if she cannot complete the assignment? What if she won't be able to finish the course because of this project? For the rest of the project I feel vulnerable and uncomfortable. I don't see her again until the day of the final screening where she shows a beautiful movie she did on her own, with the help of one of her peers. A huge wave of relief over-comes me.

With consideration of the literature on ethics in DST in teaching and learning: there are a number of assumptions these frameworks/principles and guiding questions are based upon which have no resonance in our context (as illustrated in the 'snapshot' above). Some of the most important examples of these are:

Assumption of small group and workshop context: Digital storytelling originated from a community space. Traditionally, the DST format, as promoted by the StoryCenter, includes a 3 – 5 day workshop in which a small group of participants is supported in developing digital stories, being carefully guided in sharing their story ideas, developing a script, recording a voice over, selecting images, using video editing software to assemble all these elements into a short video and finally watching the movies together. In HE, while we do run small group workshops for staff and students, DST projects realistically will be set for a whole class comprising anything from 30 to 200 students. This means adapting the workshop format in all sorts of ways, from weekly sessions over a period of several weeks (up to 10 weeks in some instances) (see for example Hardy (2017); Condy et al., (2012); or Livingston (2014)) to self-directed processes (either independent or group-based). While lecturers are creative in adapting this method to support these often large classes (from training peer facilitators to support smaller groups of students to creating digital stories in groups), this means that the level of support will be compromised in this context.

Assumption of voluntary participation/consent/right to withdraw: Traditionally, consent has been a big concern in DST. The right to consent and withdraw are essential elements of the DST process. How does that translate into the HE space where participation in DST is in general compulsory, as it is part of the curriculum and more often than not will need some form of assessment? What does that mean for students who don't feel comfortable or simply cannot or do not want to participate and share their stories, as in the story above? Is it enough to allow students to choose the story they want to share and to be as personal or impersonal as they feel comfortable with? What if there are religious reasons for students not to participate? Or medical, i.e. if students have experienced trauma and the process of DST triggers it? Can they be forced to engage in this process? Amy Hill in her 2010 chapter, for example, suggests that DST should not be used with participants who suffer from PTSD.

Assignment briefs and a careful selection of the model stories shown to students as examples of the genre will go a long way in framing stories and having an impact on the level of personal sharing students will feel able/prompted/required to do. However, anybody who has ever taken part in a story circle will be able to attest at the 'magic' of these storycircles, the core of the DST process, unearthing stories that participants would have never thought to share in the first place. Can/should these stories be limited? What would be a cause of concern for facilitators? Stories that could potentially incriminate students or trigger other students? Open wounds we are not able to heal?

What about assessment? How closely does a student have to address a brief? How much choice is there in terms of style, language, content and creativity? And how can these very personal stories be assessed? Who should assess them? Should they be assessed at all? Attempts at assessing digital stories are often done through rubrics loosely following the Seven Elements of Digital Story-telling[16], sometimes in conjunction with a reflective essay (Benmayor, 2008; Hardy, 2017; Condy et al., 2012). Other examples include drawing up a series of mile-stones students have to complete (Livingston, 2014; Stewart & Ivala, 2017) or self- and peer-assessment. Still, as Hessler and Lambert argue, these attempts "usually lead one to learn just as much about who is doing the assessment, and what they are signifying about themselves or their institutional context" (2017:28). Hill (2010) argues that the collective of stories developed in a DST process can create a collective social story of injustice or struggle, which helps to move beyond the individual trauma of a story. As such, assessment should always bear in mind that the ultimate goal of DST is to help participants become more "empathetic, attentive, and collaborative learners" (ibid:32).

Space, skills, technology: Because DST is often done in facilitated workshop settings, access to technology and the skills to use this technology are required. Facilitators should have access to a workshop space conducive to the sharing of intimate stories and a set range of technology for all participants to ensure that they acquire skills to create and share digital stories. This would offer a level playing field in terms of output. Often facilitators take over a post-production phase to guarantee a high-level outcome that can be screened or shared with a wider audience, in particular if stories were shared/produced for advocacy purposes. In HE (in particular in resource-restrained contexts such as ours) none of this is a given. Spaces are often non-conducive to group storytelling (story circles). Classrooms might have furniture that cannot be moved around, no privacy can be given or groups of students might have to tell their stories in a crowded, noisy room, sometimes even in corridors or other shared public spaces. Students most likely will have to source their own technology/equipment, leading to highly varied outputs and quality of stories. Storytelling and multimodal/digital skills will also vary among students. Lecturers might not be able to support all stu-dents in equal ways (might not even have all the skills themselves). Even though there are creative ways to engage with this (such as co-teaching with colleagues/ student assistants across courses with diverse skills sets or sourcing labs/tech-nology across departments and faculties), the quality of output will differ and will have an impact on how an audience reacts to shared stories. As Hessler and Lambert argue "[c]reating environments where all of those differences and

---

16 http://www.ucdenver.edu/faculty_staff/faculty/center-for-faculty-development/
    Documents/Tutorials/Rubrics/documents/ex_digital_storytelling.pdf

capabilities are appreciated, but where none are overly privileged, becomes the distinct challenge for the educator" (2017:32). This leads to the next point around support and facilitation of DST projects.

Support/skilled facilitators: Traditionally, DST facilitators will undergo rigorous training. The StoryCenter offers an intensive programme for facilitators, often spanning years of (costly) training. This is one of the reasons why DST is seen as an exclusive, hard to access practice. But it must be noted that this intensive training is what encourages the appropriate emotional support for participants, who often share difficult stories or trauma (see also next point around *expectations of catharsis*). In HE, lecturers often adopt DST with little exposure to good practices of DST or enough training in DST facilitation. In the best case scenario, they might have participated in a workshop themselves and created their own digital story. In many cases they might just have heard about DST at a conference or read an article about this practice.

Novice facilitators to DST struggle to understand or foresee the unintended consequences of it, which is the opening up of spaces for the sharing of personal stories that cannot be closed again. How to support students making themselves vulnerable, how to create a space that is as safe as possible, how to care for the stories told and the audience response, what to do once stories have been shared and needs for care have been expressed – these questions all remain unanswered. Where does the responsibility for a storyteller, a story and the audience end? What do we do with the stories shared? Is it enough to refer an emotionally unsettled storyteller to student counselling? The story was shared in a particular space, to a particular group of people – the trust given calls for a level of responsibility that cannot be responded to by a referral to external psychologists or counsellors. What if students are not comfortable accessing counselling services based on their cultural beliefs and practices (in African culture 'therapy' is still very much seen as a Western tradition not necessarily in line with local customs and practices to engage with emotional fallouts)? Also, while traditional workshops have a demarcated timeline and, in some ways, a clearly defined window of responsibility for the facilitator, for a lecturer running a DST project, the responsibility for students does not end with the end of the project but will continue for as long as he/she teaches the students participating in the DST project. How should I have responded to the student leaving the story circle in the snapshot preceding this section?

Assumption of story as therapy/healing/catharsis/transformation: Closely related to the above-mentioned point is the assumption that DST, or rather telling stories in general, is cathartic, healing and that they are seen as therapy. Often DST workshops are centred on difficult topics, marginalised groups (such as women suffering from gender-based violence), survivors of war trauma or patients with specific medical conditions. However, when DST is adopted in HE, the focus must move from a therapy intervention to a pedagogical space. The most consistent feedback we get from students is the importance of these kinds of projects for their own personal growth, a space that is usually not created in the often rigid HE context. However, we are first and foremost educators, not counsellors or psychologists. One of the approaches we have taken is to adopt a pedagogy of discomfort (Boler & Zembylas, 2003), which intentionally moves away from 'psychologising' individual students to an understanding of trauma as a collective, shared, constructed and inherited experience. Digital storytelling can be seen as both a transformative educational experience on an individual and social level (Hessler & Lambert, 2017), but the boundaries between therapy and education need to be clearly defined and spoken about.

4.2 DST in research in HE

Snapshot 2: Dilemma in research (Candice): Nadine is a young artist who volunteered to take part in an autobiographical DST project as part of her fourth-year final exhibition. In her digital story, she revealed that she had been sexually abused as a child. Although Nadine gladly signed the consent and release forms, and was quite happy to share her story with the class and the greater research community, I, as both facilitator and researcher of this process, couldn't help but wonder what psychological fallout could have arisen from her disclosure. The fact that I still watch her story, four years later, leaves me wondering if Nadine is OK, as I have never followed up on her wellbeing; not at the time of the writing of the story, or now, many years later. As she has left the school, I wouldn't even know how to contact her.

From its inception, DST has always been a research-based practice, often driven by an educational agenda (Meadows, 2003:189). The general principles that are adhered to in research projects can be transferred to research in DST, but there are a number of assumptions regarding research that are challenged by this practice in a HE context. These assumptions relate to the collection of data, the anonymising of that data, the manner in which the participants are sampled, the prerequisite confidentiality offered to the participants and their right to give and withdraw consent from an educational research project. The final assumption in a research context is that participants will be protected from harmful or risky situations.

Collection and analysis of data: An assumption in research is that data should be collected through a number of validated or reliable instruments. Most research ethics applications require that you provide an example of the instrument that you will be using to collect your data. But is it possible to validate or ensure that the data – in form of a digital story – is reliable, as it is by nature subjective, deeply personal and emotional? It is true that DST often provides a rich source of data for the understanding of and engagement by a diverse student body, but the niggling question at this point is: How can intensely personal stories be ethically viewed as data and how can this be collected ethically without the storyteller becoming a mere participant and the story becoming a mere artefact? When does the data from personal stories move from a personal sharing of stories space into the scholarship of teaching and learning? And is it ethical to represent and write about this data in a traditional way? At the least the researcher should state his/her positionality upfront to allow readers to understand how he/she is reading the stories collected. Also, participant checks will help ensure that storytellers are represented meaningfully and ethically (see more on representation in the community engagement section).

Anonymity and confidentiality: There is also an assumption in research that participants in a research project will be granted anonymity and that the data produced in the research context will remain confidential. Due to the nature of DST and the public dissemination of the stories, this is next to impossible. This is probably the greatest concern within the HE research contexts: Students might feel safe when sharing their stories in a story circle and may also give consent to share their story during a class screening, but what happens if their stories are shown at a conference where anonymity and confidentiality cannot be guaranteed? And how will they feel when they finally read the academic publication that resulted from a research project? How much confidentiality can thus be ensured, especially – as we will later argue – since the storyteller should be invited into the conference space, if possible to introduce her/his story?

Sampling and consent: An important assumption in qualitative research is that sampling is purposive but also voluntary. As shown in the example above, Nadine's digital story was part of her final year art portfolio, and although she had a choice whether or not she wanted to share her story with the greater community, she had no choice about the completion of her assignment. This then raises the issue of whether it is ethical to include a research component in an academic DST project, when students are forced to take part – especially if their participation in the project is not voluntary and forms part of an assessment. Lecturers may give the student the option to not have his/her story used as data in a research project, but their participation in the project is still mandatory. This leads to the questioning of power dynamics between the storyteller and the researcher (who is very often the lecturer). If a student does not have a say over whether or not they want to take part in a digital story project, how can this sampling strategy be seen as valid, especially if the student feels coerced into taking part in the project and feels as though they have lost their 'voice'? This feeds into the contentious issue of consent. How can a lecturer ask a student to give their consent to be in a project and use their artefacts when, in essence, the student has no consent to give particularly as the project is compulsory? How much choice does a student have to not participate in a study if the researcher is their lecturer, most likely the person assessing their work as well?

Because of the highly constrained format of DST (length, topic), stories have to focus on the mere essentials and often do not provide a lot of background information on the storyteller. When a story travels beyond the classroom or institution and is shared at a conference – far removed from the context where it was produced in – who will provide context? Can the researcher be relied on to provide the necessary backstory? Should Nadine be invited to co-present, co-write with me (the researcher in this case) as participatory research would suggest? And how will the story be introduced and 'read' by a conference audience? Hill (2010:138) asks for "resisting simplistic and passive readings in favour of readings that encourage viewers to reveal their own stories and open themselves to raw vulnerability (comparable to that exercised by the storytellers in sharing their lives in the first place) and a form of emotional distress or confusion which makes simplistic explanations or solutions impossible." How can this be realised in a traditional conference setting where time for presentations and questions and answers is often limited to 20 – 30 minutes?

In Nadine's case, consent was a once-off action and was never revisited. With a story of this nature, with its sensitive content and deeply personal revelations, should consent not be sought every time the story is shown, even if it is years later? What if Nadine changes her mind about her story? Layered consent is something that must be considered. What would ongoing/layered/continuous consent look like in this situation? Will this be possible if the research has been published? It would be ethically responsible to withdraw a conference presentation or an article from publication if the student changes the conditions of their consent at a later stage, but how viable is this really?

Do no harm: The final assumption regarding research is that a participant will not knowingly be put in a situation which could harm them or expose them to unnecessary risk and that the reputation of the HEI must be safeguarded. It is also known that an institution may be subject to vicarious liability if they knowingly put a student in harm's way or do not take the necessary precautions to protect a student from harm or risky situations. But, as shown in the dilemma above, is it possible for a facilitator (who is often both the lecturer and researcher) to mitigate the emotional harm that may arise from a disclosure of this nature, especially if the only ethical training that the facilitator has received is quite often perfunctory? Is the facilitator able to deal with the psychological ramifications of this disclosure, both for the student and themselves? As discussed above, is it good enough to only offer the services of the on-campus counsellor? And what about future risks? What if the student has a delayed response to her disclosure, and years later decides that she does not want her story to be told? This raises issues for researchers who should adhere to the ethical principle of 'do no harm'. We have to ask ourselves, are we properly equipped as researchers to, firstly, identify the risk and, secondly, deal with the consequences of the emotional fallout of DST, both at the time of viewing the story, and, later, when the DST process has been completed? The final question that has to be debated though, is: How is it ethically viable for a lecturer to conduct a DST workshop without being able to mitigate this possibility of harm or offer the prerequisite support?

4.3   DST in community engagement in HE

Snapshot 3 (Jacqui): My story begins with a Journalism Alumnus who approached our unit requesting logistical support for his project with the District Six (D6) community[17]. The aim of the project was to compile a film of the stories of former and current residents who had been forcibly removed. Our Cape Town campus (recently renamed as D6 campus) was built during Apartheid as the Cape Technikon, serving a predominantly white student population. At first, I delayed responding to the request as I felt that it was critical that we spend some time to engage with the community to understand the project. At the same time there was an expectation to act on the community's request that their stories be digitised. My university also

---

17   The District Six community is one of the most prominent sites of forced removals as a consequence of the Group Areas Act during Apartheid. For more information visit http://www.districtsix.co.za/

needed to display to the community (which included alumni) that we were serious about building connections to honour the history of the space occupied by the D6 campus. I felt stuck in the middle of these expectations, being both a representative of my institution and having myself family history in D6. The screening of the films was followed by an intergenerational dialogue with community members, university staff and students. Photography students developed audio-visual materials (in the form of digital stories) from their interviews with D6 community members. The project highlighted the individual agendas of the key role-players: 1) The need of the community participants to share/tell their stories; 2) The need for the journalist and filmmaker to get stories that would 'sell' and make for good viewing; 3) The need for the university to involve and conscientise students to the history of the D6 campus and to show the building of partnerships between themselves and the D6 community within this highly contested space. The stories generated a wide range of emotions from communities and students, which was expected. What was unforeseen were the political tensions that were revisited and regurgitated between the university and the external community. In retrospect, inadequate attention was given to preparing the students and the community. During the process, there were no strategies put in place to support the participants and no indication was given as to what would happen to the stories post project. One question which has sprung to mind is: How do we as the university practice DST ethically to act in the interests of all parties (staff, students and all partners), especially in highly charged political environments where we have much to lose but also much to gain?

While DST in community engagement can have many forms and can include training community members alongside students, at our institution, DST in community engagement often means students collecting stories within communities and creating digital stories on their own/back at the institution. This can lead to a number of ethical dilemmas as shown below as the usual assumptions in a DST process and community engagement practices clash.

Collaboration, trust and competing agendas: Community engagement (service-learning and civic engagement) projects, as advocated and practiced by most HEIs, are largely dependent on the building of strong partnerships between the university and society. More directly, for staff, students, community and government partners, the presence and practice of trust, empathy, transparency and respect, amongst others, are important components. Boughey (2014:105) echoes the view of Dazé, Ambrose and Ehrhart (2009:21) who describes 'development' as a "creative collaboration around an emergent agenda", based on a foundation of "relationships with individuals and communities". Collaboration becomes complicated as students, lecturers, researchers and their collaborators are motivated to engage in community engagement projects for different reasons. Students might be in it for a mark, lecturers because they have been told to and the community due to a need to share their stories. What if they encounter community members that are illiterate and do not fully understand what they are giving consent to/participating in? This might lead to unequal buy-in and a skewed sense of collaboration, where different partners contribute on different levels of emotional engagement. What might be a box-ticking-exercise for some might be deeply personal for others, thereby affecting the relationship of trust that should exist between the parties involved. As shown in the snapshot above, this can be made even more intricate by the presence of a media partner in the partnership. Trust develops overtime and the building of sustainable relationships with communities around DST projects needs to be a concerted effort between the institution and the community (Bickel, Shewbridge, Huebler & Oskoz, 2017).

Dealing with emotional responses: DST in particular as a community engagement tool may emphasise the digital aspects and film-making process rather than an engagement with the emotional responses encountered. Students may be trained in digital storytelling but not in empathetic interviewing skills. While this is highlighted in oral storytelling ethical practices, it is not given enough credence in current DST community engagement projects. Another aspect to consider is that the storytelling environment can become considerably more emotionally charged when the 'story collector' becomes/is a participant in the process. Often students collect stories in their own community, which can contribute to a sense of connection and collective caring with others. But what if they find out something about their past which is traumatic or experience some sort of cognitive dissonance? Here in the Western Cape, for example, family histories around slave heritage or forced removals are often shameful and silenced and students finding out about these aspects of their family history could present them with emotional difficulties. Another question then is: Who is responsible to respond for this emotional fallout? The lecturer, the student or the community member? All of them?

Equal partnerships: Bringle *et al.* (2009:3) and also Van Schalkwyk and Erasmus (2011:67) usefully differentiate between a 'relationship', which broadly refers to all types of interactions between persons, and a 'partnership', which refers to a relationship in which the interaction possesses the three qualities of closeness, equity and integrity. These qualities may be pertinent to consider when building an environment for engagement with communities. Closeness is a function of three components: (a) frequency of interaction, (b) diversity of activities that are the basis of the interactions, and (c) strength of influence on the other person's behaviour, decisions, plans and goals. The quality of equity is not measured by the comparison between what was invested in the project and the end result, but by the degree to which the end results are perceived as being proportionate to the initial inputs. These relationships have high levels of integrity, share deeply held internally coherent values, and propose a vision of a future transformed world.

One of the core elements in DST is the story circle, where storytellers share their initial stories. In community engagement projects, where students are sent out to collect narratives from community members, this story circle is often left out of the DST process. One might argue that this then does not count as DST, but still many lecturers refer to these projects as DST. What happens then, when certain members of the partnership have more tools/skills/power than others? Who takes decisions regarding production/pictures/the story that will be told? The students? The students in collaboration with community members? The community members? What if students do not have the time for a lengthy post-production process or consultations? Will the community members ever see the final product/the final digital story? Will they be invited to the screening? Could any costs such as transport costs be covered? Who has the final say in whether the story will be screened? The student or the community member? Could community partners be part of the assessment of the stories? And how could this be encouraged, made possible by the lecturer?

Reciprocity: In service-learning and civic engagement, the principles which influence good practice is when community relationships strive to be mutually beneficial (Clayton, Bringle, Senor, Huq, & Morrison, 2010). The concept of 'reciprocity' is on occasion utilised by practitioners to indicate this very basic commitment to a partnership that is mutually beneficial through the exchange of resources, but, a deeper and broader interpretation can be related to mutual transformation. According to Jameson *et al.* (in Clayton *et al.*, 2010:18), this understanding of the term "emphasizes shared voice and power and insists upon collaborative knowledge construction and joint ownership of work processes and products", which then creates an environment where development is inclusive of all participants. As service-learning partnerships require reciprocal partnerships, this concept should be extended to incorporate the 'reciprocity of care' as part of the partnership guidelines. In projects where students collect community narratives and produce digital stories, what participants get out of this project may differ. Are students passing on some of their skills to the community? If community members give up their time to be part of storytelling sessions, will they be remunerated? Who owns and benefits from the media products emanating from the project? And will these community members be credited in any academic or digital outputs that are produced by the project?

Dialogue and equal engagement across generations: Community engagement relies on deep dialogue and sensitive engagement with cultural context before, during and after interventions. Students might not be adequately prepared for this type of engagement (as evident in the unforeseen political fallout in the snapshot shown above), but might also not have sufficient time in projects that are often rushed to meet tight deadlines and demands of full curricula. The diverse agendas of the participants and partners may not emerge during the project but becomes evident at a screening when the end product is showcased to a broader audience. Further engagement with this particular community then becomes framed within this paradigm, which can have a negative influence on the relationships between those who are left behind. It is important to acknowledge these agendas upfront and to be open and transparent during the storytelling journey.

Representation: Having a historical bias, a particular political ideology or culture can influence the relationship between the storyteller and story collector, especially in the case of projects like the District Six one which deals with the traumatic legacy of forced removals by the former Apartheid government. When there is a strong political and cultural identification between project partners, the collector (in this case the student) can assume that he/she possesses the legitimacy to access, develop and package the stories into a final product and to own and distribute the story on behalf of the community with which he/she strongly identifies. This then also raises issues of representation of the depicted community and the potential for misrepresentation by either party, for any number of reasons, including for personal or political gain. As mentioned before, will there be time for the student to go back and do a 'participant check' with the storyteller to ensure that there is a fair representation of the community in their digital story?

4. Conclusions

In this chapter we have tried to unpack some of the ethical dilemmas we have encountered in our practice when introducing DST into teaching and learning, research and community engagement. We believe in the process of DST as a means to create a space for sharing and learning about self and other, which is rare in the HE context we operate in. However, to continue promoting this practice, we have seen the need to alert colleagues of the ethical perils they may encounter in this highly personal and powerful practice. In HE we work with many limitations and challenges that the traditional DST do not have to consider, as we have shown above, and, as such, general guidelines on ethics are not fully appropriate.

We are aware that we are asking more questions than providing answers for the moment. While we are working – in parallel to this paper – on guidelines or rather guiding questions for an ethical practice of DST in HE[18], we are hoping that this chapter may encourage educators, researchers and community engagement practitioners to take a step back, reflect on their own practices, consider some of the questions we asked and add their own. Following political philosopher Joan Tronto's 'Ethics of Care' approach, we believe that, at the end of the day, much more important than sticking to guidelines and principles, ethical practices are everyday decisions of care in caring relationships (Tronto, 1993; 2001). It is in our everyday practices of caring for ourselves and others that we most need to consider and practice ethical behaviour (Tronto, 2001). Tronto sees care as a complex ethical relationship in which all participants or actors need to be involved. There can be no one person solely responsible for decision making in a caring relationship or web of relationships such as the DST practice discussed in this chapter: All parties involved should contribute to the discussion on caring needs and how they should be met.

When storytelling enters HE (in and beyond the institution), the educator/researcher/community practitioner becomes an active participant in this process, learning from and with students/participants through dialogue and mutual respect. When DST moves into the pedagogic sphere and becomes data for research projects in the HE arena, it is essential that we as academics and researchers learn to navigate this terrain, not by consulting a checklist of ethical rules relating to gaining consent and 'doing no harm' and making the prerequisite ticks; rather, we argue, that we need to see DST and the ethics around DST from a situated practice perspective, where consent is a contextual, scaffolded,

---

18 https://docs.google.com/document/d/1sV6Dn3N_8xCTF_7kTP8p6VmoyDVMuvV4oz
    hQ-SghaUA/edit?usp=sharing

ongoing and layered process and the principles of mitigating risk and harm become embedded in the project before, during and long after the process has been completed (see also Gachago & Livingston, 2020). There is a need for 'improvisation', for flexibility, rather than rigid rules and regulations in teaching, learning and research practices of this nature (Bliss, 2017), where we as facilitators are challenged to think on our feet – together with students, participants and community members. If the ethics of care is to be embedded in a DST project, we will have to begin with an ethical appraisal of ourselves and our motives and endeavour to ensure that the entire DST process is more than just ethical – it should be ethically sustainable for the dignity of the students, especially with regards to the emotional fallout that these projects might elicit. In essence, the rules of engagement have to be negotiated and agreed upon on a continual basis, not only with regards to issues of scaffolded consent and choice, but also to those of power-sharing, ownership and digital afterlife of the stories as more-than-data.

What that means for us, is that we all – lecturers, students, researchers and community members – need to take responsibility for our DST projects and care for both ourselves and others involved in these projects. Communication, negotiation of rules, active listening and response, and witnessing become important elements in this process. Storytelling then becomes a caring, consensual mutual practice (Bliss 2017) of ethically sharing and listening, responding and acting in and beyond the HE classroom.

5.   Acknowledgements

We are deeply thankful to the Ethics Deme participants at the 2017 Untold Conference who shaped our thinking around the ethics of digital storytelling and in particular allowed us to recognise the many DST practices with all their different ethical concerns and encouraged us to work towards specific guidelines for HE. We would also like to thank the SA Story Worker Group who helped us think through some of our ethical dilemmas. And finally, thank you to our colleagues and students; without their passion and stories there would be not DST practice at our institution.

References

Ban, D. & Nagy, B. 2016. iDig stories: Digital storytelling in practice. http://idigstories.eu/wp-content/uploads/2016/09/Digital_Storytelling_in_Practice.pdf, date of access: 18th of August 2020.

Benmayor, R. 2008. Digital storytelling as a signature pedagogy for the new humanities. *Arts and Humanities in Higher Education*, 7:188-204. https://doi.org/10.1177/1474022208

Bickel, B., Shewbridge, B., Huebler, R. & Oskoz, A. 2017. Faculty reflections at the intersection of digital storytelling and community engagement. In: G. Jamisson, P. Hardy, Y. Nordkvelle & H. Pleasants (eds). *Digital Storytelling in Higher Education*, 371-389. Cham: Palgrave Macmillan. https://doi.org/10.1007/BF03033420

Bliss, E. 2017. Engaged scholarship and engaging communities: Navigating emotion, affect and disability through digital storytelling. In: G. Jamisson, P. Hardy, Y. Nordkvelle & H. Pleasants (eds). *Digital Storytelling in Higher Education*, 321-334. Cham: Palgrave Macmillan. https://doi.org/10.1007/BF03033420

Boler, M. & Zembylas, M. 2003. Discomforting truths: The emotional terrain of understanding difference. In: P. Trifonas (ed). *Pedagogies of difference: Rethinking education for social change*, 110-136. New York: RoutledgeFalmer.

Boughey, J. 2014. *A Comprehensive University at the Heart of its Communities: Establishing a Framework for Engagement*. Philosophiae Doctor in Higher Education Studies (Five-article option) in the School of Higher Education Studies Faculty of Education University of the Free State Bloemfontein January 2014.

Bringle R.G., Clayton, P.H. & Price, M.F. 2009. Partnerships in service learning and civic engagement. *Partnerships: A Journal of Service Learning & Civic Engagement* 1(1): 1-20.

Clayton, P.H., Bringle, R.G., Senor, B., Huq, J. & Morrison, M. 2010. Differentiating and Assessing Relationships in Service-Learning and Civic Engagement: Exploitative, Transactional, or Transformational. *Michigan Journal of Community Service Learning*. Spring 2010: 5-22.

Condy, J., Chigona, A., Gachago, D. & Ivala, E. 2012. Preservice students' perceptions and experiences of digital storytelling in diverse classrooms. *Turkish Online Journal of Educational Technology (TOJET)*, 11(3), 278-285.

Concordia University. 2018. Ethics. Centre for oral history and digital storytelling. Retrieved from http://storytelling.concordia.ca/toolbox/ethics

Dazé, A., Ambrose, K. & Ehrhart, C. 2009. Climate vulnerability and capacity analysis handbook. *Care International*. http://www.careclimatechange.org, date of access: 18th of August 2020.

Gachago, D. 2015. *Sentimentality and Digital Storytelling: Towards a Post-Conflict Pedagogy in Pre-Service Teacher Education in South Africa*. Unpublished PhD Thesis. School of Education: University of Cape Town. https://doi.org/10.13140/RG.2.1.4738.8403

Gachago, D., Ivala, E., Condy, J. & Chigona, A. 2013. Journeys across difference: Pre-service teacher education students' perceptions of a pedagogy of discomfort in a digital storytelling project in South Africa. *Critical Studies in Teaching and Learning*, 1(1), 22-52. https://doi.org/10.14426/cristal.v1i1.4

Gachago, D. & Livingston, C. 2020. The elephant in the room: Tensions between normative research and an ethics of care for digital storytelling in higher education. *Reading and Writing*, 11 (1). https://rw.org.za/index.php/rw/article/view/242/625, date of access: 18th of August 2020

Gachago, D. & Sykes, P. 2017. Navigating Ethical Boundaries When Adopting Digital Storytelling in Higher Education. In: G. Jamisson, P. Hardy, Y. Nordkvelle & H. Pleasants (eds). *Digital Storytelling in Higher Education*, 91-106. Cham: Palgrave Macmillan. https://doi.org/10.1007/BF03033420

Gubrium, A.C., Hill, A.L. & Flicker, S. 2014. A situated practice of ethics for participatory visual and digital methods in public health research and practice: A focus on digital storytelling. *American Journal of Public Health*, 104(9):1606-1614. https://doi.org/10.2105/AJPH.2013.301310 https://www.ncbi.nlm.nih.gov/pmc/articles/PMC4151912/

Haigh, C. 2017. 'The times are a changin': Digital storytelling as a catalyst for an ideological revolution in theal-care research. In: G. Jamissen, P. Hardy, Y. Nordkvelle & H. Pleasants (eds). *Digital Storytelling in Higher Education*, 115-130. Cham: Palgrave Macmillan.

Hardy, P. 2017. Physician, know thyself: Using digital storytelling to promote reflection in medical education. In: G. Jamissen, P. Hardy, Y. Nordkvelle & H. Pleasants (eds). *Digital Storytelling in Higher Education*, 37-54. Cham: Palgrave Macmillan.

Hessler, B. & Lambert, J. 2017. Threshold concepts in digital storytelling: Naming what we know about storywork. In: G. Jamissen, P. Hardy, Y. Nordkvelle & H. Pleasants (eds). *Digital Storytelling in Higher Education*, 19-36. Cham: Palgrave Macmillan.

Hill, A.L. 2010. Digital storytelling for gender justice: Exploring the challenges and the limits of polyvocality. In: *Confronting global gender justice*, 126-140. Oxford: Routledge.

Hill, A. 2014. Digital storytelling and the politics of doing good: Exploring the ethics of bringing personal narratives into public spheres. In: H. Pleasants & D.E. Salter (eds). *Community-based Multiliteracies and Digital Media Projects*, 39:174-178. Peter Lang Publishing.

Jamissen, G., Hardy, P., Nordkvelle, Y. & Pleasants, H. 2017. *Digital storytelling in Higher Education: International perspectives*. Cham: Palgrave Macmillan.

Jessee, E. 2011. The Limits of oral history: Ethics and methodology amid highly politicized research settings. *The Oral History Review*, 38(2):287-307, https://doi.org/10.1093/ohr/ohr098

Lambert, J. 2013. *Digital storytelling: Capturing lives, creating communities* (4th edition). New York: Routledge.

Lambert, J. 2017. Foreword. In: G. Jamissen, P. Hardy, Y. Nordkvelle & H. Pleasants (eds). *Digital Storytelling in Higher Education*, v-viii. Cham: Palgrave Macmillan.

Livingston, C. 2014. Engaging in art appreciation: A digital autobiographical perspective. In: *Fourth international conference on Design, Development and Research* (DDR) held in Cape Town on 9-10 September 2014: 107-126. ISBN 978-0-620-62981-0.

Mandal, J., Acharya, S. & Parija, S.C. 2011. Ethics in human research. Series on ethics in research. *Tropical parasitology*, 1(1):2-3.

Meadows, D. 2003. Digital storytelling: Research-based practice in New Media. *Visual communication*, 2:189-193.DOI: 10.1177/1470357203002002004

Prager, D. 2017. A guide to online images copyright and fair use laws. Retrieved from https://www.rivaliq.com/blog/guide-copyright-fair-use-laws-online-images/

Stewart, K.D. & Ivala, E. 2017. Silence, voice, and "other languages": Digital storytelling as a site for resistance and restoration in a South African higher education classroom. *British Journal of Educational Technology*. https://doi.org/10.1111/bjet.12540

StoryCenter. 2018. Ethical practice. https://static1.squarespace.com/static/55368c08e4b0d419e1c011f7/t/579134a05016e13dde264720/1469133984611/Ethics.pdf, date of access: 18th of August 2020.

Thomson Long, B. & Hall, T. 2017. From Dewey to digital: Design-based research for deeper reflection through digital storytelling. In: G. Jamissen, P. Hardy, Y. Nordkvelle & H. Pleasants (eds). *Digital Storytelling in Higher Education*, 55-72. Cham: Palgrave Macmillan.

Tronto, J. 1993. *Moral boundaries: A political argument for an ethic of care*. New York: Routledge.

Tronto, J. 2001. An ethic of care. In: M.B. Holstein & P.B. Mitzen (eds). *Ethics in Community-Based Elder Care*, 60-68. New York: Springer.

Van Luyn, A. 2011. An obsession with storytelling: Conducting oral history interviews for creative writing. *Ejournalist*, 11(1).

Van Schalkwyk, F. & Erasmus, M. 2011. Community participation in higher education service learning, *Acta Academica*, 43(3). Sun Media: Bloemfontein.

Chapter 11

Identifying and exploring possible challenges encountered by local communities regarding the conservation volunteering activities in Kruger National Park

Precious Shabalala and Joana Bezerra

UNIVERSITY OF MPUMALANGA,
SCHOOL OF HOSPITALITY AND TOURISM;
RHODES UNIVERSITY COMMUNITY ENGAGEMENT

precious.shabalala@ump.ac.za; j.bezerra@ru.ac.za

1. Introduction

The primary goal of protected areas is biodiversity conservation (Watson, Dudley & Segan, 2014). To reach national and international conservation targets, protected areas are demarcated and maintained throughout the world. The establishment and maintenance of such areas are not without conflict, ranging from buying land for conservation purposes to loss of economic opportunities for food or wood production (McCarthy *et al.*, 2012; Ruslandi & Putz, 2011; Venter, Magrach, Outram, Klein, Marco & Watson, 2018). Protected areas, however, are not just the site of biological diversity – they also have great cultural value and appeal.

The appeal of protected areas is not restricted to one group of people. Communities from different cultures use green spaces in urban and peri-urban areas. These spaces can be protected areas or private reserves and they provide a space where different cultures can be celebrated in the same space (Sustainable Tourism – Parks and Culture, 1997-2010). Parks provide a primary contact with biodiversity and natural environment for many people in their personally chosen form of interactions with a public green space. This space also often offers broader social benefits, such as acting as meeting places that give a shared focus to diverse communities (Barbosa, Tratalos, Armsworth, Davies, Fuller, Johnson, & Gatson, 2007).

Although driven by national conservation targets, the expansion of protected areas is hindered by costs (Armsworth *et al.*, 2013), which has been recognised by the conservation field (Naidoo Balmford, Ferraro, Polasky & Ricketts, 2006; Wilson, Cawardine, & Possingham, 2009). The need to counteract such costs, coupled with the rise in awareness about conservation efforts, led to the strengthening of volunteer programmes in protected areas (Halpenny & Caissie, 2003) that will provide labour for different aspects of a protected area's management. Volunteers can be involved in fundraising, habitat management (Bremer & Graeff, 2007), control of invasive species (Bryce, Oliver, Davies, Gray & Urquhart, 2011), amongst others (see, for example, Schmeller *et al.*, 2009; Silvertown, 2009; Crall, Newman, Jarnevich, Stohlgren & Waller, 2010; Ramsey & Addison, 1996). The number of volunteers can also be a good indicator of support for the protected area where they volunteer (Armsworth *et al.*, 2013). This support status can influence future planning decisions on how to maintain such support or how to increase it. As well as expressing their stewardship, protected areas volunteers are usually in better general health with less trips to their doctor (Koss & Kingsley,2010). Crucial for the survival of protected areas, the support of community members and their inclusion in the management of such spaces through volunteering can promote a sense of ownership and improve the relationship between community members and conservation institutions.

Protected areas in South Africa

The South African National Parks (SANParks) was established according to the Protected Areas Act, 2003, with the aim to manage the biodiversity conservation of South Africa and the heritage of these landscapes through national parks (Protected Areas Act 2003). Throughout its history, SANParks has had a good record of biodiversity conservation, achieved through well-defined management objectives combined with monitoring programmes (Swemmer & Taljaard, 2011).

On top of management staff, SANParks houses a volunteering programme. SANParks Honorary Rangers (SHRs) programme provides an entry point for community members and businesses to get involved in conservation initiatives in South Africa. SHRs are volunteers who dedicate their free time and skills to support the conservation of the country's national parks. Honorary Rangers are involved in different activities, from welcoming guests at entry gates to fundraising events. One of the most notable initiatives is the Junior Honorary Rangers programme that inspires youngsters to understand the value of conservation. All funds raised by the Honorary Rangers are used in strategic SANParks projects (SANParks Volunteers, 2018).

Although the Honorary Rangers initiative is well-established, limited research has been done on the impact of such programmes on the volunteers, the challenges they face to reach the programme, and those experienced during its course. Such programmes depend on their visibility to attract new volunteers, but how widespread the knowledge about such initiatives is, within the communities around protected areas as well as amongst tourism students or even tourist guides, is unknown.

The aim of this chapter is twofold: 1) to identify and explore the possible challenges encountered by local communities in conservation volunteer organisations/activities; and 2) to identify possible solutions for these challenges and equip local communities to work with SANParks and contribute towards building a broad constituency for conservation in a citizen-centred way.

Including local communities around the parks in parks' management, with communities taking ownership of the park and seeing the benefits of biodiversity conservation for themselves and for the nation, has a direct impact on knowledge production and dissemination. This is the key link between this topic and social innovation. This speaks to the social and political dimensions of social innovation (Klein *et al.*, 2013), with social change and justice at its core. By promoting social inclusion through stimulating and giving a space for knowledge from outside academia to flourish and building and strengthening social relations, social innovation continuously chips away on the apartheid of knowledge.

2. Study site and methods

2.1 A brief history of the Kruger National Park

To understand the history of the Kruger National Park (KNP), one needs to look at the history of South Africa. During apartheid, only 13% of the total territory of South Africa was set aside for black South Africans, who represented 80% of the population. In line with this legislation, black communities were forcibly evicted from their homes so that land could become a conservation area (Carruthers, 1995; Mabunda, Pienaar & Verhoef, 2003). After the democratic elections of 1994, the land restitution process aimed to restore not only land access but also dignity for communities that were wrongfully evicted (Walker, Bohlin, Hall & Kepe, 2010). Individuals, families or communities who were wrongfully evicted from their lands after 1913 and can prove so, can lay a claim to their land. If the claim is successful, claimants are allowed to have their rights to the land restored or choose financial compensation, an alternative land or a combination of these options. However, if the land claimed is now a protected area and claimants choose restoration, they and the conservation agency in charge must enter into a collaborative management agreement.

There was a time when almost half the area of the Kruger was under land claim by rural communities who were forcibly relocated from within its borders before or during the apartheid era, and presently some of the claims have been settled, some have been dismissed, with some still outstanding (Siyabona Africa, 2020). These surrounding communities are currently being assisted by the South African government to have a share in management of what was historically their land, and are engaged with KNP in joint decision-making about the land use for conservation purposes. Most of the rural people are seeking benefits and poverty alleviation as first outcomes of the land value of the Kruger and its wild animal populations. Although not directly related to the Honorary Rangers programme, the social and historical context paint a picture of the environment where such initiatives exist, and it can help explain some of the challenges therein.

Volunteers have been part of the history of the KNP since 1902 and they play a key role in sharing some of the workload with full-time staff. Today SANParks counts more than 1 600 volunteers in all of the 21 national parks (SANParks Volunteers, 2018). The study was conducted in Mpumalanga province in South Africa. **Figure 1** shows a map of the KNP. Data was collected from Matsulu Township, KaNyamazane Township and Luphisi Homeland area situated in Nelspruit on the south and south east boarders of the KNP.

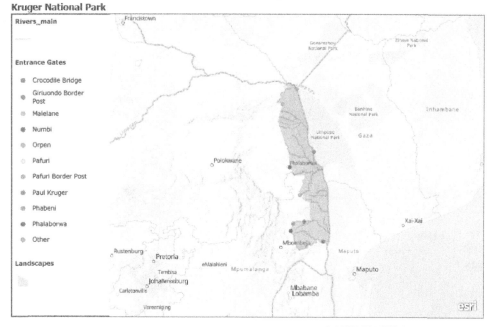

Figure 1: Kruger National Park [basemap]. Scale Not Given. March 10, 2021. Layers retrieved from SANParks Data Repository (Rivers_main, Entrance Gates, Landscapes). http://dataknp.sanparks.org/sanparks/metacat)

2.2   *Methods used*

A mixed concurrent method was adopted for the chapter. Veal (2011) posits that a mixed-method of data collection is needed for deeper data collection and ana-lyses. The research project used two different data collection tools with six diffe-rent stakeholders to develop an understanding of the different dynamics around the research problem. Data was ethically collected. A study information sheet and consent forms were used in the research project. These documents were available in English and the local language. All participants were voluntarily recruited after the study information sheet was read and explained to them. The participants also gave their approval for the interviews to be recorded (signed consent forms).

2.3   *Semi-structured interviews*

Semi-structured interviews were conducted with key informants, which consti-tuted four different groups: KNP staff members, SHRs, high school tourism educators and tourism experts. Purposive sampling was used to identify key informants to be interviewed. Different semi-structured interview guides were designed for each key informant group to achieve the objective of the study that referred to that particular group: KNP; Honorary Rangers; and tourism teachers. KNP staff members were selected as they are the custodians of the protected area, trusted by SANParks to carry out the mandate of both the people and of conservation. SHRs and tourism teachers were interviewed to determine the knowledge of volunteering initiatives amongst those groups. The interviews with SHRs were crucial in getting their input into educating the general public about conservation and determining their views on diversity in the SHR organisation. Some SHR's were interviewed over the telephone. Some of the SHR's, including the tourism experts, preferred to email their feedback. On-site face-to-face interviews were recorded using a voice recorder, while handwritten notes were made and photos were taken using an iPad. Notes were also made during each interview to serve as 'memory joggers' for the important matters or indicate the emphasis placed by each respondent in their feedback.

A total of nine interviews were conducted with SANParks staff members of the KNP (Phalaborwa, Letaba and Skukuza campsites) and another nine inter-views were conducted with senior SHRs volunteers as follows via telephone (1), email (6) and on-site interviews at Phalaborwa camp (1) and at Skukuza camp (1) in September 2014. It must be noted that the SHR that was interviewed at Skukuza was originally based at Malelane. Four tourism educators from the four local high schools teaching tourism as an elective subject were also interviewed in the month of October 2014.

2.4   Questionnaire

Probability sampling was adopted for the household survey using a structured questionnaire. A purposive sampling method was adopted for third-year and BTech Tourism students from the University of Johannesburg, also using a struc-tured questionnaire. The researcher administered the surveys. The question-naire comprised 16 close-ended and open-ended questions. Final-year students were included since, as senior students who would be working in the industry soon, their knowledge of and understanding about the SANParks Honorary Rangers programme and conservation volunteering activities would indicate the dissemination of such initiatives.

Seventy-one completed questionnaires were collected from local commu-nities from the targeted areas bordering KNP on the south and south east, namely: Matsulu Township, KaNyamazane Township and Luphisi Homeland area in October 2014. A total of 65 responses were received from the University ·of Johannesburg's third-year and BTech Tourism students.

2.5   Data analysis

The data was analysed using descriptive statistics and selective coding techniques. The analyses followed content analysis style (thematic and descriptive in nature), where coding (selective coding, axial coding and open coding) was applied using themes and sub-themes developed from research objectives. Goldman (2012) notes that axial coding takes place when data is put back together in an innovative way by making connections between categories and when axial coding categories are merged, new ones identified and categories that bore no relevance to the aim and objectives of the study are rejected. Furthermore, open coding entails careful inspection of the data, with the goal of breaking down the data into units of meaning, as it occurs through close examination of the data, and ascribing labels to concepts as they present themselves in the data. Lastly, Goldman (2012) claims that selective coding is the selection of a core category that relates to all other categories, thus selecting the real meaning of what is being investigated.

3.   Findings and discussion

Two broad themes emerged from the findings: 1) the role of education initiatives in promoting volunteering; and 2) social inclusion. The chapter provides recommendations on how to advance the state conservation authorities' objectives and how to promote equitable social inclusion on their volunteering programmes.

3.1   Education initiatives in promoting volunteering

People's actions reflect what they understand to be important and what they value. Volunteering in green spaces and protected areas can be an avenue for people who are passionate about conservation to devote some of their time to promote and strengthen such initiatives. Learning about conservation and the importance of parks for the nation but also for each individual can have positive effects on people's lives (Du Toit, Erasmus & Strydom, 2012). However, the results of the study reveal that the majority of the respondents are unaware of the conservation volunteering opportunities and biodiversity conservation. Six out of 10 community members stated that they didn't have knowledge about conservation-focused volunteer organisations in their country. The quote below illustrates this perfectly:

Group 6: *"The majority of our people lack information about conservation."*

The lack of knowledge about biodiversity conservation is not restricted to community members. Fifty-two percent (question 2) of the respondents indicated that they had the subject of Conservation or Environmental Studies at school, but some stated that it was not in the syllabus form, meaning the teacher had personally been responsible for adding the content. Eighty-six percent (question 7) of respondents indicated that they did not have knowledge about conservation-orientated volunteer organisations in the country, and only eleven percent indicated that they have some knowledge. Ninety-eight percent (question 11) of the students indicated that they think it is important for them to take part in helping to conserve and protect the parks. Furthermore, 92% (question 12) indicated that they think conservation-orientated volunteer organisations such as the SANParks Honorary Rangers can play a role in increasing South Africans' voluntary involvement and participation in protecting natural resources such as parks. In addition, 92% (question 6) indicated that they would be willing to participate should they be given a chance to get involved in conservation volunteer activities.

The lack of knowledge about the importance of biodiversity conservation amongst community members, coupled with the fact that about half of the students state that they had conservation studies at school, indicate that this is a structural problem. Furthermore, some of those community members who had an idea about conservation- orientated volunteer organisations in the country felt that it is not easy to become part of the conservation volunteer organisations. When discussing joining the SHRs or an ecotourism conservation effort with the community members, the following was stated:

Community Respondent Group 6 (different people in one household): *"We do not understand how the organisations (SHRs) operate. 2. Their application forms are not user-friendly. 3. Their way of communication is not easy for an uneducated person to understand. 4. Government must intervene through it [to make it accessible and understandable to us]."*

This suggests that conservation volunteer organisations need to make changes within their organisations in order to cater for historically disadvantaged individuals (HDIs). The other issue highlighted by these findings is the absence of biodiversity conservation studies in the high school curriculum. The current national school curriculum of South Africa aims to equip all learners – irrespective of socio-economic background, race and gender and physical or intellectual ability – with the knowledge, skills and values necessary to be meaningful participatory citizens of a free country. It can be argued that the curriculum does not always help much in aligning our students with 'meaningful participation' when it comes to conservation studies. The lack of information at high school level in some areas/rural areas may be affecting a majority of students as some only get to learn about conservation studies when pursue their tertiary education. The quote below from a tourism student suggests getting students from different educational levels together:

Tourism Student Respondent 17: *"Include modules related to conservation and get students from the high school to tertiary level involved."*

In most cases, this is too late to make an informed choice and understand the role of tourism studies, ecotourism and issues such as volunteering in parks. The lack of knowledge negatively affects students who should be motivated in tourism subjects and conservation lectures at high school – especially if they are in communities who combine their livelihoods with the success of the parks in ecotourism activities – to conduct research on conservation or local community ecotourism-related studies.

Some of community members felt that conservation education should begin at a very early age at school, as evident in the quote below:

Community respondent – Group 10: *"We think it will be better if this study can be introduced at school level so that the kids can grow up with the knowledge and it will make it easier for them to volunteer because they will grow up with the interest and love of nature."*

Conservation strategies that can be used to promote biodiversity education and hands-on experience for communities can trigger the desire and passion to protect/conserve the natural resources in the protected areas. To complement education strategies, the marketing division could develop campaigns to encourage high school learners to participate in conservation volunteering, like SHRs. Such programmes speak directly to the development of citizenship constituency in conservation. The Batho Pele White Paper (1997) is aimed at providing a policy framework and a practical implementation strategy for the transformation of Public Service Delivery. This White Paper is primarily about how public services are provided, and specifically about improving the efficiency and effectiveness of the way in which services are delivered (Department of Public Service and Administration, 1997:11). The Batho Pele White Paper signalled a strong government intention to adopt a citizen-orientated approach to service delivery, informed by the eight Batho Pele principles of consultation, service standards, access, courtesy, information, openness and transparency, redress and value for money (Department of Public Service and Administration, 1997:16-17). This infers that SANParks' activities as a public park should embrace diversity in the people who work for the parks and who visit the parks, with continuous transparent and ethical communication about why parks and wild areas are important and why volunteering plays an important role in this future.

Coding resulted in a conceptualisation of three selective key themes: 1) volunteerism and the Constitution; 2) the Department of Education's conservation education; and 3) adult conservation education. Regarding the Department of Education's conservation education and adult conservation education: the findings indicate that the theme should be taken into consideration as respondents indicated the importance of introducing conservation education in schools by the Department of Education. In addition, adult education (adults not attending school) about conservation is a matter of consideration by protected areas, possibly through SHRs and other possible conservation volunteering programmes. Furthermore, adult education should be extended to high school teachers as all interviewed teachers indicated that they have never received any formal training, including orientation about student educational programmes offered by SANParks, for example the Cape to Cairo Programme and the SANParks Junior HR Programme.

A study by Du Toit *et al.*, (2012) strongly supports the power of learning and teaching in volunteering, highlighting that the communities learn their role in supporting the park, and, by being exposed to the tourism industry, community members might also create economic opportunities from this experience. In light of this, increasing the number of HDIs in the Honorary Ranger organisation would benefit both the park and the community.

3.2   Social inclusion

The voluntary work done by the SHRs in SANParks has been praised in the SANParks' annual reports, the KNP homepage, SANParks Honorary Rangers webpage and a local newspaper (Lowvelder). Despite the success of such initiatives, the programme struggles to reach those who live on the other side of the park's fences. Local communities identified the following challenges that prevented them from volunteering: lack of knowledge, lack of skills, language/communication barrier, park access constraints and socio-economic barriers.

These challenges contribute to a lack of interest in conservation volunteering, especially in the communities where human basic needs have not been met yet. This suggests that, to attract HDIs, volunteering organisations would have to make structural changes.

A high number of volunteers indicate that there is support for the park and its conservation measures, thus the higher the number of volunteers, especially from historically disadvantaged race groups, the higher the environmental awareness and the stronger the support for the park. This is why diversity in the volunteer group is key in establishing the support for the park. Having a diverse volunteer group will ensure a brighter future for the SHRs as an organisation because every South African citizen from any background will start to see the organisation as their own and take the opportunity to serve in the organisation. In addition, this act would provide a sound succession plan as the matured volunteers oversee the junior HRs. This speaks to the educational dimension of such initiatives as a way to not only fill in a need for conservation education, but also to become attractive to different groups of people.

Over 90% of community members mentioned poverty and unemployment as some of the challenges preventing them from doing anything else, including volunteering. Conservation volunteering might not be well known, but volunteering, however, is not new to these communities. Prior to 1994, communities volunteered to fight the injustices of the apartheid system. Increased knowledge of volunteering opportunities and what volunteering entails could lead to increased numbers of volunteers in parks. Potentially, this knowledge about conservation and the tourism industry related to it could lead to community members benefiting from the tourism influx generated by the parks. However, this brings into play another barrier in that these volunteers may not have the skills to run tourism jobs. This creates a cycle that will be perpetuated as long as local community schools are unable to teach tourism and conservation studies and integrate the possibility of training at university level for a tourism/conservation-related career.

Another challenge for local communities is the cost of volunteering. Although these are non-paid opportunities, they do carry a cost that might be too expensive to some community members. To volunteer requires one to travel, which costs money. Volunteers need to have clean uniforms, which carries the underlying assumption that volunteers live in areas with a stable water supply. Thus, on top of acquiring conservation knowledge, one needs to be financially and socio-economically sound, and have time to be able to volunteer. The following excerpts illustrate how socio-economic challenges continue to prevent HDIs from volunteering:

KNP Respondent 8: *"My personal feeling is that, you can "be" a volunteer of any something if you have a passion about it. My answer will be, it must be passion driven. Volunteers in this case SHRs, we are not compensating them in any way. They volunteer while they pay their own fuel to come here, they pay for their accommodation where they are staying, while doing duties here and they pay for their meals. So if you talk volunteerism it is in the true sense of the word."*

KNP staff member: 4: *"Yes, at times it costs you in different scenarios. It will cost in a sense that you need to have transport from Phalaborwa gate to Letaba camp, the closest camp. It will also cost when doing duties at the gate which is not much, because it is at the door step. Yeah, it does cost money but you don't have to be rich to become a SHR, but you must be able to put petrol to Letaba and back let's say about R150.00."*

Communication about and dissemination of not only information but also of opportunities is another identified challenge. The importance of local language usage, especially with the HDIs, is vital, especially when communicating with illiterate elderly community members. Enhancement of marketing platforms and advertising the SHRs and KNP/its activities on local/community newspaper, national radio (Ligwalagwala FM), community radio, visits by volunteers are suggested by local community members.

HRs Respondent 3: *"Having been a SHR for many years, I think the marketing is a lot better now. However, it is still unclear to me how this appeals to local KNP communities and if the concept of volunteering in conservation appeals to them. The marketing in my opinion is not pitched at the right level and needs to be community specific."*

In addition, there seems to no marketing of volunteering programmes directed at tertiary students. The following excerpt indicates that there is no knowledge of an integrated marketing strategy/programme aimed at educating tertiary students except for the junior SHRs programme.

SHR Respondent 3: *"Within SHR I don't think there are marketing strategies for tourism students. I don't believe this avenue has been fully explored. Unless there is something specific within SHR that would attract tourism students, it is unlikely that the SHR programme would yield a sustainable interest in SHR for students. It really depends on what students are aiming to achieve. Within SHR I've always believed that what you put in is what you will get out. Like with most things in life, it's what you make of it!"*

This is a pool of potential of SHRs volunteers who already chose the field of tourism and conservation, soon to become involved in the industry. The same students can be envisaged as ambassadors of the organisations in their households and communities and amongst their peers in the university community.

4.   Conclusion and recommendations

In conclusion, challenges related to education on school and university level and social inclusion prevent a more diverse participation in the SHRs programme in the area researched. This chapter recommends socio-economic and financial solutions, eco-education programmes presented using local language/s and the establishment of communication channels suitable for average township/ homeland community members as ways to try to overcome these challenges.

To oversee the coordination and implementation of the recommendations made, a task team with local community representatives, SANParks staff and Honorary Rangers is advisable. The inclusion of local community members would promote a sense of ownership and it would establish communication between the community as whole and the institution. The team can include academics, community members' representative/s, SANPark/KNP, office of the MEC/Premier, SHRs, both primary and high school educators and the Department of Basic Education. A development of SHRs and SANParks marketing strategy, which would be specially designed to target such communities, is highly recommended. Based on the findings of this chapter, recommendations for further research are suggested to guide the contribution to and building of a diverse, knowledgeable volunteer organisation.

5. Acknowledgements

I, Precious Shabalala, would like to express my gratitude to the KNP Scientific Services Unit for trusting me to conduct this kind of research in the park. I would like to express my gratitude to the University of Mpumalanga's Research Department for the support through the writing retreat. My gratitude is extended to everyone who has supported me, including all the participants and respondents. A big thank you goes to my daughter for being the source of my strength, and my loving God, Jehovah, for making everything possible.

References

Armsworth PR, Cantú-Salazar L, Parnell M, Booth JE, Stoneman R, Davies ZG. 2013. Opportunities for Cost-Sharing in Conservation: Variation in Volunteering Effort Across Protected Areas. *PLoS ONE*, 8(1):e55395. https://doi.org/10.1371/journal.pone.0055395

Barbosa, O., Tratalos, J.A., Armsworth, P.R., Davies, R.G., Fuller, R.A., Johnson, P. & Gatson, K.J. 2007. Who benefits from access to green space? A case study from Sheffield, UK. *Landscape and Urban Planning*, 83:187-195.

Bremer, S. & Graeff, P. 2007. Volunteer management in German National Parks – from random action toward a volunteer program. *Human Ecology*, 35:489-496.

Bryce, R., Oliver, M.K., Davies, L., Gray, H. & Urquhart, J. 2011. Turning back the tide of American mink invasion at an unprecedented scale through community participation and adaptive management. *Biological Conservation*, 144:575-583.

Carruthers, J. 1995. *The Kruger National Park: A social and political history*. Pietermaritzburg: University of Natal Press.

Crall, A.W., Newman, G.J., Jarnevich, C.S., Stohlgren, T.J. & Waller, D.M. 2010. Improving and integrating data on invasive species collected by citizen scientists. *Biological Invasions*, 12:3419-3428.

Department of Environmental Affairs. 2003. Protected Areas Act. Pretoria.

Department of Public Service and Administration. 1997. The White Paper on Transforming Public Service Delivery (Batho Pele White Paper) Notice 1459 of 1997. https://www.gov.za/sites/default/files/gcis_document/201409/183401.pdf [Accessed 05 May 2020].

Du Toit, G.S., Erasmus, B.J. & Strydom, J.W. 2012. *Introduction to business management*. 8th edition. Cape Town: Oxford Press.

Goldman, G.A. 2012. Exploring academics' experiences of a merger in higher education: The reflective experience of mergers (REM) -framework. *African Journal of Business Management*, 6(14):4862-4879. doi:10.5807/AJBM11.2137

Halpenny, E.A. & Caissie, L.T. 2003. Volunteering on nature conservation projects: Volunteer experience, attitudes and values. *Tourism Recreation Research*, 28(3): 25-33.

Klein, & Klein, J.L. & Fontan, J.M & Harrisson, D. & Lévesque, B. 2013. The Quebec Model: A social innovation system founded on cooperation and consensus building. *Cheltenham Glos (UK), Edward Elgar Publishing*.

Koss, R. & Kingsley, J. 2010.Volunteer health and emotional wellbeing in marine protected areas. *Ocean & Coastal Management*, 53:447-453.

Mabunda, D., Pienaar, D.J. & Verhoef, J. 2003. The Kruger National Park: A century of management and research. In: J. Du Toit, K.H. Rogers & H.C. Biggs (eds). The Kruger experience: Ecology and management of savanna heterogeneity, 3-21. Washington D.C.: Island Press.

McCarthy, D.P., Donald, P.F., Scharlemann, J.P.W., Buchanan, G.M., Balmford, A., Green, J.M.H., Bennun, L.A., Burgess, N.D., Fishpool, L.D.C., Garnett, S.T., Leonard, D.L., Maloney, R.F., Morling, P., Schaefer, H.M., Symes, A., Wiedenfeld, D.A., Butchart, S.H.M. 2012. *Financial costs of meeting global biodiversity conservation targets: Current spending and unmet needs.* Science, 338 (2012), pp. 946-949.

Naidoo, R., Balmford, A., Ferraro, P.J., Polasky, S. & Ricketts, T.H. 2006. Integrating economic costs into conservation planning. *Trends in Ecology and Evolution*, 21:681-687.

Ramsey, C.J. & Addison, D.S. 1996. Facilitating a multiparcel land acquisition project in the western big Cypress region of Collier County, Florida, USA. *Natural Areas Journal*, 16:36-40.

Ruslandi, V.O. & Putz, F.E. 2011. Overestimating conservation costs in Southeast Asia. *Frontiers in Ecology and the Environment*, 9:542-544.

SANParks Volunteers. 2018. About us. http://www.sanparksvolunteers.org/about_us.php [Accessed 05 July 2018].

Schmeller, D.S., Henry, P.Y., Julliard,R., *et al.,* 2009. Advantages of volunteer-based biodiversity monitoring in Europe. *Conserv Biol*, 23(2):307-316. doi:10.1111/j.1523-1739.2008.01125.x

Siyabona Africa. n.d. Kruger – Into the future. http://www.krugerpark.co.za/Krugerpark_ Travel_Guide-travel/kruger-into-the-future.html [Accessed 05 May 2020].

Silvertown, J. 2009. A new dawn for citizen science. *Trends in Ecology and Evolution*, 24: 467-471.

Swemmer, L.K. & Taljaard, S. 2011. SANParks, people and adaptive management: Understanding a diverse field of practice during changing times: Essay. *Koedoe*, 53(2):1-7. doi:10.4102/koedoe.v53i2.1017

Sustainable Tourism – Parks and Culture. 1997-2010. Sustainable tourism online. http://sustain.pata.org/sustainable-tourism-online/ [Accessed 20 March 2014].

Veal, A.J. 2011. *Research methods for leisure and tourism: A practical guide* (4th edition). Harlow: Financial Times Prentice Hall.

Venter, O., Magrach, A., Outram, N., Klein, C.J., Marco, M.D. & Watson, J.E.M. 2018. Bias in protected-area location and its effects on long-term aspirations of biodiversity conventions. *Conservation Biology*, 32:127-134.

Walker, C., Bohlin, A.,Hall, R. & Kepe, T. (eds) 2010. Land, memory, reconstruction and justice. Ohio: Ohio University Press.

Watson, J., Dudley, N., Segan, D. 2014. The performance and potential of protected areas. *Nature*, 515: 67-73. www.https://doi.org/10.1038/nature13947

Wilson, K.A., Cawardine, J. & Possingham, H.P. 2009. Setting conservation priorities. *Annals of the New York Academy of Sciences*, 1162:237-264.

Chapter 12

Reflections on experiences working alongside informal traders at Warwick Junction in Durban: a human factors and ergonomics perspective

Jonathan Davy[1], Andrew Todd[1], Richard Dobson[2], Tasmi Quazi[2], Patric Ndlovu[2] and Laura Alfers[3]

[1]DEPARTMENT OF HUMAN KINETICS AND ERGONOMICS, RHODES UNIVERSITY,

[2]ASIYE E'TAFULENI, WARWICK JUNCTION,

[3]WOMEN IN INFORMAL EMPLOYMENT: GLOBALIZING AND ORGANIZING (WIEGO) AND DEPARTMENT OF SOCIOLOGY, RHODES UNIVERSITY.

jonathan.davy@ru.ac.za

1.   Human factors and ergonomics: an overview

Human factors and ergonomics (HFE), as defined by the International Ergonomics Association (IEA, 2020), refers to the scientific discipline concerned with the understanding of interactions among humans and other elements of a system, and the profession that applies theory, principles, data and methods to design in order to optimize human wellbeing and overall system performance. Articulated differently, HFE focuses on understanding the system in which humans interact with their environment, with this focus being applicable to work (Dul, Bruder, Buckle, Carayon, Falzon, Marras, Wilson & Van der Doelen, 2012), sport (Balague, Torrents, Hristovski, Davids & Araújo., 2013) or everyday life. Understanding these systems and how they either enhance or detract from the human's ability to remain safe and productive provides HFE specialists with insights into how to better design for humans, with humans (i.e. a human-centred approach is adopted).

By way of introduction to HFE, John Wilson, in his 2014 paper titled *Fundamentals of systems ergonomics/human factors* provides a framework to characterise the approach that HFE should take in order to successfully reach its dual outcomes of maintaining human wellbeing and safety and maximising performance and productivity. The first of these fundamental notions is that HFE must take a systems approach (Dul *et al.,* 2012; Wilson, 2014). This highlights the importance of identifying and understanding what components of the system a human interacts with, which can best be illustrated through the Work Systems model (Smith and Carayon-Sainfort, 1989; Carayon, Hundt, Karsh, Gurses, Alvarado, Smith & Brennan, 2006). This model (**Figure 1**) highlights five overriding components of a system (Smith and Carayon-Sainfort, 1989; Carayon *et al.,* 2006). This model is useful in that it provides a schematic map through which a system can be understood either at a micro level, where the focus is largely on the human-task interaction, at a meso level, where the interaction between teams of people and their working environment is the focus, or at a macro level, where the overall organisational design and how it is affected by the external environment becomes relevant in trying to optimise or balance system performance and human safety. Recently, Thatcher, Waterson, Todd and Moray (2018), preceded by Moray (1995), argue that HFE even has a role to play in resolving a plethora of global issues relating to food, water, energy, violence and terrorism, pollution and waste, and health and medicine.

The second notion refers to the importance of understanding the interactions between these different components of the system (Wilson, 2014) and to appreciate how these interactions (or a lack thereof) influence the different components and the overall outputs and safety of the humans within. The third notion emphasises the importance of understanding the context in which the system exists and interactions occur (Wilson, 2014). Too often, interventions or changes to an existing system are made without an understanding of the current and past ways in which and why 'people do things', which give some insights into the contextual factors that need to be harnessed to effect more meaningful change. This places an emphasis on shifting research away from the laboratory and into *in situ*, otherwise the interactions do not reflect the context within which they occur.

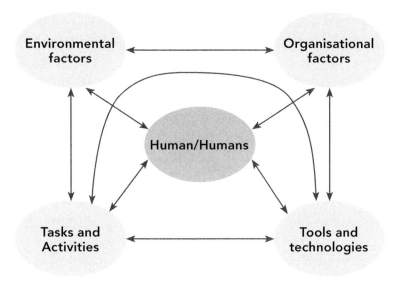

Figure 1: The work systems model (adapted from Smith and Carayon-Sainfort, 1989; Carayon et al., 2006)

Holism, the importance of understanding the system stakeholders, inputs and outputs, is the fourth notion that Wilson emphasises. Understanding the human and their interaction with the system holistically, and acknowledging the impact that it has on different human responses (physical, cognitive, social and emotional) is an important precursor to taking a participatory approach to either intervening or redesigning a system. The fifth concept is that of emergence (Wilson, 2014). This refers to the importance of constantly observing the emergent properties, behaviours or outcomes of a system and a human's interactions with it, which can, in most instances, highlight areas that present challenges to work or the use of a product or how to do work differently or better.

Lastly, Wilson argues strongly for the important role that embedding plays in understanding and modifying a system from within (Wilson, 2014). By embedding, HFE specialists are able to fulfil the requirements of the above-mentioned notions – to understand the system components and their interactions holistically, how the context shapes these interactions and the emergent properties or behaviours. While this requires time, effort and interaction with multiple levels of stakeholders, it is a critical component of an ergonomist's work, and will likely dictate the level (micro, meso or macro) and quality of the intervention.

2. HFE in the future world of work

Given the focus of the discipline, HFE is uniquely positioned to contribute to understanding and designing work systems following the rapid changes in the future world of work. Ergonomics originated out of the need to design tasks and work environments and systems to meet the needs of the humans (Kuorinka, 2000; Hollnagel, 2001) and was, in its infancy, focused predominantly on physical factors and their impact on the human and, by extension, work performance (Hollnagel, 2001). The need to optimise work systems during and after the Second World War and Industrial Revolution was also instrumental in framing the focus of the discipline. Since the 1980s, the appreciation of how technological development influenced the cognitive and psychological processes of the human resulted in the emergence of cognitive ergonomics, which was primarily focused on optimising human-technology interaction (Hollnagel, 2001). As technology continues to develop, and the way we work continues to be influenced by this, HFE's focus has been centred on work that is considered the 'norm' – where there is a defined employer–employee relationship in the context of formal workplaces, in both high-, middle- and low-income countries. Despite the fact that there have long been calls for HFE to address the multiple challenges faced by workers in low to middle income countries, now often referred to as the Global South and previously referred to as developing countries (Scott, 2009), the focus of these calls has largely revolved around formal work.

Work as we know it, the conventional 9 to 5, five days a week with weekends off, is changing rapidly and is, by and large, very different in the contemporary view of work. Recently, the International Labour Organisation has set up a commission to investigate, understand and potentially prepare for the changes in how work is being done around the world – this group, the Commission on Future of Work, has identified a number of key aspects that provide a glimpse into what the future of how we work will look like.

3. New ways of working: the gig economy, digital work and the platform economy

One consideration is found in the International Labour Organisation (ILO) reports that state that, since 2000, there has been a marked growth in the provision of services online, referred to as the platform economy or digital work, which can take the forms of crowd work or work on demand via applications that form part of the gig economy (ILO, 2018). For instance, there has been an increase in the growth of disruptive technologies and ways of doing work. Businesses such as Uber, AirBnB, TaskRabbit and other service-related industries and shared economies have upset their conventional equivalents (metered taxis, hotels and calling an electrician or plumber or other tradesperson for support). Facilitated through improved connectivity and technology, these industries provide round the clock service and accessibility to consumers, but at a cost to those who provide them. Again, the fact that these industries offer individuals the chance to work when they want means that work hours as we would know them can differ significantly both in terms of when they happen and for how long. In the ILO publication on working time and future of work, it is evident that there is concern around how technology and the new forms of work are blurring the lines between work and home life (Eurofound and the International Labour Office (2017)). The growth in these industries has been driven by the need to be able to self-regulate working time and effort, but their effect on individuals is yet to be determined, particularly around how workers in these jobs can get access to basic protections, such as insurance, leave, health and social benefits and collective bargaining, given that there is no employer–employee relationship. It is also interesting to note that these new types of work also transcend the income bracket countries fall into.

4. A different perspective on the world of work: the informal economy

For many years development economists assumed that as development progressed, low-income traditional economies, including petty trade, small-scale production and casual jobs, would be absorbed into the modern formal economy (Lewis, 1954). It became clear in the 1970s, however, that this model was not matched by empirical reality, even in countries where economic growth was occurring (ILO, 1972). The model came under further scrutiny during the 1980s and 1990s, when developed economies began to see the rise of 'non-standard' employment (an umbrella-term to cover a range of work arrangements including part-time, temporary and agency work, often with low pay, few protections and little chance of upward mobility), and economic crises in Latin America and Asia led to the growth of the informal economy.

A number of theories developed to explain the emergence, continuation and growth of the informal economy. Chen (2012) argues that the informal economy is in fact too complex and heterogenous to be encapsulated by single causal theories. While some informal workers choose to operate informally, many are forced into informal employment during economic downturns, so that it is necessity as well as choice that drives the informal economy. While the informalisation of employment relations is a characteristic of the global economy, it also has to be recognised that in many developing countries the majority of the workforce has never been formally employed. Important as well is that the informal economy is not separate from the formal economy, as the dualists would have it, but is in fact linked into it in complex ways (Chen, 2006; Meagher, 2013). This suggests that more heterodox models are needed which can better capture this complexity (Chen 2012).

4.1   *Defining and profiling the informal economy*

Despite informal employment having long dominated the labour markets of many developing countries up until recently, the informal economy was ignored by economists and policy makers. This started to change in the 1970s when the term 'informal sector' was first coined by the economic anthropologist, Keith Hart (1973), in his study of low-income activities among unskilled migrants from Northern Ghana to Accra, and later adopted by the ILO's 1972 employment mission to Kenya (Chen, 2012). 'Informal economy' is widely accepted to refer to the diversified set of economic activities, enterprises, jobs and workers that are not regulated or protected by the state (Chen, 2012).

While this definition has largely remained unchallenged, the definitional debates around the term informal employment were more complicated. In 2002 the ILO, the International Expert Group of Informal Sector Statistics (called the Delhi Group) and the global network Women in Informal Employment: Globalizing and Organizing (WIEGO) worked together to broaden the concept. In 2003, the 17th ICLS adopted a definition of informal employment which refers to all employment arrangements in which individuals do not get access to social protection through their work, whether the work is for informal enterprises, formal enterprises or households (Vanek, Chen, Carré, Heintz, & Hussmans, 2014). In summary, the three key concepts are:

- The informal sector: production and employment in unregistered enterprises.
- Informal employment: any employment outside of labour protections, whether in formal or informal firms or households.
- The informal economy: all economic activities, enterprises, jobs and workers that are not regulated or protected by the state and the output from them.

Informal employment is not uniform and incorporates a wide variety of statuses in employment, the two most significant being self-employment and waged employment. Each of these incorporates their own sub-categories as follows:

Informal self-employment	Informal wage employment
Employers in informal enterprises Own account workers in informal enterprises (self-employed workers who do not employ others) Contributing family workers (in informal and formal enterprises) Members of informal producers' cooperatives	Employees of informal enterprises Casual or day labourers Paid domestic workers Contract workers (someone who performs work under conditions of dependency, but not within a formal employment relationship) Unregistered or undeclared workers Industrial outworkers

In developed countries, the use of the terms 'non-standard' or 'atypical' work are preferred over using the term 'informal employment' to refer to employment arrangements that would fit into the definitions provided above. The term 'non-standard work' includes: own account self-employed workers, temporary (or fixed term) workers and some part-time workers (Vanek *et al.*, 2014). It also encompasses the gig economy.

In 2018, a revision of status in employment in the informal economy was on the agenda of the 20th ICLS (Carré, Negrete & Vanek, 2017). The 19th ICLS noted in 2013 that there was a strong consensus on the need to revise the International Classification of Status in Employment (ICSE-93) (Carré *et al.*, 2017). One of the suggested revisions that was accepted in 2018 is the incorporation of the concept of 'dependent contractor'. This category of informal employment is aimed at more accurately capturing workers who do not fit easily into either the self-employed or wage worker categories (Carré *et al.*, 2017). Although the definition has not yet been fixed, the working definition is as follows:

- Employed persons with no employees (currently classified as own account) whose access to the market depends on resources provided by an entity that directly benefits from the work performed by the contractor.
- These persons are dependent on another economic unit for access to raw materials, capital items or clients. Their work may be organised or supervised by another economic unit as a client or as an entity that mediates access to clients.
- They are paid for the end product (usually on a piece rate basis).

Recent statistics, released by the ILO show that over two billion of the world's population work informally, which accounts for just over 60% of people employed globally (ILO, 2018). In sub-Saharan Africa, 85.8% of workers work in the informal economy. Due to its particular economic history, South Africa has a much smaller informal economy, with 33% of workers employed informally, a lower percentage

of self-employed informal workers and a higher percentage of informally employed wage workers (Budlender, 2011). Nevertheless self-employment in the
informal sector – the part of the informal economy in which the workers in Warwick
Junction are located – plays a significant role in reducing poverty rates in the
country (Cichello & Rogan, 2017).

WARWICK JUNCTION IN DURBAN, SOUTH AFRICA

Warwick Junction is one of the largest transport nodes in the city of Durban,
KwaZulu-Natal, South Africa. On average, nearly 500 000 commuters move
through the station each day to and from their place of work. An emergent
characteristic of this number of people being in one place was the development
of a large-scale informal sector, which houses as many as 8 000 street traders,
the majority of whom are women. The junction has several markets that trade
in a variety of goods, including a fresh produce section, a bovine head market,
a general food court, the early morning market (chicken traders), the traditional
medicine market, the music bridge, a mixed strip section that sells a variety of
goods and perishables (ranging from cigarettes and snacks to hand lotions), and
finally, the Brook Street market that has bead makers, garment makers and clay
traders (Dobson, Skinner & Nicholson, 2009). The trade of certain items vary, depending on the time of day and the needs of potential customers – traders are
responsive to customer needs (Dobson *et al.*, 2009). The majority of people working in and around Warwick Junction are self-employed own account workers
who operate in public spaces and along the road sides.

Initially, in the 1990s, traders were allowed to sell at the junction but were not
provided with any amenities and trading facilities (Dobson *et al.*, 2009). Historically, African women were not permitted to live in the cities, and, as a result, they
did not acquire accommodation in the cities and most commuted between their
rural home and the city to do street trading (Dobson *et al.*, 2009; Siqwana-Ndulo,
2013). The banning of traders from the streets at night made it difficult to find
overnight accommodation as it was often expensive; this resulted in several traders sleeping in the market with their trading stock (Dobson *et al.*, 2009; Siqwana-
Ndulo, 2013).

In the present day, there are still several workers who sleep at Warwick Junction, mainly the porters and lime stone traders. The porters or barrow operators
offer their services of transporting goods around the market for traders and
customers and their working hours are from 04:00 until after 21:00 (Dobson *et al.*,
2009). The morning routine includes delivering traders' goods to the trading site
from the storage facility before the traders arrive (Dobson *et al.*, 2009). Often

times the porters will sleep in groups around their heavily packed trolleys to avoid paying for overnight storage (Dobson *et al.*, 2009).

A unique characteristic of Warwick Junction is the presence and active involvement of Asiye e'Tafuleni (AeT). AeT is a non-profit organisation (NPO) that was set up in 2009 to provide urban design solutions to informal workers in Durban, and specifically in Warwick Junction where it is based. The NPO was founded by two ex-municipal employees who had both worked on the regeneration of the Warwick Precinct during the late 1990s. The two have unique skills in architecture, urban design, participatory processes and social facilitation. These skills, combined with over 20 years of sustained relationship building with the Warwick community, have allowed them to establish a unique South African 'laboratory' for developing and testing participatory human-centred urban design solutions to support urban informal livelihoods. It is this human-centred and participatory approach to their work that attracted researchers in the field of HFE.

4.2   Why should HFE take an interest in the informal economy?

Of interest to HFE specialists, is how the characteristics of the informal economy work (the environment, the tools, tasks and activities and the organisational, social, political and economic structures and processes) affect the individuals that operate within that system. Workers in the informal economy usually use adapted technologies for the purposes of their work, which are usually small in scale but at times can be incredibly labour intensive (Alfers, Bali, Bird, Castellanos, Chen, Dobson, Hughes, Roever & Rogan, 2016). The actual individuals working in these public spaces are more often than not from a lower socio-economic status, with little formal education, which therefore drives the need to generate income through informal activities as the access to formal employment is limited. There is also a large proportion of women in the informal economy, which results from a complex interaction of social, cultural and patriarchal norms dictating that women work in low-income jobs. There is also very little in the way of support for mothers who have to work but have no-one to assist them with their children.

Informal traders are often affected by inclement weather, which can damage or destroy their goods. Furthermore, exposure to heat, cold, rain and other artificial pollutants such dust, smoke and chemicals can affect work in this context as well as the overall health of those exposed to these elements (Ametepeh, 2011). The nature of the work can be physically taxing, which, when performed in hot environments, presents additional challenges to the successful execution of the physical tasks (Lund, Alfers & Santana, 2016). Furthermore, the actual physical urban space they operate in is seldom designed with informal workers in mind, resulting in significant mismatches between the physical environment and the work. There are also many examples of how, in order to work, informal workers use a variety of adapted tools and technologies (Chen, 2016). An example of this from Warwick Junction specifically is the trolley used by the water porter, which is fashioned out of bread crates and other sourced materials. The use of industrially made shopping trolleys attracts negative attention from police who usually confiscate them, hence the innovation to fashion a self-made, functional yet rather unattractive trolley. From a social perspective, informal traders more often than not have very little social or legal protection in their work spaces, characterised by a high prevalence of abuse from city officials, police and members of the public who perceive these activities as nuisances that take up space and are unattractive. More broadly, non-inclusive city planning, design and policy-making add to the burden of trying to generate an income.

Another challenge that has emerged from previous research concerning time-use in the informal economy is the concept of time poverty. This concept refers to how competing claims on an individual's time limit the choices they make about time allocation. They usually need to make some compromise, resulting in either increased work intensity or the neglect of other important activities such as those that are economically productive or leisure- or recreation-focused or those dedicated to sleep and rest (Kes & Swaminathan, 2006; Gammage, 2010). In particular, women are restricted to activities related to or performed in the domestic sphere (this can include care work) and/or activities that warrant extended hours of work and reduced hours of rest and recovery (Gammage, 2010).

In an attempt to begin to understand the context and the systems within which the informal economy operates, specifically in the context of Warwick Junction, the Department of Human Kinetics and Ergonomics has started research into how certain aspects of working in the informal economy present challenges to the traders. These challenges will be outlined below in the form of two case studies.

4.3   Understanding work as done: examples of the application of HFE principles in the informal economy

CASE STUDY 1: Time-use survey at Warwick Junction

Following an introduction to the informal economy at Warwick Junction, we were interested in understanding the effects of one particular aspect of workers in this context: how they used their time (Hirway, 2009). Time-use surveys offer an excellent, non-invasive and easy means of gaining insight into how work is done, the time allotted to it and the value associated with the work performed. Through time-use surveys, one is able to understand the nature of the workforce and determine the wellbeing and socio-economic status of individuals, all of which can be used to support and recognise activities that are not always formally recognised, such as informal work or care work. From an HFE perspective, understanding time-use affords important insight into how work and working time is arranged and how other activities that require time (commuting, domestic and personal activities, eating and sleeping) are arranged around work. Anecdotally, informal workers are thought to work excessively long days (over 12 hours) and have limited time for personal, domestic- and sleep- related activities, which ultimately impact their ability to rest and recharge and be productive at work. As such, we sought to determine the time-use behaviours of a small cohort of traders at Warwick Junction with the help of Asiye e'Tafuleni (AeT).

Ten traders (5 males and 5 females) – including one traditional hat maker, one storage operator, one bovine head cook (this refers to a cows head, which is a Zulu delicacy), one mealie cook and vendor (mealies are also referred to as maize or corn, the cooked mealies are conveyed in and sold from supermarket trolleys), two cardboard and plastic recyclers (who use trolleys to collect and convey recyclables to central areas where they are purchased by middle-agents), one water transporter (who transports up to 400 litres of water nearly 5 km every day), one bead maker and seller and two barrow operators (who use self-made carts to transport informal traders goods from the storage facilities to their trading posts and back again every day) – were recruited from Warwick Junction.

We sought to determine their time-use by means of an activity clock – a 24-hour clock presented on a piece of cardboard, which allowed each trader to divide their day up according to the time they allocated to various activities. All traders were asked to indicate the amount of time they dedicated to the following activities on both normal and busy days: work and work-related activities, commuting, household and child care activities, personal activities (grooming, bathing, using the toilet, eating) and sleep.

What emerged was that all informal traders who were interviewed work between 53 and 87 hours per week and, on average, 12 hours per day for six and sometimes seven days per week (Davy, Rasetsoke, Todd, Quazi, Ndlovu, Dobson & Alfers, 2018). More detailed analysis of the data revealed that work duration differed between busy and normal times of the year or month, with traders working nearly 13.5 hours per day during busy periods and 10.7 hours during regular or normal periods. The most extreme example in this case was a 15.5 hour work shift, reported by a bovine head cook. These work periods were also, in some cases, preceded and followed by extended commutes home, with the worst example being 4.5 hour commute. This left traders with 6.1 hours and 7.1 hours for sleep during busy and normal periods respectively, which, according to literature in the area, can be insufficient for some adults.

A comparison between male and female traders revealed that female traders generally have longer work hours, a higher domestic load, less personal time and less time for sleep. This supports previous findings that have consistently demonstrated that female traders experience time poverty, where the competing claims (to work and fulfil the traditional responsibilities associated with the household) limit or require them to compromise on other areas (such as personal time and sleep) (Gammage, 2010; Kes & Swaminathan, 2006). Irrespective of gender, the study highlighted how, in addition to the plethora of social, economic and physical work-related challenges, informal traders likely work extended shifts, which, when combined with extended commutes and other house-related activities, limits the opportunity for adequate sleep and recovery. This may in turn affect the long-term health and work ability of these traders, which the study highlighted as a cause for concern. At the same time, this small study revealed examples of the everyday resilience of informal traders who, in spite of the systemic challenges they face, continue to work in a very routine and organised way.

CASE STUDY 2: An activity analysis of trolleys used by cardboard collectors at Warwick Junction

As part of ongoing collaboration with AeT, the Department of Human Kinetics and Ergonomics participated in research aimed at exploring whether trolleys, designed by AeT (in collaboration with informal workers), were fit for purpose when used by cardboard collectors at Warwick Junction. AeT has been working with informal recyclers (also known as waste pickers) since 2011 through a collaboration with the eThekwini Municipality. During this time they began the process of designing trolleys which would ease the load on the waste picker's bodies, with the intention of increasing collector productivity while also ensuring that the trolleys were robust enough to be used in a challenging urban environment. In 2017 AeT received a commission from the municipality to develop the trolleys beyond the prototype phase. It was at this point that the collaboration with the Human Kinetics and Ergonomics (HKE) Department was set up.

Four informal recyclers who specialise in the collection of cardboard participated in the study, which comprised an observational task and activity analysis of these traders during their use of the trolleys to collect cardboard. Task analysis refs to the observation and recording of the different components of the work, such as pushing and pulling the trolley, cutting, flattening and stacking the cardboard and selling it to the 'middleman' at the local recycling depot. The activity analysis takes this one step further by exploring the way in which the tasks are performed. For example, in order to flatten the cardboard, traders use sharp pieces of glass as opposed to a more appropriate tool such as a paper knife. The reason for this choice stems from the fact that legislation, specifically the law of Nuisances and Behaviour in a Public Places, prohibits informal traders from carrying knives or sharp objects that could be used as a weapon. Without directly observing and engaging with traders while they work, it would not be possible to understand this emergent behaviour, which is a product of the way the system is designed and organised. Additionally, the waste pickers were asked to give their feedback on the appropriateness (positive and negative aspects) of the trolleys for the job they performed.

Following the completion of the study, it emerged that the waste pickers were satisfied with the trolley design. They did, however, make important suggestions for improving the trolley design, based on their experience of using them daily. Furthermore, through the observation of the waste pickers, it emerged that, despite the good design of the trolley, the success of the cardboard collection process is influenced by many other systemic barriers and constraints. Four particular constraints were identified. The first was the weather – the wind, heat and rain can sometimes make pushing/pulling the trolleys physically challenging. Furthermore, if the cardboard gets wet, the collectors receive less money for the load, as payment is based on the mass of the cardboard collected and with it being wet the mass is not an accurate reflection of the actual mass collected. A second systemic constraint was the presence of police, who, in some cases, would confiscate goods from the collectors and sell them for their own profits. A third challenge was the terrain and the physical state of the roads or pavements on which the collectors would have to push the trolleys. The undulating terrain, combined with a loaded trolley, would at times be physically taxing, while pushing their trolleys in the road was made difficult by the presence of potholes and traffic. During periods of peak traffic, traders would be forced to push their trolleys on the pavement, which then meant they were required to navigate through many pedestrians, which also made work slow. In an attempt to avoid the traffic, collectors would also start work early.

The study highlighted that, although the intervention from AeT was successful in that it made the work of the waste collectors easier, the system in which the trolleys were being used still presents barriers to effective, safe and meaningful work for these waste pickers. This emphasises the importance of considering the broader systemic design of systems in which people work, alongside micro interventions such as the trolley design. It also emphasises the need not only to focus on the work system itself but also look at the broader picture and other stakeholders that influence the system. For example, based on both case studies presented here, it is clear that there is a need to understand and work with local municipalities and law enforcement officials.

5. Reflections on experiences in the informal economy: the importance of building bridges between the grassroots and the ivory tower

The partnership with Asiye e'Tafuleni originated from the request made by the organisation to assist with the testing and refinement of the trolleys described in the above-mentioned case study. Although the research has contributed to an improved understanding of the specific challenges relating to issues of time-use and the systemic challenges that waste pickers face, the collaboration with AeT and those involved in the informal economy has been of immense benefit to those (academics and students) involved in HFE. This section outlines some critical reflections on how these projects have shaped our view of our own discipline of HFE, how it has contextualised the notions put forward by Wilson and how it exemplifies the importance of embedded, engaged and locally responsive teaching, learning and research in preparing students to make a meaningful impact on the ever-changing South African (and global) workplace. This is followed by a set of reflections from AeT on their experiences of working with universities and students to advance the interests of informal workers.

5.1 Shifting perspectives of HFE in the world of work

Work, whether formal or informal, requires people to interact with one another and many different components of their immediate system. The interactions observed at Warwick present numerous challenges to those working there (e.g. health, social), but also constitute excellent examples of every day resilience and innovation, which should be understood better in an attempt to improve the working and ultimately living conditions of many working in the Informal Economy

5.1.1 HOW WORK IN THE INFORMAL ECONOMY HAS SHAPED HFE EDUCATION

Prior to the start of our collaboration with AeT and our exposure to informal work at Warwick Junction in particular, the focus of the Department, with respect to research, teaching and learning, revolved around more formal work, mainly because the discipline had been restricted to this context. With respect to teaching and learning and putting HFE and human-centred design into context, exposure to informality has reshaped and enhanced our ability to provide locally and contextually relevant examples of work and work systems to our students, which not only give students a different perspective of what it means to work, but also affords them a more transformed, nuanced and realistic view of what many South Africans (and Africans) face when working in the informal economy. A vital component of this journey was how the collaboration pushed the university HFE academics and students to go beyond our academic ivory towers and to engage with and recognise the reality of most people trying to make a living within South Africa. It also offered a real and, at times, raw perspective on some of the systemic barriers that some traders face on a daily basis. This was captured by one of the students who conducted his honours research project at Warwick when he wrote: "... *to be honest, it was the most eye-opening experience for me. To actually see, first-hand how difficult it is for IE workers to make a living and who have no education was hard to comprehend coming from someone (myself) who has been educated. I take a lot for granted as do other South Africans who drive past them [informal workers] without batting an eyelid or that they consider them a nuisance to our society.*" This statement from a white, privileged male, demonstrates the profound impact that spending time in this context had on the student and his preconceived ideas of those in the informal economy.

Furthermore, with reference to the work systems model (**Figure 1**), spending time in Warwick Junction allowed for us as educators to be able to give a number of examples of different components of a system and how they interact and how these interactions affect the human. Both case studies provide ample material which can be applied in a classroom setting to give context to the theory behind the work systems model. As we strive to provide students with experiences that bring home the realities of work as done rather than work as imagined, these in situ experiences are crucial. These examples are also crucial in opening students' eyes to the realities of work in South Africa and changing students' perceptions from initially seeing informal traders as a nuisance to understanding the vital role they play in the South African economy.

In terms of certain core concepts in HFE education, such as resilience, the collaboration with AeT and the traders at Warwick Junction provided novel examples that lent new meaning to the terms in the context of work. According to Hollnagel, Nemeth and Dekker (2009), for a system (and the individuals within it) to be resilient, it (they) should be able to predict what may happen, monitor what is happening, respond effectively (and appropriately) when something happens and learn from past experiences. While resilience can refer to how a system (or an individual) bounces back from acute or catastrophic shocks or challenges, a more nuanced view holds resilience as the ability to cope with and function, despite chronic challenges on a day-to-day basis. In any context, there are daily examples of resilience which provide important insights into how humans cope with, adapt and transform in order to overcome difficulties they face. The term resilience has largely been applied to the context of healthcare and aviation and has not been used in the context of the informal economy. Both the time-use and cardboard collector observation studies highlighted how, in spite of the long daily and weekly work hours, the long commutes and the physically taxing nature of some of the work and other systemic constraints, traders and in particular female traders, continued to work almost every day. The informal traders are also 'designers' in their own right, demonstrating remarkable resilience in adapting technology to suit the environment within which they operate. As such, engaging with technology at the bottom of the pyramid is a vital consideration for HFE researchers and practitioners. There is a need for a focus on high-impact low-cost technology that can easily be introduced into the informal sector to alleviate physical and cognitive strain and improve productivity.

5.1.2 THE RESHAPING OF RESEARCH IN HFE

HFE research, certainly in the context of the Department of Human Kinetics and Ergonomics, has taken a typically rigid scientific approach to studying humans, normally in the context of a laboratory setting where as many as possible extraneous variables have been controlled. In other words, the research has taken a micro view of a component of a system, not a systems approach, which Wilson (2014; p7) argues is a necessity for effective ergonomics intervention development. To this end, Wilson argued that "few if any laboratory studies are properly ergonomics because they cannot account properly for the complexity and multiple factors found in real setting" to embrace and understand complexity of systems and how they work. While laboratory research has its place, it has become evident that, in order to understand the way work is done and the inherent challenges faced by informal workers or any worker in any system for that matter, this research must be carried out in situ. Furthermore, it was refreshing to not be bound by taking hypothesis-driven/deductive-based approaches to research in this context. We entered as participants, as part of the system with the help of those who were already embedded in (AeT) the system. With their help, we approached the effort to learn more about humans in this context through different, contextually relevant yet culturally and linguistically sensitive methods which were suggested and decided upon alongside AeT and other stakeholders who had the necessary insights. This allowed us to move from hypothesis-testing research to broader problem identification and hypothesis generating research.

In the time-use survey study, for instance, the use of the activity clock was particularly effective for determining the time usage amongst the cohort of informal traders. This was attributable to its rather simple design that allowed for the traders to partition their typical (or busy) day up by drawing on the actual clock, much the same as a pie chart. This simple yet effective tool facilitated the collection of quantitative data (through interactions and conversations with the traders) so as to overcome any language or education barriers. In the second case study, activity analysis was adopted in order to investigate the tasks and activities of the cardboard collectors at Warwick Junction. Activity analysis is a method aimed at learning about an individual's conduct, work strategies, thought processes and interactions with others in a given situation. It requires long observations of different patterns of behaviour (or specific behaviours) within a system and is often accompanied by interviews of the workers in order to understand not only *what* people do but also, and more importantly, *why* they do what they do (Garrigou, Daniellou, Carballeda & Ruaud, 1995). In doing so, it became evident that the traders have developed a number of strategies and innovations to overcome certain constraints they face while working (such as not being able to carry a blade, even though it is necessary for their work, or dousing some of the cardboard in effluent to make it heavier and then placing it in the middle of the stack so as to get paid more). This was captured by a student researcher who wrote: "*Even though they [the traders] may have little education, they are still able to adapt to their surroundings with positive effects [outcomes]. So what I found that emerged from them [the innovation] was mind blowing*". These are not insights that would be immediately observable without applying this HFE method to this work context. Irrespective of the method applied, it is only through taking an embedded approach, which Wilson (2014) argues as fundamental for successful HFE, that one can truly appreciate the complexity of a system such as Warwick Junction and the people who work in it. Furthermore, the time spent there allowed for the understanding of the interactions that occur, the contextual factors that shape these interactions, the emergent characteristics or behaviours and the impact that all of the above have on the humans in the system in a holistic way.

5.2 Reflections from Asiye e'Tafuleni on working with universities

Since its inception, AeT has sought to collaborate with both academics and students. The organisation regularly hosts student interns from a range of different disciplines, for e.g. from social work through to engineering, and has worked with international universities such as Harvard and MIT, as well as local universities such as the University of KwaZulu-Natal and now Rhodes. For AeT the benefits of these collaborations are multiple.

The work of the NPO largely centres on responding to the day-to-day needs of the informal workers in Warwick. *"Too often we're in an isolated bubble with our noses to the sidewalk, dealing on a day-to-day basis with what comes up. Engaging with universities is important because they force us to think outside of ourselves,"* said an AeT staff member. Collaboration between the two can help the more practically-orientated organisation to step back from their work, think critically about what it is trying to achieve and delimit new possibilities and directions. It can also push more theoretically minded academics to think carefully about what their theory might mean in the real world and about how to move from research into action. The approach taken by AeT when collaborating with researchers and students is captured in **Figure 2**.

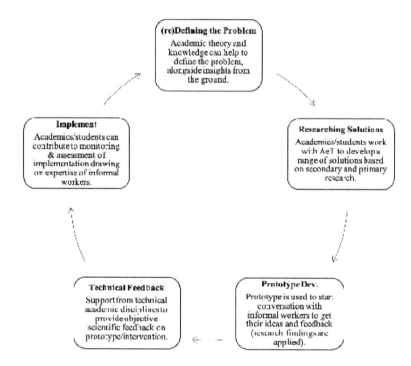

Figure 2: Collaborative model developed and applied by Asiye e'Tafuleni

For AeT, the introduction to systems thinking and a systems approach that has come through its interactions with HFE have been particularly useful. *"Informal workers struggle because they have to ward off controlling influences that are often uncoordinated. For example, the police fine traders because their goods are extending beyond their demarcated area, but at the same time the City has retrenched the team who paints the demarcation lines, so traders don't actually know where the demarcation line is,"* says AeT. The organisation believes that systems thinking and taking a systems approach could be useful in helping them articulate and advocate for the better integration of urban systems, *"to sew urban activities together in support of informal workers."* In this way, academic inputs can help to define the way in which a problem is approached.

This was similarly the case with the time-use research. *"We realized through this research that some of the waste pickers have these clockwork-like existences,"* said an AeT staff member who participated in the research. *"Work, coffee, listening to a religious programme, more work etc. These are highly ordered lives."* This is something that is often not appreciated about the informal economy. This provides another line of thinking about how to understand and approach advocacy work on integrating urban management systems so that they do not disrupt this very careful order that has been established by informal workers themselves.

The work on the waste picker trolleys has also been useful in helping AeT to think critically about the prototypes they were already producing. *"Once you've got a prototype and you've got funding to produce more, it's important to step back and see if we've got it right. We don't want to be producing something that injures or hurts people. Before production we have to be certain that we've got this as good as we can get it to be using strong scientific principles."* The testing of the trolleys, from an objective ergonomic perspective, has given AeT confidence that the trolleys are of an acceptable standard.

Finally, AeT engages with students in particular as a long-term influencing strategy, the process of which is highlighted in **Figure 2**. The organisation sees it as their responsibility to develop a new cadre of professionals from a variety of disciplines to take up the cause of supporting informal workers. Working with students on research projects, contributing to experiential teaching programmes and working with student interns are all a part of this strategy. *"It may be that HFE graduates don't work with informal workers directly, but maybe they are employed by the rail regulator which does employ HFE graduates. Rail regulators are constantly having to work with informality in a variety of ways. We're training people in all walks of life to consider informality and to think about how to work with it rather than against it."*

6.   A way forward

Despite the growing number of people working in the informal economy, this type of work remains precarious, given the prevailing negative perception of those working in this context, accompanied by the non-inclusive city planning and design. These beliefs, attitudes and policies threaten the sustainability of those who work in public spaces. Given the role that HFE is now starting to play in city planning and design, there is scope for HFE, which focuses on the needs of the humans in the system, to be involved in 'shifting perspectives' of important decision makers in municipalities and governments and helping them to recognise and be more inclusive of those operating in the informal economy. In doing so, HFE would rise to being locally responsive and advancing social justice. Given the economic, social and political challenges in South Africa, there is need to think differently and facilitate more opportunities for South Africans within the informal economy to grow their businesses and not to focus on the conventional way that work has always been structured in the attempt facilitate an upward trajectory out of poverty. If we, as those in tertiary institutions, get this right, in collaboration with those who already work in these spaces, we advance the public good purpose of universities and break down the ivory tower perceptions that have, for far too long, prevailed.

Through this experience it became evident that HFE has a lot to offer to those who work alongside and in the informal economy, as captured by one of the student researchers involved in the trolley project: "... *from an HFE perspective, I found it rather exciting because never in my life did I consider that HFE could have a huge part in the informal economy.*" Similarly, and more importantly, those that are alongside and within the informal economy can offer incredible insights to the discipline of HFE and in particular HFE education and research in South Africa. However, these insights could not have been gained without the assistance from stakeholders such as AeT. From an HFE perspective, the collaboration with this group, who are already embedded within the Warwick Junction system, facilitates important access to the traders and their work and, to some extent, their personal lives. In essence, AeT has spent years establishing trust with the traders by assisting them to improve their work. It is through such platforms that other research and advocacy groups can join in and assist in pursuit of improving the lives of many who live and work in the informal economy.

References

Alfers, L., Bali, N., Bird, M., Castellanos, T., Chen, M., Dobson, R., Hughes, K., Roever, S. & Rogan, M. 2016. *Technology at the Bottom of the Pyramid: Insights from Ahmedabad (India), Durban (South Africa) and Lima (Peru)*. Report of the WIEGO Network Component of the Technology and the Future of Work Project undertaken by Practical Action and WIEGO with support from the Rockefeller Foundation.

Ametepeh, R.S. 2011. Occupational health hazards and safety of the informal sector in the Sek-ondi-Takoradi Metropolitan Area of Ghana. *Research on Humanities and Social Sciences*, 3(20):87-99.

Balague, N., Torrents, C., Hristovski, R., Davids, K. & Araújo, D. 2013. Overview of complex systems in sport. *Journal of Systems Science and Complexity*, 26(1):4-13.

Budlender, D. 2011. *Statistics on informal employment in South Africa*. WIEGO Statistical Brief No. 3. Cambridge: WIEGO.

Carayon, P., Hundt, A.S., Karsh, B.T., Gurses, A.P., Alvarado, C.J., Smith, M. & Brennan, P. F. 2006. Work system design for patient safety: the SEIPS model. *BMJ Quality & Safety*, 15(suppl 1):i50-i58.

Carré, F., Negrete, R. & Vanek, J. 2017. *Considerations for Revision of the International Classification of Status in Employment – ICSE-93*. WIEGO Statistical Brief No. 17.

Chen, M. 2006. Rethinking the Informal Economy: Linkages with the Formal Economy and the Formal Regulatory Environment. In B. Guha-Khasnobi, R. Kanbur & E. Orstrom (eds). *Unlocking human potential: Concepts and policies for linking the informal and formal sectors*. Oxford: Oxford University Press.

Chen, M. 2012. *The informal economy: Definitions, theories and policies*. WIEGO Working Paper 26. Cambridge: WIEGO.

Chen, M. 2016. Technology, informal workers and cities: insights from Ahmedabad (India), Durban (South Africa) and Lima (Peru). *International Institute for Environment and Development (IIED)*, 28(2):405-422.

Cichello, P. & Rogan, R. 2017. *A job in the informal sector reduces poverty about as much as a job in the formal sector*. ECON 3x3 Working Paper. http://www.econ3x3.org/ [Accessed 17 January 2019].

Davy, J., Rasetsoke, D., Todd, A., Quazi, T., Ndlovu, P., Dobson, R. & Alfers, L. 2018. Analyses of time-use in informal economy workers reveals long work hours, inadequate rest and time poverty. In Bagnara, S., Tartaglia, R., Albolino, S., Alexander, T. & Fujita, T.(eds) *Congress of the International Ergonomics Association*, 415-424. Florence, Italy: Springer.

Dobson, R., Skinner, C. & Nicholson, J. 2009. Working in Warwick: Including street traders in Urban Plans. School of Development Studies University of KwaZulu-Natal, Durban:. ISBN: 978-1-86840-667-8

Dul, J., Bruder, R., Buckle, P., Carayon, P., Falzon, P., Marras, W. S., Wilson, J.R.& Van der Doelen, B. 2012. A strategy for human factors/ergonomics: Developing the discipline and profession. *Ergonomics*, 55(4):377-395.

Eurofound and the International Labour Office. 2017. Working anytime, anywhere: The effects on the world of work, Publications Office of the European Union, Luxembourg, and the International Labour Office, Geneva. http://eurofound.link/ef1658. [Accessed August 2020].

Gammage, S. 2010. Time pressed and time poor: Unpaid household work in Guatemala. *Feminist Economics*, 16(3):79-112.

Garrigou, A., Daniellou, F., Carballeda, G. & Ruaud, S. 1995. Activity analysis in participatory design and analysis of participatory design activity. *International Journal of Industrial Ergonomics*, 15, 311-327.

International Ergonomics Association. 2020. Retrieved from: https://iea.cc/ [Accessed 18 August 2020].

ILO. 1972. *Employment, incomes and equality: A strategy for increasing productive employment in Kenya.* Geneva: ILO.

ILO. 2018. *Men and women in the informal economy* (3rd edition). Geneva: ILO.

Hart, K. 1973. Informal Income Opportunities and Urban Employment in Ghana. *Journal of Modern African Studies*, 11(1).

Hirway, I. 2009. Mainstreaming time use surveys in national statistical system in India. *Economic and Political Weekly*, 56-65.

Hollnagel, E. 2001. Extended cognition and the future of ergonomics. *Theoretical Issues in Ergonomics Science*, 2(3):309-315.

Hollnagel, E., Nemeth, C. P. & Dekker, S. (eds). 2009. *Resilience engineering perspectives: preparation and restoration* (Vol. 2). Ashgate Publishing Ltd, Surrey, England.

Kes, A., Swaminathan, H. 2006. *Gender, time use, and poverty in Sub-Saharan Africa.* World Bank Working Paper, 73.

Kuorinka, I. 2000. *History of the International Ergonomics Association: The first quarter of a century.* IEA Press. International Ergonomics Association (www.iea.cc). .

Lewis, W.A. 1954. Economic development with unlimited supplies of labour. *Manchester School of Economic and Social Studies*, 23(2).

Lund, F., Alfers, L. & Santana, V. 2016. Towards an inclusive occupational health and safety for informal workers. *NEW SOLUTIONS: A Journal of Environmental and Occupational Health Policy*, 26(2):190-207.

Meagher, K. 2013. *Unlocking the informal economy: A literature review on linkages between formal and informal economies in developing countries*. WIEGO Working Paper No.27. Cambridge: WIEGO.

Moray, N. 1995. Ergonomics and the global problems of the twenty-first century. *Ergonomics*, 38(8):1691-1707.

Scott, P.A. (ed). 2009. *Ergonomics in developing regions: Needs and applications*. CRC Press; Taylor and Francis Group, Boca Raton, Florida.

Smith, M. J. and Carayon-Sainfort, P. 1989. A balance theory of job design for stress reduction. International Journal of Industrial Ergonomics, 4(1): 67–79.

Siqwana-Ndulo, N. 2013. The informal sector in South Africa: Women street traders in Durban – Part 1. Consultancy Africa Intelligence. Paper accessible: https://www.polity.org.za/article/the-informal-sector-in-south-africa-women-street-traders-in-durban-part-1-2013-05-13. (Accessed: 18 August 2020).

Thatcher, A., Waterson, P., Todd, A. & Moray, N. 2018. State of science: Ergonomics and global issues. *Ergonomics*, 61(2):197-213.

Vanek, J., Chen, M., Carré, F., Heintz, J. & Hussmans, R. 2014. Statistics on the informal economy: Definitions, regional estimates and challenges. WIEGO Working Paper No.2. Cambridge: WIEGO.

Wilson, J.R. 2014. Fundamentals of systems ergonomics/human factors. *Applied ergonomics*, 45(1):5-13.

Chapter 13

A socially innovative Employee Assistance Programme (EAP) using communities to promote societal inclusion

Kathryn Anne Nel and Saraswathie Govender

PSYCHOLOGY,
UNIVERSITY OF LIMPOPO

kathryn.nel@ul.ac.za; saraswathie.govender@ul.ac.za

1.   Introduction

Very little research has been carried out on EAPs, more recently called wellness programmes, in South Africa. The authors conducted an investigation into whether a wellness programme, implemented under the umbrella of a human resources department in a service organisation, was effective and sustainable. The programme was evaluated over an 18-month period using process evaluation. To contextualise the chapter, a brief background to EAPs is given, followed by their historical genesis in South Africa. A short account of what an EAP (or wellness programme) is is then given, followed by a description of Appreciative Inquiry (AI), which underpinned the appraisal, and the method and results of the investigation.

2. The beginnings: organisational health programmes in South Africa

According to Partington (2005), health programmes in South Africa started in the mining industry in the early 20th Century. Mines were notorious for the poor conditions in which miners worked and miners often became ill. It was therefore in the best interest of companies to keep their workers as healthy as possible by the introduction of specific interventions. The mines were hot, poorly ventilated and dust was ever-present, posing major health risks to workers (Stanton, 2004).

In 1914 the erstwhile Transvaal Chamber of Mines convened a Standing Committee on Dust and the training of dust inspectors began in 1916 (Stanton, 2004). The first legislation was enacted in 1917, which made dust inspections mandatory for mines employing more than a thousand workers. The establishment of the Mine Medical Officers Association followed in 1921. Two decades later, the Mine Ventilation Society became a professional association (1944). Occupational health practitioners formed a professional discipline in 1983, called the Occupational Hygiene Association of South Africa. Fundamentally, this led to organisational health being taken seriously in the country, and was in reaction to the global movement in introducing the EAPs in the late 1980s (Partington, 2005).

During the mid to late 1990s, after the end of apartheid, EAPs became embedded in South African organisations. Maiden (1992) commented that EAP staff in South Africa were made up of more professionals than in other countries (particularly America) and were more likely to use the services of social workers, psychologists and human resource professionals. Today, this has continued and some organisations provide medical aids that offer health incentives, for instance cheaper gym memberships (to keep the body fit). Physiotherapists and bio-kineticists have also been added to the EAP mix.

There is a difference between EAP or wellness programmes in South Africa and international programmes. South African programmes are more holistic and based on a macro-model, which takes into account systemic problems created by the long history of colonialism, separate development and apartheid (Du Plessis, 1991). European and American EAPs are typically underpinned by micro-models as they look at individuals and their problems in the work context only (Partington, 2005). According to Partington, the nationalist government put basic interventions for health and wellness into place in the work environment, but these interventions usually did not address many lifestyle and health-related issues amongst African workers.

The 21st century EAP or wellness programmes take the aforementioned into account, and, in South Africa, they often support not only employees but their families as well. Programmes deal with various work-related and other problems ranging from job-performance, vocational/career issues, financial problems, work-related stress and a wide range of psychological difficulties (e.g. relationship problems, bereavement, trauma, stress and anxiety).

3. Features of EAP and wellness programme services in South Africa

These programmes are put in place to give support to the entire workforce and, as is the case in South Africa, often their families as well. These programmes look at work-related problems such as interpersonal problems and poor job-person fit, and non-work-related issues such as familial problems and any other cognitive or emotional issues that can be addressed by advice, counselling or psychotherapy (financial and legal advice may also be incorporated). EAPs help companies to deal with workers who have emotional and/or personal issues which affect their work performance negatively. In South Africa, EAPs are also aimed at helping workers have more rounded lifestyles, as advice is also given on fitness, diet and recreational activities (Partington, 2005; Rakepa, 2012; Sheppell, 2018).

Critical elements of an EAP or wellness programme include (Awane, 2018; Partington, 2005; Rakepa, 2012; Stolfus, 2009):

a) All stakeholders must be equally committed to the programme (workers, management and unions).

b) Communication between stakeholders must be continuous and clear and all policies properly articulated.

c) There must be a workplace committee based in human resources representing all spheres of the organisation (and if the EAP is out of house (run by a service provider outside the company), it must be properly represented.

d) The EAP policy must be written and reviewed yearly to ensure all matters are properly represented.

e) EAP staff must be properly trained and should ideally be registered counsellors, social workers and/or psychologists or registered EAP practitioners.

f) The programme should be evaluated regularly in order to see what aspects need changing and if it is well-utilised and sustainable.

The programme in this evaluation focused on an in-house process which used EAP practitioners, counsellors, psychologists and social workers. Issues not related to counselling/advice/therapy were referred to appropriate professionals such as financial advisers or human resource officers who a) either worked in the organisation; b) came into the organisation at least twice a month; or c) referred them to appropriate advisers or consultants who had agreed to take part in the EAP (these were paid by the organisation or, if medical in nature, by the worker's medical aid. If the medical aid did not cover the costs, then the organisation paid if they could, otherwise the worker was referred to a public health facility).

4.   AI: an overview

According to Nel and Govender (2018), this method is grounded in action research, underpinned by social constructivism (Lewin, 1946) and first theorised by Cooperrider and Srivastva (1987). AI affirms the positives in any system by fundamentally looking at the best of *What is, What might be, What should be,* and the potential of *What will be.* This research method is mostly used in industrial/organisational psychology; however, as it focuses on the positive, it can be used in all areas of the social sciences. Tebele and Nel (2011) looked at how a woman living in poverty was able to *appreciate* the best things in her life and use them to *dream of* and implement her desired *destiny* in a sustainable manner. Nel and Govender (2018) state that AI is reinforced by the notion that internal and external truths are constructed through the social context in which they are grounded and placed within the dominant discourse of specific communities.

In this study, the researchers used AI to focus on an area of investigation (the EAP) that had been identified by stakeholders (management of the organisation). All AI investigations are collaborative in nature and people who participate in such studies are referred to as co-collaborators. According to Cooperrider and Srivastva (1987), the whole process utilises the 4Ds, which are to *discover* the best of *what is,* to anticipate or *dream* of *what might be,* to *design* what you think *should be,* and to believe in *destiny* or *what will be.*

In this investigation, supported by AI, the overall process looks at, and builds on, the *best of what is* in the EAP, as problem-solving approaches generally look for negatives and how to *fix* them, which often results in much negativity. The authors posit that by using the positives that exist in co-collaboration with all members of the workforce, an EAP that is the *best of what should be,* will ultimately become the *best of what will be.*

5.   Models of community psychology programmes as pillars of the EAP

EAPs that meet the need of a medium-sized organisation can be, for instance, central diagnostic and referral services which provide various services to different organisations (usually out-sourced); consortium models (multiple service-delivery organisations) that collaborate to offer different services, for instance financial and mental health services; independent contracts where an outside company offers its own services for use in a company and provides referrals to services outside its ambit; and finally, those who have a clinical liaison officer within the company (usually a social worker based in human resources) who offers first-line assessment and referrals as required (Partington, 2005).

An eclectic mix of community psychology models underpinned the EAP evaluation at the organisation. The Social Action Model of Community Psychology is one and is grounded in a psychosocial and socio-political context. Edwards (1999) refers to it as a reactive, critical engagement that helps communities construct definitions of self through social empowerment and transformation. In this context, the EAP evaluation was ground-breaking as it allowed participants to co-collaborate in the system at all levels and was seen as a community and not as separate workforce 'levels.' Researchers were able to use focus group discussions where participants presented views and opinions supported by their socio-political experiences in their communities.

Another community psychology model underpinning the EAP evaluation is the Mental Health Model of Community Psychology, based on what is termed the hospital model of mental health. Edwards (2002) reports that the original emphasis of this model was primary care, including primary prevention, which aimed at reducing the incidence of illness of those who were at a perceived risk (for instance, using condoms to prevent HIV infection). It focused on prevention and promotion of wellness, which is what the EAP at the company also used as its directive.

The third model is the Ecological Model of Community Psychology, which looks at how people in a specific environment interact with one another and establish harmony. It is a systemic process which looks at coalescing communities. In terms of the EAP under evaluation, the workforce was regarded as a community which was encouraged to use the programme in order to promote and prevent health-related issues. This implies looking at the workforce as a: "community as a [going] concern and intervening at multiple levels in various roles." (Edwards, 2002:16).

Lastly, the company was in an organisational setting, thus some principles of the Organisational Model of Community Psychology reinforced the EAP mix. Edwards (2002) states that this model emphasises that the workforce is a community that is vulnerable to stressors and that needs community support and team building to strengthen it. The EAP in this research was mandated to help both members of the workforce (internal community) and their families (external community).

6. Method

A mixed methods research design (convergent parallel design) was used by the authors to evaluate the EAP (**Figure 1**). Process evaluation, which investigates whether the programme was applied as intended, and outcome evaluation, which examines the overall goals of the programme, were employed (O'Neill, 2010). This type of design utilises quantitative and qualitative elements of the investigation at the same (and sometimes different) points in the research procedure (Sweeney, 2016).

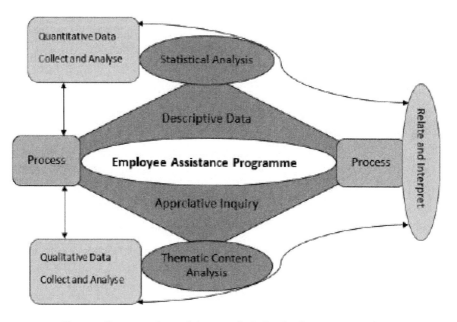

Figure 1: Convergent parallel research design for the present study

The evaluation was continuous and the workforce was looked at as a unit by utilising different lenses, for instance ethnicity and language, in order to gain more insight into their overall perceptions. (It must be noted that the financial viability of the EAP was not evaluated, as organisational management wanted this completed by their auditors. Information given to the researchers revealed that the financial audit of the EAP indicated that it was financially viable and sustainable.) Emphasis is always on the process, thus the following data was evaluated:

- Continuous time-series data from weekly reports prepared by the EAP specialist over a period of 18 months (this was used to monitor the growth and development of the programme). In this time period, around 300 people used the programme.

- A workshop given to all levels of staff in order to help them understand that using an EAP was a 'sea change' or paradigm shift in terms of support for staff. The workshop included eight focus groups (eight members in each group, thus 64 participants altogether) aimed at gaining the in-depth perceptions of the people who had participated in the EAP. In these workshops, overall health and wellness related to physical, psychological and dietary facets of health were discussed.
- Semi-structured interviews underpinned by AI were used and all interviews were conducted by the principle researchers in order to evaluate EAP outcomes.
- Surveys about how employees experienced specific workplace issues at the company comprised open-ended questions related to sensitive issues. These issues were picked up by researchers during focus group sessions and individual interviews. The design of these questions was underpinned by AI, focusing on the positives.

6.1. Population and sample

The sample was purposive in nature and consisted of all 500 members (all levels) of the workforce. The final sample of people who participated in different elements of the study amounted to 317. This was based on the numbers who attended different services offered by the EAP (over an 18-month period) and properly filled in questionnaires (overall a 79% participation rate).

6.2. Data collection

Data was collected over an 18-month period. The data included an opinion survey, a health and wellness survey, semi-structured (face-to-face) interviews, focus groups and the continuous time-series data. The self-report survey questionnaires on different topics were handed out to staff during meetings with the researchers or sent via email (at different times during the evaluation). These were filled in and put into a box outside the company's human resources offices or sent back to researchers via email. The semi-structured interviews took place nine months into the EAP evaluation, and participants were recruited through sending e-mails to all members of the workforce.

A guide was used for the semi-structured interviews so that the facilitator could remain focused (Guest, MacQueen, & Namey, 2011). The interviews lasted 40 minutes to an hour, with five minutes for building rapport and a five-minute debriefing period. They were carried out in an office in the human resources division of the company. After the individual sessions, more sessions were conducted with participants to give them feedback and to validate the transcripts. Questions in the interview guide were underpinned by AI to *discover* the positives of the workforce community. These positives were used to delineate the focus of the inquiry. Examples of questions are: *What do you appreciate (or like) about the EAP that has been introduced into the company?* And: *Explain to me what you appreciated (or liked best) about the EAP?* These types of questions helped the participant, in co-collaboration with the researchers, to think about (and appreciate) the positives in the EAP.

The EAP workshops informed the workforce about services offered through the programme, and were held every six months to find out how it was developing (focus groups were used for this). The eight focus groups consisted of six to 12 participants. Audio devices, supplemented with field notes (so that body language can be recorded), were used to collect data. All focus groups took place in the human resources boardroom at the company. Interviews were conducted in English as all communication in the company occurs in English; however, to ensure that all people were catered for, a person (from outside the company) who spoke the prevailing vernacular sat in on the sessions in case translations were required. Questions that were asked were underpinned by AI and were similar to those asked in the semi-structured individual interviews, for instance: *What positive experiences have any of you had while using the EAP?* And: *Could you tell me what you consider 'will be' the programme's overall impact on the workforce?*

Continuous time-series data was collected by the EAP professionals and counsellors who worked in the programme and collated by the researchers over an 18-month period.

6.3 Data analysis
6.3.1 THEMATIC CONTENT ANALYSIS (TCA)
TCA was used to analyse data obtained through the semi-structured interviews and the focus groups. Steps from Braun and Clarke (2006) were used, since they allow for an in-depth and rich illustration of data and the emerging patterns in participants' experiences. An outline of the steps follows:
1) Familiarisation and immersion. In this process, the researchers engaged with the textual transcripts by reading and re-reading them. Initial codes were produced and documented.

2) The second step was to induce themes. Because of the data immersion in the first step, these themes emerged in a logical and natural way from the data. As a result, themes were coded and then re-examined and subsumed into fewer groups, which allowed them to become clear, concise and integrated.

3) Step three comprised elaboration, which meant the researchers continued to code until no new themes presented themselves. The researchers followed this up with a further review of themes to ensure that nothing was missed.

4) The themes were then interpreted, checked and properly defined in terms of what researchers found thought-provoking.

5) In the last step, the researchers documented the research, in this case in the form of a chapter, in order to present the findings as part of an overall evaluation of the programme.

The interviews and focus groups were underpinned by AI and analysed using TCA. In this process, *intriguing possibilities* that created *bold statements* were derived out of the data, which allowed the workforce to *discover* their *ideal possibilities*. This allowed them to understand what outcomes they could expect (or *dream of*) in the programme (Nel & Govender, 2018). In this regard, the participants were asked to speak about what actions *should be* taken to *determine* the EAP's sustainability. They were asked for their input on the EAP *design*, to enable it to achieve *delivery* of their *anticipated* goals (*dreams*).

Descriptive statistics were used to analyse the continuous time-series data, data from the adaptability to and the opinion survey, which included frequencies, tables and figures that illustrated the data. A chi-square test was used on appropriate data to look for any significant differences between nominal variables on a survey which elicited quantitative data.

6.3.2 QUALITY CRITERIA AND RELIABILITY, VALIDITY AND BIAS

This qualitative research used quality criteria developed by Shenton (2004:1). The participants were informed of the nature of the research and their rights, and TCA and AI were used appropriately, all of which ensured the credibility of the study. The researchers also met frequently to discuss all aspects of the investigation and made adjustments when and where necessary.

Transferability was attained as the researchers used many existing studies to contextualise the study, while dependability was ensured by giving a thorough description of the research methods. Confirmability was achieved as the researchers remained objective by having frequent meetings where they discussed the ongoing evaluation and data interpretation and used each other as sounding boards for their own biases and judgements.

Bias was negated by using the same administrative methods during the evaluation and having frequent consultations (to ensure that researchers remained objective). Researchers also participated in continuing reflexivity in terms of their roles in the investigative process, which allowed them to recognise any possible bias.

6.3.3 ETHICAL CONSIDERATIONS

All members of the workforce were informed by email and during workshops, focus groups and individual interviews that participation was voluntary. They were also told that they could withdraw at any point during the study, no questions asked (Guest *et al.*, 2011). Confidentiality was discussed with all stakeholders who requested that their names were not used. The organisation also requested that their name and industry should not be made known nor the exact time of the evaluation. In this research, psychological harm was minimal; however, if any members of the workforce felt upset by any part of the research, they were informed they would be counselled. No request for this was received during or after the research process.

An explanation of the anonymity and confidentiality of the procedures was provided to all participants and informed consent forms were signed by them. Although the risks associated with participation in the evaluation were estimated as minimal, protection from any psychological harm resulting from the participation in the study was to be upheld. Psychological risk was mitigated by making counselling and debriefing available (Corbin & Strauss, 2014). All stakeholders gave permission for the evaluation of the EAP.

7. Presentation of results

Due to the extensive nature of the EAP evaluation, not all results are presented. The results selected to be outlined here indicate the successful and sustainable nature of the programme.

7.1. *Continuous time-series data (counselling/therapy/advice sessions)*

The researchers presented the results and interpretation together using different lenses in the process evaluation of the EAP. Figures and tables generated at various times during the evaluation are also used to illustrate the process. (See **Figure 2** below.)

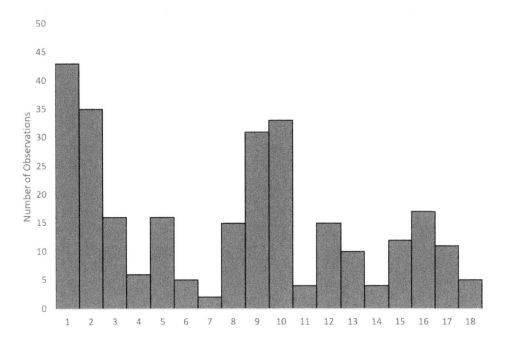

			Key	
1.	Marital	10.	Other/clinical (substance abuse included)	
2.	Depression	11.	Bereavement	
3.	Stress	12.	Feedback – profiles (assessments)	
4.	Anxiety	13.	Gambling	
5.	Career	14.	TOP – Termination of pregnancy	
6.	Hi-jack	15.	Gender issues	
7.	Abuse (physical/mental)	16.	Interpersonal skills	
8.	Family members	17.	Feedback to management	
9.	AIDS/HIV	18.	Sexually transmitted infections	

Figure 2: Mental health categories used by EAP clients over an 18-month period

During the 18-month evaluation of the EAP, the majority of sessions provided were for marital problems, depression, other clinical problems (substance abuse (alcohol, marijuana and other substances), bi-polar disorder and major depressive disorder, HIV/AIDS concerns, stress, career concerns, interpersonal skills (referred by human resources if members of the workforce had problems with communication) and visits by family members (either for marital- or child- related problems). Members of the workforce also consulted EAP professionals as a result of TOP (termination of pregnancy), gambling, gender issues (lesbian, bi-sexual, gay, transsexual and intersexual concerns), bereavement, hi-jacking, anxiety and sexually transmitted infections. Feedback to management was also conducted first on a monthly and later on a quarterly basis. This feedback was not related to members of the workforce (unless a danger to self or others) but was required in terms of how the EAP was developing.

The gender breakdown of those who attended sessions during the first nine months was 168 males (57.53%) and 124 females (42.46%) out of 292 sessions (**Table 1**). However, more males were employed by the company at the time of the evaluation. Females only constituted 19% of the workforce during the eva-luation, which indicates that they were much more likely to use the EAP than their male counterparts who comprised 79% of the workforce. During the second nine months of the EAP, figures were very similar for gender breakdown and EAP use.

Table 1: Breakdown of counselling/advice/therapy sessions by gender during the first 9 months (key for types of sessions see Figure 2)

Ethnicity	Lang.	1	2	3	4	5	6	7	8	9	10	11	12	13	14	15	16	17	18	Tot
African/ Black	N. Sotho	4	13	9	3	9	0	2	8	32	6	4	3	0	0	2	6	2	5	188
White	Eng	16	7	2	3	1	0	0	7	0	24	0	6	6	1	0	12	6	0	40
White	Afr	15	10	6	2	3	5	0	1	0	2	1	4	4	3	10	1	3	0	36
Indian /Asian	Eng	7	2	0	0	4	0	0	0	0	1	0	3	0	0	0	0	0	0	22
Coloured	Afr	0	3	0	0	0	1	0	0	0	1	0	1	0	0	0	0	0	0	6
All groups		42	35	17	8	17	6	2	16	32	34	5	17	10	4	12	19	11	5	292

Key	
African Black	N. Sotho – Northern Sotho first language speakers (SePedi and BaPedi)
White	Eng – English first language speakers
White	Afr– Afrikaans first language speakers
Indian and Asian	
Coloured	

One hundred and eighty-eight (188 = 64%) of Black African Northern Sotho speakers (which encompasses SePedi and BaPedi) used the EAP most during its first nine months of operation, followed by White English speakers (40 or 13.69%) and White Afrikaans speakers (36 or 12.32%). Twenty-two (7.53%) of the English (Indian/Asian) speakers and six (2.05%) of the Afrikaans speaking Coloured employees used it during this period. Africans were overall much more likely to use the programme than any other group; however, it is true that they made up the majority of the workforce. Nonetheless, all the other ethnic groups that were members of the organisational community utilised the EAP. Figures remained constant during the second half of the year and represented the same percentages as the first nine months.

As 60% of the workforce utilised the EAP during the time it was evaluated, it can be inferred that workers were comfortable using it. However, males were less likely to use the counselling/advice/therapy services than females (see **Table 2**), which suggested that more knowledge related to using an EAP needed imparting to the male employees, who made up the majority of the workforce. This was addressed, to some degree, through the individual interviews and focus groups; however, the aforementioned results suggest that a more concerted effort is needed to help males understand that EAPs and wellness programmes are for everyone. This result is likely due to the patriarchal nature of South African society where females are seen as more likely to 'need' and 'seek' help than males.

Table 2: Breakdown of counselling groups by ethnicity and language during the first 9 months (key for types of sessions see Figure 2)

Gender	1	2	3	4	5	6	7	8	9	10	11	12	13	14	15	16	17	18	Total
Male	25	21	11	5	9	4	1	4	18	11	2	11	8	0	12	14	10	2	168
Female	17	14	6	3	8	3	1	12	14	23	3	6	2	4	0	5	1	3	124
All groups	42	35	17	8	17	6	2	16	32	34	5	17	10	4	12	19	11	5	292

7.2. Focus group results

The meanings the workforce attributed to the EAP and how they experienced the programme are reported within the sphere of the socio-cultural and organisational context they exist in, underpinned by questions emphasising positives (underpinned by AI). Eight major themes and four sub-themes emerged from the data gleaned from eight focus groups. As reporting all of them is beyond the scope of this chapter, four major themes are presented (**Table 3**).

Table 3: Four major themes generated by focus group discussions

Theme	General meaning of the theme
Theme 1: Appreciation of the EAP	How the EAP was perceived and appreciated by members of the workforce.
Theme 2: Knowledge about health and wellness	How the workplace appreciated knowledge imparted about health and wellness generally in workshops related to the EAP.
Theme 3: Workplace as a community	The participants of focus groups appreciated their organisational community.
Theme 4: Delivery and design of the EAP	The workers appreciated the delivery and had ideas that added to the EAP design.

THEME 1: Appreciation of the EAP

Analysis of data from the eight focus groups conducted over the 18-month period revealed that the workforce overwhelmingly expressed appreciation for the EAP. Many reported *discovering* things about themselves for the first time and feeling that they *should be able* and fulfilling the potential of *what they might be*. There were many responses supporting each theme; however, for the sake of brevity, four responses for four themes are provided. The following key is used: FB = Female Black; FW = Female White; FI/A = Female Indian/Asian; FC = Female Coloured; MB = Male Black; MW = Male White; MI/A = Male Indian/Asian; and MC = Male Coloured.

Participant 1: Focus group 3 FB: *"You know, it was great to go to someone and talk about my family problems. I felt it was good – you know I really felt that the company was doing something for me and I was appreciated."*

Participant 4: Focus group 7 MB: *"You see, I didn't think it would work, my friend said I should go because of my feelings [father had recently passed on]. I thought it was for the girls, but it helped, I even had someone speak my language. Yes, it is a good thing, I know that the company values me by doing this."*

Participant 8: Focus group 2 FW: *"I wasn't sure where to turn, my child had become unmanageable. I thought she was just going to leave home and drop out of school. The doctor told me there was nothing wrong with her and it was our [husband and herself] parenting that was a problem. I saw a psychologist then took my daughter and she was referred to a psychiatrist. My daughter was diagnosed* with ADD (Attention Deficit Disorder). Now, you know, with medication and therapy she is fine, what a change. The programme (EAP) is really wonderful."

Participant 4: Focus group 4 MI/A: *"My marriage was breaking up because I was gambling a lot because I was stressed at work. My wife said she would leave if I didn't do something. I went to see the counsellor and I see that I do have a gambling problem. The counselling is helping and I was referred to a Gamblers Anonymous group which has really helped me more. I don't go to counselling anymore but I do attend the group ... if I hadn't gone to the counsellor my wife would have left and I think I would have gambled away everything. Ya, it is a really good thing to have at work [the EAP]."*

THEME 2: Knowledge about health and wellness
Another prevalent theme was how the workforce appreciated the workshops on health and wellness in general in relation to the EAP.

Participant 1: Focus group 3 MC: *"My Dad had diabetes and he died when I was young. It was only when the presenter told us about it and said sometimes tiredness, drinking lots of water and being too fat might be, what do you say, symptoms? Ya, symptoms – I thought perhaps I might have it. The doctor told me it was good I came in because I would have had a collapse if I didn't. Yes, I have it – but I am losing weight and eating better as well as having injections. I feel lucky that I listened cos I didn't want to go – I thought it was a waste of time."*

Participant 6: Focus group 3 MW: *"Ya, I know what you mean [referring to afore-mentioned participant] I know that I am overweight and when I heard about the things that can happen like strokes and heart-attacks I decided to try and eat better and try and get fitter. It's not so easy at my age but the counsellor said that with my medical aid I could join a gym at a cheaper rate. I think the programme is a good thing."*

Participant 8: Focus group 1 FB: *"I worried at first, I thought that the EAP woman would tell others but because I had problems with my boss I decided to go. She was very helpful and my boss and me had a meeting with her and we came to understand that the problems we had could be made better. Yes, work is much better now."*

Participant 5: Focus group 4 MB: *"It was a positive experience this thing – it made me feel good and helped me a lot. I can say that it is something that our work should have done long ago."*

THEME 3: Workplace as a community

During the process of evaluating the EAP, many members of the organisation *discovered* and appreciated that, in spite of age, gender, ethnic and workplace levels (management through to workers on the ground), their workplace was a community situated within their outside social context.

Participant 8: Focus group 4 MW: *"I spend most of my life at work, somehow I didn't realise that this was a community until the facilitator at the workshop explained how systems fit into each other. It was a sort of revelation, a good one – I feel more positive as I never liked people saying the workplace is a family … it isn't, it is a community and we all need to understand its different parts."*

Participant 3: Focus group 2 FB: *"It was when my friend told me I needed help because I was robbed coming to work and others told me the same … I thought, you know, they care about me not just because of the work I do because I am someone they work with and talk with – Ya, we are all people who work here and live in the town."*

Participant 2: Focus group 5 FW: *"My mother died recently and I did not appreciate how much my colleagues cared. Management allowed me time off [more than was allowed by the policy] and my colleagues took up a collection which really helped [the funeral was on the other side of the country]. It was like you said [facilitator] in the workshop, we are a community. You know some Whites don't understand us but most of the people here do."*

Participant 6: Focus group 7 FI/A: *"I don't have any family here they are all in KZN – I struggled at first but now my work friends are a big part of my life. I really appreciate them and what is it, you know … Yes, it is the organisational community where we work."*

THEME 4: Delivery and design of the EAP

This theme recounts how participants who took part in the focus groups found being a client of the EAP a positive thing which they felt they had helped *deliver* (by their participation). It also indicates that participants felt like co-collaborators and part of the overall EAP process as they felt they could add to its *design* by making suggestions as to what they thought *should be* in terms of adding to, or extending, the programme.

Participant 3: Focus group 5 FB: *"This programme makes me feel part of the workplace and it must go on. I think we should add a gym [in-house], it can be small. Those of us who work at night could come in early and use it or before we go home … I don't have time to go to gym when I go home … it is impossible."*

Participant 6: Focus group 5 BM: *"Yes, that is a good idea – it takes me long to get here and get home and I can't afford to go to gym … anyway there are no gyms where I live [informal township]. That would really help us – this is the best idea we need it in the programme."*

Participant 2: Focus group 4 FB: *"I think we need a nurse to come in – you know those who can give out injections and drugs because some of us who earn little don't have a medical aid. This would be a good thing, they could come in once a week for those of us who earn little. That would help us a lot."*

Participant 5: Focus group 4 FB: *"That would be really good, even those with medical aids sometimes need to consult and our funds have run out. This is something we should discuss more, I am sure that many will agree. You know this EAP thing could be even be better than it is."*

The themes indicate that when people feel that they belong to an organisational community and appreciate the best of *what is* and *what should and will be* and appreciate the potential for *what will be,* they are able to *discover, design and dream* and find their *destinies.* Researchers found that during this evaluation, the use of AI helped the workforce to focus on positives and not dwell on any negatives.

7.3. *Semi-structured interviews*

There were six themes, three of which are presented in this chapter, elicited from the data of the individual semi-structured interviews underpinned by AI. These themes demonstrate elements of the four Ds (discover, dream, design and destiny). Twenty-five individual interviews were undertaken, representing 5% of the entire workforce. The same key used for the focus groups was used to identify the ethnicity and gender of respondents.

THEME 1: Individual interviews: Positive feelings

Interviews with participants in the EAP identified responses which elicited the above-mentioned theme. Three responses will be given for each theme.

Interviewee 6 FB: *"I think this is a good thing [the EAP]. I have trouble with my husband so this helps me a lot."*

Interviewee 8 FW: *"It is something that will help a lot of people in the company. I really support it."*

Interviewee 10 MB: *"I don't like coming somewhere for help – but I did and it was a good thing that I experienced. We should not let this thing die [end]. I came because some of the bosses are racist."*

THEME 2: Individual interviews: Help available

Interviewee 12 MW: *"I come to work early and leave late, and on the weekends I shop, rest and take my family out … getting help for problems is not easy. Here at work they let us go to the EAP if we have a problem – this for me, lets me get help for different things."*

Interviewee 15 MC: *"My wife came here because she didn't have to pay and our medical aid ran out. They helped her a lot. This is helpful to me as I didn't have to worry about my wife getting the help she needed."*

Interviewee 3 FB: *"I had many loans and they were taking all my money [garnishing her wages], I did not have enough for food and my children. I went to look for help at the EAP and the lady sent me to a finance person at a bank. That helped a lot and now I pay everything back in one payment a month but I have money left for food and my children."*

THEME 3: Individual interviews: No fear, no stigma in the organisational community

This theme from data indicated that interviewees were comfortable with the EAP and felt that their confidentiality was respected in their organisational community. This suggested that they anticipated the EAP to be discreet and that they were of the opinion that their visits would remain anonymous.

Interviewee 21 MB: *"A lot of people come here I have heard about it from many – it is an acceptable thing. Nobody fears coming because of that thing, you know [discrimination]."*

Interviewee 23 FB: *"I have told others that I attended because I have been feeling down [depressed]. I don't feel judged at all which is good. Some of my colleagues tell me they are going to attend."*

Interviewee 9 FC: *"You know I attended because I needed someone to talk to about my problems at home with my husband. He hits me when he gets drunk, the children too. You know I am still going because I want to get on with my life and I think one-day I can leave. The counsellor did not judge me and I wasn't scared of going because my husband knows I'm at work. I really appreciate her help."*

These themes relate to and integrate well with the focus group themes in terms of their ability to indicate how the workforce community appreciated, understood and *discovered* the EAP outcomes and it being a process which helped them in terms of their overall health and wellness.

7.4. Self-report surveys

These surveys were used to support data collected through focus groups and individual interviews as well as the time-series data.

7.4.1. SELF-REPORT 'OPINION' SURVEY

This brief survey was returned by 150 members of the workforce (30%). It elicited the respondents' opinions about a variety of issues related to health, wellbeing and the usefulness of an EAP in the workplace. This survey was quantitative in nature, using 'Yes' and 'No' and 'Not Applicable' responses. It was based on issues reported in the interviews and focus groups. This survey was distributed and returned during the last three months of the evaluation. A chi-square test was used to determine if there were any differences between the responses of White and Black groups (Indian/Asian and Coloured respondents were subsumed under Black for this survey as only two from the first group and one from the second group completed this questionnaire).

A discussion of the results from the 10 questions (statistically significant if $p = <0.05$) hence follows.

Question 1 asked if respondents thought communication was good in the organisation. There was no statistical difference between Black and White respondents as both groups reported that communication was good in the organisation. Question 2 asked whether respondents felt that people who attended the EAP were likely to suffer from discrimination. A statistically significant difference was found between the responses of Black and White members of the workforce, with Black members saying that it was likely that they would be discriminated against for attending the EAP (p = 0.2324). Question 3 asked if respondents thought racism existed in the organisation. The results were not statistically significant; however, 57% of the Black respondents perceived racism in the workplace, while 33% of White respondents did not. This is likely due to the legacy of apartheid. Question 4 asked if respondents had difficulty with the English language (as most of the communication in the organisation was in English). A significant difference was noted with 71% of the Black respondents having experienced problems with English (p = .000816), while 25% of the White respondents also had problems (Afrikaans first language speakers). Question 5 asked if respondents had utilised the EAP. The vast majority of the respondents (70%) had utilised the EAP. There was no significant difference between Black and White respondents in this regard. Question 6 asked if respondents had received adequate help from the EAP if they had attended it. Sixty-eight percent (68%) of respondents answered that they had received adequate help, while 2% said that they had not and 30% selected 'Not Applicable'. There were no significant differences between Blacks and Whites on this question. Question 7 asked if the respondents understood the notion of AI. Ninety-five percent (95%) said 'Yes' and 5% said 'No'. There were no significant differences between the groups on this question. Question 8 asked if respondents understood that they were co-collaborators with the researchers in this research. Ninety-eight (98%) answered 'Yes' and 2% answered 'No'. No significant differences were found between Blacks and Whites on this question. The last two questions may appear contentious, but as issues of race were noted in the focus groups and interviews, they were thought appropriate by the researchers. Question 9 asked if Whites understand Blacks. Seventy percent of the Black respondents stated 'No' they did not, while 30% (mostly White) of the respondents stated 'Yes' they did. There was a significant difference between groups here (p = .03253). The last question asked if Black workers were discriminated against in terms of Whites getting promoted before them. Again there was a significant difference between White and Black respondents. Seventy-five percent of Black respondents stated that 'Yes', this is true, while 25% of the respondents (mostly White) stated 'No', this was not true.

These results gave the researchers some clarity in terms of where the EAP needed expanding. It was apparent that Black and White opinions differed in terms of racism and in terms of the English language. Workshops on cultural diversity and racism were advised as was the use of the prevailing vernacular in communiques.

7.4.2. PERCEPTIONS OF HEALTH AND WELLNESS
OPEN-ENDED QUESTION SURVEY

This survey utilised open-ended questions underpinned by AI to elicit perceptions about health and wellness. Two hundred and fifty members of the workforce returned this survey which was given out three months before the end of the evaluation (per email). There was a good response rate of 51%. This was a brief survey as it required answers that were fairly long. The answers were analysed using TCA. Three major themes emerged from the data.

THEME 1: Health and wellness survey:
Life at home and work are indivisible

Participants in this survey found that they appreciated their lives both at home and at work and noted that if they felt appreciated in both social contexts they were more likely to *discover* and *dream* about the best of *what is, might be, should be and will be.* The following responses illustrate this theme. The same codes were used as in the focus groups and individual interview results.

Participant 1: Health and wellness survey FB: *"If my husband is cross I feel angry and sometimes I bring this to work and take it out on others. The EAP workshop helped me understand that I need to sort out things at home otherwise my colleagues will suffer."*

Participant 25: Health and wellness survey FW: *"I find myself very stressed when my children have trouble at school and this stress carries over to my work. Sometimes this stress gives me headaches before I get to work. I learned how to de-stress by using different things like breathing properly or using things like putting happy thoughts into my head by using a technique the counsellor taught me."*

Participant 30: Health and wellness survey MB: *"When my wife complains all the time in the morning this makes me tired when I get to work. We talked about this when I was in a group and I saw I was not the only one. I went to the counsellor and he told me to ask my wife to discuss things that were stressful on Saturdays so it won't affect work. My wife told me she felt very tired when we argue in the* mornings, it makes her tired, so we agreed to try this. It has worked and we argue less now as well."

THEME 2: Health and wellness survey: Obesity is not a good thing
Participants reported that being fat (obese) was *"not a good thing"*, as it led to illnesses such as diabetes, heart disease and generally feeling tired and unwell.

Participant 5: Health and wellness survey FB: *"I always struggled to be a small size even as a child. As you see me now I know that I am too heavy. I already have diabetes and my doctor says I must be careful otherwise my heart will suffer. The lady who talked about food (dietician) really helped me when I was referred to her. She has given me an eating programme she said I shouldn't use the word diet. I am managing to stick to it and hope I will become healthier."*

Participant 40: Health and wellness survey MW: *"I got divorced last year and have struggled to get out of bed I just want to sleep. I also don't want to go out with my friends and I put on a lot of weight. When the EAP lady gave that presentation in the workshop I realised I was depressed. Since then I have gone to my doctor and he has advised me to exercise and has given me anti-depressants – I am starting to feel better now."*

Participant 100: Health and wellness survey MI/A: *"My mother-in-law is very difficult and now my wife wants her to come and live with us as she is old. I feel very depressed about this but didn't tell my wife. I just started to eat a lot and put on weight. This affected my work. The good thing was I went to see the counsellor and he told me to bring my wife in so we could discuss the issue. She came in and we are beginning to see what we can and what we can't do. It is very useful and I feel better at work and not depressed anymore."*

THEME 3: Health and wellness survey: Counselling services help reduce stress levels
Anxiety is usually what we experience in the short term; however, long-term anxiety results in high stress levels (Partington, 2005). Chronic stress can result in illnesses both psychological and physical, for instance depression and high blood pressure. Stressors occur both in and out of the workplace. The following responses support this theme.

Participant 7: Health and wellness survey MW: *"My stress levels are very, very high. My wife and I used to get into heated arguments resulting in that we don't speak for days or even weeks. We hurl insults at each other and also pick on other family members. I also noticed that our kids were being affected by this as were my relationships with my colleagues. My wife was equally unhappy so we went to see the psychologist at the EAP, we have been going for four months and everything is going better. We are starting to speak to each other with respect."*

Participant 120: Health and wellness survey MB: *"I had trouble with my boss [a White male]. We were both frustrated. He suggested we go and speak to someone at the EAP and I agreed though, at first, I wasn't happy. I went because I was too stressed. It has been good though we have learned to understand each other and there is a pleasant atmosphere at work – and at home because before I was getting home upset and angry and I took it out on my family."*

Participant 250: Health and wellness survey FB: *"Counselling services have helped me on a personal level as I was very stressed before I went. I had stress everywhere at home, at work and when I went out [social events]. I couldn't control it I just wanted to cry because of the stress I felt. When I went for counselling I found that some of the health issues I have were stressing me and they didn't need to. When things were explained to me about those things I started feeling better straight away. The counsellor told me to visit some websites which would give me more information; this really helped."*

The high response rate and long answers to questions revealed that many members of the workforce had been helped through using the EAP. This survey was distributed during the last three months of the 18-month evaluation process, which suggests the programme had developed well and was effective and sustainable.

8. Conclusion

The holistic evaluation, a multi-method approach underpinned by AI using focus groups, individual interviews, surveys and continuous time-series data, reveals that the EAP used by the organisation was effective and sustainable. Workforces are both organisational communities and part of the broader social context, thus an EAP is likely to have a ripple effect on empowering and enabling all community contexts by the transfer of knowledge and skills. The EAP evaluated by the authors was found to be a powerful tool for both community and organisational wellbeing and community empowerment in general. The programme supports its workforce which, in turn, is likely to lead to better production and better overall health and wellness for all. Recommendations included giving workshops on cultural diversity and racism and expanding the EAP to include nurse practitioners and the construction of a small gymnasium.

References

Awane 2018. *Five critical parts of an EAP.* https://www.awane.com/blog/5-critical-parts-employee-assistance-program [Accessed 18 July 2018].

Braun, V. & Clark, V. 2006. Using thematic analysis in psychology. *Qualitative Research in Psychology*, 3(2):77-101.

Cooperrider, D.L. & Srivastva, S. 1987. Appreciative inquiry in organisational life. In: R. Woodman & W. Pasmore (eds). *Research in organisational change and Development*, 1:129-169. Greenwich, CT: JAI Press.

Corbin, J. & Strauss, A. 2014. *Basics of qualitative research: Techniques and procedures for developing grounded theory.* London: Sage.

Edwards, S. 1999. Cultural psychology: Cultural counselling in a community context. *Health promotion: Community psychology and indigenous healing*, 1:15-23.

Edwards, S. 2002. Models of community psychology. *Health promotion: community psychology and indigenous healing, 1,* 3-20.

Du Plessis, A. 1991. *A society in transition: EAPs in South Africa.* EAP Digest, March/April: 35-62.

Employee Assistance Professionals Association – South Africa (2018). *EAPA-SA website.* Retrieved from https://www.eapasa.co.za/# (accessed 23.7.2018).

Guest, G., MacQueen, K.M. & Namey, E.E. 2011. *Applied thematic analysis.* London: Sage.

Lewin, K. 1946. Action research and minority problems, in G.W. Lewin (Ed.), *Resolving social conflicts.* New York, NJ.: Harper & Rowe.

Maiden, P.R. 1992. *Employee assistance programmes in South Africa.* New York: Haworth Press.

Nel, K. & Govender, S. 2018. Transformative research methods: Appreciative inquiry. *Research Methods in South Africa: Theory & Application.* Johannesburg: Wits Press (In process) (Accepted DHET).

O'Neill, G. 2010. *Programme design – programme evaluation.* http:www.ucdie/teaching [Accessed 20 July 2018].

Partington, K. 2005. An evaluation of the Ticor SA Holdings (Pty) Ltd. Employee assistance programme. Unpublished PhD. University of Zululand, KwaDlangezwa.

Rakepa, T.T. 2012. *The implementation of employee assistance programme of the Department of Education: A case study of Motheo District in the Free State Province.* file:///C:/Users/kathryn.nel/Downloads/rakepa_implementation_2012.pdf [Accessed 9 July 2018].

Shenton, A.K. 2004. Strategies for ensuring trustworthiness in qualitative research projects. *Education for Information*, 22:63-75.

Sheppell, M. 2018. *Your employee and family Employee Assistance Programme.* https://www.shepell.com/en-ca/totalhealthsolutions/yourefap/ [Accessed 19 July 2018].

Stanton, W.D. 2004. *Promoting occupational hygiene in Africa and globally.* https://www.saloh.org [Accessed 14 July 2018].

Stolfus, E. 2009. *Access to wellness programmes and employee assistance programs in the United States.* https://www.bls.gov/opub/mlr/cwc/access-to-wellness-and-employee-assistance-programs-in-the-united-states.pdf [Accessed 18 July 2018].

Sweeney, T.B. 2016. A convergent parallel mixed methods investigation into the role of mindfulness in moderate to severe, persistent depression. http://eprints.nottingham.ac.uk/37603/1/Timothy%20Sweeney%20Thesis%20PDF.pdf [Accessed 11 June 2017].

Tebele, C., & Nel, K. A. 2011. *Appreciative inquiry: A case study of a woman's experience of poverty.* Journal of Psychology in Africa, 4, 607–609.

Chapter 14

Facilitating Local Social Innovation by Appreciating Glocal Community–Higher Education Partnerships

Deidré van Rooyen and Karen Venter

CENTRE FOR DEVELOPMENT SUPPORT;
COMMUNITY ENGAGEMENT,
UNIVERSITY OF THE FREE STATE

griesd@ufs.ac.za

1.   Introduction

Across the globe, the reality of unmet human needs (United Nations Development Programme (UNDP), 2015) in greater society remains a challenge. Often, it is a lack of quality education that hinders sustainable development in society. However, scholars such as Cooperrider, Whitney and Stavros (2008), who work from an appreciative perspective, would rather reframe the previous statement, namely that quality education can facilitate (Fredrickson, 2006; Seligman, 2010) the wellbeing of people and the planet and profit-making (Whitney, Trosten-Bloom & Rader, 2010). By making use of PERMA (positive emotion, engagement, relationship, meaning-making and accomplishment), people can contribute to a positive society (Seligman, 2010).

To enable the delivery of quality education, Boyer (1990, 1996) advised scholars in Higher Education Institutions (HEIs) to become responsive towards societal challenges by revisiting their scholarship. By making use of four interlocking scholarly functions, namely discovery, integration, knowledge sharing and application, scholars and practitioners can deliver an integrated and engaged scholarship (Sandmann, Saltmarsh & O'Meara, 2016). Zuber-Skerritt, Wood and Louw (2015:3) also advised scholars to follow a participatory paradigm of engaged scholarship towards rendering a "holistic and actively engaged scholarship that integrates the three core functions of higher education – teaching-learning, research and community engagement."

In the same manner as Boyer, the South African government called upon scholars in HEIs to become responsive to pressing social challenges and engage in their surrounding communities (Republic of South Africa (RSA), Education White Paper 3, 1997). However, it seems that the ideal practice of engaged scholarship remains at the margins of some HEIs (Albertyn & Daniels, 2009; Council of Higher Education (CHE), 2016; Erasmus, 2014; Petersen & Osman, 2013).

One of the reasons for the marginalisation of engaged scholarship is a lack of available funding for enabling inquiry with the community (Kearney, Wood & Zuber-Skerritt, 2013; Wood, Louw & Zuber-Skerritt, 2017; Zuber-Skerritt et al., 2015). This challenge has opened the agenda for scholars to establish a partnership project, named Common Good First, funded by the European Union and the Erasmus+ Programme. The aim of the project is to support and grow the emerging South African social innovation sector by creating a digital network through Common Good First for connecting social change champions and HEIs around the world.[1] This funding opened doors for capturing and showcasing innovative social impact in existing community–higher education partnerships (CHEPs).

As a result, not only local, but also global partnerships have been established to enable scholars and practitioners to augment their responsibility for engaged scholarship. On the basis of their experience of more than ten years in community engagement, three engaged scholars who serve as key role players in the project at the University of the Free State (UFS), South Africa, formed a core CHEP to conduct an Appreciative Inquiry (AI). The question that defined the inquiry was: *How can we facilitate local social innovation by appreciating glocal community–higher education partnerships?* By making use of a semi-structured triad appreciative conversation, the scholars co-discovered their best practices, character strengths and positive values. The discovery of this positive core served as a foundation for collectively designing a strategy to facilitate the establishment and development of two digital storytelling labs.

The scholars applied PALAR (Zuber-Skerritt et al., 2015) to advance social change. It is argued that PALAR can facilitate the co-construction and generation of knowledge (Bushe, 2007; Gergen & Gergen, 2008) to provide a preferred future for the common good of the greater society. It is suggested that collaborative

---

1   www.commongoodfirst.com

inquiry for learning in a CHEP should start with the identification of a relevant societal challenge and end with the dissemination of the knowledge generated (Tandon, Singh, Clover & Hall, 2016). Furthermore, the outcomes of the research should generate user-centred knowledge to influence policy and to develop the capacity of scholars and practitioners. The aim of such collaborative inquiry is to sustain the ability of all the participants in a CHEP for improving their current practice.

Here, the theme of social innovation for advancing transdisciplinary inter-institutional and glocal networking can be fostered to inform future inquiry. Such learning can also stimulate and sustain diversity, social inclusion and citizenship (Elliot, 2013). Moreover, when the positive design and methodology of AI (Cooperrider *et al.*, 2008; Stavros, Godwin & Cooperrider, 2016) is applied to guide the scholarship of engagement, PALAR is placed in a positive context. The application of PALAR calls participants to continuously and critically reflect on the quality of their practice for enabling holistic (affective, social and cognitive) and emergent professional learning and development (Zuber-Skerritt *et al.*, 2015) in a CHEP.

Therefore, in this chapter we will illustrate how a positive scholarship of engagement can be enhanced through the establishment of local and global CHEPs for networking. Firstly, the reader will be informed as to what is meant by the concepts 'facilitate', 'PERMA' and 'scholarship of engagement'. The essence of funding for community engagement projects will be discussed, with a focus on glocal partnership building to advance social innovation. Local social innovation projects are highlighted within the global Common Good First project. Lastly, the findings of the above-mentioned inquiry will be shared as a strategy to guide holistic learning in a CHEP, with the intent to stimulate the growth of a project beyond sustainability. Here, the concept of emergent learning will be discussed (Taylor, 2011).

2. Imagining a positive future in which societal wellbeing flourishes

Leaders from across the globe united with the hope to inquire on how to create a better future for a human and non-human society (UNDP, 2015). However, it seems that scholarly inquiry mostly focuses on minimising the challenges in society, rather than focusing on imagining and generating a "positive human future" (Seligman, 2010:231).

When engaged scholars work from a positive framework, the intent is to facilitate the growth of society beyond sustainability. Such a positive intent can contribute towards creating a common good for all. In fact, if the focus falls on enabling conditions for people, the planet and the economy, the positive side of life can be built through application of the acronym 'PERMA' (Seligman, 2010). When PERMA is applied, the aim is to create conditions in which humans can flourish by finding sources for (1) more positive emotion, (2) more engagement with people we care for, (3) building better relationships with people, (4) finding more meaning in life, and (5) creating more positive accomplishments. In summary, a flourishing human system portrays positive social change as a result of collective action, which in turn brings goodness, generativity, growth, and resilience (Fredrickson, 2006) into society.

Thus, when scholars and practitioners (hereafter referred to as scholar-practitioners) engage for collective inquiry on a topic from an appreciative stance (Cooperrider *et al.*, 2008), positive learning and development occur at the 'heart' of an organisation or a partnership. Here, the positive core of the whole system is discovered to create an awareness of the collective thoughts, habits and actions of participants. Such inquiry can allow for appreciation of human connectivity and collaboration in a CHEP to become "universes of strengths" (Stavros *et al.*, 2016:97) for enabling scholar-practitioners to develop a positive scholarship of engagement.

3.   A positive scholarship of engagement

When scholar-practitioners engage for inquiry in the community, resources should be shared, and knowledge exchanged in order to address the most pressing social, public and ethical challenges in society (Boyer, 2016; RSA, 1997).

From a positive PALAR perspective, it can be argued that personal and practical wisdom (Taylor, 2011) emerges from participants' knowledge sharing and experiential learning in a CHEP. Hence, it can be anticipated that positive practical learning "gives life" (Stavros *et al.*, 2016:97) to pure scientific theoretical assumptions. In the whole system of a CHEP, engagement in collaborative learning (community and scholarly) occurs when participants connect to co-generate socially innovative ideas. Then, positive theory becomes grounded in best practices for humans (Grieten, Lambrechts, Bouwen, Huybrechts, Fry & Cooperrider, 2017) by discovering the positive core of participants, which leads to the development of caring human capitalism.

Therefore, as a global movement in support of engaged universities, the Talloires Network (2018) envisions HEIs around the world becoming "a vibrant and dynamic force in their societies, incorporating civic engagement and community service into their research and teaching mission". Inspired by the global vision, engagement embraces an integrated reciprocal, two-way exchange (Sandman, 2008) of resources between communities and HEIs, within the context of CHEPs.

After more than 20 years since the birth of democracy in South Africa, scholars now need to critically analyse the public educational service rendered by HEIs. With a focus on the history and current practice as it is, scholars can re-imagine and plan for decisive actions to improve educational practices for the future. Such appreciative reflection can lead to a better understanding of the whole system.

In their pursuit of strengthening sources of income, HEIs mostly focus on pure scientific research to address the important gaps needed for the advancement of future economic wellness in society. However, such research often only offers ideal theoretical frameworks as solutions and fails to discover the potential of existing social innovations created amongst and by communities themselves (the heart of human capital).

On the other hand, by assessing the positive core of people at the heart of society and creating common awareness of challenges, policy can be informed to make the necessary choices needed to ensure the creation of an ideal future. Here, the South African Higher Education Community Engagement Forum played a pivotal role over the past nine years in facilitating debate, informing policy, networking and expanding the existing knowledge base of engaged scholarship.

Therefore, engaged scholarship has been recognised in South Africa. Since 1997, HE scholar-practitioners aimed to establish community engagement and service-learning initiatives at their different institutions. Engaged scholarship foregrounds the knowledge developed for a public purpose. It involves (1) discovery that mimics pure research but pushes back the "frontiers of human knowledge" (Boyer, 2016:21); (2) application of knowledge to address societal issues; and (3) knowledge sharing and exchange to facilitate collective learning. The scholarship of engagement requires scholars who continuously reflect critically on their practice and act as members of society who commit themselves to develop knowledge for the wellbeing of society, rather than for their own sake (Checkoway, 2013).

This is why, in 2010, Prof Mabel Erasmus from the service-learning division at the office of Community Engagement at the UFS applied for funding from the NRF to support the initiative called *Knowledge as enablement: NPO focus (2011 – 2013)* (Erasmus, 2014). This initiative aimed to establish a long-term collaborative research platform for the reciprocal building, sharing and utilisation of knowledge, used for mutual enablement and capacity building between a limited number of HEIs, a selection of participants from the NPO sector and relevant public sector role players. By publishing *Knowledge as enablement: Engagement between higher education and the third sector in South Africa* (an edited scholarly book by Erasmus and Albertyn (2014)), this project laid the foundation for community engagement research in the Free State Province.

In the same way, Prof Annemarie Joubert from the Faculty of Health Sciences, School of Nursing, UFS (Mulder, 2016) applied for funding in the NRF Community Engagement Programme (2015 – 2017) for the *Knowledge sharing through rural-based health dialogue in action project* (NRF, 2015/2016). Venter, Holtzhausen and Erasmus (2018) established that long community–higher education partnerships are fundamental to growing community engagement. Taking these two examples of case studies into consideration, the assumption seems clear that funding plays a prominent role in developing flourishing partnerships.

4. Funding through partnerships

The question is what sources of funding are available in South Africa and abroad to assist and develop engaged scholarship. In 2016, the Glasgow Caledonian University in Scotland partnered with six South African and six European universities in a three-year (2016 – 2019) programme, the Erasmus+ Funding Programme of the United Union (European Commission, n.d.). The partnership manifested the Common Good First project that created a digital network to identify, showcase and connect social innovation projects in South Africa to one another and to universities around the world for research, community engagement and teaching-learning. Apart from building a digital platform, the team collected 100 social innovation profiles from CHEPs across South Africa. To make the Common Good First funded storytelling lab at the UFS worthwhile and sustainable, the office of Community Engagement partnered with the team members from the Centre for Development Support to form part of the Common Good First project.

Thirty social innovation profiles of partnerships were compiled in the Free State Province. Furthermore, Venter *et al.*, (2018) shared that there is a need for reciprocal and inclusive capacity building for all stakeholders (internal and external) involved in CHEPs. Thus, to continue with the excellent foundation that was laid for CHEPs since 2011 at the UFS, in line with the opportunity that Common Good First (middle-2016 – 2019) has created, a positive engaged scholarship through social innovation within glocal community–higher education partnerships was spawned.

A partnership is an alliance between two or more organisations that commit themselves to work together towards a common goal, share risks and benefits and review the partnership when necessary (UFS, 2006). At the heart of a good partnership are relationships characterised by values such as closeness, equity and integrity (Bringle, Clayton & Price, 2009). Scholar-practitioners engaged in long-term partnerships need to establish strategies for extending and developing social networks that would facilitate learning and development. Such networking will depend on the "context, goals and needs" of all partners in the partnership (Bringle *et al.*, 2009:15).

Therefore, building on the previous principles to guide knowledge sharing in CHEPs, the four Cs of "connection, collaboration, continuous communication and change" (Venter, Erasmus & Seale, 2015:157) have already created meaningful conversations and relationships. The glocal partnership between international role players, national community engagement forums and local cooperation through digital storytelling to showcase social innovation and entrepreneurship has opened doors for continuous collaborative action through a multi-interdisciplinary approach (Cooperrider *et al.*, 2008). "Universities need to use the opportunities presented by the National Development Plan (2030), and the recognition of major challenges facing the globe, to position engaged scholarship as a key strategy for strengthening the contribution of universities towards addressing national and global challenges" (CHE, 2016:269). Therefore, partnerships are key in establishing an effective engaged-generative scholarship.

Furthermore, Nikula, Kopoteva, Niska, Butkeviciene and Granberg (2011) have distinguished three perspectives on partnerships that can be viewed as a way of action or as a process or structure. Also, partnerships have been viewed as a site of action (Seddon, Lewis, Freeman & Shanks, 2004). When a partnership is viewed as a structure, the focus is (1) on the diversity, skills, local knowledge and leadership of the partners; (2) on the complexity, delegation, management or staff competence of the organisations; and (3) on the organisational and institutional arrangements of the state and the non-state actors.

When partnerships are viewed as a process, the focus is on the formation of partnerships and their development, strategic planning, networking and local decision-making. Here, James (2002:19) defined a partnership "as a process involving an inter-organisational arrangement that mobilises a coalition of interests around shared objectives and a common agenda as a means to respond to a shared issue or to realize specific outcomes". This is then a process of integration of actors across different sectors: their joint working, pooling of resources, integrating 'top-down' and 'bottom-up' interests, experimentation and innovation.

Partnerships can further be viewed as a space or a site of action in which people and organisations from some combination of public, business and civil constituencies come together to engage in voluntary, mutually beneficial, innovative action (Seddon *et al.*, 2004). Social innovation in current societies is an "essential factor for fostering sustainable growth, securing jobs and increasing competitive abilities" (Howaldt & Schwarz, 2010:6-7). It is clear that social innovation aims at enhancing the common good of greater society and tends to be grounded in moral values, more than on exclusively economic criteria.

Wenger and Wenger (2015) described such a collaborative environment as a community of practice, of "groups of people who share a passion for something that they know how to do and who regularly interact in order to learn how to do it better." In South African community engagement, the triad partnership model mimics such a community of practice and serves as a vehicle to connect HEIs and the community. Knowledge sharing can occur within such communion (Venter *et al.*, 2015). Langergaard (2008) distinguished two kinds of knowledge: 'know-what' (explicit knowledge) and 'know-how' (tacit knowledge). Both explicit and tacit knowledge facilitate the creation of social innovations. When local knowledge is shared in a CHEP, it can create a pool of knowledge which, again, creates an opportunity for synergistic effects. Such a pool of shared knowledge in a CHEP can foster discovery, design and development of social innovations.

5. Social innovation

The term 'social innovation' has overlapping meanings, such as open-source methods of innovation, innovations with a social purpose and social entrepreneurship or innovation in public policies and governance (Chesbrough, 2006; Von Hippel, 2005). Social innovation results from the construction and integration of new knowledge. According to Dees, Anderson, and Wei-Skillern (2004), this could be programmes, organisation models of a set of principles and other means to utilise a local response to positive and negative results.

According to Howaldt and Schwarz (2010:16), "A social innovation is new combination and/or new configuration of social practices in certain areas of action or social contexts prompted by certain actors or constellations of actors in an intentional targeted manner with the goal of better satisfying or answering needs and problems than is possible on the basis of established practices."

Social change can then be accentuated and provides improved solutions, compared to already established solutions, to meet one or more common goals to help create a future for a society (Adams & Hess, 2010; Gillwald, 2000; Ogburn, 1964; Pol & Ville, 2009).

Furthermore, social innovation can be seen as the generation and implementation of new ideas about how people should organise their interpersonal activities or social interactions. This is not necessarily societal improvement, but improvements in such things as the actions, organising and know-how of a group of people are the goal, measured at the group's horizon of experiences and thus based on the existing know-how and experiences of the group involved (Moulaert, Martinelli & Swyngedouw, 2005; Mumford, 2002). This field has evolved from the classical sociology of social change *(Marx, Weber, Durkheim, Schumpeter)* to the practically inclined orientation more likely to be directly linked to the interest of "caring capitalism" (Jessop, Moulaert, Hulgård & Hamdouch, 2013:111). Here, change champions interact with their social context, transforming from being transformed by it, as they promote social change through this innovation (Cajaiba-Santana, 2014) and appears as an interactive bottom-up collective learning process (Rao-Nicholson, Vorley, & Khan, 2017).

A connected 'difference theory' can be emphasised because these social innovations usually combine new or existing elements, practice cross-cutting disciplinary boundaries and leave behind compelling new social relationships. The critical aspect is the 'connectors' in these networks that bring together the people, ideas and money (Mulgan, 2007).

According to Hart, Ramoroka, Jacobs and Letty (2015), social innovations are new products, services models and practices that meet social requirements and involve new social collaborations. They furthermore state that there are three lenses through which social innovation is adopted. Firstly, individuals usually have excellent communication skills to transfer good ideas with practical abilities. These individuals have inspiring, energising and impressive stories to prove that persistence and dedication against all odds can change society radically. Secondly, movements for change, such as environmentalism, feminism and disability rights, root their ideas in discontent. The third lens is the organisation. New and existing organisations can be renewed through radical possibilities for future planning.

According to Mulgan (2007), online networks are becoming essential innovation drivers. Global links therefore also make it easier to share the lessons learned. The Common Good First digital platform will allow the social innovation profiles, established within an HEI, to promote their positive impact through digital stories. The connectivity and enhancement of these projects should not stop there. Therefore, the aim of the positive engaged scholarship through social innovation within glocal community–higher education partnerships project is to enable positive engaged scholarships through supporting the thirty partnership projects to an advanced stage of creating flourishing livelihoods and, ultimately, social change.

Despite the legislation and introduction of social innovation (RSA, 2017), the concept has not been actively implemented outside of the policy realm in South Africa. According to Hart *et al.,* (2015), the emphasis has shifted to inclusive development, which also supports the underserved people in society as innovators and allows for social and economic development. The trends of social innovation in South Africa were highlighted by Junge (2015) from the Social Innovation Exchange (SIX) initiative. These trends showcase that social innovation is driven by determination, improves access to information, is human-centred and community-based, and listens to the hidden voices – all of which facilitate a movement towards inclusive, integrated, collaborative and holistic learning.

6.   Holistic learning

From a PALAR perspective, grounded in neuroscience, it is of essence to respect and address the service and learning needs of the individual, social group, cultural backgrounds, economic state and even the environment. To ensure the effective collective generation of knowledge when creating a social innovation design that ensures wellness in a CHEP, such a complex, whole system learning platform calls for a holistic learning strategy. Fletcher (2015) described such a holistic and inclusive learning framework as the affective-socio-cognitive model for learning where the brain is seen as an emotional, social and cognitive organ for enablement of learning (Fletcher, 2015).

Learning is rooted in the affective domain of the brain (Zull, 2002). Through a continuous interplay between the physical perception through senses of the body and mental experience, perceptions are processed in the brain. Neural learning pathways become engrained in the brain through repetitive exposure to experiences, leading towards the development of patterns for combining thought, action and habits. These patterns are influenced by an integration of primary (innate emotions), secondary (emotions influenced by the limbic system) and tertiary processes (neo-cortical cognition, reflection and decision-making). Throughout the developmental stages, from birth to adulthood, these processes first start from a bottom-up response to emotion (underpinned by reliance on positive or negative affect), to a top-down response, underpinned by complex cognitive and reflexive control. Emotions include systems of seeking, rage, fear, lust, care, grief and play (Panksepp, Asma, Curran, Rami, and Greif, 2012). Stemming from the emotion of seeking, curiosity and motivation to seek out new experiences, aligned with networking, understanding and learning follow.

To create social innovation, it is of essence that expectations are met. Therefore, ethical and moral principles for collaborative inquiry – such as gaining informed consent, doing good, applying justice, valuing freedom, building trust, practicing the Golden Rule[2], respecting human rights and diversity, serving

2   *"Do unto others as you would have others do unto you"* (Máhrik, 2018)

others with integrity, being honest and acting with care (love for others) – should be followed (Venter *et al.,* 2018). In brief, these principles could be summarised as the philosophy of life in African societies – Ubuntu: *"I am because we are"* (Nzimakwe, 2014: 31). If these principles are not met, it can hinder the development of equity, closeness and integrity.

With regard to the social domain of learning, Lieberman and Eisenberg (2009) state that the human brain is wired to connect and interact with others in order to learn. By making use of thinking, we as humans can choose how we respond to and reflect on emotions and we can learn new ways of thinking, doing and being (Rock, 2008). Therefore, in a partnership, it is essential to appreciate and value the positive core of scholar-practitioners and to allow for inclusive discovery and creative imagination and design of innovative solutions for a preferred future (Cooperrider *et al.,* 2008).

The cognitive domain of learning involves awareness of knowing ourselves and enables our understanding of others (Damasio, 2010). Because our cognitive brain decides on how we will act, it is essential to develop a sense of self-awareness and social awareness when learning with others in a CHEP. Here the new sensory sources which enter our environment, such as listening to the diverse perspectives of other participants or observing behaviour different to ours, might seem a threat to our existing frame of knowledge and worldview. Relational learning should allow for the development of empathetic understanding to guide our actions. If we know ourselves well, we can become willing to develop the ability to manage our feelings and reflect before, during and after we act (Gregory & Parry, 2006). By knowing ourselves and focusing on information received during social interaction, we can learn from how we differ from others and evaluate if such new information should be added to our existing frame of knowledge. Therefore, cognitive and emotional intelligence should guide our actions when generating social innovative solutions for advancement of a well-functioning society (Fletcher, 2015).

Such integration of theory and practice, research and development, thought and action, is described in the literature as praxis (Zuber-Skerritt, 2001). When scholar-practitioners have developed praxis, they progress to a level of learning beyond knowledge acquisition called wisdom. Wisdom can stem from emergent learning in a CHEP. Therefore, a CHEP can help scholar-practitioners to learn and develop in a holistic way when making use of PALAR for development of positive engaged scholarship.

7. Methodology

Working from a synthesis of a positive, social constructionist and generative paradigm, the design and methodology of AI was applied in the PALAR. Here, the research process followed the steps of discovery, dream, design and destiny.

Drawing from their experience of more than ten years in community engagement, three engaged scholars who serve as key role players in the project at the UFS, South Africa, formed a core CHEP with which to conduct an AI. The main question that guided the inquiry, was: *How can we facilitate local social innovation by appreciating glocal community–higher education partnerships?*

As mentioned earlier, the PALAR was framed in a positive paradigm, because the participants wanted to generate a socially innovative solution (by the community for the community) and did not try to solve a problem. By making use of a semi-structured triad appreciative conversation, facilitated by one of the scholars, the participants inquired into their best practices, character strengths and positive values. The discovery of this positive core served as a foundation to collectively dream forward and design a strategy to facilitate the establishment and development of the Common Good First initiative in two digital storytelling labs. The dialogue in these conversations called for active, respectful and compassionate listening.

During the data generation, an empathetic understanding of the participants' stories about their careers emerged. Their appreciative trialogue created a feeling of interconnectedness and a profound understanding of their commitment to the development of a positive, engaged scholarship.

The appreciative conversation enabled the participants to 'enter' into each other's worlds. During the conversations, a sense of inspiration resulted from a spontaneous surge of excitement, characterised by positive thinking, feelings of joy, hope and resilience (Cooperrider, 2013; Fredrickson, 2003). It was a challenge to remain objective amidst their subjectivity, especially when they became excited and energised by the learning experience, but they guided each other to stay focused on their factual generation of data during the appreciative conversation.

The data was transcribed, coded and analysed by two of the participants. Thematic inductive analysis was applied by making use of the holistic learning model of Fletcher (2015). Furthermore, it was possible to generate an innovative strategy for facilitating the establishment of the two digital storytelling labs.

8.   Findings

The findings will be reported on under the phases of the process.

8.1   Discovery

Table 1 displays a summary of the positive core portrayed by the participants in the CHEP. As mentioned, the characteristics and values that were described by the participants when they reflected on the high points of their careers – when they experienced successful partnership project outcomes – were framed according to the affective-socio-cognitive model for holistic learning.

Table 1: Summary of the positive core of the CHEP

AFFECTIVE	SOCIAL	COGNITIVE
Citizenship	Relationship | Partnership |	Innovation
Care/love	Friendship	Unlock potential
Trust	Adaptable & flexible	Sustainable development
Honesty	Connect	Lifelong learning
Democracy	Collaborate (purpose-driven)	Funding
Safety	Coordinate (glocal networking)	Framework & structure
Appreciation	Continuous dialogue	Employability
Asset-based	Change	Flourish
Commitment	Socio-economic environmental	Academic grounding
Making a difference	challenges	Knowledge dissemination
Willingness	Enough time	Academic networking
Humble	Mindful listening	Implementation
Equality	Engagement	Applicability
Acceptance	Enablement	Practical example (pilot)
Authenticity	Transformation	Interdisciplinary
Common good	Mentorship	Research
Empathy	Access	Capacity building
Compassion	Inclusivity	Marketing
	Dynamic	Inform policy
Knowledge sharing	Reciprocity & mutuality	Holistic approach
	Engaged scholarship (theory & practice = PRAXIS) Critical thinking PALAR Trialogue	

(Source: Authors' own (2018))

As portrayed in the last column of **Table 1**, it seems that knowledge sharing, reciprocity and mutuality and the use of a holistic approach can contribute to the success of a partnership project. Positive engaged scholarship thus calls for an integration of theory and practice (praxis). It can be assumed that praxis, or practical wisdom, stems from collaborative learning that emerges at the heart of human interaction in a partnership.

In the practice of PALAR, the participants portrayed that an innovative initiative to conduct collaborative inquiry can be applied. The concept of trialogue explains the idea that emerged when the participants engaged to generate data. One of the participants advised that rather than doing two paired conversations, one triad conversation can be conducted. This method not only saved time but provided the opportunity for all the participants to be in the room at the same time. As a whole system change strategy (Stavros *et al.,* 2016), AI is about the discovery of the positive core in people, their organisations and the strengths-filled, innovative, opportunity-rich world around them. AI "is not so much a shift in the methods and models of organisational change, but a fundamental shift in the overall perspective taken throughout the entire change process to see the wholeness of the human system and to inquire into that system's strengths, possibilities, and successes." (Stavros *et al.,* 2016, p. 97).

It further appeared that an array of affective, social and cognitive characteristics in a CHEP can serve as a holistic framework for facilitating inquiry and advancing the project.

8.2   Dream, design and delivery

Collaborative inquiry and knowledge sharing in a CHEP needs principles and a caring mentorship by a change champion to enable relationship and character building and to facilitate learning. As portrayed in **Table 1**, and confirmed by Zuber-Skerritt *et al.,* (2015), PALAR portrays seven Cs, namely communication, collaboration, commitment, coaching and learning from another, critical and self-critical attitude, competence in facilitating PALAR and character building. Such character building should be portrayed by role modelling trust and being trusted, honesty, reciprocal respect, diversity and cultural difference, resilience, integrity and openness to new perspectives for enabling the creation of innovative solutions to deliver a preferred society. Furthermore, three Rs – relationship, reflection and recognition – can serve as guiding principles for relationship and partnership building.

It also seems that the skills of adaptability and flexibility are needed for collaborative inquiry.

Of interest is that the values of partnerships, inclusion, democracy, engaged citizenship, social responsibility, respect, reciprocity and lifelong learning are embedded in the framework.

The characteristics mentioned in **Table 1** portray various elements of emergent learning, which Taylor (2011: 3) defines as follows:

> Emergent learning arises from our direct experience of the practical world; it is triggered by an unpredicted event. The process that follows has the possibility to create not only knowledge but also wisdom we need to engage productively and effectively in a world of uncertainty. Learning that leads to wisdom involves the whole person and new dimensions that have been banished from public life in the modern era. It requires attention to our right-brain processes – sensing, feeling, imagination, metaphor, and context – as well as left-brain processes – analysis, logic, strategy, and application.

Therefore, it is suggested that the holistic strategy of emergent learning (Taylor, 2011) can be followed to facilitate collaborative learning in a CHEP, no matter what the goal of the project is.

9. Conclusion

We argued that, in order to facilitate the growth of a project, glocal partnerships and collaboration should be established. Without the contribution of committed change champions (community and HE stakeholders), society as a whole will not grow beyond viability. Furthermore, the Common Good First project funded by the European Union supports social innovation by creating a digital network to showcase the social impact of community projects in South Africa. In this way, partnership building can take place in South Africa, as well as with international collaborators. Because of the globally funded network initiative, the building of appreciative local CHEPs have evolved into an ideal practice where scholar-practitioners could engage for PALAR in CHEPs.

Partnerships are therefore key in developing positive engaged scholarship. This is also true in converse, because engaged scholars create relationships that spawn community development. Reciprocal and collective knowledge sharing, exchange, generation and dissemination would then always be ideal; to improve relationship and partnership building and allow community and HEIs to function as a collective whole system.

The ultimate goal for investments such as the Common Good First and the partnership building of the CHEP, is to engage practitioners from vulnerable and marginalised groups as participants in participatory research. This can be made possible through PALAR and community engagement initiatives. It is suggested that the focus should be shifted from only developing an individual scholar, to rather creating the wellbeing of the greater society. Each and every scholar should take up the responsibility to not only develop their own scholarly achievement, but also to contribute to the common public good. Glocal citizenship can be coined by integrating academic champions' critical reflective questioning with their role as citizens and members of society at large. In this way, engaged researchers can acknowledge their role in social accountability and civic responsibility.

References

Adams, D. & Hess, M. 2010. Social innovation and why it has policy significance. *Economic and Labour Relations Review*, 21(2):139-155. https://doi.org/10.1177/103530461002100209

Albertyn, R. & Daniels, P. 2009. Research within the context of community engagement. In: E. Bitzer (ed). *Higher education in South Africa: A scholarly look behind the scenes* (409-428). Stellenbosch: SUN Media.

Boyer, E.L. 1990. *Scholarship reconsidered: Priorities of professoriate*. A special report. New York: The Carnegie Foundation for the Advancement of Teaching. http://www.hadinur.com/paper/BoyerScholarshipReconsidered.pdf. [Accessed 18 April 2018].

Boyer, E.L. 1996. The scholarship of engagement. *Journal of Higher Education Outreach and Engagement*, 1(1):10-20. https://www.files.eric.ed.gov/fulltext /EJ1097206.pdf

Boyer, E.L. 2016. The scholarship of engagement. *Journal of Higher Education Outreach and Engagement*, 20(1):15-28.

Bringle, R.G., Clayton, P.H. & Price, M.F. 2009. Partnerships in service learning and civic engagement. *Partnerships: A Journal of Service Learning & Civic Engagement*, 1(1):1-20.

Bushe, G.R. 2007. Appreciative inquiry is not (just) about the positive. *Organization Development Practitioner*, 39(4):30-35.

Cajaiba-Santana, G. 2014. Social innovation: Moving the field forward. A conceptual framework. *Technological Forecasting and Social Change, 82*, 42-51. doi: 10.1016/j.techfore.2013.05.008

Checkoway, B. 2013. Strengthening the scholarship of engagement in Higher Education. *Journal of Higher Education Outreach and Engagement*, 17(4):7-22.

Chesbrough, H. 2006. *Open business models: How to thrive in the new innovation landscape*. Boston, MA: Harvard Business School Press.

Cooperrider, D.L. 2013 (October 2). *The power of resilience: David Cooperrider at TEDxUNPlaza*. TEDx Talks [Video file] https://www.youtube.com/watch?v=-SoAKaTKAYA [Accessed 16 April 2018].

Cooperrider, D., Whitney, D. & Stavros, J. 2008. *Appreciative inquiry handbook. For Leaders of change* (2nd edition). London: Berrett-Koehler.

CHE (Council of Higher Education). 2016. *South African higher education reviewed – Two decades of democracy*. Pretoria: Author.

Damasio, A. 2010. *Self comes to mind: Constructing the conscious brain*. New York: Pantheon Books.

Dees, J.G., Anderson, B.B. & Wei-Skillern, J. 2004. Scaling social impact strategies for spreading social innovations. *Stanford Social Innovation Review*, 1(4): 24-32.

Elliott, G. 2013. Character and impact of social innovation in higher education. *International Journal of Continuing Education and Lifelong Learning*, 5(2):71-84. ISSN: 1997-7034; Online: 2071-1158.

Erasmus, M. 2014. The political unconscious of higher education community engagement in South Africa. In: M. Erasmus & R. Albertyn (eds). *Knowledge as enablement: Engagement between higher education and the third sector in South Africa* (100-114). Bloemfontein: SUN MeDIA.

Erasmus, M. & Albertyn, R. (eds) 2014. *Knowledge as enablement: Engagement between higher education and the third sector in South Africa*. Bloemfontein: Sun Media.

European Commission. n.d. *About the Erasmus+ funding programme*. https://ec.europa.eu/info/education/set-projects-education-and-training/erasmus-funding-programme_en. [Accessed 16 April 2018].

Fletcher, M. 2015. Professional learning. In: O. Zuber-Skerritt, M. Fletcher & J. Kearney (eds). *Professional learning in higher education and communities: Towards a new vision for action research* (41-75). London: Palgrave.

Fredrickson, B.L. 2003. Positive emotions and upwards spirals in organizations. In: K.S. Cameron, J.E. Dutton, & R.E. Quinn (eds). *Positive organizational scholarship: Foundations of a new discipline* (163-193). San Francisco, CA: Berrett-Koehler.

Fredrickson, B.L. 2006. Unpacking positive emotions: Investigating the seeds of human flourishing. *The Journal of Positive Psychology*, 1(2):57-59.

Gergen, K.J., & Gergen, M.M. 2008. Social construction and research as action. In: P. Reason & H. Bradbury (eds). *The Sage handbook of action research: Participative inquiry and practice* (150-170). London: Sage Publications.

Gillwald, K., 2000. Konzepte sozialer innovation, Working paper. Wissenschaftszentrum Berlin für Sozialforschung, Berlin.

Gregory, G. & Parry, T. 2006. Designing brain-compatible learning. (third edition). Cornwin Press: California.

Grieten, S., Lambrechts, F., Bouwen, R., Huybrechts, J., Fry, R. & Cooperrider, D.L. 2017. Inquiring into appreciative inquiry: A conversation with David Cooperrider and Ronald Fry. *Journal of Management Inquiry*, 27(1):101-114. doi: 10.1177/1056492616688087

Hart, J., Ramoroka, K., Jacobs P. & Letty, B. 2015. Revealing the social face of innovation. *South African Journal of Science*, 111(9/10):1-6.

Howaldt, J. & Schwarz, M. 2010. *Social innovation: Concepts, research fields and international trends*. Aachen IMA/ZLW. http://www.asprea.org/imagenes/IMO%20Trendstudie_Howaldt_englisch_Final%20ds.pdf. [Accessed 15 April 2018].

James, J.E. 2002. Third-party threats to research integrity in public-private partnerships. Addiction, 97(10):1237-1360.

Jessop, B., Moulaert, F., Hulgård, L. & Hamdouch, A. 2013. Social innovation research: A new stage in innovation analysis. In F. Moulaert, D. MacCallum, A. Mehmood, & A. Hamdouch. The International Handbook on Social Innovation. Edward Elgar Publishing: Cheltenham, UK.

Junge, J. 2015. 10 trends of social innovation in South Africa. *Social Innovation Exchange*, 20 April 2015. https://www.socialinnovationexchange.org/insights/10-trends-social-innovation-south-africa [Accessed 26 July 2018].

Kearney, J., Wood, L. & Zuber-Skerritt, O. 2013. Community-university partnerships using Participatory Action Learning and Action Research (PALAR). *Gateways: International Journal of Community Research and Engagement*, 6:113-130. doi:10.5130/ijcre.v6i1.3105

Langergaard, L.L. 2008. Social entrepreneurship and capitalist crisis. *Nordicum-Mediterraneum*, 9(3) (Online). Icelandic E-Journal of Nordic and Mediterranean Studies. http://nome.unak.is/nm-marzo-2012/vol-9-no-3-2014/73-conference-paper/493-social-entrepreneurship-and-capitalist-crisis

Lieberman, M.D. & Eisenberger, N.I. 2009. Pains and pleasures of social life. *Science Mag*, 323:890-891.

Máhrik, T. 2018. The golden rule of morality – an ethical paradox. *Ethics & Bioethics*, 8(1-2): 5-13.

Moulaert, F., Martinelli, F. & Swyngedouw, E. 2005. Towards alternative model(s) of local innovation, *Urban Studies*, 42(11):1969-1990.

Mulder, M. 2016. *School of nursing: Annual progress report*. https://www.ufs.ac.za/docs/librariesprovider25/school-of-nursing-documents/all-documents/2016-annual-report.pdf?sfvrsn=4edd721_0 [Accessed 29 July 29].

Mulgan, G. 2007. *Social innovation. What it is, why it matters and how it can be accelerated*. Skoll Centre for Social Entrepreneurship, Oxford Saaid Business School, Working Paper. The Young Foundation. London: Basingstoke.

Mumford, M.D. 2002. Social innovation: Ten cases from Benjamin Franklin. *Creativity Research Journal*, 14(2):253-266.

Nikula, J., Kopoteva, I., Niska, M., Butkeviciene, E. & Granberg, L. 2011. Theoretical and methodological context. In: J. Nikula, I. Kopoteva, M. Niska, E. Butkevicience & L. Granberg (eds). *Social innovations and social partnerships in Finland, Russia and Lithuania.* (11-54). Finnish Centre for Russian and Eastern European Studies, University of Helsinki, Finland. http://www.helsinki.fi/aleksanteri/english/ publications/files /Nikula_Social_ innovations.pdf . [Accessed 16 April 2018].

Nzimakwe, T.I. 2014. Practising Ubuntu and leadership for good governance: The South African and continental dialogue. *African Journal of Public Affairs,* 7(4):30-41.

Ogburn, W.F. 1964. *On culture and social change*: Selected papers. Duncan, O.D. (ed). Chicago: University of Chicago Press.

Panksepp, J., Asma, S., Curran, G., Rami, G. & Greif, T. 2012. The philosophical implications of affective neuroscience. *Journal of Consciousness Studies,* 19(3):6-48.

Petersen, N. & Osman, N. 2013. An introduction to service learning in South Africa. In: R. Osman, & N. Petersen (eds). *Service learning in South Africa,* (2-32). Cape Town: Oxford University Press.

Pol, E. & Ville, S. 2009. Social innovation: buzz word or enduring term? *The Journal of Socio-Economics,* 38(6):878-885.

Rao-Nicholson, R., Vorley, T. & Khan, Z. 2017. Social innovation in emerging economies: A national system of innovation based approach. *Technological Forecasting and Social Change,* 121:228-237. doi:10.1016/j.techfore.2017.03.013

Rock, D. 2008. SCARF: A brain-based model for collaborating with and influencing others. NeuroLeadershipJournal. https://www.epa.gov/sites/production/ files/2015-09/documents/thurs_georgia_9_10_915_covello.pdf. [Accessed 18 April 2018].

RSA (Republic of South Africa), Department of Science and Technology. 2017. *White paper on science, technology and innovation.* Pretoria. https://tbcsa.travel/ wp-content/uploads/2018/02/NEW-White-Paper-Draft-1.5-V2-as-at-24- November-2017.pdf. [Accessed 16 April 2018].

RSA DoE (Republic of South Africa, Department of Education). 1997. *A program for the transformation of higher education. Education White Paper 3, Notice 1196 of 1997.* Pretoria: DoE.

Sandmann, L.R. 2008. Conceptualization of the scholarship of engagement in higher education: A strategic review, 1996–2006. *Journal of Higher Education Outreach and Engagement,* 12(1):91-104.

Sandmann, L.R., Saltmarsh, J. & O'Meara, K. 2016. An integrated model for advancing the scholarship of engagement: Creating academic homes for the engaged scholar. *Journal of Higher Education Outreach and Engagement,* 20(1):157-174.

Seddon, P.B., Lewis, G.P., Freeman, P. & Shanks, G. 2004. The case for viewing business models as abstractions of strategy. *Communications of the Association of Information Systems*, 13:427-442. http://aisel.aisnet.org/cais/vol13 /iss1/25 . [Accessed 18 April 2018].

Seligman, M. 2010. *Flourish: Positive psychology and positive interventions*. The Tanner Lectures on Human Values. The University of Michigan. https://tannerlectures.utah. edu/_documents/a-to-z/s/Seligman_10.pdf [Accessed 29 July 2018].

Stavros, J.M., Godwin, L.N. & Cooperrider, D.L. 2016. Appreciative Inquiry: Organization development and the strengths revolution. In: W.J. Rothwell, J.M. Stavros & R.L. Sullivan (eds). *Practicing organization development: Leading transformation and change* (fourth edition) (96-116). New Jersey: Wiley.

Tandon, R., Singh, W., Clover, D. & Hall, B. 2016. Knowledge democracy and excellence in engagement. In: M. Leach, J. Gaventa & K. Oswald (eds). Engaged excellence. *IDS Bulletin*, 47(6):19-36. doi:10.19088/1968-2016.197

Taylor, M.M. 2011. *Emergent learning for wisdom*. New York: Palgrave-McMillan.

The Talloires Network. 2018. *Who we are – Our vision*. Tufts University, Medford, MA. http://talloiresnetwork.tufts.edu/who-we-are/. [Accessed 15 April 2018].

UNDP. 2015. *Sustainable development goals*. http://www.undp.org/content/dam/undp/ library/corporate/brochure/SDGs_Booklet_ Web_En.pdf [Accessed 16 April 2018].

UFS (University of the Free State) 2006. *Community Service Policy*. (Policy 06.1). https:// www.ufs.ac.za/supportservices/departments/community-engagement-home/ community-engagement/policy-definition. [Accessed 16 April 2018].

Venter, K. Erasmus, M. & Seale, I. 2015. Knowledge sharing for the development of service learning champions. *Journal for New Generation Sciences*, 13(2):147-163. DSpace Repository, Central University of Technology, Free State. http://hdl.handle.net/11462/772. [Accessed 18 April 2018].

Venter, K., Holtzhausen, S. & Erasmus, M. 2018. Appreciating integrated service-learning praxis for flourishing of engaged scholarship in community-higher education partnerships (Submitted for publication).

Von Hippel, E. 2005: *Democratizing innovation*. Cambridge: MIT Press.

Wenger, E. & Wenger, B. 2015. *Communities of practice: A brief introduction*. EB Wenger-Trayner: http://wenger-trayner.com/introduction-to-communities-of-practice [Accessed 15 July 2018].

Whitney, D., Trosten-Bloom, A. & Rader, K. 2010. *Appreciative leadership*. New York: McGraw Hill.

Wood, L., Louw, I. & Zuber-Skerritt, O. 2017. Enhancing postgraduate learning and development: A participatory action learning and action research approach through conferences. *Action Learning: Research and Practice*, 14(2):120-135. doi:10.1080/14767 333.2017.1295361

Zuber-Skerritt, O. 2001. Action learning and action research: Paradigm, praxis and programs. In: S. Sankara, B. Dick & R. Passfield (eds). *Effective change management through action research and action learning: Concepts, perspectives, processes and applications* (1-20). Lismore: Southern Cross University Press.

Zuber-Skerritt, O., Wood, L. & Louw, I. 2015. *A participatory paradigm for an engaged scholarship in higher education. Action leadership from a South African perspective.* Netherlands: Sense.

Zull, J. 2002. *The art of changing the brain: Enriching teaching by exploring the biology of learning.* Sterling VA: Stylus Publishing.

Printed in Great Britain
by Amazon

81764330R00197